Prehistoric Maritime Adaptations of the Circumpolar Zone

# World Anthropology

*General Editor*

SOL TAX

*Patrons*

CLAUDE LÉVI-STRAUSS
MARGARET MEAD
LAILA SHUKRY EL HAMAMSY
M. N. SRINIVAS

MOUTON PUBLISHERS · THE HAGUE · PARIS
DISTRIBUTED IN THE USA AND CANADA BY ALDINE, CHICAGO

# Prehistoric Maritime Adaptations of the Circumpolar Zone

WITHDRAWN

*Editor*

WILLIAM FITZHUGH

MOUTON PUBLISHERS · THE HAGUE · PARIS
DISTRIBUTED IN THE USA AND CANADA BY ALDINE, CHICAGO

# General Editor's Preface

Students of the Arctic are an interdisciplinary and international circle of colleagues who have for forty years increasingly worked together on common problems. The present book is a unique summation of what specialists know of the archaeological and historical adaptations of our species to the interesting complex of environments which surround the North Pole. The Editor's Introduction not only excellently assesses the results but also described the history of theory concerning the area, this latest phase being inspired by a unique Congress which brought together for such summations an assemblage of scholars from every part of the world.

Like most contemporary sciences, anthropology is a product of the European tradition. Some argue that it is a product of colonialism, with one small and self-interested part of the species dominating the study of the whole. If we are to understand the species, our science needs substantial input from scholars who represent a variety of the world's cultures. It was a deliberate purpose of the IXth International Congress of Anthropological and Ethnological Sciences to provide impetus in this direction. The *World Anthropology* volumes, therefore, offer a first glimpse of a human science in which members from all societies have played an active role. Each of the books is designed to be self-contained; each is an attempt to update its particular sector of scientific knowledge and is written by specialists from all parts of the world. Each volume should be read and reviewed individually as a separate volume on its own given subject. The set as a whole will indicate what changes are in store for anthropology as scholars from the developing countries join in studying the species of which we are all a part.

The IXth Congress was planned from the beginning not only to include as many of the scholars from every part of the world as possible, but also with a view toward the eventual publication of the papers in high-quality volumes. At previous Congresses scholars were invited to bring papers which were then read out loud. They were necessarily limited in length; many were only summarized; there was little time for discussion; and the sparse discussion could only be in one language. The IXth Congress was an experiment aimed at changing this. Papers were written with the intention of exchanging them before the Congress, particularly in extensive pre-Congress sessions; they were not intended to be read at the Congress, that time being devoted to discussions — discussions which were simultaneously and professionally translated into five languages. The method for eliciting the papers was structured to make as representative a sample as was allowable when scholarly creativity — hence self-selection — was critically important. Scholars were asked both to propose papers of their own and to suggest topics for sessions of the Congress which they might edit into volumes. All were then informed of the suggestions and encouraged to re-think their own papers and the topics. The process, therefore, was a continuous one of feedback and exchange and it has continued to be so even after the Congress. The some two thousand papers comprising *World Anthropology* certainly then offer a substantial sample of world anthropology. It has been said that anthropology is at a turning point; if this is so, these volumes will be the historical direction-markers.

As might have been foreseen in the first post-colonial generation, the large majority of the Congress papers (82 percent) are the work of scholars identified with the industrialized world which fathered our traditional discipline and the institution of the Congress itself: Eastern Europe (15 percent); Western Europe (16 percent); North America (47 percent); Japan, South Africa, Australia, and New Zealand (4 percent). Only 18 percent of the papers are from developing areas: Africa (4 percent); Asia-Oceania (9 percent); Latin America (5 percent). Aside from the substantial representation from the U.S.S.R. and the nations of Eastern Europe, a significant difference between this corpus of written material and that of other Congresses is the addition of the large proportion of contributions from Africa, Asia, and Latin America. "Only 18 percent" is two to four times as great a proportion as that of other Congresses; moreover, 18 percent of 2,000 papers is 360 papers, 10 times the number of "Third World" papers presented at previous Congresses. In fact, these 360 papers are more than the total of ALL papers published after the last International Congress of Anthropological and Ethnological

Sciences which was held in the United States (Philadelphia, 1956). Even in the beautifully organized Tokyo Congress in 1968 less than a third as many members from developing nations, including those of Asia, participated.

The significance of the increase is not simply quantitative. The input of scholars from areas which have until recently been no more than subject matter for anthropology represents both feedback and also long-awaited theoretical contributions from the perspectives of very different cultural, social and historical traditions. Many who attended the IXth Congress were convinced that anthropology would not be the same in the future. The fact that the next Congress (India, 1978) will be our first in the "Third World" may be symbolic of the change. Meanwhile, sober consideration of the present set of books will show how much, and just where and how, our discipline is being revolutionized.

Readers of this volume will be interested in a number of others in this series on maritime anthropology in other contexts; archaeological and population studies of areas adjacent to the Arctic; and studies of early man, population biology, and migration as a continuing species phenomenon.

*Chicago, Illinois*                                                      SOL TAX
*September 3, 1975*

# Table of Contents

General Editor's Preface     v

Introduction     1
  by *William Fitzhugh*

PART ONE: SCANDINAVIA

Agriculture, Inland Hunting, and Sea Hunting in the Western and
  Northern Region of the Baltic, 6000–2000 B.C.     21
  by *Stig Welinder*

The Rock Carvings at Nämforsen, Ångermanland, Sweden, as a
  Problem of Maritime Adaptation and Circumpolar Interrelations     41
  by *Mats P. Malmer*

Prehistoric Coastal Settlement on the Upper Bothnian Coast of
  Northern Sweden     47
  by *H. Christiansson* and *Noel D. Broadbent*

Use of Slate in the Circumpolar Region     57
  by *Kristen R. Møllenhus*

When and Why Did Occupational Specialization Begin at the
  Scandinavian North Coast?     75
  by *Povl Simonsen*

Maritime Adaptations in Northern Norway's Prehistory     87
  by *Gutorm Gjessing*

Circumpolar Adaptation Zones East-West and Cross-Economy
  Contacts North-South: an Outsider's Query, Especially on
  Ust'-Poluj     101
  by *Carl-Axel Moberg*

PART TWO: NORTH PACIFIC AND BERING SEA

Problems of the Origin of the Ancient Sea Hunters' Cultures in the
Northern Pacific                                                        113
by *R. S. Vasilievsky*
The Okhotsk Culture, a Maritime Culture of the Southern Okhotsk
Sea Region                                                             123
by *Haruo Ohyi*
Stability and Adaptability in the Evolution of Hunting Tools in
Ancient Eskimo Cultures                                                159
by *S. Arutiunov* and *D. Sergeev*
Coastal Adaptation and Cultural Change in Alaskan Eskimo
Prehistory                                                            167
by *Don E. Dumond*
Aleut Adaptation and Evolution                                         181
by *William S. Laughlin* and *Jean S. Aigner*
Technological Continuity and Change Within a Persistent Maritime
Adaptation: Kodiak Island, Alaska                                      203
by *Donald W. Clark*
Marine Transgressions and Cultural Adaptation: Preliminary Tests
of an Environmental Model                                               229
by *G. F. Grabert* and *C. E. Larsen*

PART THREE: NORTHWEST ATLANTIC

Maritime Adaptation on the Northwestern Atlantic Coast                 255
by *James A. Tuck*
Demography and Adaptations of Eighteenth-Century Eskimo
Groups in Northern Labrador and Ungava                                 269
by *J. Garth Taylor*

PART FOUR: COMPARATIVE STUDIES

Maritime Adaptations in Cold Archipelagoes: An Analysis of
Environment and Culture in the Aleutian and Other Island Chains   281
by *A. P. McCartney*
A Comparative Approach to Northern Maritime Adaptations               339
by *William Fitzhugh*

Biographical Notes                                                     387

Index of Names                                                        393

Index of Subjects                                                     399

# Introduction

WILLIAM FITZHUGH

The occasion of the IXth International Congress of Anthropological and Ethnological Sciences, held in Chicago in 1973 under the direction of Dr. Sol Tax, offered a unique opportunity to explore global anthropological issues. Formerly, works contributed to the Congress varied widely, and it was rare to assemble a group of specialists who had agreed beforehand to apply themselves to a single topic. The decision that the 1973 Congress would be organized around topical symposia and would publish volumes with substantive papers of general as well as specialized interest provided a structure by which the Congress could serve more usefully as an educational forum for focused scholarly discussion while also making available to the public a synopsis of the current state of knowledge in a given field.

These changes in Congress format provided the impetus for a new departure in the traditional quintennial colloquy of circumpolar archeologists. The existence of this fraternity of northern specialists has been a distinctive feature of circumpolar studies, and one wonders if their solidarity accrues from a combination of common historical and methodological problems or from a huddling effect instilled by inurement from mosquitos and common tastes for bakeapple *(Rubus chamaemorus)* and fresh fish. Aside from these proclivities, however, there is no doubt that Marshall and Fulbright fellowships and the history of Danish research in the North American Arctic, together with exchanges of Russo-American research in Alaska and Siberia, have resulted in an unusual kinship of scholarly enterprises and associations which has promoted the development of crossties in circumpolar anthropology. The reasons, of course, go far beyond this and include both scholarly traditions and the continuity of arctic and subarctic environments around the Arctic Basin.

The decision to prepare a Congress session on circumpolar maritime adaptations grew from developments in the general field of northern anthropological research over the past century. These trends are useful to note, for they document the intertwined nature of ethnological and archaeological theory in arctic studies. Besides the obvious environmental similarities, three factors seem to have been predominant influences: speculation on the relationship between ethnographic Eskimos and Paleolithic cultures of Western Europe, the diffusion of cultural elements within the circumpolar tundra-taiga zone, and the functional question of cultural and biological adaptations. Cross-cutting each of these research topics was the fundamental question of whether the basis of circumpolar anthropological theory is the result of environmental reductionism and cultural simplification or whether observed similarities result from a basic historical relationship linking Scandinavia with Eurasia and the American Arctic.

Present circumpolar theory can be traced to the nineteenth-century discovery of Ice Age man and his hypothesized relationship to Eskimo culture. The knowledge that man was once adapted in Western Europe in the height of the last glaciation, surrounded by animals now either extinct or restricted to northern environments, posed a major interpretive problem at that time. Contemporary acculturated or economically transformed cultures of northern Scandinavia and those of northern Asia did not provide useful analogy to this problem, and it was not until the availability of information on Eskimo culture that a suitable model of Pleistocene human existence was found. Thus, it was just a century ago that Dawkins (1874) established the first link in circumpolar research by proposing a direct genetic link between the ethnographic Eskimos and European Paleolithic cultures. This idea, later developed by Sollas (1915), suggested that Eskimo culture represented a living relic of these early hunters who had followed the retreating reindeer herds north at the end of the Ice Age. Since that time, the origins and antiquity of the Eskimo have been closely associated to (as well as modified by) conceptions of European and Asiatic prehistory. This theme, after a period of eclipse by Birket-Smith's inland North American origin of Eskimo culture, is still very much alive in current interpretations of Paleo-Eskimo origins (cf. Irving 1968; Laughlin 1963, 1967).

An outgrowth of the belief in historical continuities was the translation of speculative theory into the more scientific distributional studies based on early archaeological excavations in the north. The work of archaeologists such as Bøe, Brøgger, Schmidt, and others in north Scandinavia; of Dall, Hrdlička, and Collins in the Bering Strait and Aleutians; of Mathiassen in the Canadian Arctic and Greenland, and Ritchie and Wintemberg in the Northeast, together with distributional compendia, such as Leroi-Gourhan (1946) and de Laguna (1947), resulted in recognition of early Eskimo-like cultures throughout most areas of the North and raised most directly the problem of historical connections. Similar questions were being considered in ethnological studies of northern peoples (Cooper 1946).

The result of this trend was the crystallization of the Circumpolar Stone Age concept by Gjessing (1944). As envisioned by Gjessing, cultures adapted to the ice-bound fringe of the polar sea had existed for millennia with a stone age technology, maintaining low population densities and traveling widely in search of food. During these movements similar groups were encountered and ideas were exchanged which eventually resulted in a common pool of adaptive elements including the core features of sledges, skin boats, ground slate technology, semi-lunar knives, toggling and nontoggling harpoons, and oil lamps. These groups were thought to have extremely conservative cultural traditions, isolated from neolithic and other innovative developments to the south, and many of the adaptive traits in question seemed to be traceable from Mesolithic cultures of northern Europe to contemporary ethnographic peoples.

Gjessing's Circumpolar Stone Age was based on the belief that the ecological requirements of an arctic adaptation led to the need for similar technological and social solutions; hence, as these forms were developed — presumably in northern Europe — they spread by a combination of diffusion and population movements throughout the circumpolar region, eventually reaching Eskimo and Laurentian cultures by way of the arctic sea coast. Given the great distances, the lack of archaeological evidence from central Eurasia, and the impressive time differentials involved, one cannot help but be awed by Gjessing's faith in cultural transmission and retention. However, the less faithful were soon to appear, and archaeologists more concerned with documentation, such as Spaulding (1946), Rudenko (1961), Gebhard (1946), Møllenhus (1958, this volume), and Moberg (1960), began to point out the significant gaps in distribution of many of the key complexes, especially of ground slate and toggling harpoons, between Scandinavia and the Pacific coast. Many of these problems are evident in the proceedings of the Circumpolar Conference of Copenhagen held in 1958 (Birket-Smith 1960).

By this time fragmentation of the diffusionist aspect of the circumpolar concept had become clearly evident. Continued regional documentation and more refined dating pointed to further problems with historical explanations. By the end of the following decade we have the somewhat plaintive note:

Has more than a generation of research brought us no closer to a solution, than to the dispersal of too hastily formed theories about cultural Arctic Circumpolar contacts? Do we merely end up with a general picture of cultural convergence in which the same kinds of materials are used for similar purposes, the fashioning of implements into shapes rational to their use, ending up with a frame-constructed skin boat in two different Arctic areas? (Nordland 1968: 306).

Trying to revive interest in the comparative ethnological studies, Nordland noted the widespread complexes and similarities in shamanism, beliefs concerning the Aurora Borealis, rock art, and certain rituals concerned with the increase of game. These and other widespread forms, such as raven myths, have not been adequately studied by ethnologists, but their citation in support of a circumpolar culture base presently remains at the search-and-find level of isolated comparison similar to that found in early archaeological diffusion studies. Without utilizing new methods, perhaps based on structural and linguistic analyses (cf. Kleivan 1971), this approach does not appear to offer new hope for circumpolar ethnological theory.

However, during the past decade the intensification of archaeological research in many northern areas has produced information with which the question of historical diffusion can be more scientifically assessed, and at the same time has opened a number of new themes diversifying the web of circumpolar archaeology beyond its original conception. Several articles in this volume reflect these new concerns, such as questions of cross-cultural comparison and cross-economy contacts with technologically "advanced" societies south of the boreal-taiga zone.

## CIRCUMPOLAR DIFFUSION

As we have noted, the Circumpolar Stone Age concept was based on ethnological theory of northern hunting cultures and their distribution within a relatively homogeneous environment. Recently, the cultural basis for this formulation has been amplified in a provocative paper by Simonsen (1972) in which questions of general circumpolar research are approached by way of Simonsen's archaeological research in North Norway. Speaking from the local level, Simonsen points out the semi-

nomadic nature of these cultures and the lack of environmental boundaries throughout much of this area. Difficulty in defining ethnological
cultures from archaeological complexes leads him to the belief that
cultures adapted along an ecological continuum, such as found in North
Norway, display gradual shifts in cultural elements and settlement
patterns which make definition of specific regional groupings almost
impossible. At the far end of an ecological continuum new elements
appear while many of the dominant features at the other end will either
be present or show minimal modification. Two factors modifying this
tendency for cultural continuities are suggested: ecological breaks and
population replacement. Significant ecological boundaries include the
one between North and South Scandinavia discussed by Moberg (1960);
the break between coastal and interior mountainous regions from which
semi-nomadic occupation by coastal peoples is impossible; and the
more dramatic winter ice boundary existing further east along the Kola
peninsula, where open water winter fishing cannot be practiced and a
settlement pattern reversal similar to Eskimo adaptations north and
south of the Alaskan peninsula is found. The second factor of change is
the replacement or amalgamation of peoples from across a transition
zone. Under these general conditions Simonsen sees the north Scandinavian and adjacent regions as exhibiting diffusion of selective elements
along gradual ecological transitions on an east-west axis while more substantial economic and cultural modifications or actual migrations occur
along the north-south lines (1972: 166).

In Scandinavia, Simonsen suggests that contacts between stone age
peoples and Neolithic or sub-Neolithic societies resulted in the dissemina-
tion of innovations into the epi-Mesolithic cultures of intellectually and
materially starved northern peoples eager to add new and useful elements
to their otherwise narrow form of adaptation. Further, he suggested that
these innovations subsequently spread to the east on a basic circumpolar
current largely as envisioned by Gjessing (Simonsen 1972: 168).

In terms of intercultural relationships within the Scandinavian area
Simonsen's statement is supported generally, especially given the abundant evidence of northern diffusion and trade from northern Europe.
However, Simonsen broadens this into a general theory of circumpolar
diffusion in which a number of assumptions remain hypothetical, including (1) temporal priority for innovations in the west, (2) the inevitable
flow of innovations from technologically advanced to technologically
simple societies, (3) receptivity of innovations in hunting cultures, and
(4) the lack of creative ability in hunting societies.

While there may be validity in these assumptions, they remain unproved and are part of the intellectual baggage from the early Dawkins time-slope hypothesis and our own relativistic ideas of the superior efficiency of a donor culture's technology in subsistence adaptations. There is no question about individual traits and sometimes technologies, such as metallurgy, being introduced, but it is questionable if significant adaptive elements were introduced into northern cultures independently from more advanced southern groups. Rather it seems likely that they developed in their northern contexts (Fitzhugh 1975). Of Gjessing's original list only the bone harpoon occurs in all northern complexes, and its history is certainly older than the other elements that comprise Gjessing's Arctic Stone Age complex.

By far the greatest problem is the continuing theoretical nature and lack of specificity of the circumpolar diffusion question. When proposed by Gjessing the concept was of necessity a collage of ethnological and archaeological facts unrelated in time and context. Subsequent research, however, has not produced a more culturally coherent formulation; nor has it produced new traits by which cross-cultural comparisons could be made. Distribution gaps, chronological gaps, lack of typological specificity, and other problems result in the present soft underbelly of circumpolar diffusion theory, where available evidence is either negative or inconclusive and where negative evidence is of assumed importance.

Despite the absence of substantiating data, however, the circumpolar diffusion concept shows no sign of drifting into anthropological oblivion. There is some possibility that development and cross-correlation of regional prehistories will provide the necessary data for documenting contacts through the circumpolar region. Both the boreal and arctic coastal routes should probably be maintained as possible conduits despite the ecological and ethnological bias currently favoring the former (cf. Spaulding 1946; Clark 1952). Further research along the Eurasian arctic coast may indicate alternatives to the present understanding of exclusively north-south riverine adaptations in this area, and the possibility that coastal ice conditions and ecology may have been significantly different during the Hypsithermal should be considered. Finally, the current tendency toward independent origins of circumpolar cultures does not necessarily invalidate Gjessing's entire thesis; rather, it suggests that contacts may have been significant at a much earlier time period and that if the individual elements suggested by Gjessing were never linked in a single donor culture, at least some aspect of the adaptive complex, such as bone harpoons, may well be the only surviving element of an original circumpolar dispersion. This idea had considerable support among the conference participants.

## CROSS-ECONOMY TRANSFORMATIONS

In the face of negative evidence for east-west diffusion it is natural that north-south contacts should be more intensively studied. This second theme of circumpolar research has been developing gradually over the past twenty years and was initiated in Scandinavia by Moberg's (1960) paper on the boundary between hunting and farming cultures. The isolated study of northern hunting and fishing peoples is no longer considered a valid basis for research since there is abundant evidence that they participated to varying extents in other social and economic systems. In southern Scandinavia the incorporation of neolithic elements was made selectively and did not greatly alter the hunting and fishing basis for society in the Younger Stone Age for many years. Increased trade and communication seem to have been the result of these changes which eventually brought new ideas and produced economic markets even in the Arctic cultures (cf. Simonsen, Christiansson and Broadbent, Malmer, this volume). The investigation of these cross-economy contacts has raised new problems of wide anthropological interest, such as its relation to Marxist theory; and the varying degrees of Neolithic influence in northern societies has also stimulated discussion about taxonomic units and description, such as whether a northern culture should be termed "Neolithic," "sub-Neolithic," "epi-Mesolithic," or "Mesolithic," (cf. Meinander 1961 as quoted in Simonsen 1972).

Further study of these north-south linkages is needed to determine if they demonstrate population movements or routes of massive cultural introductions to the north, as suggested by Simonsen. The methods of modern archaeology will serve to enhance cross-economy linkages which have been eclipsed for so long by the isolationist view of northern cultures and the question of east-west diffusion. Faunal analyses and settlement pattern approaches will be especially important additions together with the social and economic implications of trade nets now becoming documented in Scandinavia. The former emphasis on isolation in northern cultures is being replaced by a more dynamic set of explanatory models. The importance of these cross-economic, north-south contacts is not only evident in Scandinavia, but in the central Soviet Union north of Ust'-Poluj (Moberg, this volume; Cernetsov 1953; Moshinskaya 1970) and also in the Far East, as for example in the role of domestic animals in the Okhotsk culture (Ohyi, this volume). Characteristically, these contacts run along north-south coastlines from temperate to arctic zones at the edges of the northern continental margins, or along major river systems transecting taiga and tundra zones in the Soviet Union.

Few natural barriers are noted along these routes. In fact, they tend to follow ecological gradients through which cultural transmission might occur among groups sharing elements at a basic adaptation type, be it taiga or maritime hunting. These socioeconomic trendlines, providing communication routes between more developed southern societies and markets and natural resources of northern peoples, often through a water-transport medium, are as important as east-west environmental and cultural continuities. Together they constitute the warp and weft of circumpolar cultural relations.

## COMPARATIVE STUDIES

The third theme of circumpolar research evident in recent literature and in the articles of this conference relates to comparative studies of archaeological and ethnological cultures of the North. While the nature of these comparative projects varies from the investigations of functional parallels, evolutionary development, and questions of cross-cultural generalization, they all depend to some extent on Gjessing's idea of an adaptive technological complex including his core elements and the leveling effect of harsh environmental conditions on social organization, settlement patterns, and other aspects of northern cultural adaptations. Regardless of the fate of circumpolar diffusion, Gjessing has advanced a more fundamental problem which deserves careful attention by archaeologists concerned with cultural processes. Such an approach is particularly germane in the north where environmental conditions are more homogeneous and where complicating historical and acculturation questions are at a minimum.

An initial approach to these comparative studies is to ask how similar two cultures or complexes are, whether they are independent developments or the result of diffusion or other historically attributed causes; and, if independent, why have they developed similar forms or structures within their respective adaptations? Once independent origins are established for two or more cultures, responses to environmentally-related problems and the corresponding adaptation types are emphasized in the comparative approach.

Several factors have contributed to the interest in comparative studies in northern archaeology. Foremost among these is the lack of evident historical contact between those cultures of Scandinavia, the North Pacific, and northeast North America which were presumed to share Gjessing's circumpolar adaptive complex. If this current view is correct we must then begin to consider convergent development as similar adaptive responses. Secondly, as previously noted, the relative simplicity of these cultural systems offers more chance of isolating common features of an evolutionary or functional type. Finally, this process involves a systematic approach by which one can assess the relative merits of explanation across cultural boundaries within ecosystems which share common structural features.

Two adaptation types are commonly encountered in the circumpolar region. The most conspicuous of these is the taiga-steppe variety which was found ethnographically in the Tungus, Yukaghir, and Chukchi of the central and eastern Soviet North. These groups had, however, been substantially altered economically by metallurgical introductions from the south and by reindeer domestication presumably spreading during the last 2,000 years through the taiga from Scandinavia and northwestern Russia. Less acculturated interior hunting economies are found in the Alaskan and Canadian boreal forest among the Tulareumiut, Kutchin, Chipewyan, Cree, and Montagnais-Naskapi. These eastern hunters had an adaptation which is presumed to be closer to that of Paleolithic man in the Old World than other groups for which ethnographic documentation is known and consequently have been used as models for cultural reconstruction and analogy (cf. MacDonald 1968; Campbell 1968; Nelson 1973). Very little is known of the cultural ecology of these groups, and yet they are frequently used as models of adaptations in other environmental zones and eras. Unfortunately, economic and social changes have nearly completely transformed these societies today so that we shall now have to investigate these problems through historical documentation.

Archaeologically, the peoples of the northern forests and tundra ecotones are poorly known largely because of their low population density, their dispersed and transient settlement pattern, and the insatiable appetite of podsols for organic cultural and faunal remains. Geographically, the boreal corridor has presented barriers to archaeological investigations which are only recently beginning to erode with the discovery of stratified sites in eastern Asia and Alaska. Heretofore, the problems of interpreting relatively undifferentiated lithic industries, often of mixed components and in shallow deposits, have not stimulated research compared to the more productive sites of the northern coastal margins. The coastal cultures have always been better known ethnographically and archaeologically, and it is ironic that most of Gjessing's circumpolar complex was drawn from northern maritime cultures, not from the taiga and boreal hunting cultures which, according to

Spaulding, were the more likely conduits for circumpolar diffusion throughout the vast continental interiors.

Attention to the coastal aspect of circumpolar theory drew support from Clark's (1952) analysis of Mesolithic seasonal coastal adaptations in northern Europe and from Bryan's (1957) suggestion that, as a global phenomenon, the circumpolar distribution of ground slate industries was associated more with maritime adaptations than with interior hunting patterns. However, Bryan felt that many of the circumpolar traits noted by Gjessing and Spaulding must once have been historically related and that their lack of association as a single complex was due to selective diffusion and acceptance at an early time. This diffusionist cast, attributable to current beliefs, should not diminish Bryan's reaffirmation of Gjessing's coastal association of circumpolar Stone Age complexes, which, following Spaulding's boreal thesis, represented an important clarification. If, in fact, these complexes were associated with historically independent northern maritime adaptations along the continental margins, this opened a new query in circumpolar research: to what extent were they attributable to evolutionary processes and adaptive efficiency in these zones? Do northern maritime adaptations evolve through time toward the use of skin boats, oil heating, ground slate and bone technologies, harpoon complexes, and the use of semi-lunar knives? If so, what could be the causal trends and how have they operated in producing similaritity and diversity in northern cultures? What is the time frame of these developments, and how do they reticulate with local environmental and regional historical conditions? Do these phenomena represent purely regional trajectories or are they interrelated perhaps as the result of global climatic conditions or culturally-achieved plateaus? In short, the possibility that maritime adaptations have common functionally-related similarities in Scandinavia, Northeast Asia, Bering Sea and the North American Arctic, the Northwest Coast, and the American Northeast presented archaeologists with a new problem of more theoretical interest than in proving or disproving circumpolar diffusion. It introduced environmental and adaptive variables of more general anthropological significance than the mechanical transmission of ideas assumed under historical explanations (Fitzhugh 1975). Ethnological and archaeological cross-cultural studies of arctic and subarctic maritime adaptations, and of adaptation types not restricted to the circumpolar area (Fitzhugh, McCartney, this volume), provided a method of determining the variables and causal factors involved in the development and testing of anthropological theory. Initial attempts in this direction should promote further interest in comparative archaeology and will produce insight into the very real needs for methodological refinements in definitions and the comparability of cultural complexes, adaptations, and units of reference in general. The wealth of time depth available in archaeological studies suggests that greater scientific rigor can be applied to comparative studies of this type and that the use of the method of cross-cultural comparison should not be restricted to historical periods. Further, by the use of adaptation types it permits comparative studies beyond similar environmental zones to more diverse ecosystems of the temperate and tropical regions, and an investigation of the influence of environmental and historical diversity on functional adaptations, and religious, demographic, and other cultural subsystems. The growing recognition of a discrete field of maritime anthropology is signal to the potential future of archaeological and evolutionary studies of this economic adaptation type and its relationship to agricultural adaptations in anthropology.

The Chicago Congress seemed to be an ideal forum to reopen discussion of circumpolar issues with specialists from all segments of arctic anthropology. The decision to focus on northern maritime adaptations grew from my own research in coastal Labrador which, with new information on the Moorehead and Maritime Archaic cultures of the Northeast (cf. Tuck 1971, this volume), gave a more complete view of this maritime adaptation type than that previously available. Further, the research of the past decade, principally by Simonsen (1961, 1963), into Stone Age cultures of northern Scandinavia provided the basis for comparative study of these two similar environments, their respective culture histories, and possibilities of historical contacts across the North Atlantic (cf. Ridley 1960; Kehoe 1962, 1971). The results of this work suggested no concrete evidence for such contacts, and for this reason the importance of convergent development and functional equivalency in northern sea mammal hunting and fishing cultures needed investigation. The symposium was called, therefore, to reassess the circumpolar diffusion question from the new perspective of maritime adaptations from both a historical and comparative basis.

Several definitional problems beset this approach. As used here, northern maritime adaptations are generally restricted to the subarctic and arctic coasts and archipelagoes where marine productivity and concentration is high and is seasonally available with aboriginal exploitative techniques. Sea mammals, available anadromous and demersal fishes, and estuarine vertebrate and invertebrate resources are important in these northern adaptations. Questions about the proportion of marine and interior resources, of sea mammal hunting ("catching") versus fishing, of the duration and season of coastal settlement, and of the dispersed or nondispersed nature of coastal settlements provide other problems in the definition of this adaptation type. For the present, these have been avoided in favor of a broader preliminary approach to northern maritime adaptations. The point, however, must be stressed, that the topical restriction of the conference imposed an arbitrary isolation of maritime from interior economies, which, in most areas, is not a self-sufficient economic pattern. Only in the Aleutians and possibly the Kurils are maritime and coastal adaptations of almost exclusive importance. In all other areas settlement patterns include interior hunting and fishing adaptations as a vital supplement to coastal resources, either through direct exploitation or by indirect means of trade and exchange. In southern Scandinavia and the Baltic, maritime economies for the past 6,000 years have been seasonal activities and cannot be considered apart from farming and animal husbandry, as noted by Clark (1952), Moberg (1960), and Welinder (this volume). A similar dual economy is present in the Okhotsk culture (Ohyi, this volume).

Despite these caveats, the widespread distribution and similarities in northern maritime adaptations suggest that it is methodologically sound to investigate their origins and function as a separate adaptation type, and to determine their evolutionary roles, as a self-sufficient economic strategy, as a subsystem within both mixed Neolithic and maritime economies, and as a seasonal partner to coastal-interior adaptations of the northern seacoasts and forests. Such an approach should not and cannot be confined to prehistoric times. Although much of the emphasis on circumpolar diffusion has been confined to the prehistoric period, historic and demographic data is becoming more important in analogic and functional studies (cf. Taylor, this volume).

The articles presented here demonstrate the variety of problems under consideration in the circumpolar area. All of these are original contributions to the Congress with the exception of the translation of Møllenhus' original paper of 1958 which reflects the concern at that time with the diffusional aspect of Gjessing's hypothesis and which is not generally known outside Scandinavia. The content of the other articles shows a movement away from problems of circumpolar diffussion to diverse regional issues. For this reason the presentation of the articles here is organized by geographic groups rather than by thematic content. Each group reflects the problems which have dominated research in its areas, as well as the state of archaeological information. The articles of Part One concern Scandinavia and northern Russia and demonstrate the importance of trade, cross-economic and social ties with Neolithic societies, of rock art and cultural reconstruction, and exhibit a relatively advanced understanding of culture history and environmental relationships. This is compared with, for instance, the dominance of culture-historical questions in the articles of Part Two, the North Pacific-Bering Sea, or Part Three, the Northwest Atlantic regions where, except for later Eskimo development, very little information is available for studying cultural transformations. The final section, Part Four, contains articles of a more general nature not confined to specific geographic regions. Unfortunately, the balance in these sections is uneven, with underrepresentation of current work in the Bering Sea and northern Eskimo cultures.

This introduction has presented the background and development of circumpolar archaeology and the major issues which were of concern to the conference participants. While I will not attempt to summarize the contributions and new ideas which are better presented by the authors herein, I do feel it is useful to conclude with a brief enumeration of salient points about which a consensus now seems to exist. There are also several areas of disagreement especially noted in a post-Congress communication by Aigner on the rigor of explanation and the admissibility of certain cross-cultural procedures which unfortunately could not be included here. I must emphasize that these are my understandings and are not necessarily shared by the conference members, whose opinions, however, I hope to have reflected accurately.

1. It is evident that Gjessing's circumpolar diffusion hypothesis as initially proposed and as modified by Spaulding is not supported by present evidence; nor does it seem likely that confirmation of diffusion will be forthcoming even from the poorly-known regions of Eurasia and North America.

2. Gjessing's constellation of traits (ground slate tools, oil heating, skin boats, ulu-type knives, toggling harpoons) is not found in interior taiga of boreal regions but does occur in subarctic and arctic maritime hunting and fishing cultures.

3. These similarities appear to develop independently in maritime settings in Scandinavia, the Northern Pacific-Bering Sea zone, and the northwestern Atlantic. In Scandinavia, the Northwest Coast and the Northeast, these trends converge during the Hypsithermal and reach their greatest point of similaritity during the temperature peak circa 4000 to 5000 B.P.

4. Blade and burin industries are not usually associated with ground slate technology of the maritime zones.

5. In accordance with the traditional hypothesis, ground slate tools

appear to have their most likely prototypes in ground and honed bone, or possibly shell industries.

6.   An early wave of diffusion, perhaps by an original population spread west to east, may have carried the prototype bone industries into North America at a Paleolithic or Mesolithic cultural level, preceding the convergent development noted in northern maritime regions.

7.   The role of maritime adaptations cannot be understood in isolation from other economic types; however, as a group they form a distinct class of subsistence strategies which share a number of common features and have similar social and cultural implications which facilitate cross-cultural examination.

8.   Common solutions to problems of northern maritime adaptations, rather than common histories, are the most likely causes of cultural convergences in these areas.

9.   Considering the limited evidence of east-west cultural contacts, the north-south contacts appear to have been more meaningful in terms of northern cultural developments; many of these contacts involve cross-economy exchanges which result in transformation of more isolated northern cultures.

10.   Seasonality, especially utilization of interior resources, is an almost universal feature of northern maritime adaptations. Economic transformations of northern cultures often proceed along lines of least resistance, replacing mobile interior adaptations with more intensive maritime exploitation or substitution by seasonal farming or animal husbandry.

11.   Northern maritime adaptations often provide greater demographic stability and seasonal permanence of settlement not encountered in post-Pleistocene interior hunting cultures. Riverine exploitation may provide similar stability, although riverine adaptations are not necessarily a precursor to coastal or maritime adaptations.

12.   Although sea mammal products are important sources of food, heat, and technological materials in northern maritime societies, the presence of dependable supplies of fish protein and carbohydrates is the sustaining element in most of these economies.

13.   Northern maritime adaptations tend to exhibit recognizable cultural continuities over long periods of time. In most of these areas population stability is suspected for many millennia, and persistence of the cultural system is noted.

14.   Cultural stability, seasonal sedentariness and productive economies have permitted a greater elaboration of artistic, social, and economic systems as compared to interior hunting cultures. There is a tendency

toward increased trade and perhaps craft specialization.

15.   The development of intensive maritime adaptations as early as 5000 to 6000 B.P. has resulted in a great loss of data due to the submergence of coastal sites under rising sea levels (cf. Grabert and Larsen, this volume). Local geological conditions vary, but extensive inundation is evident especially at the margin of isostatic rebound. Site destruction will have to be considered when comparing the apparent boundary between northern coastal regions with large semi-permanent settlements and more southernly zones, where large coastal populations are less frequently encountered archaeologically.

In conclusion, the study of circumpolar anthropological problems has evolved through a number of stages over the past hundred years since Dawkins first proposed a link between Paleolithic and ethnographic Eskimo cultures. In tracing these developments we have noted the importance of a number of studies initiated by Gjessing, Spaulding, Bryan, Moberg, Møllenhus, Simonsen, and others which bring this field of research to the present day. The concern of this volume with northern maritime rather than interior adaptations is due to the occurrence of many of the traditional circumpolar trait complexes within coastal contexts. Unfortunately, it was not possible to include works which would have provided a more balanced geographic coverage. Even so this collection demonstrates many of the kinds of research that are now being conducted within the circumpolar areas. While concern with northern diffusion routes has waned, a number of new research problems has emerged dealing especially with local culture history, environmental relationships, acculturation phenomena across economic and ecological boundaries, and cross-cultural comparisons. Though often regional in scope, the implications of these studies generally transcend local problems and demonstrate the continuing usefulness of a widely disseminated circumpolar dialogue combining anthropological, archaeological, and environmental interests. The future development of circumpolar theory and the testing of hypotheses on northern cultural development will depend on our ability to integrate these fields and to define problems for future investigations. These articles identify a number of problem areas, such as the need for field research in northern Eurasia, the origin of the early North Pacific maritime adaptations including the more restricted problem of Eskimo and Aleut origins, relationships between maritime and interior adaptations within cultural systems, and the establishment of baselines for cross-cultural research in northern maritime adaptations. More important than all others, however, is the need for rapid expansion of the data base of northern archaeology by new scientifically adequate excavations and thorough analysis and publication. It is remarkable that so many totally unknown regions still exist, while others, like the Bering Sea area, are becoming well known. Finally, we must confront the important question of evolutionary developments in maritime adaptations both as they relate to explainable diversity in cultural and environmental settings and to the causes and extent of convergence. The northern regions offer excellent testing ground for developing evolutionary theory, and it is beginning to appear as though maritime adaptations have played a central role in cultural development by virtue of providing a more stable economic base for reduced seasonal nomadism and maintenance of larger, more permanent seasonal settlements than possible in the northern interior. Such problems have only begun to be explored. It is hoped that these articles will contribute to this end.

## REFERENCES

BIRKET-SMITH, K., *editor*
  1960   The Circumpolar Conference in Copenhagen. *Acta Arctica* 12.
BRYAN, ALAN L.
  1957   Results and interpretations of recent archeological research in Western Washington with circum-boreal implications. *Davidson Journal of Anthropology* 3(1):1–16.
CAMPBELL, J. M.
  1968   "Territoriality among ancient hunters: interpretation from ethnography and nature," in *Anthropological archeology in the Americas.* Edited by B. J. Meggers, 1–21. Anthropological Society of Washington.
CERNETSOV, V. N.
  1953   Ust'-Polyeskoe Vremya v Priob'e. *Materialy i Issledovaniya po Arkheologiyi SSR* 35.
CLARK, J. G. D.
  1952   *Prehistoric Europe: the economic basis.* London: Methuen.
COOPER, J. M.
  1946   "The culture of the northeastern Indian hunters: a reconstructive interpretation," in *Man in northeastern North America.* Edited by F. Johnson, 272–305. Papers of the R. S. Peabody Foundation, 3.
DAWKINS, W. BOYD
  1874   *Cave hunting.* London.
DE LAGUNA, FREDERICA
  1947   *The prehistory of northern North America as seen from the Yukon.* Society for American Archaeology Memoir 3.

FITZHUGH, W. W.
1975 Ground slates in the Scandinavian Younger Stone Age with reference to circumpolar maritime adaptations. *Proceedings of the Prehistoric Society*.

GEBHARD, PAUL H.
1946 "Stone objects from prehistoric North America with respect to distribution, type, and significance." Unpublished doctoral dissertation, Department of Anthropology, Harvard University.

GJESSING, GUTORM
1944 The Circumpolar Stone Age. *Acta Arctica* 2.

IRVING, W. N.
1968 The Arctic small tool tradition. *Proceedings of the VIII International Congress of Anthropological and Ethnological Sciences* 3:340–342. Tokyo and Kyoto.

KEHOE, A. B.
1962 A hypothesis on the origin of northeastern American pottery. *Southwestern Journal of Anthropology* 18(1):20–29.
1971 "Small boats upon the North Atlantic," in *Man across the sea*. Edited by C. Riley, 275–292. Austin: University of Texas Press.

KLEIVAN, INGE
1971 Why is the raven black? *Acta Arctica* 17.

LAUGHLIN, WILLIAM S.
1963 Eskimos and Aleuts: their origins and evolution. *Science* 142(3593): 633–645.
1967 "Human migration and permanent occupation in the Bering Sea," in *The Bering Land Bridge*. Edited by D. M. Hopkins, 409–450. Stanford: Stanford University Press.

LEROI-GOURHAN, A.
1946 *Archéologie du Pacifique Nord*. Paris: Institut d'ethnologie.

MAC DONALD, G.
1968 Debert: a Paleo-Indian site in central Nova Scotia. *Anthropological Papers of the National Museum of Canada* 16.

MOBERG, CARL-AXEL
1960 On some circumpolar and Arctic problems. *Acta Arctica* 12:67–74.

MØLLENHUS, KRISTEN R.
1958 *Steinalderen i Søndre Helgeland*. Det Kongelige Norske Videnskabers Selskabs Skrifter 1. Trondheim.

MOSHINSKAYA, V. I.
1970 The Iron Age in the north of western Siberia and its relation to the development of the circumpolar region cultures. *Proceedings of the VII International Congress of Anthropological and Ethnological Sciences* 10:411–413. Moscow.

NELSON, R. K.
1973 *Hunters of the northern forest*. Chicago: University of Chicago Press.

NORDLAND, O.
1968 Folklore and religion among the northern peoples; a contribution to the discussion of the Arctic Circumpolar theory. *Proceedings of the Eighth International Congress of Anthropological and Ethnological Sciences* 3:305–309. Tokyo and Kyoto.

RIDLEY, F.
1960   Transatlantic contacts of primitive man: Eastern Canada and North-western Russia. *Pennsylvania Archaeologist* 30(2):46–57.

RUDENKO, S. I.
1961   *The ancient culture of the Bering Sea and the Eskimo problem.* Arctic Institute of North America, Translations from Russian Sources 1. Toronto.

SIMONSEN, P.
1961   *Varanger-funnene II: fund og udgravninger på fjordens sydkyst.* Tromsø Museums Skrifter 7(2). Tromsø, Oslo: Universitetsforlaget.
1963   *Varanger-funnene III: fund og udgravninger i pasvikdalen og ved den østlige fjordstrand.* Tromsø Museums Skrifter 7(3). Tromsø, Oslo: Universitetsforlaget.
1972   "The cultural concept in the Arctic Stone Age," in *Circumpolar problems.* Edited by G. Berg, 163–169. New York: Pergamon Press.

SOLLAS, W. J.
1915   *Ancient hunters and their modern representatives.* London.

SPAULDING, A. C.
1946   "Northeastern archaeology and general trends in the northern forest zone," in *Man in northeastern North America.* Edited by F. Johnson, 143–167. Papers of the R.S. Peabody Foundation 3.

TUCK, J. A.
1971   An archaic cemetery at Port au Choix, Newfoundland. *American Antiquity* 36(3):343–358.

# PART ONE

*Scandinavia*

# Agriculture, Inland Hunting, and Sea Hunting in the Western and Northern Region of the Baltic, 6000-2000 B.C.

STIG WELINDER

## ENVIRONMENTAL BACKGROUND

The development of land forms in the Baltic region (see Figure 1) is complicated because of the isostatic land upheaval, the eustatic rise of the sea, and the succession of plants after the melting of the ice sheet. These factors must be considered when dealing with the Stone Age.

### Geological History of the Baltic

Immediately following the ice sheet, the Baltic depression was filled with meltwater, forming the Baltic Ice Lake by 8200 B.C. When the ice sheet left the Middle Sweden Lowlands, the ice lake was connected with the sea across the Scandinavian peninsula. There was salt water, known as the Yoldia Sea, at least in the northern part of the Baltic depression, for some hundreds of years, from 8200 to 7800 B.C. Because of the isostatic land upheaval, the Yoldia Sea was cut off and the Ancylus Lake was formed where the Baltic is now situated. This important fresh water stage lasted from 7800–6500 B.C.

By 6500 B.C. the eustatically rising sea reached the edge of the Ancylus Lake and the Baltic depression became the Littorina Sea. During the first stage of the Littorina Sea, called the Mastogloia Sea, the Baltic depression was connected with the ocean through narrow sounds and the water was only slightly brackish with a salinity of less than 0.5 percent.

The sea level rose in a series of transgressions, the first of which occurred in 5000 B.C. in the Littorina Sea. From then on the salinity of the Littorina Sea was higher than today, probably above 0.7 percent, and the water was

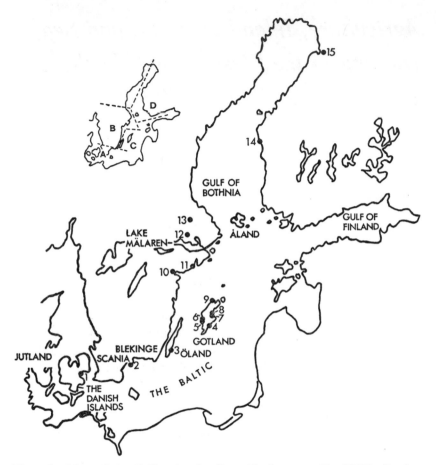

Figure 1. Map of the Baltic. A = the Scano-Danian area, B = Middle Sweden, C = the Baltic islands, D = Finland; 1 = Ølby Lyng, 2 = Siretorp, 3 = Alby, 4 = Hemmor, 5 = Visborgs Kungsladugård, 6 = Visby, 7 = Västerbjers, 8 = Svalings, 9 = Norrbus, 10 = Norrköping, 11 = Överåda, 12 = Åloppe, 13 = Svartmyra, 14 = Närpes, 15 = Oulujoki

warmer. The last transgression maximum of the Littorina Sea occurred about 2000 B.C. From then on the salinity and the warmth of the water in the Baltic depression have decreased to today's levels (Fredén 1967; Königsson 1968; Nilsson 1968; Åse 1970; Mörner 1969; Berglund and Liljegren 1971).

## Vegetation Development

About 8300 B.C., when the ice sheet still covered northern Scandinavia the first forest – with juniper, aspen, and birch – appeared in southern

# Plates

STIG WELINDER
Agriculture, Inland Hunting, and Sea Hunting (pp. 21–39)                    iii

POVL SIMONSEN
Occupational Specialization at the Scandinavian North Coast
(pp. 75–85)                                                               iv/viii

G. F. GRABERT, C. E. LARSEN
Marine Transgressions and Cultural Adaptation (pp. 229–251)        ix/xi

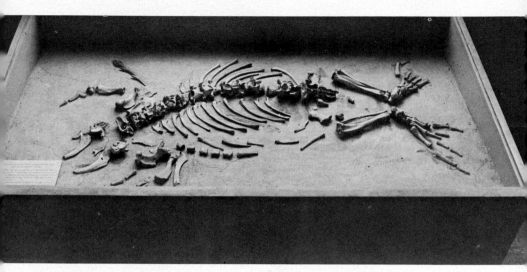

Plate 1.   Ringed seal, found in 1907, when excavating for the foundations of the new
city hall of Norrköping, Östergötland, Sweden, together with a bone harpoon head.
(Photo Nils Sagergren in the former exhibition of Statens Historiska Museum,
Stockholm)

Plate 1.

Plate 2.

Plate 3.

Plate 4.

Plate 5.

Plate 6.

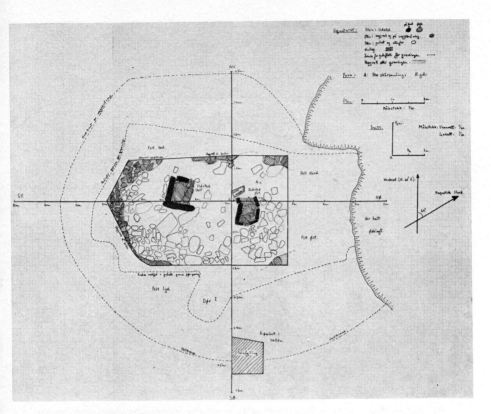

Plate 7.

Plate 8.

Plate 9.

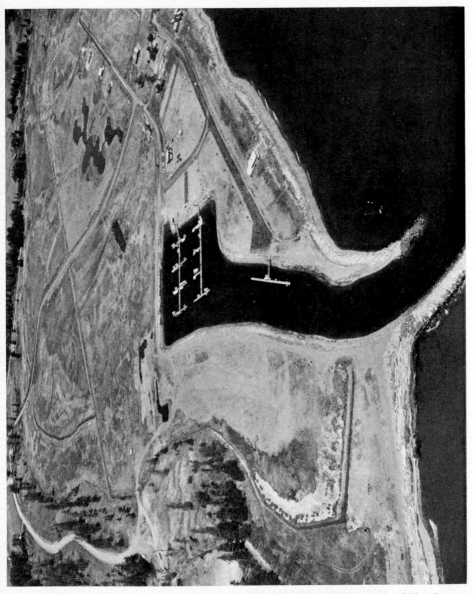

Plate 1.   Aerial view of the Birch Bay Village sites. 45-WH-11 shell midden is visible at the beach immediately to right of marina entrance channel and extends off right of photograph. 45-WH-24 lies on terrace edge where road divides, and 45-WH-24L lies at edge of creek delta. The intertidal hearth lies at the corner of the boat-launching ramp. 45-WH-29 occupies the top of the headland off the left of the photograph. (Photograph courtesy of Northwest Air Photos)

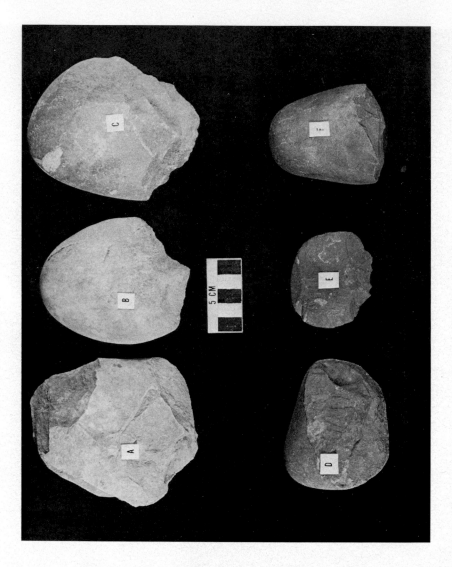

Plate 2.   Cobble and pebble implements. A, B, and C are from 45-WH-24. A is a randomly struck core. All three are of quartzite, predominant at this site — an approximate balance between basalt and quartzite was noted at 45-WH-24L nearby. Specimens D, E, and F are of basalt, and came from the lower cultural stratum at 45-WH-1. The tools from the latter component show a high frequency of edge use; basalt is the compositional material

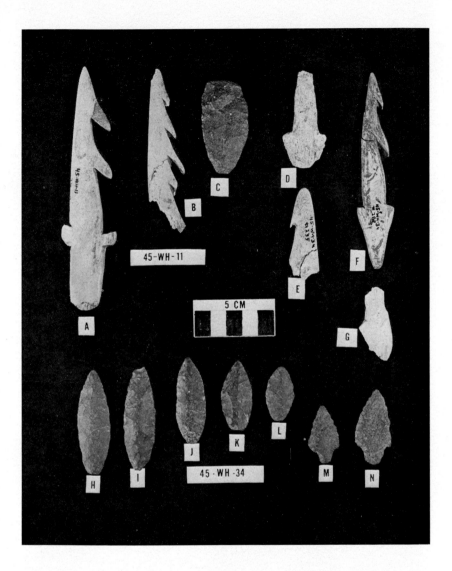

Plate 3. Harpoons and chipped stone projectile points from Birch Bay sites and 45-WH-34 (inland). Specimens A–C from Birch Bay, and D–N from 45-WH-34. Specimen C came from the tidally flooded hearth exposed in the marina; the two antler harpoons were found at the base of the more recent shell midden. The harpoons from the two sites strongly resemble each other and appear similar to Fraser Delta Marpole Phase forms. Projectile points of smaller leaf shape and stemmed forms tended to occur in strata associated with the antler harpoons

Scandinavia. Vegetation development within the forest is less dependent on the climate than on rate of spread, competition among the species, and edaphic factors such as flooding. The first more or less stable forest on high grounds was boreal, dominated by pine, hazel, and elm. It was established in the Scano-Danian area by 7500 B.C. and in Middle Sweden and southern Finland as the land was raised above the Ancylus Lake and Mastogloia Sea.

The boreal forest was followed by the Atlantic climax forest with the introduction of linden. This dense type of wood was dominated by linden and elm. The climax forest was established in southern Scandinavia by 6000 B.C., in the northern part of the Swedish west coast by 5000 B.C., and in Middle Sweden around Lake Mälaren by 4500 B.C. It never played an important role in northern Sweden and Finland. During the Atlantic period, low, marshy grounds were occupied by alder, while pine and birch were to be found along the coast and at high altitudes inland.

After 4500 B.C. in south Scandinavia and after 4000 B.C. in Middle Sweden the frequency of oak increased and after 3300 B.C. in all of southern and middle Scandinavia, the frequency of elm decreased according to pollen profiles. There is still not absolute agreement about the reasons for this phenomenon. Several possibilities have been pointed out: the deterioration of the post-glacial climate; edaphic factors such as increasing acidity; forest clearance by Neolithic man; the establishment of the climax forest on marshy grounds.

From 3000 B.C. to 2000 B.C. the woods in Scano-Dania, the Middle Swedish plains, and other fertile areas were growing more open as a result of the introduction of agriculture and stock raising (Iversen 1960, 1967; Fries 1965; Berglund 1966; Ten Hove 1968; Digerfeldt 1971).

*Fauna*

Associated with the boreal forest was a big game fauna with elk (moose) and aurochs. This fauna disappeared on the Danish islands and became less frequent in the southernmost part of the Scandinavian peninsula at the end of the boreal period – by 6500 B.C. North of this area the aurochs survived to the end of the prehistoric time and the elk well on to today.

The animals of the Atlantic period were red deer and wild boar. Reindeer are not known in southern and Middle Sweden during postglacial times.

Today there are three species of seal in the Baltic: harbor seal, ringed seal, and gray seal. The harbor seal is most common in the southwestern part of the Baltic. It is possible that it was present in the Ancylus Lake. From the Littorina Sea it is known to have been common further to the north than today, at least as far as the archipelago of Stockholm.

The ringed seal is the most common in all of the Baltic and in the Gulf of Bothnia. The ringed seals in the Baltic and the lakes Ladoga, Onega, Saimen, and others are local subspecies. The main species lives only in arctic water. The southern subspecies are interpreted as relics from the late glacial Baltic Ice Lake. They may have migrated through the outlets of the ice lake across Finland to the White Sea.

The gray seal today is most common in the northern part of the Baltic and in the Gulf of Bothnia. It is known as a fossil at least from early Littorina times.

It is of importance that during the time of the Littorina Sea a fourth species was common in the Baltic – the Greenland seal. Today it is present only in the Arctic Ocean. It is rare even on the coast of northern Norway. Subfossils of Greenland seal have been found in late glacial deposits from 10,000–8,200 B.C. on the Swedish west coast. It is probable that its occurrence in the Littorina Sea is to be looked upon as a relic from this time. Part of the year the Greenland seal wanders over extensive areas in herds of hundreds of animals, so another possibility is that a single herd may, by chance, have come to the Littorina Sea and adapted itself.

In any case it does seem curious that the Greenland seal was common in the warm Littorina Sea. This was, however, due to the higher salinity of the water which causes stratification with surface water of less salinity than today. This favored a greater ice formation than today, and this, in turn, was favorable for the Greenland seals (Ekman 1922; Degerbøhl and Krog 1959; Ahlén 1965; Degerbøhl and Fredskild 1970; Liljegren and Welinder 1971; Møhl 1971a, 1971b).

*Summary*

The possibility of sea hunting has been present in the Baltic since 6000 B.C. – that is, since the ingression of salt water. After 5000 B.C. – the time of the maximum transgression – a rich maritime fauna including Greenland seal appeared in the warm and salty Littorina Sea. There have been seals in the Baltic depression during the entire post-glacial period. Whether this includes the Greenland seal, too, is problematic.

The establishment of the Atlantic climax forest resulted in a change in the big game fauna. Elk and auroch disappeared from the Danish islands and decreased in number in the southernmost part of the Scandinavian peninsula. North of this area there was no important change.

During the period from 6000 to 2000 B.C. the land fauna do not seem to have changed very much in the western and northern region of the Baltic, while the maritime fauna were affected by the transgression of the Littorina Sea in 5000 B.C.

## CULTURAL BACKGROUND

The following chronology is a trial use of a radiocarbon time-scale common to all of the Scandinavian area ($T^1/_a = 5730$ years, no correction for the de Vries effect) (Siiriäinen 1969; Tauber 1971; Welinder 1973a).

### Stages in the Expansion of Farming: 3400–2000 B.C.

Farming here includes agriculture as well as stock raising. The conclusions presented are based solely on evidence from pollen analysis (M.-B. Florin 1958; Berglund 1969; Königsson 1970; Ahlonen 1970; Vuorela 1970; Welinder n.d.).

STAGE I: 3400–3100 B.C.  The first expansion of farming was restricted to the Danish islands and Scania. It is connected with the Funnel Beaker culture Stage A. Barley and several kinds of wheat were cultivated. According to one theory the cattle were pollarded and kept in stable the whole year.

There is no agreement as to whether the first farmers were invaders or sedentary food gatherers adapting to a new economy (Becker 1947; Troel-Smith 1953; Salomonsson 1970).

STAGE II: 3100–2700 B.C.  The second stage of expansion of farming is a continuation of the first – farming spread to the north, to southern Norway and the northern side of Lake Mälaren. It is connected with the Funnel Beaker culture Stage C. Extensive clearing to provide pasture is known to have occurred in the Atlantic climax forest during this stage. It was probably accomplished by burning (S. Florin 1958).

This second stage of expansion, which was the first one north of Scano-Dania, was of short duration except in the most fertile areas. After 2700 B.C. there are no traces of farming in the pollen profiles from most of the Scandinavian peninsula with the exception of Scania, parts of western Sweden, and the Island of Öland. The exceptions coincide with the area of distribution of passage graves. However, in these areas, there was less farming activity during the period 2500–2200 B.C.

STAGE III: 2200–2000 B.C.   The third expansion stage was the one reaching farthest north. Farming was brought to western Norway, southern Finland, and the western coast of the Gulf of Bothnia. This stage is connected with the Battle-Axe culture. The people of the Battle-Axe culture have been said to be invaders with a more or less nomadic way of living. Probably they were farmers as sedentary as those of the Funnel Beaker culture. The same types of cereals were cultivated as before, but sheep and goats seem to have increased in comparison with cattle (Malmer 1962; Becker 1967; Edgren 1970).

*Expansion of Neolithic Technology (Manufacturing of Pottery):*
*3800–2000 B.C.*

EXPANSION FROM THE SOUTH: 3800–2000 B.C.   The oldest pottery in south Scandinavia is the Ertebølle pottery. It is known to come from all of Denmark, Scania, westernmost Blekinge, and the Island of Öland. It dates from 3800–2600 B.C. in the Danish islands, and may be 200 years older in Jutland. On the Scandinavian peninsula it is not known to be older than 3100 B.C. This pottery is connected with the food-gathering Ertebølle Culture.

On the Scandinavian peninsula north of the above-mentioned area, the oldest pottery is connected with the Funnel Beaker culture Stage C and Stage II of the expansion of farming. The Funnel Beaker culture disappeared when farming ceased to be practiced after 2700 B.C. but the manufacture of pottery continued within the food-gathering Pitted Ware culture datable to 2600–1900 B.C. Food-gathering sites with pottery contemporary with the Funnel Beaker Stage C farming sites are not known. However, from the period 2800–2600 B.C., hunting sites with pottery similar to both the older Funnel Beaker pottery and the younger Pitted Ware are known. The northern limit of the Pitted Ware culture extends from Dalarna to the southern part of the Gulf of Bothnia. It is remarkable that north of this limit pottery was not introduced until the Bronze Age except for a few sites with Battle-Axe culture pottery from the expansion Stage III of farming (Brinch Petersen 1971; Königsson, Königsson, and Lepiksaar 1971; Salomonsson 1971; Welinder 1971).

EXPANSION FROM THE EAST: 3500–2000 B.C.   The Neolithic techniques spread to the eastern and northeastern coasts of the Baltic earlier than to the northwestern coast. After 3500 B.C. the southern and western coasts of Finland were dominated by the food-gathering Comb-Ornamented Pottery culture. This extended in the west to the Island of Åland.

The expansion Stages I–II of farming never reached Finland, and Stage III was of short duration, 2200–1800 B.C. (Meinander 1961, 1964).

*Inland Hunting Sites:* 6000–3000 B.C.

The economy of a hunting site must be determined with the aid of the preserved bones. The possibilities of preservation are quite uneven in the area under discussion.

The bedrock in most of Denmark and Scania and in small areas around Lake Mälaren consists of chalk or limestone. The Baltic islands are built up completely of limestone. In northern Sweden, limestone occurs in several places along the foot of the mountains. Outside the areas mentioned the bedrock consists of very old rocks. Calcareous deposits of the Quaternary Age are found in large areas in the parts of the coastal regions submerged during early stages of the history of the Baltic.

At sites in the Scano-Danian area, bones are regularly preserved. The coastal sites with deposits in sand or gravel are an important exception.

In Middle Sweden, sites with preserved bones are extremely rare. Burned fragments of bones do occur regularly and occasionally they may be identified.

In the Baltic islands the possibilities for preservation of bones are the best in the Baltic region. Sites on beach ridges may be exceptions.

In Finland the situation is the same as in Middle Sweden, or perhaps even worse.

SCANO-DANIAN AREA   Denmark and Scania were occupied by the Early Coastal culture (6000–4500 B.C.) and the Late Coastal culture (4500–2600 B.C.). From the Early Coastal culture, both inland and coastal sites are known. Both types of sites are dominated by red deer, roe deer, and boar.

From the Late Coastal culture (the late stage of which is called the Ertebølle culture), several types of sites are known. Both inland and coastal sites are dominated by the same fauna as the sites of the Early Coastal culture. The kitchen middens of the Late Coastal culture consist primarily of oyster shells. The mammal bones of the middens are dominated by the same species as the inland sites.

The presence of seal bones in Coastal culture sites will be discussed later (Althin 1954; Troel-Smith 1960; Jørgensen 1961; Kapel 1969).

MIDDLE SWEDEN   In Middle Sweden no bones are preserved at sites from this period. A few burned fragments of bones are available from one site dating to 4000 B.C. at the northern side of Lake Mälaren, which in those days formed part of the Littorina Sea. Deer, elk, beaver, marten, boar, and seal have been identified.

The excavated sites are characterized by hearthpits with a thin charcoal layer at the bottom and large amounts of burned stone chips. The sites are datable to 5000–4000 B.C. The same features are seen at the inland hunting sites in northern Sweden.

These scanty indications suggest that inland hunting was dominant in Middle Sweden before the Neolithic Stone Age (Welinder 1973b).

FINLAND   The faunal remains from the Finnish pre-Neolithic sites consist solely of burned bones which have not been examined (Luho 1967).

*Summary*

In those areas where an estimate is possible, inland hunting seems to have been absolutely dominant in the western and northern region of the Baltic during the period 6000–3500 B.C., that is during the pre-Neolithic period.

Neolithic techniques spread to the coast area from the Danish islands to Finland by 3500 B.C. and to the coast area from Scania to the Island of Öland during the period 3500–3000 B.C.

Farming was introduced in the Scano-Danian area in 3400 B.C. and in the rest of southern and Middle Sweden in 3100–2700 B.C.

During the period 2700–2200 B.C. the area of farming was reduced to certain fertile locations. The coastal areas of the Baltic were inhabited by hunting people using Neolithic techniques.

A second expansion of farming, 2200 B.C., reached Middle Sweden, the coast of northern Sweden, and southern Finland.

## OLDEST KNOWN SEAL-HUNTING SITES

As seen in the preceding section, the fact that a site is located on the coast does not mean that seal hunting was important at that site. However, seal hunting sites ought to be located on the coast. Baltic coastal sites are available for scientific research with the following important exceptions: in the southern Danish islands the Stone Age coasts were submerged;

in the northern islands and in Scania the shorelines older than 5000 B.C.
are submerged; sites from the period 5000–3000 B.C. are usually
covered by sediments deposited during the transgression maximum
of the Littorina Sea. North of the Scano-Danian area the coasts
are raised and in this area the coastal sites regularly are available
to research. Now and then sites covered by Littorina Sea deposits are
found, mostly from the periods 6000–5000 B.C. and 3100–2700 B.C.

*Scano-Danian area:* 3600–2000 B.C.

At Danish inland and coastal sites of the period 7000–3600 B.C. seal bones
are found now and then but never more than a few. Seal hunting seems
to have been insignificant. The oldest known site with traces of a more
intensified seal hunting is the late pottery-containing Ertebølle site,
Ølby Lyng, datable to 3600–3400 B.C. Fragments of the fauna from
Ølby Lyng have the following frequency:

| | |
|---|---|
| Red deer | 48 percent |
| Roe deer | 24 percent |
| Seal | 11 percent |
| Boar | 10 percent |
| Tame dog | 3 percent |
| Porpoise | 2 percent |
| Other | 3 percent |

In addition, many bones of birds and fish, mostly cod, have been found.
Among the seals, the Greenland seal was the most numerous. Gray seal
was less common and ringed seal was identified with some uncertainty.
The site has been interpreted as a hunting site inhabited in the months of
November and December when the porpoise and Greenland seal are
wandering northward through the Danish Sounds.

Thanks to the Ølby Lyng site, it is known that sea hunting by boat and
harpoon late in the year may have been part of the annual cycle of the
Ertebølle people. Seal bones are regularly found at the coast sites of the
Ertebølle Culture but seldom more than a few. The seals were hunted
partly because of the blubber. Blubber lamps like those of the Eskimos
are found with the Ertebølle pottery.

Seal hunting on a large scale is known only since a somewhat advanced
stage of the Neolithic period from 3100 B.C. Siretorp in westernmost
Blekinge is a typical site from the period 3100–1900 B.C. Only burned

fragments of bones are preserved. Out of some tens of thousands, only 1,496 have been identified. It must be stressed that bones of seal are the easiest bones to identify in small fragments. The fauna of the site are distributed as shown in Table 1, divided according to the different cultures.

Table 1.  Distribution of fauna at the sites

|  | Pitted Ware culture 2500–1900 B.C. | Funnel Beaker culture 3100–2800 B.C. | Ertebølle culture 3100–2800 B.C. |
|---|---|---|---|
| Seal | 1202 | 26 | 7 |
| Domesticated pig | 83 | | |
| Cattle | 77 | 2 | |
| Sheep/goat | 15 | | |
| Deer | 10 | 2 | |
| Others | 39 | | |

The people of the Funnel Beaker culture were the farmers of expansion Stages I–II of farming. Funnel Beaker pottery is regularly found at coastal sites. Thus one may assume that the economy of the Funnel Beaker culture was based upon farming as well as hunting, as seen, among others, at the Siretorp seal hunting site.

The Pitted Ware pottery is not found on farming sites. The people of that culture were food gatherers and pig herders. At the sites of the Pitted Ware culture around the Baltic coasts of Scano-Dania, bones of seals and pigs are dominant. From the inland sites of the Pitted Ware culture seal bones are known. Thus one may assume that the seal hunting sites of the Pitted Ware culture at the Baltic were seasonal in the annual cycle of the people (Bagge and Kjellmark 1939; Becker 1951; Brinch Petersen 1971; Møhl 1971b).

*Middle Sweden:* 2500–2000 B.C.

The oldest sites in Middle Sweden with preserved bones are a few Pitted Ware sites from the period 2500–1800 B.C. For example, there are Åloppe and Svartmyra at the inner part of the bay of the Littorina Sea formed by Lake Mälaren and Överåda in the outer archipelago south of Stockholm.

Seal bones dominate at these sites and a rough estimate of the quantity can be gained from the Överåda site. The bones found there were distributed among 142 find numbers. The number of finds with identified species was as follows:

| | |
|---|---|
| Seal | 90 |
| Fish | 42 |
| Birds | 3 |
| Domesticated pig | 1 |
| Elk | 1 |
| Hare | 1 |
| Deer | 1 |
| Marten | 1 |

Greenland seal has been identified in a couple of cases, and several of the seal bones were identified as coming from young animals. Some bones are split to get at the marrow. The site may be interpreted as a specialized seal hunting site inhabited part of the year when the hunting of Greenland seal was most favorable.

At the sites in the inner part of the bays ringed seals are dominant, but elk and boar are a considerable part of the game. These sites may have been inhabited for a longer part of the year. Domesticated pig occurs more or less regularly at the Pitted Ware sites, while cattle are rare. This is especially true for the late sites which are contemporary with the Battle-Axe culture and the expansion Stage III of farming.

Sites with Funnel Beaker pottery from the period 2800–2500 B.C. are found in the same terrain as the younger Pitted Ware sites. The fauna of these sites are, however, not known. Most probably seal hunting was carried out within the Funnel Beaker culture. This may also be true of the pre-pottery sites.

The complete skeleton of a ringed seal (Plate 1) found in Littorina deposits at Norrköping, Östergötland in 1907 together with a harpoon head is not precisely datable. Probably it belongs to the Neolithic Stone Age (Almgren 1906; Lönnberg 1908; Ekholm 1918; Welinder 1971).

*The Baltic Islands:* 5500–2000 B.C.

During the period 5500–2500 B.C. there are sporadic traces of seal hunting at the sites of the Island of Gotland. At the site Svalings on the eastern coast a few bones of gray seal were found together with a couple of flint flakes in a stratum below Littorina shore gravel. The site is older than the first transgression of the Littorina Sea about 5000 B.C.

At a big group of Gotlandic sites, which are hard to date more exactly than to the Late Mesolithic or Early Neolithic period 4000–2500 B.C., fragments of harpoons and some seal bones, mostly gray seal and ringed seal are regularly found. These sites include Visborgs Kungsladugård, and Norrbus. It is remarkable that fish bones are never found at these sites. The site, Alby, on the eastern coast of the island Öland, dates from about the same period, 4500–2800 B.C. At this site Ertebølle pottery and early Funnel Beaker pottery are found. The fauna have the following distribution (number of finds):

| | |
|---|---|
| Ringed seal | 57 |
| Gray seal | 23 |
| Greenland seal | 4 |
| Harbor seal | 1 |
| Seal, undetermined | 846 |
| Porpoise | 19 |
| Red deer | 6 |
| Elk | 1 |
| Boar | 7 |
| Fox | 8 |
| Bear | 4 |
| Other (Besides the mammal bones a great many fish bones are present, mostly cod) | 37 |

Thus there is clear evidence of seal hunting on the Baltic islands during the period 5500–2500 B.C. The site at Alby may be interpreted as a specialized seal hunting site inhabited in the late autumn and winter.

The fauna of the Pitted Ware sites from the period 2500–1800 B.C. on Gotland are well known. The sites Västerbjers and Visby on the eastern and western coasts respectively are typical and have percentages of species as shown in Table 2.

Table 2.   Fauna from two Pitted Ware sites (in percent)

| | Visby | Västerbjers |
|---|---|---|
| Ringed seal | 20.8 | |
| Gray seal | 1.9 | |
| Greenland seal | 3.6 | |
| Seal, undetermined | 9.4 | 11.1 |
| Porpoise | 0.1 | |
| Fox | 0.9 | 0.8 |
| Beaver | 0.1 | |
| Hare | 0.1 | 0.2 |
| Domesticated pig | 51.6 | 73.1 |
| Sheep/goat | 1.1 | 3.4 |
| Cattle | 6.4 | 3.2 |
| Domesticated dog | 3.2 | 6.9 |

Fish and birds play an insignificant role at these sites. Domesticated pig is dominant, while seal are a minor part of the fauna. The seal hunting of the sites may be interpreted as part of an economy which has been based mainly on pig breeding. At other sites, for example Hemmor, the Greenland seal is the most common species among the seals. At the sites with Greenland seal considerable quantities of cod bones are found. Specialization of seal hunting seems to have been different at different sites (Nihlén 1927; Stenberger 1943; Königsson, Königsson, and Lepiksaar 1971).

*Finland:* 6000–2000 B.C.

At the Suomusjärvi culture sites along the coasts of the Gulf of Bothnia and the Gulf of Finland, roughly datable to 6000–3500 B.C., slate knives with broad blades and a few bone harpoons occur. This may be an indication of seal hunting. The broad-edged knives may have been used when cutting and flaying the seals.

From the Neolithic Period, 3500–2000 B.C., only a small quantity of burned bones have been identified at the Comb-Ornamented Pottery sites. Most common among the identified species are ringed seal, beaver, and elk. In addition to these, domesticated dog and maybe cattle occur. The economy of the Comb-Ornamented Pottery culture seems to have been based on seal hunting as well as inland hunting.

Two important finds of complete skeletons have been made: one of Greenland seal at Närpes and one of ringed seal at Oulujoki. A harpoon was found with each skeleton. Both skeletons have been dated by pollen analysis to the time of the Comb-Ornamented Pottery culture (Ailio 1909; Leppäaho 1937; Luho 1967).

## PROBLEM OF MARITIME ADAPTATION IN THE WESTERN AND NORTHERN REGION OF THE BALTIC

From the period 6000–3600 B.C. there is very little evidence of sea hunting in the Scano-Danian and Middle Swedish area. For Middle Sweden this is at least partly due to the lack of preserved bones at the sites, and for south Scandinavia it is at least partly due to the submergence of the coastal sites. However from the sites available with fauna remains it is seen that seals are an insignificant part of the game mammals.

The importance of sea hunting in Finland before 3500 B.C. is hard to estimate. On the Island of Gotland seal hunting is proven to have occurred before 5000 B.C., but the evidence is too scanty for an estimation of the importance of seal hunting before 3500 B.C.

During the period 3600–3000 B.C. seal hunting is known to be part of the economy of the Ertebølle culture on the Danish islands. Seal and porpoise were hunted late in the autumn and in the winter. Inland hunting was, however, the most important activity during these same months.

During the period 3500–2500 B.C. seal hunting seems to have been of importance all around the Baltic in more or less the same way as within the Ertebølle culture of Denmark at the Ertebølle sites of south Scandinavia, the coastal sites of Gotland and the Comb-Ornamented Pottery sites of Finland. The situation on the Swedish east coast is unknown.

Farming was introduced in extensive areas of south and middle Scandinavia in the period 3500–2700 B.C. by the Funnel Beaker culture. Hunting and maybe seal hunting in particular seems to have been part of the economy of the Funnel Beaker culture.

During the period of decreased farming intensity, 2700–2200 B.C., and during the third stage of expansion of farming 2200–2000 B.C., the coasts of the Baltic were inhabited by the people of the Pitted Ware culture and the Comb-Ornamented culture. Seal hunting was of importance within all these cultures, but it was never a dominant part of the economy. Seal hunting seems to have been part of the annual cycle along with other activities.

The preceding statement seems to be valid for the sea hunting around the coasts of the western and northern Baltic during all of the Stone Age in spite of the fact that seals have been present in the Baltic ever since the time of the Yoldia Sea and that many sea fauna were present in the Littorina Sea during the period 5500–2000 B.C.

In south Scandinavia sea hunting began to be part of the hunter's annual cycle around 3500 B.C., but in more northerly parts of the Baltic, seal hunting must already have been of importance around 6000–5000 B.C. The date of the beginning of sea hunting in south Scandinavia is astonishingly late, while the rough dating from the northern part of the Baltic coincides with the development of the Littorina fauna. During all of the Mesolithic period, however, inland hunting has been of greater importance than sea hunting all around the Baltic.

Within the Funnel Beaker culture the sea hunting was of less importance than farming. At the hunting sites around the Baltic, which were Neolithic without farming, sea hunting was part of the economy based on pig-breeding in the southern part of the Baltic and on the Baltic islands and on inland hunting in the northern part of the Baltic.

Clark's conclusion from 1946 can now be revised in some respects. According to Clark the big development of seal hunting in Scandinavia coincided with the establishment of Neolithic farming cultures. A system of trade between inland farmers and sea hunters was developed as a stimulus for sea hunting. Such a system may have been in operation in the Scano-Danian area, Middle Sweden, and on the Baltic islands but not until the time of the third expansion of farming 2200–2000 B.C. During the period 2200–1800 B.C. the Battle-Axe culture seems to have been solely a farming culture. Contemporary with this were the Pitted Ware and Comb-Ornamented Pottery sites, where seal hunting was carried on. The few Battle-Axe shards regularly found at the coastal sites may be traces of trade.

The oldest Neolithic farmers of Scandinavia, the Funnel Beaker culture 3400–2700 B.C., seem to have supported themselves with game from the sea. It is, however, remarkable that the earliest seal hunting in the Scano-Danian area is technically connected with the earliest Neolithic Stone Age. At the oldest pottery-containing sites all around the Baltic one finds considerable traces of seal hunting too. It is, however, only in the Scano-Danian area that it is evident that seal hunting first became an important part of the economy at the time of the introduction of pottery. In fact, it seems more likely that seal hunting as an important occupation is older in the northern part of the Baltic and on the Baltic islands than in the southern part.

There is no group of Stone Age sites around the western and northern coasts of the Baltic of which it can be said that its inhabitants were completely adapted to maritime hunting. During the Stone Age, sea hunting seems to have been a seasonal occupation of secondary importance compared to inland hunting and farming.

# REFERENCES

AHLÉN, I.
  1965  Studies on the red deer, *Cervus elaphus* L., in Scandinavia, part one: History of distribution. *Viltrevyn* 3:1.
AHLONEN, P.
  1970  "En pollenanalytisk undersökning vid stenåldersboplatsen Perkiö i Hauho sn, Södra Finland," in *Studier över den snörkeramiska kulturens keramik i Finland*. Edited by T. Edgren. *Finska Fornminnesföreningens Tidskrift* 72.
AILIO, J.
  1909  *Die steinzeitliche Wohnplatzfunde in Finland*. Helsinki: Finska Fornminnesföreningen.

ALMGREN, O.
1906   Uppländska stenåldersboplatser. *Fornvännen* 1.
ALTHIN, C.-A.
1954   Man and environment: a view of the Mesolithic material in southern Scandinavia. *Meddelanden från Lunds universitets historiska museum.*
ÅSE, L.-E.
1970   Mälardalens lägre liggande strandlinjer. *Geologiska Föreningens i Stockholm Förhandlingar* 92:1.
BAGGE, A, K. KJELLMARK
1939   *Stenåldersboplatserna vid Siretorp i Blekinge.* Stockholm: Kungl. Vitterhets Historie och Antikvitets Akademien.
BECKER, C. J.
1947   Mosefundne lerkar fra yngre stenalder. *Aarbøger for Nordisk Oldkyndighed og Historie.*
1951   Den grubekeramiske kultur i Danmark. *Aarbøger for Nordisk Oldkyndighed og Historie.*
1967   Gådefulde jyske stenaldergrave. *Nationalmuseets Arbejdsmark.*
BERGLUND, B.
1966   Late-Quaternary vegetation in eastern Blekinge, southeastern Sweden: a pollen-analytical study, part two: Post-glacial time. *Opera Botanica* 12:2.
1969   Vegetation and human influence in south Scandinavia during prehistoric time. *Oikos*, supplement 12.
BERGLUND, B., R. LILJEGREN
1971   Littorina transgressions in Blekinge, South Sweden: a preliminary survey. *Geologiska Föreningens i Stockholm Förhandlingar* 93:3.
BRINCH PETERSEN, E.
1971   Ølby Lyng – en østsjaellandsk kystboplads med ertebøllekultur. *Aarbøger for Nordisk Oldkyndighed og Historie.*
CLARK, J. G. D.
1946   Seal-hunting in the Stone Age of northwestern Europe. *Proceedings of the Prehistoric Society* 11.
DEGERBØHL, M., B. FREDSKILD
1970   The urus (*Bos primigenus Bojanus*) and Neolithic domesticated cattle (*Bos taurus domesticus Linné*) in Denmark. *Det Konglige Danske Videnskabernas Selskabs Biologiske Meddelelser* 17:1.
DEGERBØHL, M., H. KROG
1959   The reindeer (*Rangifer tarandus* L.) in Denmark. *Det Konglige Danske Videnskabernas Selskabs Biologiske Meddelelser* 10:4.
DIGERFELDT, G.
1971   "The Post-Glacial development of Lake Trummen, Småland, Central South Sweden, part one: The regional vegetation development." Unpublished dissertation. Lund.
EDGREN, T., editor
1970   *Studier över den snörkeramiska kulturens keramik i Finland. Finska Fornminnesföreningens Tidskrift* 72.
EKHOLM, G.
1918   Två nyupptäckta uppländska stenåldersboplatser. *Upplands Forminnesförenings Tidskrift* 33.

EKMAN, S.
1922   *Djurvärldens utbredningshistoria på Skandinaviska halvön.* Stockholm: Bonniers.

FLORIN, M.-B.
1958   "Pollen-analytical evidence of prehistoric agriculture at Mogetorp Neolithic settlement," in *Vråkulturen. Stenåldersboplatserna vid Mogetorp, Östra Vrå och Brökvarn.* Edited by S. Florin.

FLORIN, S., *editor*
1958   *Vråkulturen. Stenåldersboplatserna vid Mogetorp, Östra Vrå och Brökvarn.* Stockholm: Kungl. Vitterhets Historie och Antikvitets Akademien.

FREDÉN, C.
1967   A historical review of the Ancylus Lake and the Svea River. *Geologiska Föreningens i Stockholm Förhandlingar* 89:3.

FRIES, M.
1965   The Late-Quaternary vegetation of Sweden. *Acta Phylogeographica Suecia* 50.

IVERSEN, J.
1960   Problems of the Early Post-Glacial forest development in Denmark. *Danmarks Geologiske Undersøgelse* 4(4):3.
1967   "Naturens udvikling siden sidste istid," in *Danmarks Natur 1.* Edited by A. Nørrevang and T. Meyer. Copenhagen: Politikens.

JØRGENSEN, S.
1961   "Zur Frage der ältesten Künstenkultur in Dänemark," in *Bericht über den V. internationalen Kongress für Vor- und Frühgeschichte Hamburg.* Edited by G. Bersu. Berlin: Verlag Gebr. Mann.

KAPEL, H.
1969   En boplads fra tidlig-atlantisk tid ved Villingeback. *Nationalmuseets Arbejdsmark.*

KÖNIGSSON, E.-S., L.-K. KÖNIGSSON, J. LEPIKSAAR
1971   Stenåldersboplatsen i Alby på Öland. *Fornvännen* 1971:1.

KÖNIGSSON, L.-K.
1968   The Ancylus transgression in the Skede Mose area, Öland. *Geologiska Föreningens i Stockholm Förhandlingar* 90:1.
1970   "Traces of Neolithic human influence upon the landscape development at the Bjurselet settlement, Västerbotten, northern Sweden," in *Bjurselet settlement I.* Edited by Hans Christiansson, 13–30. Kungliga Skytteanska Samfundets Handlingar 7. Umeå.

LEPPÄAHO, J.
1937   Närpiön ja Oulujoen kivikauden hyljelöydöt, part one: Löydöt muinaistieteelliseltä kannalta tarkasteluina. *Suomen Museo* 42.

LILJEGREN, R., S. WELINDER
1971   Pollen-analytical dating of the skeleton of an aurochs. *Geologiska Föreningens i Stockholm Förhandlingar* 93:3.

LÖNNBERG, E.
1908   Om några fynd i Litorinalera i Norrköping. *Arkiv för Zoologi* 4:22.

LUHO, V.
1967   Die Suomusjärvi-Kultur: die mittel- und spätmesolitische Zeit in Finnland. *Finska Fornminnesföreningens Tidskrift* 66.

MALMER, M.
1962   Jungneolitische Studien. *Acta Archaeologica Lundensia* 80(3).
MEINANDER, C. F.
1961   De subneolitiska kulturgrupperna i Europa. *Societas Scientarium Fennica* 39 (B):4.
1964   Smikärr. *Finskt Museum* 49.
MØHL, U.
1971a  Oversigt over dyreknoglerne fra Ølby Lyng. *Aarbøger for Nordisk Oldkyndighed og Historie*.
1971b  Fangstdurene ved de danske strade. *Kuml* 1970.
MÖRNER, N.-A.
1969   The Late-Quaternary history of the Kattegat Sea and the Swedish west coast: deglaciation, shore level displacement, chronology, isostasy and eustasy. *Sveriges Geologiska Undersökning* C:640.
NIHLÉN, J.
1927   Gotlands stenåldersboplatser. *Kungl. Vitterhets Historie och Antikvitets Akademiens Handlingar* 36:3.
NILSSON, E.
1968   Södra Sveriges senkvartära historia. *Kungl. Svenska Vetenskapsakademiens Handlingar* 4 12:1.
SALOMONSSON, B.
1970   Die Värby-Funde: ein Beitrag zur Kenntnis der ältesten Trichterbecherkultur in Schonen. *Acta Archaeologica* 41.
1971   "Malmötraktens förhistoria," in *Malmö stadshistoria I*. Malmö: Allhems.
SIIRIÄINEN, A.
1969   Über die Chronologie der steinzeitlichen Küstenwohnplätze Finnlands im Lichte der Uferschiebung. *Suomen Museo* 76.
STENBERGER, M.
1943   *Das Grabfeld von Västerbjers auf Gotland*. Stockholm: Kungl. Vitterhets Historie och Antikvitets Akademien.
TAUBER, H.
1971   Danske kulstof-14 dateringer af arkaeologiske prøver. *Aarbøger for Nordisk Oldkyndighed og Historie*.
TEN HOVE, H.
1968   The Ulmus Fall at the transgression Atlanticum-Subboreal in pollen diagrams. *Paleogeography, Paleoclimatology, Paleoecology* 5.
TROEL-SMITH, J.
1953   Ertebøllekultur – bondekultur: resultater af de sidste 10 aars undersøgelser i Aamosen. *Aarbøger for Nordisk Oldkyndighed og Historie*.
1960   Ertebølletidens fangstfolk og bønder. *Nationalmuseets Arbejdsmark*.
VUORELA, L.
1970   The indication of farming in pollen diagrams from southern Finland. *Acta Botanica Fennica* 87.
WELINDER, S.
1971   Överåda: a Pitted Ware Culture site in Eastern Sweden. *Meddelanden från Lunds universitets historiska museum*.
1973a  The radio-carbon age of the Pitted Ware Culture in Eastern Sweden. *Meddelanden från Lunds universitets historiska museum*.

1973b  Boplatsen Dalkarlstorp. *Västmanlands Fornminnesförenings Årsskrift* 52.

n.d.  Bebyggelsehistoriska studier i Badelundaåsens dalgång.

# The Rock Carvings at Nämforsen, Ångermanland, Sweden, as a Problem of Maritime Adaptation and Circumpolar Interrelations

MATS P. MALMER

The study of rock carvings is all too often isolated from other aspects of prehistoric research (Moberg 1970). Of course petroglyphs are the main base for the study of prehistoric religion and art. But the great quantities in which they occur and their wide geographic distribution make them suitable also for chronological studies and for all kinds of environmental research. And such facts are important also for the study of prehistoric religion: it is necessary, at least, to ask whether a certain motif had the same meaning in northern Norway as in Denmark or Karelia.

The rock carvings of northern Europe are usually divided into two groups: a southern group, attributed to a Bronze Age farming population, and a northern group, attributed to a Stone Age hunting population. There is nothing like a sharp frontier between the two groups. On the contrary, motifs from the southern group occur in the northernmost parts of Norway. The question of whether motifs from the northern group influence the southern group has been less intensely discussed. However, a study of the south and middle Scandinavian rock carvings of the southern group shows that there are more pictures of wild animals among the middle than the south Scandinavian carvings The wild animal is the main theme of the northern group. Thus it is fairly clear that the southern and northern groups mutually influenced each other, which also means that the northern group must belong, at least partly, to the Bronze Age (Malmer i.p.).

The rock carving site of Nämforsen (63°26'40" North latitude) shows some rather unusual traits. Containing about 1,750 figures, it might be the biggest agglomeration of rock carving in northern Europe. Geographically it is rather isolated, the nearest rock carving sites to the west and east being situated at a distance of sixty and seventy kilometers, respectively. Both have a distinctively "northern" character. The nearest rock carving site in the south, which is also "southern" in character, is as far away as 400 kilometers. Nämforsen itself is dominated by pictures of animals (mostly elk) of a northern character. But also several distinctively southern motifs are represented, such as ships, foot-soles, circles, and cup-shaped hollows (Hallström 1960).

Quite near the rock carvings, on the southern bank of the Ångerman-älven River, there is a dwelling site with Stone and Bronze Age finds, no doubt inhabited during the time the rock carvings were made. This close and sure connection between rock carvings and habitation site is very unusual. During the past few decades some 3,000 Stone and Bronze Age sites have been found along the rivers and lakes of northern Sweden, during investigations in connection with the construction of power plants. The site at Nämforsen is one of the biggest, and upstream from Näm-forsen there is a remarkable concentration of dwelling sites (Janson and Hvarfner 1960).

The rock carvings at Nämforsen are no doubt a circumpolar phenom-enon inasmuch as they must be seen against the background of the Norwegian carvings in the west, but they also have to be compared with the Finnish rock paintings and the Karelian carvings in the east. Quite unmistakably, it is a question of east-west connections in the subarctic zone. On the other hand, the influences from the south Scandinavian rock carving area are very obvious at Nämforsen.

Nämforsen is the name of a rapids in the Ångermanälven River. The rapids have a length of some 500 meters, and the height of the fall is 17 meters. The carvings are found on small islands in the river and on both banks. This is a natural place for these rock carvings depicting game and hunting, and probably with a magic purpose. Elk, which were hunted down in the rapids, were attracted by the water to the rocky shores, where they made an easy target for the hunters. More unusual is the fact that these rock carvings in the Stone and Bronze Ages were actually situated quite near a bay of the Baltic. The distance from Nämforsen to the mouth of the Ångermanälven River is now about 40 kilometers, but at least in the Stone Age the mouth must have been just below the rapids (Hallström 1960: 373).

Now our problem is clear. Stone and Bronze Age habitation sites, belonging to populations of hunters and fishers, are found in great numbers in northern Sweden, mainly inland, along lakes and rivers. Of all the rapids suitable for hunting, only Nämforsen has rock carvings with a probably magic purpose. At the same place we find one of the richest habitation sites. In the rock carvings we find an admixture of south and north Scandinavian motifs. Is it mere chance that this remarkable place is situated quite near a bay of the Baltic, possibly with easy, direct communication with south Scandinavia? Or is this a case of maritime adaptation? Have the hunters and fishers of an inland culture chosen a site near or at a bay of the sea, with the explicit wish for contact with the sea and its possibilities for good communication with the south?

It is probable that the habitation site of Nämforsen to some extent could help to answer these questions. However, the material is not yet published, and moreover there seems to be no significant stratigraphy, so we have to rely on the rock carvings. For them we need a chronology. We cannot content ourselves with the statement that northern and southern elements are mixed at Nämforsen. We must know whether it is possible to trace a development among the northern motifs, the animal figures, and further, whether the southern motifs were present from the beginning or if they appeared only at a later stage.

Because no stratigraphy and no sealed deposits in any sense of the word are present, we have to base our investigation on the distribution of the various motifs. It is not a hopeless task because the number of figures is so great. We also need a division of the vast carving area. Hallström (1960) presented such a three-part division. Nämforsen I comprises the rock carvings of the banks of the river. Nämforsen II is the easternmost island, Notön, and Nämforsen III is the central island, Brådön. They contain 567, 795, and 380 figures respectively.

The petroglyphs depicting quadruped animals may be divided into four groups (Malmer i.p.):

A. Outline carving
B. Outline carving with an inner design of lines
C. Scooped-out body
D. Single lines forming the body

Table 1 shows the distribution of these four types.

Table 1. Distribution (in percentages) of the four types of petroglyphs depicting quadruped animals

|  |  | A | B | C | D | Total |
|---|---|---|---|---|---|---|
| I. | River banks | 24.5 | 2.5 | 72.5 | 0.5 | 100 |
| II. | Notön | 43 | 7 | 43 | 7 | 100 |
| III. | Brådön | 51.5 | 24 | 24.5 | – | 100 |

The A and B animals are more frequent on the islands, and especially on the central island, Brådön, than on the river banks, which are dominated by C animals. A and B are large animals in outline carving. These traits are typical for a large portion of the Norwegian figures, and especially for the carvings in Nordland, which for several reasons, may be considered to be oldest. In contrast, the small, naturalistic C animals with scooped-out bodies are rare or absent in northern Norway. So we may conclude that carving in Nämforsen started on the islands, especially on the central island Brådön, and later spread to the river banks. This is in accord with the fact that animal carvings of the northern group in the terrain often are found in places difficult to reach.

We also have to study the occurrence of southern motifs at Nämforsen. There are more than 350 ships and boats, of which only a few are of a distinctively southern type, and those are exclusively found on the islands, Brådön and Notön. On the river banks only naturalistic pictures of boats occur. These are usually considered to be older and belong to the Stone Age. But another hypothesis is possible. These naturalistic boat pictures may be influenced by the rather stylized southern Bronze Age ship picture, modified to achieve greater resemblance to the local boats which were actually used on the Ångermanälven River and in the bays of the Baltic.

The pictures of foot-soles at Nämforsen belong to a type which for several reasons may be dated to an early part of the Bronze Age; other types of foot-sole are more recent. Of a total of twenty-eight foot-soles, twenty-two belong to the central island, Brådön, and three each to Notön and the river banks.

The only possible explanation seems to be that Nämforsen started as a normal, northern rock-carving site, influenced by the west. Rather soon strong influences reached the site from the south. The result was that southern motifs were accepted, and that rock carvings were made in great quantities on the more accessible river banks, both in accordance with a southern tradition. However, the southern motifs soon lost their importance. Ships and foot-soles and other early types disappeared without being replaced by newer southern types. What was left was boats of the local type and masses of animals of group C, small naturalistic elk with scooped-out bodies.

The A and B animals, made in outline carving in Norway and Sweden, are so few in number that it is hard to think that they were dispersed over a very long period. If our hypothesis concerning Nämforsen is right the oldest naturalistic animals cannot date from the Mesolithic, but must belong to a late phase of the Stone Age. From that period a rich inventory of naturalistic sculptures in slate and other stone is well known.

There is little reason to believe that motifs from the south Scandinavian Bronze Age rock carvings could have penetrated as far north as Nämforsen solely on the basis of their religious significance. It is more probable that Nämforsen was a place where merchants from the south bought furs from the north. The great importation of bronze from continental Europe to south Scandinavia had to be paid for in some way, and furs were a more probable payment than the products of south Scandinavian farming.

Is it possible to hypothesize on where the supposed southern merchants came from? The naturalistic animals of group C with scooped out bodies might be a clue to this problem. Such animals are found in Krelia (with traces also among the rock paintings of Finland), although not always in the small size of Nämforsen (Ravdonikas 1936, 1938).

In south Scandinavia the C animals have a very uneven distribution. They dominate in the eastern provinces, such as Östergötland, where they are 68.5 percent of the total number of animals, or in the Mälar provinces, where they are 90 percent. But in the west they are few: in Denmark and Østfold none; in Bohuslän only 13 percent. Here they are replaced by group D.

It appears that the eastern provinces of south Sweden, together with Nämforsen and Karelia, show a remarkable unification in rock carving art during the Early Bronze Age, and that Östergötland and the Mälar Provinces were the center of fur trade from both the northern Swedish provinces and Karelia.

Thus one may suspect, that hunting tribes near Nämforsen to some extent actually changed their way of living and made a maritime adaptation for the sake of trade with the south. This conclusion may be reinforced by other findings, for instance, the cairns which in great numbers line the coasts of Ångermanland and Finland (Baudou 1968; Meinander 1954). They belong to the Bronze Age and show that people in the coast regions adopted that part of the southern burial rites which they could afford, namely, the cairns, whereas the bronzes in the graves are few.

The great distances were obviously no serious obstacle. In view of recently published findings, there can be no doubt that the south Scandinavian depiction of ships penetrated to the west Siberian region, where it is found among the Tomsk rock carvings (Okladnikov and Martynov 1972).

## REFERENCES

BAUDOU, E.
   1968   *Forntida bebyggelse i Ångermanlands kustland* [Prehistoric settlements in the coastal area of Ångermanland]. Härnösand.
HALLSTRÖM, G.
   1960   *Monumental art of northern Sweden from the Stone Age.* Stockholm.
JANSON S., H. HVARFNER
   1960   *Från norrlandsälvar och fjällsjöar.* Stockholm.

MALMER, M. P.
i.p.    *Kommentarer till bergkonstens korologi.*
MEINANDER, C. F.
1954    *Die Bronzezeit in Finnland.* Helsinki.
MOBERG, C. A.
1970    *Regional och global syn på hällristningar.* Århus: Kuml.
OKLADNIKOV, A. P., A. I. MARTYNOV
1972    *The treasure trove of Tom petroglyphs.* Moscow.
RAVDONIKAS, W. J.
1936    *Les gravures rupestres des bords du lac Onéga et de la mer Blanche,*
volume one: *Les stations néolithiques du rivage oriental du lac Onéga.*
Leningrad.
1938    *Les gravures rupestres des bords du lac Onéga et de la mer Blanche,*
volume two: *Les gravures rupestres de la mer Blanche.* Leningrad.

# Prehistoric Coastal Settlement on the Upper Bothnian Coast of Northern Sweden

HANS CHRISTIANSSON and NOEL D. BROADBENT*

It is only within the last few decades that the northern area of the Swedish coast on the Gulf of Bothnia has been systematically investigated. Since 1962, the Nordarkeologi Project, under the leadership of Docent Hans Christiansson of Uppsala University, has carried out an investigation of the prehistoric settlement in the area of Skellefteå *kommun* in northern Västerbotten, latitude 65° North longitude 21° East. The chronological framework of this investigation is built upon shoreline displacement, which has provided a system of relative chronology for the different phases of prehistoric settlement in the area. This positive shoreline displacement is due primarily to the continuous land rise which has followed glacial melting and retreat. Although this land rise has been continuous, there was a degree of irregularity in the sequence due to local differences in geological structure. At present, there is a rise of about one meter per century in middle Norrland where the uplifting has been greatest. This rate decreases somewhat toward the south and north. The process of land uplift has been decreasing since the glacial melting.

The most important archaeologically investigated sites in the Nordarkeologi investigation are Lundfors at seventy-eight meters, Heden at sixty-five meters, Bjurselet at fifty-two meters, and Fahlmark at forty meters above sea level. The succession of settlement can be traced in this series for a period of approximately 3,000 years, from 4000 to 1000 B.C. The following is a discussion of the Late Mesolithic and Middle Neolithic settlement of Västerbotten's coast.

---

* Noel D. Broadbent is responsible for the section of this article titled "The Mesolithic Settlement," and Hans C. Christiansson is the author of the section titled "Neolithic Coastal Settlement."

## THE MESOLITHIC SETTLEMENT

The existence of a Mesolithic settlement in Norrland has long been a controversial issue. As late as 1966, the authors of *Ancient hunters and settlements in the mountains of Sweden* expressed the opinion that there was no conclusive proof for settlement in Norrland before Neolithic times, 3000–1500 B.C. (Janson and Hvarfner 1966: 21). This book, first published in Swedish in 1960, was the result of the cultural-historical investigations in northern Sweden, which were started in 1942 in connection with extensive hydroelectric projects.

There have certainly been numerous finds of artifacts which bear Mesolithic affinity (especially keeled scrapers), not to mention crude implements which have been compared with the Komsa culture of Finnmark (Bagge 1937). But because of the dearth of stratigraphic contexts and a preponderance of open living sites and stray finds, no convincing proof could be provided.

The situation has been altered since then, and a number of recently excavated sites have provided the evidence for an early postglacial occupation of the Swedish north. Needless to say, the existence of such cultural horizons has long been established in Norway and Finland. The Swedish discoveries were long overdue.

Basically, there are three routes by which man could first have entered northern Sweden and through which cultural influences could have passed and helped shape cultural development there. The first possibility is the southern route through central or coastal Sweden; a second, from the west (Norway), through passes and along the river valley system of interior Norrland; the third, from the east or northeast across the land bridge between Scandinavia and Finland or by sea or sea ice across the Gulf of Bothnia. After the retreat of the continental ice sheet to the mountainous areas of interior Norrland around 6000 B.C., there was no real barrier to man other than man himself.

The archaeological picture which is slowly materializing points, in part, to all the possibilities within respective areas of contact. South Scandinavian influences can be traced penetrating the interior all the way up to Västerbotten. These groups, perhaps originating on the Swedish west coast, are characterized by very typical keeled cores and microliths, and a preference for flint and flintlike stone, dating perhaps to 6000–3000 B.C. Contact with Norway has also taken place. This could have occurred through contact with interior Fosna groups and, it is increasingly clear, among the slate-bearing cultures. The use of slate in northern Scandinavia is represented by an early, well-developed slate-quartz technology in interior central Norrland, dating to 4000–3000 B.C. This slate technology spread, in turn, both to the west and south. A third early archaeological horizon is the subject under discussion here: namely, a slate-quartz horizon on upper Norrland's coast which bears strong resemblance to the Finnish Suomusjärvi culture, dating to 3500 B.C.

The Nordarkeologi project has concentrated upon the investigation of the succession of coastal settlements in the province of Västerbotten. The framework of the approach to Upper Norrland's prehistory is built upon shoreline displacement. Despite the obvious drawbacks of this method (the assumption that sites are contiguous to water levels), an excellent series of homogeneous archaeological sites has been encountered. The highest sites are associated with two levels: seventy-eight and sixty-five meters above sea level. Surface collections from approximately twenty sites and two excavations have provided enough material to begin a characterization of settlement at these levels and, equally important, of the differences between them. The oldest sites in this series (Lundfors Complex) are situated seventy-eight meters above present sea level in a valley of silty sediment located some twenty kilometers inland from the present Baltic shoreline, near the city of Skellefteå. These sites were located on the eastern side of a sheltered inlet with access to the open sea and the Skellefteå River estuary. Dating is around 4000–3500 B.C. The second horizon of settlements (Heden Complex) is associated with the sixty-five-meter curve. The sites are situated in a stream valley of sandy sediments. The dating is about 2000–3000 B.C. Both of these archaeological horizons were associated with phases of the Litorina sea and late Atlantic climate conditions.

The physical remains of the culture consist of the little organic material that has survived podzolization and the effects of time: hard-burned bone carbon, pollen, and artifacts of stone. Only limited results of physical analysis are presently available. Most illuminating at the present time is the species identification of animal remains from the two settlements, Lundfors and Heden.

The principal game captured was the ringed seal (*Pusa hispida*). The importance of this game is manifested in nearly all the Skellefteå coastal settlement finds and continues through time to be the economic foundation of prehistoric settlement in this area. The ice-calving *Pusa hispida* is most successfully taken during late winter when it is most vulnerable and least likely to sink if seized in open water. It is not known exactly how this game was taken, but an enormous number of heavy, notched-stone sinkers have been recovered on and around the settlements. Some form of fixed netting would seem the most likely explanation. The coastal inlets and archipelago near the estuary of the Skellefteå River would provide the ideal conditions for capturing the ringed seal, by nature a bay-loving species (thus the Swedish name *Vikare* [bay-dwelling]).

A critical point of difference between the Lundfors and Heden settlements is that beaver and elk (moose) bones are present only at Heden. The question of seasonal specialization is obscured by the presence of this terrestrial and traditionally inland game. An interesting detail reflecting upon the importance of elk in these later settlements is seen in a remarkable find of a notched-stone sinker found near Heden with an elk head clearly carved on it — a curious ornament for seal or fishing equipment.

Fishing was also practiced although it is difficult to judge to what extent. Several bones of pike (*Esox lucius*) have been recovered from both Lundfors and Heden. More extensive excavation will be carried out in 1973, and it is hoped the picture will become more complete and definitive as more material is recovered.

The lithic material may be summarized in three categories: (1) artifacts of slate, including knives, projectiles, and roughly hewn and partially ground axes, (2) miscellaneous artifacts of stone, including whetstones, notched sinkers, etc., and (3) artifacts of quartz.

Most noticeable are finds of finely made implements of slate. Long considered to be a late, although characteristic, element in Norrland's prehistory, it has become increasingly obvious that a well-developed slate technology was an early manifestation. The oldest established slate complex in northern Europe is the Finnish Askola-Suomusjärvi culture. Large lanceolate and stemmed knives are characteristic of this sea-hunting complex, which dates from 6500–3000 B.C. This early complex was no doubt the stimulus behind the development of indigenous slate groups within Sweden and Norway. Recent investigations of Early Norrland NTB, a Norrland research group led by Docent Evert Baudon of Stockholm University and the Central Office of National Antiquities, have given stratigraphic and carbon-14 evidence for a slate technology as early as 4000 B.C. This dating is in full accord with the shoreline displacement evidence on the Västerbotten coast.

The early Swedish slate material is rich in small, barbed, and tanged projectile points. The Lundfors and Heden material has such points, as well as single-edged knives, including some with double notches and knobs for thong attachment. Much of this material is from surface collections, however, and it is difficult to assign specific forms to separate horizons although the small projectiles and single-edged knives belong to both.

The working of slate takes other forms on the Lundfors and Heden settlements. Roughly flaked green and black amphibolite schist axes are found on all horizons. Considerable numbers of the distinctive "North Bothnian Implements" form a major find group in surface collections in the area; in terms of raw material and manufacturing technique they are indistinguishable from the smaller axes.

The axes associated with the higher settlements are flaked and have pointed butts and sparsely ground and polished edges. They are irregular in form, somewhat plano-convex, retaining in large part the form of the slabs from which they were made. One example, excavated at Heden, is more refined; it has a squared-off form and pointed oval cross section. The butt end has been flaked thin and both the working end and sides have been polished. The axe is small, measuring only fourteen centimeters in length. This axe is clearly of the Österbotten type. The axe tradition, as a whole, is strongly linked with Finnish influence and goes back to the Askola-Suomusjärvi complex. Several other traits also fit the Finnish pattern. They include several distinctive sandstone whetstones (one triangular; one oblong and bone-shaped, with a long groove for polishing points), a discoid club with a biconical hole, and, finally, red ochre pigments which have been excavated in respectable amounts at the Lundfors settlement.

Although there is a developed slate aspect in the early archaeological horizons, the main raw material used was quartz. The artifact inventories of the Lundfors and Heden horizons are very similar. The largest proportion of implements is flake-derived and includes scrapers, especially short end-scrapers, backed knives, borers, and gravers. Core implements are also represented and consist primarily of scraper-planes and, on the Lundfors settlements, keeled core-scrapers. The actual quartz core-working techniques have given the best chronological foothold for this stone material. The Lundfors settlement quartz finds are dominated by numbers of splintered pieces (*outils écaillés*). These special cores have helped us to identify contemporaneous quarries which were located about ten kilometers southeast of the settlements. These quarry sites were linked by a water passage with the sea level seventy-eight meters higher than it is today. Furthermore the former Skellefteå River estuary was located almost exactly the same distance to the northwest of the settlements. Splintered pieces were not found at the Heden settlement although stone had been worked there. The *outil écaillé* therefore has a chronological as well as a functional significance within this area (Broadbent 1973).

To summarize, shoreline displacement has provided the opportunity for analyzing the cultural stratigraphy of the earliest settlement on the Västerbotten coast in Upper Norrland. Taken as a whole, the pattern has much in common with Finnish influences. The settlement represents, however, an indigenous adaptation — an adaptation and development which remained characteristic of settlement in coastal Norrland for thousands of years. The economic basis, once established, remained largely the same even despite the introduction of limited agriculture and livestock raising in Neolithic times.

The advantages of slate technology within such an economy were recognized very early, and the techniques spread rapidly throughout central Norrland, to Norway and even to the south to the sea-hunting Pitted Ware complex. As a result, regional patterns and styles have developed.

The present job within the archaeology of Norrland is to unwind and more deeply analyze these patterns and influences within the context of the environment in which they developed.


## NEOLITHIC COASTAL SETTLEMENT


Although no true *kamkeramik* settlement has been found in Sweden, there were cultural contacts between Sweden and Finland during the Neolithic period. This is evidenced by numerous stray finds and influences of *kamkeramik* character in interior and coastal Norrland. This influence most probably came from the Finnish coastal area on the Bothnian Gulf through the seal-hunting *kamkeramik* peoples (Christiansson 1969). Distinctive Finnish cultural elements also appear in the epi-Neolithic sites of Hedningahällen (Arbman 1945) and Darsgärde (Ambrosiani 1959).

In late middle Neolithic times a remarkable importation of flint goods took place in the coastal area of Västerbotten. Flint does not occur naturally in Västerbotten and the closest flint source area is the Silurian region of the southern Baltic basin. Isolated stray finds of ice-transported flint occur along the Norwegian coast but not to the extent needed to explain the Västerbotten imports. It is clear, in other words, that there was contact between the south Baltic cultural area and Västerbotten during middle Neolithic times.

The flint, which was imported to the northern area, came in the form of half-fabricated, thick-butted adzes or as raw flint nodules. It seems unlikely that any of the adzes were made in Norrland. Most are hollow-edged and unpolished, although some ground and polished examples do occur along with several tanged and triangular cross-sectioned points (Becker's type C). In addition, some transverse arrowheads of flint and numerous flint scrapers (mainly blade scrapers) have been found. Altogether, several hundred flint adzes have been found at some ten localities along the Västerbotten coast. No larger flint sites have been found between the north and south although smaller way stations may be marked by several stray finds along the Bothnian coast. For example, a recent find was a boat Axe whetstone located in Medelpad near Sundsvall.

The largest and best known flint site is Bjurselet in northern Västerbotten, Skellefteå *kommun*. This site was excavated by Christiansson during the years 1962–1969 (Christiansson 1965: 91–111). Numerous interpretations have been made in an attempt to explain the background of the flint imports ever since the first finds in 1830. The artifacts of flint have generally been made in caches. The largest consisted of approximately seventy axes and the smallest contains four axes and an unworked flint nodule. Until the Bjurselet excavation no dwelling sites had been previously recorded.

In recent years, the Västerbotten flint problem has been discussed primarily by Becker (1952) and Malmer (1962). Becker tried to show that it was the Pitted Ware culture that was responsible for the northern trade or immigration. Malmer, on the other hand, opted for the Swedish-Norwegian Battle-Axe culture. The theories have centered around the question of whether the imports resulted from trade aimed at selling flint to the subarctic peoples of Norrland or whether the flint was a by-product of fishing trade from the Atlantic coast to the Baltic and further south. Others believe the flint finds represent an agricultural colonization.

Excavation at Bjurselet established the settlement as a seal-hunting site with the ringed seal (*Pusa hispida*) as the principal game. This fact established the site's coastal provenience, which was not previously known. Nevertheless, the osteological material, which was hard burned, indicated that domesticated animals, including sheep or goats and possibly cattle, had been kept (Lepiksaar n.d.). Of further interest is the fact that no elk bones were found — normally these are very common in north Swedish sites.

Pollen and macrofossil samples were taken from a small fen located by the site. This fen had once been a small lagoon. The analysis of this material has shown that barley (*Hordeum*) was cultivated and that *svedje* [slash and burn] agriculture was practiced (Königsson 1970).

Although agriculture and animal husbandry were practiced, seal hunting was the main economic activity, and it was this resource that stimulated the cultural expansion to this northern area. It is likely that the Bjurselet site was first occupied by a seal-hunting group of Mesolithic character before the Neolithic settlement. This occupation was terminated by the flint-bearing peoples. The horizontal distribution of quartz scrapers and detritus is concentrated fifty centimeters to one meter higher than the corresponding flint finds.

The flint artifact material, as previously mentioned, consists of adzes and scrapers. The majority of the axes have reworked edges, which leads me to suspect they were used as heavy scrapers for skinning and skin preparation. The scrapers have concave and convex edges. Several burins have also been found. We are obviously dealing with a seal-hunting people from the south Baltic who, already well-acquainted with flint-working techniques, settled in the north. I, nevertheless, consider it too early to determine categorically whether these people were Pitted Ware or Boat Axe folk.

Some details, nevertheless, imply that it was the Boat Axe people who settled in Västerbotten. One boat axe has been found at Bjurselet and another has been found at a more inland site, Strandholm. The boat axe find from Bjurselet is not completely authenticated, representing an older surface find.

Several potsherds from Bjurselet also seem to be more like that of the Boat Axe culture than Pitted Ware. The shards lack ornament, however, and cannot be assigned with certainty to any particular group.

Whatever the final results, it is clear that a migration took place from the southern Baltic area. Just where these people came from is still unknown; possibly they came from Skåne, but if the Boat Axe people were the bearers, they were not from Denmark because the boat axes in Norrland are not of Danish type.

The probable background for this emigration, as I see it, was the scarcity of seals in the southern Baltic, possibly due to overkill, most probably due to climatic fluctuations which forced the seals north. The ring seal requires ice for calving. Warm winters with ice-poor seas, such as occurred this winter (1973), have demonstrated the scarcity of seals taken by hunters in the south Baltic and the corresponding abundance of them in the north. A succession of ice-poor winters could have forced the seal hunters far to the north, where new colonies were established on the Bothnian coast.

## REFERENCES

AMBROSIANI, BJÖRN
  1959   Keramikboplatsen på Hamnbrinken vid Darsgärde. *Tor.*
ARBMAN, HOLGER
  1945   Hedningahällen. *Finska Fornminnesföreningens Tidskrift* 45.

BAGGE, AXEL
1937   Stenåldern vid Torne Träsk. *Norrbotten.*
BECKER, C. J.
1950   Den grubekeramiske kultur i Danmark. *Aarbøger for Nordisk Old-kyndighed og Historie.*
1952   Die nordschwedischen Flintdepots. Ein Beitrag zur Geschichte des neolitischen Fernhandels in Skandinavien. *Acta Archeologica* 23.
BROADBENT, NOEL
1973   Prehistoric quartz quarrying in Norrland. *Fornvännen.*
CHRISTIANSSON, HANS
1965   "Flint finds in Västerbotten," in *Hunting and fishing.* Luleå: Norrbottens Museum.
1969   Kankeramiska influenser i Norrland och norra Svealand. *NordSvensk Forntid.*
JANSON, SVERKER, H. HVARFNER
1966   *Ancient hunters and settlements in the mountains of Sweden.* Stockholm.
KÖNIGSSON, LARS-KÖNIG
1970   "Traces of Neolithic human influence upon the landscape development at the Bjurselet settlement, Västerbotten, northern Sweden," in *Bjurselet settlement I.* Edited by Hans Christiansson, 13–30. Kungliga Skytteanska Samfundets Handlingar 7. Umeå.
LEPIKSAAR, JOHANNES
n.d.   "Bjurselet osteological material." Unpublished manuscript.
MALMER, MATS
1962   Jungneolitische Studien. *Acta Archaeologica Lundensia* 80(3).

# Use of Slate in the Circumpolar Region

KRISTEN R. MØLLENHUS

As the theory of a common circumpolar Stone Age culture (Gjessing 1942) with a distinctive use of slate as one of its most important characteristics has not been critically considered elsewhere in archaeological circles, it is of interest to examine this theory rather more closely, though I am aware that the concept "slate culture" in its usual sense embraces a complex of which slate itself is only a part. I will concern myself especially with the Eurasian area which should produce an important part of the necessary material for a theory of this kind.

Especially since the last war certain Russian work has been published which gives a fairly good reorganization of Stone Age material, especially from the European part of the Soviet Union. There is less published material relevant to our inquiry about the areas further east, from the Urals to the Pacific. It is also true, of course, that there has been less archaeological research in these areas.

We shall deal individually with the various areas and cultures as they have appeared in publications from Soviet Russia and base our considerations of the problem on this material. In order to show the particular characteristics of the material in the various cultures, it will be necessary to give a brief review of the entire material in each culture.

The Kola peninsula, lying nearest to Norway, has been the special field of research of Gurina, and one should also mention the excavations of Schmidt (Schmidt 1930). There are settlement sites along the whole coast, but they are particularly concentrated along the Barents Sea to the north

This article is a translation of part of "Steinalderen i Søndre Helgeland" in *Det Konge-lige Norske Videnskabers Selskabs Skrifter* (1958). It is reprinted with the kind permission of Det Kongelige Norske Videnskabers Selskabs.

and around Kandalak Bay to the south. According to Gurina these are sites that were in use for shorter periods during the hunting season. The major part of the collection consists of the relatively rich quartz material, this domination being due to the scarcity of flint in these regions.

On the Kola sites, quartz has been used almost exclusively for scrapers. Hammerstones and projectile points have been worked from various sedimentary rocks which must not, however, be confused with "slate," which the Russians keep separate. Naturally enough, mistakes can occur when the Stone Age material is judged solely from illustrations, and Gjessing, for example, is occasionally guilty of such misunderstandings when he refers to photographs of "slate arrowheads" in Russian publications. It is clear that these are not necessarily made from slate, but from other types of rock, such as nephrite which has a completely different composition and degree of hardness from slate and so demands a different technological treatment.

Moreover, these arrowheads have forms that on the whole are missing from our slate types. The arrowheads are most often of a pointed oval type, with more evenly rounded contours and a more pointed base than the hornstone example that Gjessing illustrates as a typical pointed oval arrowhead from northern Norway (Gurina 1951a: 155, Figure 3; Gjessing 1942: Figure 142). Barbed arrowheads are not found at all, but the spearheads can have a weak, sloping turn toward the tang. A very few examples of this type are made from slate, but we cannot say that they show any connection with the Scandinavian forms.

A few single-edged stone knives also come from Kola, and here we find greater similarity with the Scandinavian material, as some of the knives can best be classified as Skånland type or one of its variations. But the knives from Kola are usually somewhat smaller and are, moreover, shaped in a different way. The Scandinavian types when fully formed have ground sides while the back can often be unpolished, whereas the Kola knives are only ground along the edge. This gives them a rather rough appearance, which in itself points to the distance from the Scandinavian slate area with its highly developed technique.

Although bone and horn comprise only a small part of the material, horn arrowheads are relatively numerous. They are long and narrow, oval in cross-section and thicker toward the base. Some of the flint arrowheads, of which there are not many, have basically the same shape as the horn points, but are more usually blade-shaped with a weak tang.

In addition to the heavier tools of sedimentary rock, there are also large mace-heads in granite, often with a worked groove for fixing the shaft.

The pottery from the Kola settlement sites deserves a chapter to itself and in the present context 1 will give a mere summary. It consists of two groups, asbestos ware and a less widespread ware mixed with quartz. In the north the asbestos ware is quite plain, but along the south coast it can have a comb-stamped or linear decoration. In the second group, the decoration covers the whole surface and consists of pits and a kind of combed pattern. So far, this type is known largely from sites along the north coast of Kola.

On Reindeer Island and Katarina Island, Schmidt and Gurina have investigated a number of graves which date from the end of our Bronze Age and the Early Iron Age. A good deal of the material here is of various types of stone, but there is nothing of slate. Daggers and arrowheads of flint with notches above the base show an affinity with the somewhat older flint and quartz cultures from this area (Gurina 1953: 359). Otherwise, there are a number of arrowheads and other tools of bone, including compound fishing hooks. Two or three T-shaped bone objects can be interpreted as shaman drum sticks. Moreover, decoration on the pottery and a number of the bone objects shows a great similarity to finds from Kjelmøy, which are fairly contemporary.

On the dunes along the southeast coast of the White Sea, from the Onega river eastward to Mezen, settlement sites have been located and excavated over a period of years particularly by Foss, and they have produced rather homogeneous material. He has therefore coined the term White Sea culture for this group. Its particular characteristic lies in its widespread use of flint. The material includes a large number of arrow-heads of the type accordingly known to the Russians as the 'White Sea type': leaf-shaped, nicely worked points with a straight base and toothed edges. Similar types in flint are also found in other places, including the Scandinavian area, but there are stronger grounds for drawing attention to the north Scandinavian quartzite points with a straight base. Further-more, there is a pointed oval type as well as examples with concave bases. Finally, of the flint material one should mention the scrapers, often made from poor flakes or waste material.

But slate tools are lacking. The very few implements of other stone are limited to axes, some of them related to our West Coast type (Foss 1952: 127). On the whole the material lacks hammerstones and other heavier implements.

The pottery has pitted or comb-stamped decoration and is closest to that which the Russians call pit-combed ware, the first phase of combed pottery where the pit decoration is predominant.

Foss dates the White Sea culture from the beginning of the second mil-lennium to the end of the first millennium B.C., which should thus partly cover the period of our own slate culture except that we are not able to track down any connection in the slate material.

When we come down to the Karelian area, we have at once material that in many ways is closer to the Finnish material. In the Karelian culture, we find a great many parallels to the Later Finnish Stone Age and similarly many of the eastern forms which we know from Norway. It should not therefore be necessary to give a summary of the entire Karelian material: we can simply mention that we find the well-known forms of hollow-bladed adze, the Finno-Karelian (Sandhamn) type, the Rovaniemi pick, the transverse chisel, the Karelian pick (Ilomantsi type), and the cruciform pick. This applies in particular to the western part of Karelia; towards Onega, the types are a good deal more restricted.

The pottery shows strong affinities with the Finnish pottery, as is to be expected. Working from the pottery, the Russian archaeologists have been much concerned in finding connections between Karelia and the Volga-Oka region. Brusov (1940: 36), Gurina (1951b: 2, 95), and Foss (1952: 146) all go in for a theory of immigration from the latter area with a strong influence from its pit-combed ware as a result. Äyräpää has previously claimed a similar influence also on Finnish combed ware from the central Russian area.

We are familiar with an amount of slate material from Karelia: the single-edged "boot-shaped" knife, the Nyelv arrowheads (Pyheensilta type), points with a notch between blade and tang, and the long, leaf-shaped spearheads which Brusov dates to the second millennium B.C. (Brusov 1940: 303, 310), although in Finland they are particularly known from the sites of the Suomusjärvi culture, even though there are some rare examples from the combed-ware period.

However, slate implements do not occur in larger numbers here in Karelia, and it is obvious that we are already getting near the boundary of the true slate area. Brusov (1940: 20) says of the Nyelv arrowheads:

Slate arrowheads are far from characteristic in the northern Soviet Union. Among the Stone Age material from Karelia they are found only at Besoviye Sledki (two examples) and on a small settlement-site on this island (one example).

Furthermore, he says,

Exactly the same can be said of the slate points with a rhomboid cross-section [and rebate toward the tang — K.R.M. footnote] which in every detail are the same as the Scandinavian type which are found from Trondheim to Løfoten, as well as in Jämtland, but of which there have not been found any more in Karelia.

One should emphasize here that the overwhelming majority of Norwegian slate arrowheads have no rebate but in fact are properly barbed. All the same, this is of little importance, merely demonstrating that the Karelian slate material is first and foremost related to the Finnish material, which is only natural.

In the area east of Onega, towards the lakes Lacha, Ken, and Vozhe, the Russian archaeologists have found some eighty sites from the Neolithic period, many of which have been excavated. The culture of which these sites are representative is known as the Kargopol culture and seems to have lasted over a thousand years, from the end of the third to the middle of the first millennium B.C. It can be called a typical inland culture with sites spread along the rivers and lakes.

Flint is the dominant raw material, and the rich flint complex is the most characteristic feature of the Kargopol culture. Moreover, Foss is of the opinion that the flint found to a lesser extent in Karelia and Finland must have been imported from the Kargopol area (Foss 1952: 198). The flint is used especially for arrowheads whose entire surface is worked. Here again we find the White Sea type with a straight base, as well as points with a concave base, and a pointed ovate type with notches towards the triangular tang. Besides, there are scrapers from both flakes and blades and occasional examples of crescentic knives or "saws" (Foss 1952: Figures 61–63).

Of other stone we also get the Russo-Karelian axes and the Karelian pick, as well as thick-butted axes, curved chisels, and shaft-hole axes (Foss 1952: Figures 58–59). Bone and horn are represented by a number of harpoons, including some of the Kjelmøy type, as well as long arrowheads with a triangular tang and no notches. From one of the later sites comes a Mälar-type celt. Small idols of clay, bone, and horn are very similar to those known earlier from Honkaniemi and Jettbøle, for example (Foss 1952: Figure 66).

Pottery with its many variations would make up quite an extensive chapter. The most obvious elements are still pitted and combed decoration and, just as with the Karelian pottery, there is a clear influence from the pottery of the Volga-Oka region. There is also an amount of textile ware.

The only slate object found on an ordinary site is a fragmentary slate ring with an incised diamond pattern. Otherwise there are three knives of unspecified stone. This lack of slate can be explained quite naturally by the rich occurrence of flint, which makes slate superfluous as a material for arrowheads and knives. The connection with Karelia and Finland that we can detect in much of the other material does not lead to the adoption of a second-rate material when a better one is available, even though the natural environment and occupation conditions are very similar.

Finally we will draw special attention to a remarkable find within the Kargopol culture, namely a settlement on the banks of the river Modlona with building remains that Brusov interprets as original stake-dwellings (Brusov 1951: 71ff.). Up to 1951, four separate buildings had been found of irregular rectangular shape and with walls up to 5 meters long. Between the houses were remains of "platforms" or wooden paving. It seems that these stake-dwellings became flooded and buried and that at a higher level a new settlement came with a different building technique.

In both the lower and the upper layers, flint was predominant, but on the whole it was of an obviously poorer quality than on the other Kargopol sites, though there were the usual Kargopol culture forms. There were also many examples of flint sculpture (Brusov 1951: Figure 13). Because of good preservation conditions, the list of characteristic equipment is augmented by wooden objects of various uses, including wooden vessels with carved handles. Amber is not found on Kargopol sites elsewhere, but here by the Modlona there were a number of individual amber objects for personal adornment (Brusov 1951: Figures 9–10).

The only reference to a slate arrowhead within the Kargopol culture is, in fact, from the earliest occupation level at Modlona — a long, narrow example without barbs. There was also a small piece of slate which Brusov interprets as a stamp for decorating pottery. Of other stone, there were only a few picks and maces.

The two layers produced quite different pottery which at the same time is clearly separate from the rest of the Kargopol pottery. From the stake-dwelling period the decoration consists to some extent of the typical combed pattern, while the later pottery has, as well as larger and smaller pits, only small thin tooth stamps (Brusov 1951: Figures 7–8). Textile ware is also represented in the upper occupation layer.

The stake-dwellings at Modlona are dated archaeologically and by pollen analysis to not later than the first centuries of the second millennium B.C. The difference between the occupation material from this level and the rest of the contemporary Kargopol culture has led Brusov to suggest that the Modlona and the immediately adjacent area were occupied by a foreign and partly isolated people.

As the last culture within the European area of the Soviet Union we shall take the so-called Pechora culture whose settlements lie along the river Pechora and its tributaries northwest of the Urals. The culture dates from the end of the second millennium B.C. to around the beginning of our era.

The collection is completely dominated by flint which comes in the form of erratic flint pebbles from the coast. Most characteristic are the arrowheads worked all the way around, which we have met in the cultures already described. Particularly widespread are the points with a triangular tang, both with and without notches; next are those with a concave base; and there are also some few examples of the White Sea type. Of slate, I know of only one single example together with a few fragments of others, and all of the same narrow form with short triangular tangs and no notches. This type is also known on Kola and by the lower Ob (Foss 1952: 139, 249, Figure 77, 1) and its shape is reminiscent of some of the slate points in the Fenno-Scandian area which belong to the Nyelv or Pyheensilta type. But the Pechora type has a form that in fact appears heavy and is strange in our slate culture: the edges of the tang are blunted and the blade itself is specially ground, added to which the flattened part of the tang continues right up the ridge of the blade. Foss groups it with the bone points of the "gorodish" type which he dates to the end of the second and beginning of the first millennium B.C., which corresponds to the earliest material of the Pechora settlements.

Otherwise, sedimentary rock is used very little. Along with granite, it can be used for heavier implements, but this group is extremely poorly represented. Of axe forms, one can mention the Russo-Karelian type. One can say that a characteristic feature of the Pechora culture is that slate implements are quite unknown.

Even though both pitted and combed decorations occur on Pechora pottery, they are clearly different from the northern pottery types we have touched on earlier. In fact, it is impossible to detect any relationship with the so-called pit-combed ware of the Volga-Oka area which has exerted such a strong influence over the pottery of Karelia and the Kargopol region. On the contrary, one can point to an obvious connection between the decoration on the Pechora wares and the decoration in western Siberia, the Urals and along the Ob. Foss suggests that the people of Pechora have an eastern Siberian origin.

On the other hand there is also evidence for further contact with the western coastal area along the Arctic Ocean. As already mentioned, a few typical White Sea culture flint points have been found at Pechora, and two highly characteristic patterns of decoration from the oldest phase of the Pechora culture and from western Siberia have both been found individually on two settlement-sites by the White Sea (Foss 1952: Figure 77, 10–11). The latest phase of the culture, however, produces certain short linear patterns which can be compared with Kandalak and Kjelmøy (Foss 1952: Figure 77, 6, 7, 9).

The Ural region itself can be divided into two separate main groups, namely the western slopes of the Urals and the upper course of the Kama, and the eastern slopes with the immediately adjacent steppes. As yet, relatively little research has been done on the Neolithic of the Urals, but the material which is available should nevertheless be adequate for our purposes.

The material from the western sites is almost totally characterized by flint. There are arrowheads of pointed oval form, and leaf-shaped arrowheads with a rounded base, as well as a number of flint scrapers and knives made from flakes. The larger implements are made from various rock, and the site of Bor II by the Kama includes several hollow-edged chisels (Bader 1954a: 1, Figure 19). From the site at Lake Borovoye on the Chusovaya river comes a thick single-edged knife of sedimentary rock with a narrow handle (Bader 1951: Figure 15, 13). Similar but simpler knives are also known from a couple of other settlement sites in the Urals.

Comb-stamped ware dominates the pottery of the west Urals, although the grouping of the patterns is distinctive on the local level.

Remarkably enough it is the eastern Ural region that is best known and investigated. Along the eastern slopes of the mid-Urals, Dmitriev through his excavations has been able to group the Neolithic material under the name of the Shigir culture. Dmitriev himself dates this culture to the period 1300–800 B.C., i.e. Bronze Age according to the Scandinavian pattern, but recent finds have shown that its beginning must be taken back to the third millennium B.C. (Dmitriev 1951: 2, 28, 35).

Probably contemporary with the later part of the Shigir culture, in which bronze objects are known, is the so-called Andreyev culture. It extends on to the steppes a little east of the Urals and the area of the Shigir culture. But as the material from these two cultures — apart from the pottery — shows very great agreement, I find it more satisfactory to treat them together in this context.

The most dominating feature in both cultures is the large role that bone points play. These arrowheads can have rather different forms, but the predominant form has a point with a thickened conical head. There are also broad spearheads and harpoons of bone. The next largest group comprises arrowheads of flint, usually triangular, with a short tang and with barbs or notches. There are also a number which are lance-formed with a straight or concave base.

Another widespread type consists of small tools, narrow and flakelike, which can possibly be interpreted as a kind of knife (Dmitriev 1951: 2, Figure 1, 14). They are worked in both flint and sedimentary rock, including slate, and are worked along one or both of the long sides. It is, in fact, a type that is special to the east Urals.

The axes consist for the most part of the simple thick-butted type with a rectangular cross-section, while hollow-edged chisels, for example, are extremely rare. In fact, only one example has been found on a Shigir culture site.

One should mention that, among the more unusual objects, remains of both sledges and skis have been found on the settlement sites where preservation conditions are favorable. Similarly, fragments of a bow have been found as well as idols and small wooden vessels with shaped handles.

We have already mentioned the remarkable knife-like tools that were made from slate. From the area of the Shigir culture, I know of only three other slate objects — all arrowheads. The first is of simple form, almost leaf-shaped with a rhomboid cross-section; the edges are curved and the base is rounded with no particular features. For the nearest parallels to this arrowhead, Dmitriev turns to northern Europe, "especially Norway" (Dmitriev 1951: 2, Figure 1, 16, 41). The other two examples are of the Sunderøy type with a concave base and grooved shaft and come from settlement sites which can be dated to early in the second half of the second millennium B.C. Brusov, who describes these finds, refers to Gjessing's comment that this type of arrowhead shows cultural connections with the north. But, says Brusov,

I know of no other arrowheads of this type from the whole of the extensive area from the mid-Transurals to Norway, and therefore I do not think it possible on the basis of such finds to suggest a cultural link between two areas so widely separated (1955: 85).

One of the settlement sites within the Andreyev culture has also produced a single slate arrowhead. This has a split base with deep grooves down the center of the blade. From the description this could in fact also be a Sunderøy type. It is true that Dmitriev says that such arrowheads are not found on other sites east of the Urals (Dmitriev 1951: (2) 41), but as there has been a series of investigations in these areas since his work was written, there may well have been new finds.

The pottery of the Shigir and Andreyev cultures, I do not intend to discuss further. Both cultures include pitted and comb-stamped ware, but there is quite a variation in the type of decoration.

The Bronze Age of the southeastern and southern Urals is represented by the Andronovo culture. Like so many other Bronze Age cultures this contains a mixture of stone, flint, and bronze material. Arrowheads are made from bone and flint while the heavier implements are made from various stone. However, there does not seem to be a single typical slate implement known (Salnikov 1951: 130). Nor, as far as I can see, do the Russian publications mention slate implements from the previous pure Neolithic cultures in the same area.

From the Ob basin we know of an amount of Stone Age material. There is a relatively large number of axes; the majority seem to be of stone other than flint. Many of the forms have parallels in Fenno-Scandia: one finds the Russo-Karelian type and the round-backed hollow-edged chisel. In the Tomsk region Komarova has investigated a burial site with a number of graves from the Neolithic, Bronze Age, and Early Iron Age (Komarova 1952). Although Komarova does not give any specification of the material, it appears from the illustrations that all the arrowheads and spearheads are made of flint. Knives of stone are completely lacking. From the Lower Ob, including the area around Sosva, Ailio, however, specifies spearheads of slate (Ailio 1922: 19).

Near Yenesey, there are many of the same axe forms as along the Ob, as well as lugged axes. Flint points are for the most part leaf-shaped or triangular with a concave base (Rygdylon 1953: Figures 1–2). I know of no slate arrowheads from here.

A little further east, we have an area that has been subject to rather intense investigation, and that also lies within the area which, according to Gjessing, is covered by the slate culture. It includes the northern area of Lake Baikal, especially the upper reaches of the Angara River (Oklad-nikov 1950). The Neolithic material from here is grouped into various cultural stages from the fifth millennium to about 1000 B.C., and this material is so extensive that we cannot treat the various periods in detail but merely sketch the characteristic features in the list of implements on the basis of raw material.

Flint in these areas was difficult to obtain and has been used almost exclusively for the fabrication of arrowheads and, to a lesser extent, spearheads. But these tools were especially common in the earliest Neolithic period; later flint arrowheads were a rarity.

The raw material which on the whole was dominant in the production of implements was nephrite. This is a fine crystalline rock that is very hard and demands its own particular and difficult technique. But there are widespread deposits of nephrite in the Baikal area, and especially towards the end of the Neolithic period it was used for such widely ranging objects as axes, rings and not least, small models of fish in great quantities. These were used for fish bait and are also known from Eskimos and some North American Indians (Okladnikov 1950: 250, 257, Figures 72–80).

The axes on the whole are the thick-butted adze-type, occasionally hollow-edged, while knives are most often of remarkable forms for which there are no parallels in Norway.

Bone was also widely used, first and foremost for harpoon points, of course, but there are also a number of bone knives with flint insets, as well as fish hooks and plain bone points.

I have not succeeded in finding more than three slate objects mentioned in the various cultural levels of these areas, and all three were slate arrowheads — or rather one was a spearhead with a weakly curving edge and with a pointed oval cross-section and an almost straight base (Okladnikov 1950: Figure 16, Plate 6). Direct parallels within our own slate material are lacking, but its form can be roughly compared with the Norwegian and Finnish examples of Gjessing's Trollholmsund type. The three points are all from the early Chinsky phase of the fifth millennium B.C.

As far as pottery from these distant areas is concerned we need only mention that textile ware and asbestos ware are known.

The great north Siberian tundra eastward to Kolyma has been little investigated. This is essentially an area where the climatic conditions are completely unfavorable for settlement, and this was also certainly so in the prehistoric period, although to a lesser extent in the milder Neolithic period. These conditions are, of course, just as unfavorable for archaeological investigation.

When we come as far east as Kolyma, we eventually encounter smaller slate objects, for example, a single-edged knife where the upper edge of the handle is a direct continuation of the blade (Beregovaya 1954: Plate III, 4). It more or less resembles certain knives of Gjessing's Røsås type (Gjessing 1942: Figure 72). From the islands off the mouth of the Kolyma comes a two-edged stone knive that can be compared with the Eskimo man's knife (Beregovaya 1954: 304). One can also mention some short, partly crescentic edged tools, similar to the Eskimo ulu (Beregovaya 1954: Plate III, 1–3).

These sites around the mouth of the Kolyma are classified by the Russian archaeologists mainly with the old Eskimo Birnirk culture, which most researchers now date to the first half of the first millennium A.D., while Rudenko, for example, dates it to the second half of the same millennium (Beregovaya 1954: 310; Rudenko 1947: 108). The above-mentioned slate knife belongs nevertheless to a type more characteristic of the rather later Punuk culture.

Eskimo knife types are also found on the Chukotsky peninsula in the Bering Sea: single-edged polished stone knives, for example, which also have parallels in the Punuk culture as well as the later phases of the Eskimo culture (Beregovaya 1954: 304). Similarly, here we find the crescentic tools mentioned above which can best be described as scrapers (Beregovaya 1954: 306).

A large amount of Neolithic material is known from Kamchatka, but unfortunately only a small amount is published (Orlova 1955; Rudenko 1947). Nevertheless, it seems clear that obsidian, flint, and quartz are basically used for arrowheads and daggers, while flint and to some extent other sedimentary rock are used for heavier tools. We have not found slate mentioned in the published material, but one should not exclude the possibility of its use, as it is used in areas both north and south of the peninsula.

Although the distances are quite great, one does find typical slate tools in the Sakhalin area and to the south between the Amur and Vladivostok. The slate implements date to the end of the second millennium and to the first millennium B.C. — i.e. the Bronze Age and Early Iron Age according to the Montelian system. Although slate arrowheads should be found on the settlement sites in this area, I have not found a single illustration, with the exception perhaps of a little spearhead of unusual form made from unspecified stone (Ivanev 1952: 202, Figure 2.1).

On the other hand some very interesting Chinese accounts are preserved from the time of the Han Dynasty (206 B.C. – 9 A.D.) which describe the tribes north of the mouth of the Amur where they make their spearheads of "dark stone and smear them with poison so that the wounded will die immediately" (Okladnikov 1954: 253). This agrees very well with the archaeological finds from these areas where the slate points are made of such dark material. The information that poison was used on slate spearheads is important, suggesting that we can also consider its possible use on our own local material.

Otherwise there are both harpoons and daggers of slate. Harpoons here are of exactly the same form as some Eskimo examples (Okladnikov 1954: 249, 250), a simple type with two parallel slots near the point. The daggers show, for their part, clear influences from the contemporary bronze daggers which were in use in central Asia, around Lake Baikal and in southern Siberia (Okladnikov 1954: 252). Some have the same form as the bronze daggers from China and the Asiatic steppelands, belonging to the thirteenth and twelfth centuries B.C. Others can be compared with daggers from the rich finds of the Scythian times in Altai, Kazakhstan, and Mongolia (Okladnikov 1954: 252).

The phenomenon we encounter here can also be recognized in the Later Stone Age in Scandinavia, with flint daggers, for example, but our slate culture does not show the same clear influence from metal forms. Here in the Vladivostok area, slate is used as the raw material, while the forms really belong to a foreign, but geographically relatively close, metal culture.

In this survey of the Neolithic and to some extent Bronze Age material from the northernmost part of Eurasia, we have been able to provide an overall picture of the importance of slate in the various cultures within this period. We believe that this survey clearly points in a single direction: that in the large area from Karelia to the Pacific, slate has played a much smaller role than is asserted so strongly by Gjessing. Even taking into account the individual slate objects that we have not been able to consider, the picture has nevertheless been quite different from the close similarity of slate objects we have in Fenno-Scandia. There has, in fact, been a characteristic lack of similarity.

With the exceptions of a few scattered examples, it is only in the inland areas around the Urals that we encounter concentrated deposits of slate. Yet slate becomes more general when we come as far east as Kolyma and especially along the Pacific coast from the Bering Straits to at least as far south as the Amur. Although we must consider the great Siberian area as sparsely investigated, there are, however, so many finds from sealed sites here that they should give a representative picture of the material culture. Flint and bone are the dominant raw materials for points and knives, while stone, to some extent laminated, has often been used for axes and hammerstones, although in many cases we are unable to give an exact petrographic description.

The axe material should play a less significant role in our thesis. It is the widespread use of slate for arrowheads and spearheads and for knives that has been used as the criterion for the so-called Slate culture by all those who have concerned themselves with this question. It was Gjessing especially who introduced into the picture the variety of axe types that make up an important part of the equipment of the slate culture in northern Scandinavia. For some of these axes, Gjessing has tried to trace their distribution across vast areas, in some instances halfway around the world. I think that the most doubtful consequences are involved when dealing with these few individual axe forms as a basis for postulating a cultural connection between areas 10,000 kilometers apart.

As an example of the difficulties involved in such material, we can quote the example of the round-backed hollow-edged chisel. According to Gjessing, this chisel is widespread from the Norwegian coast to the Atlantic coast of North America. The whole area from northern Norway eastward produces typical examples but in addition produces axes that are less recognizable as typical. As evidence that the type has an eastern origin, Gjessing discusses the locally characteristic but less typical forms in the area between northern Norway and the coast of Møre. It is only to be expected that the forms become less typical in the marginal areas, and it is probable that the type has its origin somewhere to the east of Norway. But what about all the other less characteristic forms in the enormous area to the east? And can we be sure that the type originated at a single place within this area? Which of the places shall we choose as the one where the shape is more characteristic?

Nor can there be any doubt that in any case some of the distribution maps that Gjessing uses give a biased and to some extent false picture of the real situation. As far as typical slate objects are concerned, we have tried to give evidence for this here. Another example is his map of the distribution of the so-called Eskimo harpoon (Gjessing 1942: Figure 229) where the whole of the Arctic coast from the White Sea to Greenland in the east is carefully marked. According to the Russian Rudenko, who is familiar with the Eskimo culture, the conditions are quite different:

On one of his bold cartograms, Gjessing gives the geographical extent in the Arctic region of "Eskimo-harpoons" and refers to the whole of the Arctic coast of Siberia and Europe from Cape Dezhneva in the east to the White Sea in the west. At the moment we do not yet know of a single find of the reversible harpoon-tip, nor are we aware of any trace of Eskimo culture in north-west Asia west of the Kolyma (1947: 111).

Rudenko maintains in complete contrast to Gjessing that neither the harpoon points from Scandinavia nor those from Schmidt's excavation on Kola can be considered as Eskimo harpoons.

Slate implements are so well known as elements in Eskimo equipment that we do not need to discuss them further here. There is, however, another point in this connection to which we have good reason to draw attention.

The question of the origin of the Eskimo culture has for a long time been the object of all kinds of theories and hypotheses. However, in the last decades, most researchers have come to the conclusion that the cradle of Eskimo culture should be sought in the west, on the Asiatic mainland. There is, nevertheless, divergence of opinion as to whether it extended along the Arctic coast of Siberia westward from the Lake Baikal area in the south-west, or northward along the Pacific coast. Rudenko, a spokesman for the latter theory seems for the time being to have the best arguments (Rudenko 1947: 12ff.), based partly on the results at which Okladnikov has previously arrived. He has found characteristic elements that have their parallels in the Eskimo culture southward as far as Kamchatka and the Amur area, as well as on the Japanese islands. Incidentally, it includes the Eskimo harpoon.

In my opinion, the widespread use of slate which we have been able to demonstrate southward along the east Asiatic coast can also be included in Rudenko's theory. As we have seen, the use of slate in these areas is a striking feature in the equipment which is thus isolated from the rest of the material from northeast Asia. We recall that around Kolyma and the Bering Straits where the old Eskimo culture has been found, we also have a good many slate objects, including some Eskimo forms. The slate objects southward along the Pacific coast form a natural continuation of these northern finds. Also, the natural conditions for settlement are the same and have given rise to the same occupations of fishing and hunting for sea animals. Among the more abstract elements, one can mention the old Eskimo depiction of the original female deity and her marriage with the dog, which is widespread down the Pacific coast as far as south China.

On the other hand, I do not believe one can speak of influences between the Later Stone Age culture of Norway and the Eskimo culture. The distances are too great and the areas where finds are lacking are too large. A slate arrowhead made by a hunter on the Norwegian coast need not necessarily be so very different from an Eskimo arrowhead made in North America when both have the same purpose. And the fact that slate where it existed, was a suitable material, was discovered in both places. Because of the lack of connecting finds one cannot really postulate any connection between the three slate arrowheads from Lake Baikal and the contemporary Finnish slate arrowheads of the Suomusjärvi culture.

## REFERENCES [1]

AILIO, J.
1922  *Fragen der russischen Steinzeit.* Helsinki.

BADER, O. N.
1951  Stoyanka nizhneadishevskaya i Borovoye Ozero I na r. Chusovoy [The lower Adishev site and Lake Borovoy on the Chusovaya River]. *MIA* 22: 7–32.
1954a Stoyanka Bor II i predananinskoye vremya v Prikame [The Site of Bor II and the pre-ananian time by the Kama]. *SA* 20: 180–212.

[1]  Abbreviations:
Kratk. soobsh.: Kratkiye soobshcheniya o dokladakh i polevykh izyskaniyakh instituta istorii materialnoi kultury [Short reports about the lectures and field findings of the Institute of the History of Material Culture].
*MIA*            : Materialy i issledovaniya po arkheologii SSSR [Materials and investigations on archaeology in the USSR].
*SA*             : *Sovetskaya arkheologiya* [Soviet Archaeology].

1954b Zhertvenneyo mesto pod Pisanym kamnem na r. Vishere [The place of sacrifice near the Pisany stone on the Vishera River]. *SA* 21:241–258.

BEREGOVAYA, N. A.
1954   Arkheologicheskiye nakhodki na Ostrove Chetyrekhstolbovom [Archaeological finds on Chetyrekhstolbovy Island]. *SA* 20:288–312.

BRUSOV, A. J.
1940   *Istoria drevnei Karelii* [History of ancient Karelia]. Moscow.
1951   Svayniye poseleniya na r. Modlone [Stake-dwellings on the Modlona River]. *MIA* 20:7–76.
1955   Eines der Merkmale des gemeinsamen Ursprungs der vorgeschichtlichen Stämme im europäischen und westsibirischen Teil der Sovjetunion. *Finskt Museum* (1955): 79–89.

DMITRIEV, P. A.
1951   Shigirskaya kultura na vostochnom sklone Urala [Shigir culture on the eastern slope of the Urals]. *MIA* 21:28–93.

FEDOROV, V. V.
1953   Plechanovskaya neoliticheskaya stoyanka [The Plechanovsky Neolithic site]. *MIA* 39:293–331.

FOSS, M. J.
1947   Neoliticheskiye kultury Severa evropeiskoi chasti SSSR [Neolithic cultures of the northern European part of USSR]. *SA* 9:29–46.
1952   Drevneishaya istoriya Severa evropeiskoi chasti SSSR [Prehistory of the northern European part of USSR]. *MIA* 29:5–280.

GJESSING, G.
1942   *Yngre steinalder i Nord-Norge.* Instituttet for Sammenlignende Kulturforskning, series B, 39. Oslo.

GURINA, N. N.
1950a Nekotoriye danniye o zaselenii yuzhnovo poberezha kolskovo poluostrova [Some data about the settlement on the south coast of the Kola Peninsula]. *SA* 12:105–127.
1950b Rezultaty arkheologicheskovo obsledovaniya srednevo techeniya reki Msty [Results of archaeological investigation of the middle current of the Msta River]. *SA* 13:292–310.
1951a Neoliticheskiye poseleniya severnovo poberezha kolskovo polustrova [Neolithic settlements on the north coast of the Kola Peninsula]. *MIA* 20:143–167.
1951b Poseleniya epokhi neolita i rannevo metalla na severnom poberezhe onezhskovo ozera [Settlements of the Neolithic Early Metal epoch and on the north coast of Lake Onega]. *MIA* 20:77–142.
1953   Pamyatniki epokhi rannevo metalla na severnom poberezhe kolskovo poluostrova [Relics of the Age of the Early Metal on the north coast of the Kola Peninsula]. *MIA* 39:347–407.

IVANEV, L. N.
1952   Arkheologicheskiye nakhodki v okrestnostiyakh Vladivostoka [Archaeological finds around Vladivostok]. *SA* 16:289–298.

KOMAROVA, M. N.
1952   *Tomskii mogilnik* [The Tomsk sepulcher]. *MIA* 24:7–50.

OKLADNIKOV, A. P.
1950   Neolit i bronzovyi vek Pribaikaliya [The Neolithic and Bronze Age of the Lake Baikal region]. *MIA* 18:5–412.
1954   *U istokov kultura narodov dalnego Vostoka. Po sledam drevnikh kultur* [At the sources of the culture of the Far East nations]. Moscow.

ORLOVA, J. P.
1955   Arkheologicheskiye nakhodki na Kamchatke [Archaeological finds on Kamchatka]. *Kratk. Soobsh.* 59:163–166.

RUDENKO, S. I.
1947   *Drevnaya kultura Beringovo Moriya i eskimoskaya problema* [Ancient history of the Bering Sea and the Eskimo problem]. Moscow-Leningrad.

RYGDYLON, E. R.
1953   Novye sledki poselenii kamennovo veka v basseine srednevo Yeniseiya [New traces of the Stone Age settlements in the basin of the mid-Yenisei River]. *MIA* 39:276–285.

SALNIKOV, K. V.
1951   Bronzovy vek yuzhnovo Zauraliya [The Bronze Age of South Zauralia]. *MIA* 21:94–151.
1952   K voprosy o neolite stepnovo Zauraliya [On the question of the Neolithic of the steppe Zauralia]. *Kratk. Soobsh.* 47:15–23.

SCHMIDT, A. V.
1930   Drevnii mogilnik na Kolskom zalive [The ancient sepulcher on the Bay of Kola]. *Kolskii sbornik.*

# When and Why Did Occupational Specialization Begin at the Scandinavian North Coast?

POVL SIMONSEN

In Scandinavian prehistory it has been nearly a dogma that the pre-agrarian, food-gathering society had no professional handicraftsmen or other specialists, except the shaman. In my work with the sub-Neolithic culture of northernmost Scandinavia I have found many confirmations of this view, but also a few remarkable exceptions. These will be published here for the first time.

The pattern of settlement among the hunters and fishers of the late Stone Age in the county of Finnmark, farthest north in Norway, normally was the little fishing village on the coast and in the inland scattered and lonely huts. We must think of coast and inland as two seasons for the same individuals. In the excavations of the last twenty years (Figure 1) we have paid special attention to two areas: The Varangerfjord in the east, up to the Soviet border, and the island of Sørøy in the north, a little west of Northcape. Figure 2 is a map of a village, Gressbakken, which is surveyed and in part excavated. It is late in the sub-Neolithic, and the modern house type then was a large, semisubterranean turf house, presumably for an extended family. But earlier (Figure 3) the little house of the nuclear family dominated, here from Gropbakkeengen. The finds demonstrate that these villages were inhabited in the winter, which in Varanger is the season for cod fishing as well as for seal hunting. The same house types existed alone or two to three together scattered over the inland areas, where the finds point to the summer season, and to hunting in small bands. Chronologically the whole of this sub-Neolithic period is later than the beginning of agriculture and husbandry further south in Scandinavia. Our oldest fishing village is presumably from around 3000 B.C.; the latest is from near the beginning of the Christian era.

Figure 1.   North-Scandinavia

If now we look at the house itself and not at its position inside the village and first turn to Gropbakkeengen (Figure 3) from about 2000 B.C.,
it is obvious that all excavated house grounds are of dwellings, and all are
in principle alike. Each house (Figure 4) has an interior space of about 15
square meters and a fireplace in the center of the floor. Houses with specialized furnishings, barns, or boathouses, etc. do not exist. Turning to the
locality of Gressbakken (Figure 2) we encounter nearly the same picture.
The houses certainly are of the other main type, about 50 square meters
in floor space, with two to three fireplaces and an entrance corridor (Figure 5), but out of the thirteen houses in the village nearly all — eleven —
are also identical and are exclusively dwellings. Normally nearly all the
houses at each locality are of a similar type and point to an unspecialized
society.

I say "nearly all," because exceptions exist. As seen on the map of
Gressbakken (Figure 2) there are two deviating houses, numbers 7 and
12. They are circular and only seven to fifteen square meters in floor
space. Excavations have demonstrated that they have no fireplaces and

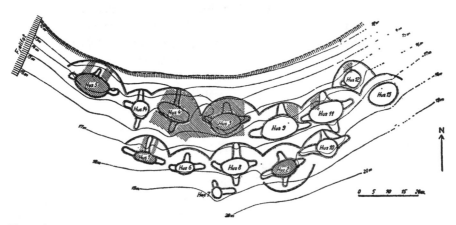

Figure 2.

none of the refuse layers with organic refuse which invariably are found
in all of the other houses. So they scarcely are dwellings. On the floors
we found a large amount of quartz and quartzite chips, half-fabricates,
and tools of types which we are accustomed to find on the so-called
"workfloors" in open air. The most probable explanation is that in the
winter people made their stone implements indoors in special workshop
houses, and in summer outside in the open. Such houses as these from
Gressbakken have been found at other places, for instance at Sandbukt
and Slettnes on Sørøy. They are always placed in connection with the village, but peripherally in relation to the dwelling houses. Sandbukt is from
about 2000 B.C., Slettnes from about 1500 B.C., Gressbakken from about
1000 B.C. These finds confirm our traditional view of the inhabitants as
hunter-fishers, with every man fabricating his own tools.

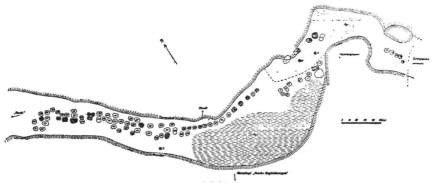

Figure 3.

We now turn to the new finds telling us the opposite, namely, that in this society, there were individuals — at least before the end of the Stone Age — who did not take very much part in the food gathering, but produced special goods and delivered these to the active hunters and fishermen.

First, there is the SHAMAN: Naturally it is completely impossible to find out how early shamans came into existence, and still more impossible to record the date when they became "full-time shamans." Many of my colleagues have supposed that the Paleolithic cave paintings in Western Europe were painted by a few specially gifted artists in every society, that is to say, a sort of shaman. But others have held the opposite view. They look upon the naturalistic, physioplastic art as the product of every single hunter, but take the stylization as a proof of the professionalizing of art and as a result of this also of magic. Gutorm Gjessing has maintained this point of view in relation to the north Scandinavian material. Here I will

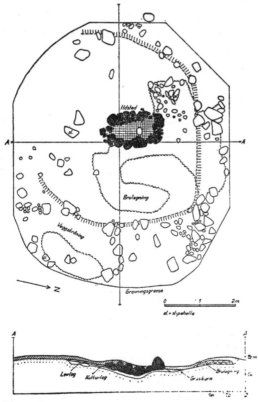

Figure 4.

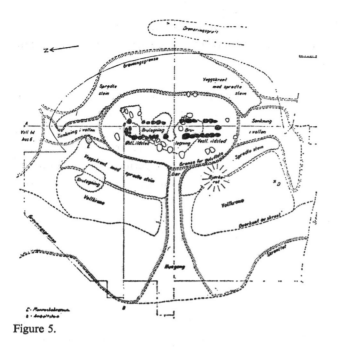

Figure 5.

stick to his line of argument. In the culture complex here mentioned, the sub-Neolithic slate complex, there are two types of art, the rock carvings and paintings and the small sculptures of slate and bone. Both use animals as their motifs. Both begin with the pure and simple naturalistic or physio-plastic style (Plates 1–2). But halfway through the sub-Neolithic period, around approximately 1500 B.C., they begin to differ from each other. The *Kleinkunst* continues unaltered through the remaining part of the Stone Age, whereas the rock art relatively quickly changes over to a stylized, ideoplastic style (Plate 3). Gjessing thinks that the reason must be that the shaman was professionalized just then. After that time, his relation to the animals was not so direct as that of the hunter. His relation to the powers tended toward a special, secret figurative language. His full-time occupation with art furthered simplification and symbolism. Out of all this a new style grew, whereas the hunters, generation after generation, still made their small sculpture naturalistic, which in reality was no style, but an imitation of nature. If this theory holds, the professionalizing of the shaman's task took place round 1500 B.C. Then it is surely not by coincidence that the three to four known examples of sacrificial places in Finnmark — mountaintops and small islands, on which fireburning and sacrificing repeatedly took place (Plate 4) — are later than that. My conclusion is that the shaman as a specialist in his society appeared at the latest in the middle of the sub-Neolithic and at any rate existed as such before the end of the north Scandinavian Stone Age around the beginning of the Christian era.

The TRADESMAN must have existed also. From the Mesolithic of north Scandinavia we have no examples of raw materials or implements transported more than some tens of kilometers from the production area. But immediately after the beginning of the sub-Neolithic, around 3000 B.C., the picture changes completely. From the following periods we find a number of things of foreign origin in Finnmark, and on the other hand some north Scandinavian products have been found far away in countries to the south and southeast. Among the imported pieces are an amber trinket from the southeast Baltic area found at a dwelling place in Varanger, a Danish amber trinket from a house site on Sørøy, two Danish flint arrowheads excavated from two house sites on Sørøy (Plate 5), fragments of two north Swedish slate ornaments from another house site on Sørøy, and so on. Besides these finds there are a number of loose finds found scattered over the whole of the area: axes, battle-axes, flint daggers, spearheads, etc., originating in Russia, the southeast Baltic, south Scandinavia, and Denmark. Most recent in this category is an iron razor from the first century A.D., found together with stone implements in a tomb at Kvalnes in Varanger, but fabricated on the island of Gotland in the Baltic. It is evident that during the whole of the era an active trade connected Finnmark not only to the agrarian societies of south Scandinavia, but also to the nonagrarian ones of northern Russia. Yet, this does not necessarily mean that professional, traveling tradesmen took the goods from their place of production and delivered them where they have been found today. It is just as reasonable to imagine a barter-trade, the single item changing owners many times, and going from hand to hand, ending its journey on the finding spot quite by random.

It is a different matter when we can demonstrate a mass transportation of raw materials, which surely were rarer and more precious than the local ones, but in relation to finished implements they must have been cheap mass goods. In Finnmark this description fits for three raw materials — south Scandinavian flint, Russian flint, and Finnish asbestos. In the opposite direction they transported the pumice of the Atlantic and Arctic coasts to the interior of northern Sweden and Finland. Here I must say that south Scandinavian flint as well as that from Russia greatly surpasses all local stone types as raw material for implements. South Scandinavian flint has been found in the form of a number of chips in nearly every excavated houseground on Sørøy and in many other places in west Finn-

1. ——    *Jutland amber.*
2. ——    *Baltic amber.*
3. ⫽⫽⫽   *South-Scandinavian*
            *flint.*

4. ⫽⫽⫽   *Russian flint from Olonetz.*
5. ⟍⟍⟍   *Large flint-depots.*
6. ▨▨▨   *Asbestos.*

Figure 6.    Neolithic trade in Scandinavia

mark and in the district round Tromsø. The finding places are sites from about 2300 B.C. down to about 500 B.C. Finished, imported implements of this same material are also found in these house grounds, but infrequently. But, as is well known, mass transportation of axe blanks of flint took place from south to north through the whole of the Baltic Sea in the period around 2000 B.C. (Figure 6). The large cache finds from the northernmost part of the Swedish east coast bear witness to that. Here we can be quite sure that we are dealing with an organized transportation of goods, originating in a farm district and sold to nonagrarian populations.

South Scandinavian imported flint has never been found in the Varanger district. There, however, we found a relatively large amount of the red, Russian flint from the Province of Olonetz between the two large lakes Onega and Ladoga. In the dwelling-place finds from Varanger there are many red and rose-colored flint chips, but there are also arrowheads and scrapers of the same material and of the Russian types. Obviously they all were imported between 2300 and 1800 B.C. This is also the peak of Russian flint export to Finland and of the amber trade from the southeast Baltic to Finland, Varanger, and northwestern Russia, so it was a very active period for trade along the whole eastern side of the Baltic. As far west as Sørøy — and in general in west Finnmark and the Tromsø area — Russian flint had not been found prior to 1971. But this year we excavated five house sites at the locality of Hellefjord on Sørøy, a dwelling place from about 2000 B.C. There we found south Scandinavian and Russian flint.

The third raw material, asbestos, is a necessary ingredient for tempering the clay in the asbestos pottery and part of the textile pottery, i.e. in the ceramics from the last millennium B.C. Asbestos has been found over the whole of north Scandinavia, partly as an ingredient in potsherds, partly as lumps of raw asbestos, found in the latest Stone Age house grounds, where it was taken for pottery production. An implement of asbestos has been found only once in north Norway, that is at Vatnan on Sørøy. In Scandinavia asbestos ceramics are widely dispersed over the whole of northern Norway, north Sweden, and Finland. Analyses have demonstrated that all this asbestos had one single area of origin, the eastern part of the Finnish province of Savolax. Mining there produced two types of asbestos, one was made by crushing it into stiff staffs or sticks, the other was a weak fiber. These two types were exported to different markets, the staff to northern Sweden and the Norwegian counties south of Tromsø, the fibers to Finnmark, north Finland, and the adjacent parts of Russia. Again, we cannot doubt the existence of professional traveling tradesmen who bought the asbestos near the mines and knew the far-away markets. But in contrast to the south Scandinavian flint, the asbestos as well as the Russian flint had to be fetched in nonagrarian or half-agrarian districts. Even if the tradesman himself had his home near the production centers, he may have come from a nonagrarian milieu.

This trade had hardly come into existence before 2300 B.C., i.e. some centuries later than the barter in finished implements. During the rest of the Stone Age it increased in extent.

The third specialist to be recorded was the POTTER. In the Varanger material we have no hints as to how pottery making took place. Diatom analyses from potsherds found on the coastal sites prove that the pots were not fabricated on the same site but inland and, therefore, in another season of the year. This sounds quite natural because the coastal dwelling places were winter places and the potter's clay was inaccessible in winter because of frost and snow. Accordingly raw asbestos is not found in the winter houses, but now and then it is found in the summer houses of the inland. On Sørøy there is no inland season. The distance to the coast is so short that no one was forced to change dwelling places, and the island conditions obviously brought about a concentration of resources, permitting people to live at the same place all, or almost all, year round. Even the summer occupations took place in the houses near the coast, and raw asbestos is found in them. But other remains from the production of pots are only found once, at the locality of Risvåg. I intend to describe this place in detail (Plate 7).

At Risvåg there is a "village" consisting of twenty house sites from the latest period of the local Stone Age. Each house is rather large, approximately 4 by 6 meters inside, i.e. 25–30 square meters of floor space. The houses are rectangular and each contains two fireplaces. All are furnished alike, except for house D. This house is in the center of the village. Only half of the house was a dwelling with a fireplace and with cultural layers. The other half of the room was a complete potter's workshop (Plate 8). Where the fireplace ought to be, we see the kiln, made with a thin slate flagstone at the bottom, three vertical flags at the sides, and one more covering the top of the construction. One side is open. The interior space was half filled with ash and charcoal. All the stone flags have been destroyed by a heat which must have been much higher than in the normal, open fireplaces. Every time the bottom flag was cracked by the heat they put in a new one, so we found more flags at the bottom, separated by accumulated ash layers. On the floor around the kiln we found sherds of smashed pots, pieces of oven-burnt pottery, lumps of unburnt clay, raw asbestos, charcoal, and ash. No doubt this house was once the domicile of a pottery in the last millennium B.C. Because none of the other excavated houses at Risvåg had such arrangements, we concluded that we had found the house of the professional village potter, who provided the other households with pots.

I have now reached my fourth and up to now most recent specialist, the ARROWSMITH: The finding place in this case is at Kuvika on Sørøy. This is a locality where you would never think of finding house sites or other types of dwelling places. There are no marine terraces with dry plains or ridges, but there is a sloping bog with water everywhere and much solifluction. There is no shelter against the northwestern wind and no open brook with fresh water during the winter. And yet here were remains of a Stone Age house. Isolated houses have been found only twice on Sørøy, two house sites out of 450 registered. This in Kuvika is one of them. But the house was superficially seen to be of a quite normal type, rectangular, with gravel and stone walls and a central fireplace. The excavation brought to light a very abnormal construction — the whole of the interior had been filled in with stones, making a pavement, elevated half a meter above the ground, and the fireplace had been placed upon this floor (Plate 9). That is to say, they had made an enormous effort to protect people as well as fire from the humidity of the terrain. What kind of man lived here in the final stage of the Stone Age, having settled quite alone in a very unsuitable place and having done a lot of work to make it suitable for living? The finds were just as unusual. Apart from one sinking stone for fishing, all other finds in and around the house were related to the production of arrows. There were arrow blanks of slate, half-finished and finished slate arrows, polishing stones of flagstone, and whetstones of pumice. In addition there were arrow straighteners of pumice. I do not see any explanation other than that the Kuvika man was a professional stonesmith, specializing in arrows and perhaps also bows. But the bows naturally are not preserved. The attraction of the locality must have been the good summer water supply and, then as now, the presence of willow scrub supplying the material for the arrow shafts and the bows. Because the house was also a dwelling, it was not a communal workshop as those described earlier to which the men came from the village each intending to produce his own arrows. The workshop houses were not only constructed in another way, but they also always will be found on the outskirts of the village, not far away from it. Kuvika can be dated to the last millennium B.C.

When I try to explain these finds, I presuppose that the traditional dogma is correct and that the North Scandinavian food gatherers lived in unspecialized societies. Why did exceptions to this come into existence on the Finnmark coast during the millennium from 1000 B.C. to the beginning of the Christian era? A definite answer is not obtainable, but I should like to point to three reasons which together or separately may have caused this development:
1.   The food gatherers in the north had regular contact with the farmers in the south. Among the latter professional craftsmen are thought to have

come into existence at a much earlier date. The trade created a channel for diffusion, and the concept of specialization was taken over by the hunters and fishermen. Personally, I do not believe in this explanation. I think that we are dealing here with a cultural trait not apt to be diffused to people not already motivated for it. But we cannot deny that chronologically it is possible.

2. The reason may be the presence of the tradesman, and his coming into existence may very well be due to cultural impulses from the south. Once he is established as a permanent member of society, he supplies the village regularly with flint and asbestos, exactly those raw materials used by the stonesmith and the potter. It is quite natural that his business connections in the village establish a kind of monopoly of local improvement of these materials, just as it is natural that his south Scandinavian providers are professional miners. In this explanation we find motivation as well as an impulse from outside.

3. We can look for a motivation springing out of the north Scandinavian society itself. Normally we explain the process towards specialization in the farmer's society as arising from the more settled life together with the creation of a surplus of food resources in relation to the number of hands available. But outside the food gathering society you will never find people closer to meeting these two criteria than in the fishermen's villages along the arctic coasts. Here many individuals live together, and there will be more people here in the fishing season than are needed to nourish the whole village. So, some individuals are able to do other things. In Varanger this is only true for some seasons, because the population in other seasons is scattered in such small bands that specialization is impossible. But on Sørøy, people presumably were more settled, because of the better resources and the shorter distances. So, the advantages of the fishing and sealing seasons became spread out over the whole of the year.

As a hypothesis for further investigation, I postulate a tendency to occupational professionalism in north Norway in the last millennium B.C. due to three collaborating reasons: the surplus of food resources in some seasons of the year, the more settled life along the coast, and the tradesman delivering special raw materials.

# Maritime Adaptations in Northern Norway's Prehistory

GUTORM GJESSING

Before and during World War II, when I worked mainly on the northern Norwegian and Arctic Stone Age, I often stumbled onto a curious paradox without being able to give a plausible explanation, namely, the remarkable cultural conservatism met with in spite of wide-ranging geographical contacts. For example, the Swedish archaeologist Arne published an article on a west Siberian cemetery from the ninth to the eleventh century A.D. at Barsoff Gorodok with pottery very strongly related to Neolithic comb ceramics, and exactly the same as was found by Valery Černetzov in his excavations at Jamal, dating from the eleventh century A.D. In other words, the comb ceramics had survived between three and three and a half millennia! This conservatism is found also in other Arctic regions and for this reason I have never been able to evaluate the material according to conventional chronological standards. According to Fitzhugh (1972: 191 ff.) marine adaptations are likely to be more stable and less subject to periodic collapse than interior ones.

The explanation, however, may be found partly, at any rate, in Marshall Sahlin's idea of "the original affluent society," which means simple hunting and/or gathering societies having no material needs extending beyond what can be procured from the ecological niche exploited. Invention is the mother of necessity. Inventions, of course, satisfy immediate needs, but then they create new needs demanding more inventions. As arctic and subarctic peoples have their material needs satisfied, they do not need the dynamics originally emerging from Gordon Childe's "food-producing revolution." This means that there was even less need for changing their social organizations. Karl Marx pointed to the fact that the evolution of technology and forms of production generally precede the evolution of social organization, and Leslie White claims that technology represents the drive of culture.

It may perhaps be necessary at the outset to mention the Gulf Stream running along the Norwegian coast which makes the climate much milder than at comparable latitudes elsewhere in the circumpolar region. Thus the northernmost birch forests in Norway are to be found at the same latitude as the southernmost part of Novaya Zemlya and at Point Barrow. Only a very narrow strip of northernmost Finnmark has an arctic climate. However, the very short distance between the mild Atlantic climate at the coast and the dry and cold continental climate in the interior causes the coast, particularly in Finnmark, to be one of the most stormy in the northern hemisphere. Moreover, the dense fog banks that are suddenly cast upon the shore often make fishing and sea hunting extremely risky and dangerous.

The maritime adaptation along the western part of the Arctic Ocean, that is, from Finnmark and along the Kola Peninsula, apparently coincides with the first settling of the area. The so-called Komsa culture, discovered in Finnmark, Petsamo, and Kola, and, according to rather conservative data, ranging from about 8000 to 2500 B.C., was decidedly maritime. Its numerous sites are without exception situated near the shore, partly farther up the fjords, partly by the seashore, the latter ones generally on small islands or on hills which at the time of settling must have been islets. This, of course, indicates that craft were used, probably skin boats, because dugouts were the only alternative, provided that the climate of the earlier phases of the culture permitted wood as a suitable material.

From Neolithic petroglyphs we know, however, that skin boats of the *umiak* type were employed along the coast of the entire northern part of the country, even in a relatively warm and calm sub-Boreal climate. Moreover, along the stormy coast of Finnmark dugouts probably would not be feasible, whereas skin boats could be really sea-going craft. Because of their minimal weight, they float upon the waves, which is very advantageous, particularly when landing the craft. On the stormy and rugged west coast of Ireland sea-going skin boats, *currachs*, even of types related to the *umiak*, have been used into modern times.

One of my younger colleagues, Knut Odner has made a thorough study of Komsa sites within the limited Varanger area, the easternmost part of Finnmark. He states that the settlements far up the fjords are much larger than those at the sea coast, suggesting that the population sought their living high up in the fjords for most of the year, but during late spring and early summer made for the outer coast. If this is right, their migratory cycle corresponded more or less to that of the coast Saames right up to the introduction of stock farming, say, in the seventeenth century, and partly even much later. (I prefer the name Saames, which is the people's own name for themselves, to Lapps, which is a derogatory term. Saames, therefore, is the official name in Norway and the Soviet Union, and now predominates in Sweden and Finland as well.) In fact, even as late as 1938, I found some houses in the vicinity of the North Cape. Here people fished and hunted sea mammals in the summer while living most of the year in the nearby Porsangerfjord.

Only surface finds of lithic materials have been known from the Komsa culture, although implements of quartzite, flint, and other hard stones clearly show that in their kits tools of antler and bone must have been extremely important. Hearths have been found at more sites, but in only one of them was charcoal from dwarf birch and polar willow preserved. I dug this site in 1938, but unfortunately the charcoal disappeared during the evacuation during World War II, and with it even the possibility of getting at least one radiocarbon dating of the Komsa culture.

If the most common view of the chronology holds water, the Komsa culture demonstrates in a conspicuous way the conservatism of hunter-fisher sociocultures, as it has proved extremely difficult to establish a chronological sequence on the basis of the morphology. Consequently the reconstruction of the available resources must be based on present conditions and must be utterly hypothetical, because the climate during the Komsa period changed from pre-Boreal (if not Late Glacial) through Boreal, Atlantic, and early sub-Boreal types of climate. According to Dekin (1972), however, these changes may have been even greater than I have suggested, but even so, the changes are not easily demonstrated in the archaeological material. And in any case, this may have meant more for the terrestrial resources than for the marine fauna, which probably was of greater importance to the Komsa people.

Yet in the county of Nordland, where the Komsa culture is not represented, to be sure, we have a group of petroglyphic panels, whose dating has recently been disputed, but which I still hold to be Mesolithic. These petroglyphs represent a wide range of animals, mainly big game such as whales (among them an old male killer whale [*orcinus orca*] in natural size), seals, halibut, reindeer, elk, polar bear, but also birds (swans or geese). Reindeer are by far the predominant species. These petroglyphs, however, are generally situated in the inner parts of big fjords, and therefore probably give a different inventory of resources than would be met with at the seacoast. Mesolithic sites have been discovered on quite a few islands at the outer coast, including some far out in the high seas.

From this we can reasonably deduce that in the Mesolithic period there was in Finnmark as well as in Nordland, and certainly also in Troms county in between, a seminomadic population who in the winter fished in the fjords and hunted in the woodlands and mountains, and in late spring and summer lived on the seacoast, fishing, sealing, whaling, and catching birds and gathering down and eggs. Thus the population exploited different ecological zones, which probably made relatively large groups possible.

In the Neolithic period, which in northern Norway lasted from about 2500 B.C. and probably well into our era, we are certainly much better equipped with data in terms of house sites; artifacts of stone, bone, and antler; refuse from meals; and finally quite a few petroglyphs and pictographs representing different kinds of game, boats, and even fishing and hunting scenes. One panel depicts a man in his skin boat and, in another boat on the same panel, a line and sinker with a halibut that has been caught. Another panel shows a man in his skin boat hunting seal. In this panel are also two ski-runners, apparently with horned-animal masks for decoys during the hunt.

Obviously, people who exploit resources from the sea, the woodlands, and the mountains have to lead a seminomadic way of life, with a fairly extensive migratory cycle. Admittedly, the investigations of the inland have barely begun, so we do not know yet how intensive the settling of the inland might have been, or to what extent the hunting inland could be conducted from the settlements farther up the fjords. As Simonsen has observed until now the known inland dwellings were single houses, in any case partly of the same types as the dwellings of the maritime villages. This may suggest that the hunting inland was conducted from the winter villages far up the fjords. The seminomadism is reflected, in part at any rate, by the types of settlements, which can be divided roughly into three main, more or less distinctive, types.

The great majority, found by the hundreds, are open sites, often extending over a considerable area and comprising several hearths, but with no signs of dwellings of any kind. The next group consists of clusters of house sites, the houses having been built from turf or stones. Finally, there are the cave dwellings. It may be practical to concentrate mainly on two different areas, namely Varanger in easternmost Finnmark, the same area in which Odner's investigations of Komsa sites were conducted, and Traena in Nordland, situated on the Arctic Circle.

In 1935 the late Anders Nummedal, the discoverer of the Komsa culture, found several house sites on an old shore terrace at the six meter level at Gropbakkeengen, in Karlebotn, on the inner part of Varanger fjord. In the course of the next few years he excavated some of the houses, revealing semisubterranean houses, square and rectangular with rounded corners, and with dimensions ranging from four by four to eight by five meters, in other words, of a size suitable for one nuclear family (Nummedal 1938).

In 1937 I visited the locality along with Nummedal and surveyed the village, the plan showing seventy-two unquestionable sites, and some others which I found too questionable to be mapped. In 1952 the Tromsö Museum continued the excavations, and some other dwellings were discovered, among them some of the ones I had not ventured to accept as houses. There are now in all eighty-eight known sites arranged in a single row, in part double, and even triple rows, along the edge of the terrace (Simonsen 1954).

Two of the sites were found to have been inhabited at two different periods. The upper stratum yielded artifacts from the same period as the sites excavated by Nummedal, that is, a period corresponding to the end of the Stone Age and beginning of the early Bronze Age in southern Scandinavia. Beneath this layer was found a neatly paved floor with a hearth, and below this more artifacts, snails, and bones above another paved floor with another hearth.

The morphological difference between the two strata is quite distinct, insofar as the older stratum contained crude implements of flint and quartzite, apparently dating from before the introduction of the so-called slate culture. On the whole, a village of eighty-eight houses with 350 to 400 people probably could not have been inhabited during only one period. These houses, built from stones and turf, cannot have lasted so long — at a guess, a maximum of thirty years, which is a span of time that in this region can scarcely be discerned by archaeological means, not in the least because of the conservatism already mentioned. But obviously it was a very good hunting place where people had their winter sites through many generations.

At another location nearby, Gressbakken, Nummedal discovered fourteen sites of subterranean houses dug into the steep edge of a terrace, and apparently having entry passages very much resembling Eskimo winter houses. At two additional localities, Advik and Bugöyfjord, Simonsen dug four house sites of precisely the same type. These yielded crude, and what are generally called "degenerate" implements of slate and quartzite, and of antler, and shards of pottery of two types (thick undecorated ware and thin ware mixed with asbestos), showing that this type of house is younger than the site at Gropbakkeengen.

Moreover, the habitation of the locality must have coincided with a sea level of not more than thirteen meters above the present one, suggesting a considerably later date than at Gropbakkeengen. In one of these sites was found a *Rovaniemi* pickax of greenstone, dated to a period corresponding to the later Bronze Age (Tallgren 1911; Nordmann 1927). The houses had posts at the four corners and probably an entrance in one or both ends. Simonsen has said that he cannot accept the above-mentioned passage in the long walls as an entrance, whatever else it may have meant, but he seems later to have changed his mind on this point.

As it is quite impossible to mention all the dwelling places in Varanger, which is, because of Simonsen's and Odner's intensive fieldwork, probably the best-investigated Stone Age area in Norway (Simonsen 1961), let it suffice here to point out that there are not only several open sites with an abundance of hearths, masses of artifacts, objects of slate, flint, and quartzite, pottery, and so on, but also some more clusters of house ruins. There is one open site on the terrace above the dwellings at Gropbakkeengen (Nummedal 1938). It has not been accurately surveyed, but on my visit there in 1937 I noted: "On the big shore terrace above the house sites are an abundance of hearths and masses of stone artifacts. The open site extends over the whole terrace and in considerable width. It is terminated by a low kernel of stones, 5.20 by 3.90 metres." Another corresponding site, close to the village at Gropbakkeengen excavated by Nummedal and myself, extended about seventy meters and included a considerable number of hearths, many objects of flint and slate, besides almost innumerable shards of comb ceramics (Nummedal 1937, 1938), showing that the site was considerably older than the houses. I shall not go deeper into the whole problem of the Varanger Neolithics published by Simonsen and collaborators in a series of volumes. Instead I shall mention the other area in which I am now interested, Traena.

During the summers of 1937–1939 I did some excavations on the small island of Sanda, in Traena in Nordland, far out in the main ocean. This island is very rugged and has several caves. I noted in all nineteen in the lofty cliffs that rise up to 338 meters. At least four of these caves have been inhabited for shorter or longer periods. One of them, Kirkhellaren [the cathedral cave], is impressively monumental: forty-five meters deep, thirty-two meters high, and twenty meters wide. It contained a culture sequence reaching from before the introduction of the slate culture, which happened about 2300 B.C., through the Stone Age and up to the sixth century A.D. The stratigraphy was relatively clear and some of the strata could be dated by objects imported from more southern parts of the Scandinavian peninsula (Gjessing 1943: 136 ff.). Tremendously rich archaeological material was dug out, including harpoons for sealing and whaling, fishhooks, spear- and arrow-heads and ornaments of antler and bone, axes, knives and points of slate and quartzite, a great number of potsherds, and many other artifacts. Moreover, there were thick layers of snails and shells, and bones of mammals, birds, and fishes. The other excavated caves and the archaeological material found were much less significant. They were probably visited quite occasionally.

Only some few hundred meters from Kirkhellaren, at least thirty ruins of several huts and houses of two entirely different types were discovered. One of semicircular type, to be reconstructed almost as a coast Saamish *bæl'lje* [hut] (Gjessing 1943: Plate 6) belongs to the Atlantic period. The one excavated was interesting because a paved path could be followed from the hut to what at that time had been a small, narrow creek, and in a little cleft, sheltered by the cliffs, the paved boat yard could still be discerned.

Other dwellings, which belonged mainly to sub-Boreal times, were long, rectangular houses built of stones, and later, in sub-Atlantic times, of turf, with two rows of posts supporting the roof. The oldest of them was from about 2300 B.C. At still another locality on the island, at Rösnesvalen, twelve house sites were discovered, nine of which were set side by side with the main walls facing one another at the foot of a sixty-five meter crag.

The question now is, what can be deduced from this material in terms of social systems? It is very possible, indeed probable, that the two areas presented represent different ethnic groups. The material from Varanger is closely related to Finnish and north Russian Neolithics, whereas the eastern relationship, although traceable, is not very conspicuous as far as Traena is concerned.

The large open dwelling sites with numerous hearths are common not only in northern Norway but, in fact, along the whole Norwegian coast. The same is true of cave dwellings (Gjessing 1945: 109 ff.), whereas the clusters of houses — the villages — are, at any rate up until now, to be considered a specific northern trait. Stone Age house ruins, however, are known from the western as well as the eastern part of the country. The first conclusion to be drawn, then, is that we are dealing with relatively small social groups from some dozen households, though the upper limit is difficult to determine. Groups of eighty to ninety dwellings housing some 350 to 400 people may easily have far surpassed the ecological resources.

In this connection it may be mentioned that about 1550 the entire Saamish population of the interior of Finnmark amounted to only 150 persons (Smith 1938: 293), and that according to a census from 1690

(Adelaer 1938), the coast Saames of Finnmark numbered only 654 persons. The ecological conditions certainly were far more favorable in the coastal area, also because the area of exploitation comprised not only the land, but also the sea, which provided probably the greatest part of the resources. Yet Rasmussen reports (1934: 247) that the Netsilik Eskimo hunting over an area of 12,500 square kilometers numbered only 259 persons.

The prehistoric groups in northern Norway alternated between different types of dwellings during the various seasons. The open sites with many hearths must represent tent villages or hamlets, obviously summer dwellings, whereas the houses indicate winter settlements. In Sanda the cool caves were summer dwellings and the houses even here were winter houses. The interpretation of the caves as summer dwellings is supported by the osteological material from other caves, not only in northern Norway but also in western Norway.

Apart from osteological evidence, it is, of course, entirely impossible to heat a cave of the dimensions of Kirkhellaren and with an entrance opening of thirty-two by twenty meters, particularly on an island where fuel, apart from blubber, always has been extremely scarce, or nonexistent. When we did the excavations, there was one single, lonely, little bush of wild white currants! It should also be noted that generally the inhabited caves are found close to the coastline, and that, according to the osteological evidence, maritime harvesting was the absolutely predominant occupation.

Concerning the houses, it could be substantiated that in the transition from the relatively dry sub-Boreal to the moist and cool sub-Atlantic climate the material for houses was changed from stones to turf, which is a very good insulating material. The correlation between a seminomadic way of life and an economic system involving both hunting in the mountains and such maritime activities as fishing, sealing, and whaling is only too conspicuous and is clearly ecologically conditioned. (By the way, several years ago one of the amateurs in northern Norway made a very painstaking investigation of the weights of Neolithic sinking stones for fishing lines; he found that the Neolithic fishermen must have been fishing at the same depths as modern fishermen, that is, to around 170 meters.) This seminomadic system, moreover, was so firmly integrated and traditional that it operated even on small islands in the main ocean like Sanda. Yet, because of its isolated situation and its topographical conditions, the migration cycle had to be restricted to some few hundred meters.

In any case we are confronted with seminomadic, subarctic hunting-fishing populations. In the spring and summer their economy was based primarily on fishing, sealing, and whaling, bird catching, and the gathering of eggs and down, and in some periods, of snails and shells. In the winter, hunting reindeer, elk, bear, and other game and fresh-water fishing through the ice were important pursuits. The main game is ascertained not only through petroglyphs and pictographs, but also by the role played by reindeer antler as material for fishhooks, harpoons, and many other implements and utensils. The importance of the elk can be seen in the slate daggers and combs made from antler (and, in one instance, from walrus ivory) which have handles terminating in sculptured elk's heads (Gjessing 1943: 395 ff.; Simonsen 1954).

Permit me now to mention some very general requirements in arctic and subarctic hunter-fisher sociocultures.

The correlation between ecological environments and social systems has long been firmly established by Steward and others, and Clark is obviously correct in writing: "Yet it remains true that the economy of any community at any moment of time is necessarily the product of an adjustment between culture and environing nature" (1952: 7). What is important in this connection is that environmental factors such as those in northern Norway prevent large aggregations, whereas the cooperation in fishing and hunting and the rapid mobilization which is often necessary make settling in clusters a necessity. It is interesting that even the Norwegian settlements in Finnmark from the sixteenth century on almost invariably took the shape of villages.

The depth of time, important in unilineal, agricultural sociocultures, is not pertinent to the sociocultures with which we are concerned. Life along the Arctic Ocean is hard and hazardous. The ecology prevents the emergence of large local groups, and often situations arise when the group must acquire new members or when some members have to emigrate owing to scarcity of food. The group territory cannot be divided into small household plots, functional in many agricultural sociocultures, because game is the chief determinant besides edible plants, and game migrates. Therefore, the whole group must have access to the entire group territory. Furthermore, an able leader is needed, one who knows the land and the migratory routes of the animals and one who is a meteorologist, according to circumstances, in order that the hazards of life can be reduced to a minimum. He must also have sufficient prestige to be able to mediate in disputes with neighboring groups. This makes for an egalitarian society with emphasis on achieved status, while in unilineal systems ascribed status and rank are most often stressed. Simonsen deals with another important social aspect, occupational specialists, including shamans, tradesmen, potters, and arrowsmiths. But we should not think of these specialists as relying exclusively on their specialties. Some kind of division of labor is as old as man himself, but all over the nonindustrialized world specialists have been particularly talented people who have had the same occupations as others in addition to their specialties.

In sociocultures of this nature unilineal systems are not very functional because their weakness is their rigidity and inflexibility in changing situations — bilateral systems give much more pliability. As they do not have the same time depth, kin traditions come to be of less importance. Thus, while the structure of unilineal systems is vertical, it is horizontal in bilateral systems, hence solidarity and loyalty are not primarily tied to previous generations, but rather to one's own. Sibling solidarity, including siblings-in-law and cousins, predominates; it is functional in an economic system based more or less on hunting and fishing on the open sea, or the hunting of big game in winter; it also explains the gerontocide encountered as an absolute necessity in some arctic sociocultures. Moreover, such a kinship system can be manipulated in many ways. By means of local exogamy, necessary if these small groups are to persist through time, various classificatory kinship relations, and ritual kinships of various kinds (godparenthood, adoptions, etc.), the solidarity can be extended to other local groups, facilitating the migration from one group to another.

When, therefore, Steward, Eggan, and Radcliffe-Brown seem to conceive a unilineal descent as a necessary condition for the persistence of such small groups (Steward 1937; Eggan 1955: 42; Radcliffe-Brown 1952: 46 ff.), this must be due to the strikingly little interest anthropological theorists have previously taken in bilateral kin groups. Eskimo, Chukchee, Koryak, Kamtchadal, and Yukhagir (Gjessing 1960) have or have had bilateral descent. Forde writes on unilineal transmission of rights and status and on unilineally related kin groups: "Below a certain level of scale and stability ... this type of organization does not emerge" (1951: 8).

Because of the long, cold, and particularly dark winters in arctic and subarctic regions, the winter settlements usually have a more stable and permanent character, and here the most important social and ritual life is conducted. Thus there is much to suggest that the rituals involving petroglyphs and pictographs have been performed at the winter settlements, which is, at least to some extent, substantiated by the localization of the petroglyphic art, and also by the ski-runners mentioned.

Hallowell's study of Algonkian hunting territories (1949: 40 ff.) has brought out clearly that the ratio of active hunters to other persons is fairly constant, being on the average 1 hunter to 3.3 other persons — which means a nuclear family with two to three children — and furthermore that there is a relationship between the size of the group and the abundance of game. This hypothesis was followed up by Cooper, who suggested that the social gradient depended on the ecological gradient. This means that the relatively small bilateral groups are to be found in the tundra zone to the north with its migratory herds of animals. But further south in the richer woodlands with their more stable fauna, a tendency emerges toward larger local groups with patrilocal systems and patrilineal transmittal of property, while the ratio of hunters to other persons remains the same (unpublished master's thesis, as quoted by Eggan 1955).

In 1926 the Skolte-Saamish population in Petsamo was distributed in three *sits* [villages], with an average ratio of 1 hunter to 3.1 other persons (Tanner 1929: 305). It is to be remarked that the Skolte-Saames kept their seminomadic way of life at least up to World War I, partly even later. According to a 1690 census from Finnmark the average ratio was 1:2.9 (Adelaer 1938), and almost the same ratio seems to have occurred among the Kola-Saames before reindeer breeding became the dominant means of subsistence. We should, therefore, with some circumspection, be permitted to suppose that the size of the families in Neolithic times was more or less the same.

There is much to suggest that these prehistoric people in northern Norway, particularly those of the Varanger district, are to be considered the direct ancestors of the Saames as socioculturally defined. Within the same part of Varangerfjord where the villages occur, the earliest known Saame burials have been excavated, dating from sometime within the two centuries before and after the beginning of our era, and with an inventory closely related to that of the youngest houses. Moreover, the well-known finds from Kjelmöy, a small island, also in Varanger, being firmly established as Saamish but deriving mainly from the third and the fourth centuries A.D. (although the oldest strata may be somewhat older), have provided an extremely rich repertoire of implements for fishing and maritime hunting as well as pottery.

The whole complex has essentially the same cultural stamp as the youngest of the known Neolithic sites (Solberg 1909, 1916; Gjessing 1942). The relationship here has been drawn still closer by some of the more recent finds from Simonsen's excavations (Simonsen 1961). It is also becoming more and more clear that these population groups in northern Norway have been intimately related to, if not ethnically identical with, the comb-ware population groups in the north of Finland and Russia. It even has been more or less proved that the Saames once extended over most of Finland, as far south as the vicinity of Helsinki, and in northern Russia to Lake Onega.

The coast Saamish character of the Kjelmöy finds has not been seriously doubted since the late Ole Solberg cleared up the matter in 1909. The site represents the summer dwelling, where all sorts of maritime activities took place, whereas the osteological material also reveals that the reindeer hunts occurred somewhere else, certainly on the mainland. Thus the finds represent a seminomadism of the same kind as that of the Stone Age sites.

The ethnic character of the hunters and fishers at Traena is much more problematic. Even here eastern influences were discernible, particularly as far as the pottery was concerned, but imported objects from the south also occurred. In particular, the type of the houses from the later periods of settlement are with difficulty explained as Saamish — although this is, of course, no watertight proof. In fact, nothing definite can be said of the ethnic character of this people. There is also the possibility that the hunters and fishers from Traena were a branch of the pre-Indo-European populations of southern Norway. The Indo-Europeanization of northern Norway probably started only with an immigration from the southwestern part of the country from the third century A.D. on.

# REFERENCES

ADELAER, HENRICH
  1938   Finmarken 1690. *Nordnorske Samlinger utgitt av Etnografisk Museum* 1 (7). Oslo.
ARNE, TURE J.
  1935   *Barsoff Gorodok*. Stockholm: Kungliga Vitterhets Akademien.
BÖE, JOHS., A. NUMMEDAL
  1936   *Le Finmarkien*. Instituttet for Sammenlignende Kulturforskning, series B, 32. Oslo.
ČERNETZOV, VALERY
  1935   Dvernaja primorskaja kul'tura na poluostrove Ja-mal. *Sovjetskaja Etnografija* 4–5.
CLARK, J. GRAHAME
  1952   *Prehistoric Europe: the economic basis*. London.
DEKIN, ALBERT A., JR.
  1972   Climatic change and cultural change: a correlative study from eastern Arctic prehistory. *Polar Notes* 12:11–31.
EGGAN, FRED
  1955   "The ethnological cultures and their archaeological background," in *Archaeology of the eastern United States*. Edited by J. Griffin, 35–45. Chicago: University of Chicago Press.
FITZHUGH, WILLIAM W.
  1972   *Environmental archaeology and cultural systems in Hamilton Inlet, Labrador*. Smithsonian Contributions to Anthropology 16. Washington, D.C.

FORDE, DARYLL
1951 The integration of anthropological studies. *Journal of the Royal Anthropological Institute of Great Britain and Ireland* 27.

GJESSING, GUTORM
1932 *Arktiske helleristininger i Nord-Norge.* Instituttet for Sammenlignende Kulturforskning, series B, 21. Oslo.
1942 *Yngre steinalder i Nord-Norge.* Instituttet for Sammenlignende Kulturforskning, series B, 39. Oslo.
1943 *Traenfunnene.* (with contributions by Ole T. Grönlie, Oluf Kolsrud, and K. E. Schreiner.) Instituttet for Sammenlignende Kulturforskning, series B, 41. Oslo.
1945 *Norges steinalder.* Oslo: Norsk Arkeologisk Selskap.
1960 Circumpolar social systems. *Acta Arctica,* fascicle 12. Copenhagen.

HALLOWELL, A. I.
1949 The size of Algonkian hunting territories: a function of ecological adjustment. *American Anthropologist* 51:35–45.

NORDMANN, C. A.
1927 "Den yngre stenåldern i Mellan-, Väst- och Nordeuropa," in *De förhistoriske tiderna i Europa.* Edited by K. Friis-Johansen. Stockholm: Bonnier.

NUMMEDAL, ANDERS
1937 Yngre stenaldersfund fra Nyelv og Karlebotn I, Oslo. *Universitetets Oldsaksamlings Årbok* 1935–1936.
1938 Yngre stenaldersfund fra Nyelv og Karlebotn II, Oslo. *Universitetets Oldsaksamlings Årbok* 1937.

ODNER, KNUT
1964 Erverv og bosetning i Komsakulturen. *Viking* 28. Oslo.
1966 *Komsakulturen i Nesseby og Sör-Varanger.* Tromsö-Oslo-Bergen: Universitetsforlaget.

RADCLIFFE-BROWN, A. R.
1952 *Structure and function in primitive society.* London: Cohen and West.

RASMUSSEN, KNUD
1934 *Fra Grønland til Stillehavet.* Copenhagen.

SIMONSEN, POVL
1954 Karlebotn: en steinaldersby ved Varangerfjorden. *Ottar* 1. Tromsö Museum.
1961 *Varanger-funnene II: fund og udgravninger på fjordens sydkyst.* Tromsø Museums Skrifter 7(2). Tromsø, Oslo: Universitetsforlaget.

SMITH, P. LORENTZ
1938 *Kautokeino og Kautokeinolappene.* Instituttet for Sammenlignende Kulturforskning, series B, 34. Oslo.

SOLBERG, O.
1909 Eisenzeitfunde aus Ostfinnmarken. *Det Norske Videnskabsselskabs Skrifter* 2. Hist-Filos Kl 1909 (7). Kristiania.
1911 Ein neuer eisenzeitlicher Fund aus Ostfinnmarken. *Praehistorische Zeitschrift* 3. Berlin.
1916 Mennikafundet. En boplads ved Pasvikelven. *Oldtiden* 7. Kristiania.

STEWARD, JULIAN H.
1937 Ecological aspects of southwestern Society. *Anthropos* 32. Vienna.

1938   *Basin-Plateau aboriginal socio-political groups.* Bureau of American Ethnology Bulletin 120. Washington, D.C.

TALLGREN, A. M.
1911   Die Kupfer- und Bronzezeit in Nord- und Ostrussland. *Finska fornminnesföreningens Tidskrift* 25. Helsinki.

TANNER, V.
1929   Skoltlapparna. *Fennia* 49 (4). Helsinki.

# Circumpolar Adaptation Zones East-West and Cross-Economy Contacts North-South: an Outsider's Query, Especially on Ust'-Poluj

CARL-AXEL MOBERG

When discussing prehistoric maritime adaptations of the circumpolar zone, contacts BETWEEN coast-adapted populations and other nonmaritime populations ought to be considered. Some circumpolar maritime adaptations are such that neither their genesis nor their function can be understood except on the basis of their internal structure. The questions to be asked here necessarily reflect the author's preoccupation with mixed adaptations in northern Europe.

To begin with Scandinavia, the relative importance of agricultural food production in prehistoric times should not be exaggerated. A full agrarian adaptation was established only in comparatively small areas in the southwest, mainly in Denmark. In extreme northern coastal and inland areas, unmixed food-collecting survived during by far the longest part of the time up to the present (Moberg 1970). Within the chronological limits of first food production (4000 B.C. or later), a mosaic of mixed economies seems to have occupied very much larger areas (Moberg and Olsson i.p.). It is understandable but unfortunate if students from the outside have difficulties realizing this situation, owing to the approach, more natural on the European continent, of emphasizing either "food collection OR food production" (Waterbolk 1968). The exact time positions of these oscillating limits are not very well known. Observations and arguments of later years point toward earlier datings than hitherto assumed of northernmost agriculture (for instance Malmer 1962; Königsson 1970; Baudou and Biörnstad 1970). By A.D. 600, the maximal extension seems to have passed 70° North (Sjövold 1962). The controversial question of how long unmixed food collection did survive (Moberg 1965, 1966) is not settled. A main obstacle is the difficulty in evaluating the role of seasonality.

In later centuries, in Scandinavia as well as in large northern Eurasian areas, the picture changed and was complicated by the introduction of a quite special pattern of food production: reindeer nomadism with larger herds. This later period will be omitted here and questions are concentrated on preceding periods.

To what extent did contacts exist between maritime-adapted populations and their more or (mainly) less agricultural neighbors in the south with their mixed economies? For an important period — during the first millennium B.C. — some answer is given by the appearance in the north of imported bronze artifacts and of local bronze casting (see Meinander 1954: 44–49, 58–60; Gjessing 1942: 256–257; Solberg 1909: 80–81; Munch 1966). Examples in this paper will be mainly from situations of this kind.

But in principle, an analogous situation might have existed between A.D. 1000 and 1500 in the westernmost part of Denmark, in Greenland. In clearly food-collecting sites, for instance Sermermiut (Mathiassen 1958), there are European traits connecting them with contemporary mixed-economy sites in the south, for instance Brattahlid-Qagssiarssuk (Nørlund and Stenberger 1934); but in such sites, there occur also non-European traits (e.g. Roussell 1936: 122). It is well known that such contacts are regarded as of little or no importance, except when it comes to the question of causes for the extinction of the Norse settlements (Nørlund 1934: 121–132; Meldgaard 1965: 87–100; Persson 1969).

Might it not be rewarding if such data were studied with less emphasis on choosing to study EITHER Eskimo OR Norse archaeology, as if they were by definition different and incompatible spheres? Such an attitude is often expressed. For instance, in the article on Greenland in the magnificent *Handbuch*, the thousands of years of pre-Norse occupation of Greenland are not even mentioned; Eskimos appear as if they were a foreign intrusion during the fifteenth century A.D. (Filip 1966: 1, 437). In a recently published popular dictionary of the *ABC of archaeology* for Denmark, even sites outside Denmark, in Norway and Sweden, are included; but there seems to be just an occasional, brief mention of the Greenland part of Denmark — and then again only in connection with Norse settlement (*Arkaeologisk ABC* 1972: 339). With such ethnocentric attitudes, problems of general importance may not get their due share of attention — in this case the possible types of interaction between maritime-adapted food collectors and maritime-adapted food producers (direct interaction, or ecologically intermediated interaction).

With such problems in mind, a parallel research situation appears further west. Then the important question is not whether the inhabitants of

L'Anse aux Meadows were Norse (Ingstad 1970; for the dating, see also Waterbolk 1971: 22–23), or something else, mixed or unmixed, but whether they really had small cattle, and what else they did in order to survive; and whether there was contact with others, or not. But we shall not be able to generalize about this as long as the ethnic questions are allowed to dominate entirely. What we need instead is a comprehensive survey of environmental archaeology and cultural systems in Newfoundland — as it exists for an area in Labrador (Fitzhugh 1972a).

Certainly, this set of questions changes in character in other regions of North America — not least because the possible contact areas in the south have food production systems considerably different from Old World patterns. With some oversimplification, one can distinguish a large set of east-west lines of research. Such lines can be global, as the circumpolar studies are, linking America with Eurasia. Arctic archaeology is a subset of this set. Other east-west lines are more limited geographically. In Eurasia, there are several such. One of them is the full-plow-agrarian zone of southwestern Asiatic type between the Atlantic Ocean and the Pacific. Another is the bronze-metallurgy zone, joining eastern Asia with Europe via and north of central Asia, partially coinciding with the steppe zone of large-scale nomadism, and studied by Tallgren, Merhart, Jettmar, Gimbutas, and Watson among others (Gimbutas 1956, 1958; Watson 1971).

Along such research lines, there have been numerous and important studies, and remarkable results have been achieved. But the general picture resulting from such studies is biased: (1) because of the dominating interest in diffusionist and migrationist explanations of change, and (2) because the transverse north-south threads of cross-contacts are not woven enough into the fabric. This does not mean that interest in such contacts is lacking, but it is concentrated on situations which might be explained in terms of, for instance, migration, and which thus are regarded as relevant for the great historical image; or it is concentrated on questions of chronology as a goal *per se*. Compared to this, there is less interest in the role of economic and social systems among populations — and this is what we need for our problems.

Being aware of the quite superficial and fragmentary character of my readings in regional archaeology of the pertinent areas, I must limit myself to asking questions again.

For example: what is the contact pattern between early food-producing groups in Japan and the islands in the north, with the Sakhalin and Aleutian branches, and with Kamchatka?

On the Eurasian mainland, contact situations developed in the coastal provinces of the Union of Soviet Socialist Republics, and in the Amur area (Andreeva and Pronina 1968: 261–265).

Farther west, from Jakutija to Scandinavia, a special opportunity for study is offered by several groups that, more or less, share many features, such as maritime adaptation, pottery, importation of bronze artifacts, and local bronze casting. Bronze artifacts with — very broadly speaking — relationships to Tagar-Anan'ino types reach the border zone of the Arctic Ocean at more than one point; this is a much more northern extension than is sometimes indicated (Childe 1954: Plate 1; Gimbutas 1956: 155; Watson 1971: 43).

In Jakutija contacts are established by bronze casting above 70° North, in the lower Lena region (Okladnikov 1955: 75). Whether these bronzes really indicate contact with populations of maritime adaptation does not seem clear, however.

Of central interest in this context is the area in the Lower Ob — Ob estuary, characterized by Ust'-Poluj and related sites (Chernecov 1953a, 1953b; Moshinskaja 1953a, 1953b, 1965, 1968: 234–237; 1970; Okladnikov 1960: 38–39). There, also, iron is frequent. In spite of the difficulties for study and publication of the Ust'-Poluj finds, caused by World War II, publications have given considerable opportunities for insight in this important complex. The natural result is that one would like to know more.

The main questions regarding Ust'-Poluj can be summarized thus:

a.   Chronology: (1) 500–200 B.C.? (Chernecov 1953c: 228; Moshinskaja 1965; accepted, mainly, by Okladnikov 1960; Shimkin 1960: 654). (2) "Early Iron Age" (300 B.C.–A.D. 300)? (Sulimirski 1970). Or (3) A.D. 600–800? (Grjaznov 1956: 137–140; accepted by Vajda 1968: 244–246).

b.   Homogeneity of the eponymous site Ust'-Poluj itself — of course, crucial for answers on the preceding as well as the following questions.

c.   The fortifications at Ust'-Poluj (and, according to Chernecov, at the earlier settlements at Iavnovka, Sortynja I, and Evi-Vozh [Chernecov 1953a: 63 ff.]) and the contemporary ones (Moshinskaja 1965) at Sortynja II, Njaksimvol', and Nizjama. Of course, the existence of this type of settlement is very important for implications in terms of settlement pattern and social organization — especially if there really is contemporaneity and thus coexistence of unfortified sites and one fortified "central site" (Moshinskaja 1965: 17).

d.   Connected with this, but regarding Ust'-Poluj itself, is the question of the distribution of artifacts within the site, interpreted as reflecting a ceremonial activity area (Moshinskaja 1965: 14–17); with interesting similarities to features in north and south Scandinavia.

e.   Graves? Brief indications in summary reports give the impression that distinct graves can be added to the trait list of sites of the Ust'-Poluj type (Troickaja and Molodin 1971; see also Moshinskaja 1965: 14, on a possible grave in excavation area I). It is with much interest that one awaits confirmation with details.

f.   Subareas within the Ust'-Poluj culture area? A distinction is made between a northern and a southern sub-area — as it seems with good reasons (Moshinskaja). In northern Ust'-Poluj, the adaptation is to a considerable extent maritime, whereas the south is more riverine and lacustrine. But what about sites north of northern Ust'-Poluj where one would expect an even fuller maritime adaptation to a more Arctic ecology? The question is focused upon the dune site on the promontory Tiutej-sale, on the western side of the Jamal peninsula, at 71°21' North. When first published, it was dated to "the end of the first — beginning of the second millennium A.D." (Chernecov 1935: 123). Later, the same author refers to it as belonging to the Early Iron Age, preceding the period of Ust'-Poluj (Chernecov 1953a: 65–66). This date seems to be the one quoted by Vajda (1968: 243). Possibly it was included among the "sites of Jamal, Tazov Bay and Javaj," according to Chernecov inhabited by "neighboring maritime arctic people" who would have "been deeply influenced by the Ust'-Poluj culture" (Chernecov 1953c: 241). On the other hand, in the most recent survey of the Ust'-Poluj culture, Tiutej-sale seems not to be included (Moshinskaja 1965). For the correct assessment of the character of the Ust'-Poluj culture and its context, an up-to-date evaluation of these northernmost sites would be most welcome. Perhaps recent investigations on the Tajmyr peninsula (Khlobystin and Gracheva 1970) will be important in this connection.

g.   Degree of maritime adaptation? From faunal lists in the publications used here, one can get only general impressions of the relative importance of maritime and nonmaritime food sources. More specification and, especially, more quantification toward the standards of, for instance, the Varanger publications (Olsen 1967) would contribute much to a better understanding of the Ust'-Poluj culture.

h.   If one accepts the early dating and the general picture, with due reservations about questions (f) and (g), the following north-south sequence in the Ob area could be used:

| | |
|---|---|
| Food collection with full maritime adaptation | (maritime arctic people; Tiutej-sale?) |
| Food collection with partial maritime adaptation | Northern Ust'-Poluj |

Food collection with                Southern Ust'-Poluj
riverine/lacustrine adaptation
Mixed economy                       Potshevash


With Potshevash (Moshinskaja 1953c), seafood can have no importance. In our context, there is no need to follow the continuation of the sequence upstream toward or beyond cattle breeding dominated Bol'shaja Rechka (Grjaznov 1956), into the central Aisatic world in its conversion from agriculture and pastoralism to nomadism; one has to remember, however, that it is from or via this zone that ideas and goods ultimately came to Ust'-Poluj.

i.   In a recent study on the sociological problems of the northern Eurasian Neolithic, Khlobystin has expressed his opinion that the introduction of bronze and so on "did not bring about sharp-cut changes in the economy" (Khlobystin 1972: 33, Note 6). Nevertheless, the differences between the earlier adaptations he analyzes and Ust'-Poluj are considerable; he admits the "development in interchange contacts." Our question must be: to what extent was this development, with accompanying changes in means of production, of real adaptive importance?

There has been argument on similarities between Ust'-Poluj and Eskimo cultures (especially in connection with the appearance of dog traction at Ust'-Poluj [Moshinskaja 1970; Vajda 1968: 244–246]) on whether or not there was reindeer breeding; and also on the identification of Ust'-Poluj people with historically known ethnic and linguistic groups. These questions have been left out here, as we are focusing on other types of problems — problems where Ust'-Poluj seems to give information of much interest.

Finally, omitting the White Sea region (the author is not prepared even to ask questions on it), and returning to Scandinavia, the circumpolar circle can be closed: the author is convinced that closer comparison between Ust'-Poluj and Varanger/Gressbakken Stage, at 70° North (Simonsen 1961: 482; 1963: 274–276), would be rewarding. Also here in north Scandinavia, bronzes of the latter half of the first millennium B.C. approach the Arctic Ocean. But when they reach its shore north of Narvik (Munch 1966), they are from a south Scandinavian source different from the Tagar-Anan'ino complex, which also is represented in north Finland, for instance (Meinander 1954: 48, with map from Zbrueva), but so far only in inland and Bothnian areas. These areas, however, are probably within the range of seasonal movements of semimaritime populations.

The research situation can be delimited figuratively on two levels:
a. A fabric of problems is emerging where specialists in Arctic archaeology and other east-west extensions, together with regional specialists in south-north prehistory — for instance in Scandinavia or in western Siberia — have to interweave their warp or weft.
b. The questions summarized here might indicate some points where more of this interweaving would be useful.

# REFERENCES

ANDREEVA, ZH. V., G. I. PRONINA
  1968  "Dal'nij vostok v rannem zheleznom veke," in *Istorija Sibiri*, volume one: *Drevnjaja Sibir'*. Edited by A. P. Okladnikov et al., 261–265. Leningrad: Nauka.
ARKAEOLOGISK ABC
  1972  *Håndbog i dansk forhistorie.* Copenhagen: Politiken.
BAUDOU, EVERT, MARGARETA BIÖRNSTAD
  1970  *Norrlands tidiga bebyggelse.* Årsberättelse.
CHERNECOV, V. N.
  1935  Drevnjaja primorskaja kul'tura na poluostrove Ja-mal. *Sovetskaja Ètnografija*, 109–133. (Résumé).
  1953a  "Drevnjaja istorija Nizhnego Priob'ja," in *Drevnjaja istorija nizhnego Priob'ja*. Edited by A. V. Zbrueva, 7–71. Materialy i issledovanija po arkheologii SSSR 35. Moscow: Akademii Nauk SSSR.
  1953b  "Bronza ust'-polujskoj kul'tury," in *Drevnjaja istorija nizhnego Priob'ja*. Edited by A. V. Zbrueva, 121–178. Materialy i issledovanija po arkheologii SSSR 35. Moscow: Akademii Nauk SSSR.
  1953c  "Ust'-polujskoe vremja v Priob'e," in *Drevnjaja istorija nizhnego Priob'ja*. Edited by A. V. Zbrueva, 221–241. Materialy i issledovanija po arkheologii SSSR 35. Moscow: Akademii Nauk SSSR.
CHILDE, V. GORDON
  1954  The socketed celt in upper Eurasia. *University of London Institute of Archaeology, Annual Report* 10:11–25.
FILIP, JAN
  1966  "Grönland," in *Manuel encyclopédique de préhistoire et protohistoire européennes. Enzyklopädisches Handbuch zur Ur- und Frühgeschichte Europas*. Edited by J. Filip, 437. Prague: ČSAV.
FITZHUGH, WILLIAM W.
  1972a  *Environmental archeology and cultural systems in Hamilton Inlet, Labrador: a survey of the central Labrador coast from 3000 B.C. to the present*. Smithsonian Contributions to Anthropology 16. Washington, D.C.: Smithsonian Institution.
  1972b  Open letter to invited participants of the International Union of Anthropological and Ethnological Sciences conference on "Prehistoric

maritime adaptations of the circumpolar zone: a comparative approach." September 28, 1972.

GIMBUTAS, MARIJA
1956   Borodino, Seima and their contemporaries: key sites for the Bronze Age chronology of Eastern Europe. *Proceedings of the Prehistoric Society* 22:143–172.
1958   Middle Ural sites and the chronology of northern Eurasia. *Proceedings of the Prehistoric Society* 24:120–157.

GJESSING, GUTORM
1942   *Yngre steinalder i Nord-Norge.* Instituttet for Sammenlignende Kulturforskning, series B, 39. Oslo.

GRJAZNOV, M. P.
1956   *Istorija drevnikh plemen verkhnej Obi po raskopkam bliz s. Bol'shaja Rechka.* Materialy i issledovanija po arkheologii SSSR 48. Moscow and Leningrad: Akademii Nauk SSSR.

INGSTAD, ANNE STINE
1970   The Norse settlement at L'Anse aux Meadows, Newfoundland: a preliminary report from the excavations 1961–1969. *Acta Archaeologica* 41:109–154.

KHLOBYSTIN, L. P.
1972   "Problemy sociologii neolita Severnoj Evrazii," in *Ochotniki sobirateli rybolovy: problemy social'no-èkonomicheskikh otnoshenij v dozemledel'-cheskom obshchestve.* Edited by A. M. Reshetov, 26–42. AN SSSR Institut ètnografii im. N. N. Miklukho-Maklaja. Leningrad: Nauka.

KHLOBYSTIN, L. P., G. N. GRACHEVA
1970   "Issledovanija v central'noj chasti Tajmyra," in *Arkheologicheskie otkrytija 1969 goda.* Edited by B. A. Rybakov, 192–193. AN SSSR Institut arkheologii. Moscow: Nauka.

KÖNIGSSON, LARS-KÖNIG, H. CHRISTIANSSON
1970   "Traces of Neolithic human influence upon the landscape development at the Bjurselet settlement, Västerbotten, northern Sweden," in *Bjurselet settlement I.* Edited by Hans Christiansson, 13–30. Kungliga Skytteanska Samfundets Handlingar 7. Umeå.

MALMER, MATS P.
1962   Jungneolithische Studien. *Acta Archaeologica Lundensia* 80(3). Bonn: Habelt; Lund: Gleerups.

MATHIASSEN, THERKEL
1958   *The Sermermiut excavations 1955.* Meddelelser om Grønland 161(3). Copenhagen: Reitzel.

MEINANDER, C. F.
1954   Die Bronzezeit in Finnland. *Finska Fornminnesföreningens Tidskrift* 54. Helsinki: Suomen muinaismuistoyhdistyksen aikakauskirja.

MELDGAARD, JØRGEN
1965   *Nordboerne i Grønland: en vikingebygds historie.* Copenhagen: Munksgaard.

MOBERG, CARL-AXEL
1965   "How long did unmixed food-collection survive in Northern Europe? A case study of archeological observation, radiocarbon determination and archeological inference," in *Proceedings of the Sixth International*

*Conference on Radiocarbon and Tritium Dating held at Washington State University, Pullman, Washington, June 7–11, 1965, USAEC CONF-650652.* Edited by R. M. Chatters and E. A. Olson, 245–255. Springfield, Virginia: United States Department of Commerce.

1966 Spread of agriculture in the north European periphery. *Science* 152: 315–319.

1970 "Remarques pragmatiques sur quelques problèmes théoriques dans l'archéologie de la Scandinavie occidentale aux environs de 1300 av. J.-C.," in *Archéologie et calculateurs: problèmes sémiologiques et mathématiques.* Edited by J.-C. Gardin, M. Borillo, and A.-M. Richaud, 25–43. Colloques Internationaux du Centre National de la Recherche Scientifique. Sciences Humaines. Paris: Centre National de la Recherche Scientifique.

MOBERG, CARL-AXEL, ULF OLSSON
i.p. *Ekonomisk historisk början 1.* Stockholm: Wahlström and Widstrand.

MOSHINSKAJA, V. I.
1953a "Material'naja kul'tura i khozjajstvo Ust'-Poluja," in *Drevnjaja istorija nizhnego Priob'ja.* Edited by A. V. Zbrueva, 72–106. Materialy i issledovanija po arkheologii SSSR 35. Moscow: AN SSSR.

1953b "Keramika ust'-polujskoj kul'tury," in *Drevnjaja istorija nizhnego Priob'ja.* Edited by A. V. Zbrueva, 107–120. Materialy i issledovanija po arkheologii SSSR 35. Moscow: AN SSSR.

1953c "Gorodishche i kurgany Potshevash (K voprosu o potshevashskoj kul'ture)," in *Drevnjaja istorija nizhnego Priob'ja.* Edited by A. V. Zbrueva, 189–220. Materialy i issledovanija po arkheologiii SSSR 35. Moscow: AN SSSR.

1965 *Arkheologicheskie pamjatniki severa zapadnoj Sibiri.* Svod arkheologicheskich istochnikov D3-8. Moscow: Nauka; Arkheologija SSSR.

1968 "Plemena lesostepnoj i lesnoj polosy zapadnoj Sibiri v I tys. do n.è.," in *Istorija Sibiri, 1, Drevjaja Sibir'.* Edited by A. P. Okladnikov et al., 233–242. Leningrad: Nauka.

1970 "The Iron Age in the north of western Siberia and its relation to the development of the circumpolar region cultures," in *Trudy VII Mezhdunarodnovo Kongressa Antropologicheskikh i Ètnograficheskikh Nauk* [Proceedings of the Seventh International Congress of Anthropological and Ethnographical sciences] 10:411–413. Moscow.

MUNCH, JENS STORM
1966 Et nytt bronsealderfunn fra Troms. Summary. *Viking* 30:61–76.

NØRLUND, P.
1934 *De gamle nordbobygder ved verdens ende. Skildringer fra Grønlands middelalder.* Copenhagen: Gad.

NØRLUND, P., M. STENBERGER
1934 *Brattahlid.* Meddelelser om Grønland 88(1). Copenhagen: Reitzel.

OKLADNIKOV, A. P.
1955 "Jakutija do prisoedinenija k russkomu gosudarstvu," in *Istoria jakutskoj ASSR 1.*

1960 "Archaeology of the Soviet Arctic," in *The Circumpolar Conference in Copenhagen 1958.* Edited by H. Larsen, 35–45. *Acta Arctica* 12. Copenhagen: Munksgaard.

OLSEN, HAAKON
    1967    *Varanger-funnene IV: osteologisk materiale. Innledning – Fisk – Fugl.*
            Tromsø Museums Skrifter 7(4). Tromsø, Oslo: Universitetsforlaget.
PERSSON, IB.
    1969    Nordboblod. *Skalk* 2:10–13.
ROUSSELL, AAGE
    1936    *Sandnes and the neighbouring fams.* Meddelelser om Grønland 88 (2).
            Copenhagen: Reitzel.
SHIMKIN, DEMITRI B.
    1960    "Western Siberian archeology: an interpretative summary," in *Selected
            papers of the Fifth International Congress of Anthropological and
            Ethnological Sciences. Philadelphia, September 1–9, 1956.* Edited by
            A. F. C. Wallace, 648–661. Philadelphia: University of Pennsylvania
            Press.
SIMONSEN, POVL
    1961    *Varanger-funnene II: fund og udgravninger på fjordens sydkyst.* Med
            et bidrag af Knut Odner. Tromsø Museums Skrifter 7(2). Tromsø,
            Oslo: Universitetsforlaget.
    1963    *Varanger-funnene III: fund og udgravninger i pasvikdalen og ved den
            østlige fjordstrand.* Med et bedrag af Knut Odner. Tromsø Museums
            Skrifter 7(3). Tromsø, Oslo: Universitetsforlaget.
SJÖVOLD, THORLEIF
    1962    *The Iron Age settlement of arctic Norway: a study in the expansion of
            European Iron Age culture within the arctic circle,* volume one: *Early
            Iron Age (Roman and migration periods).* Tromsø Museums Skrifter
            10:1. Tromsø, Oslo: Universitetsforlaget.
SOLBERG, O.
    1909    *Eisenzeitfunde aus Ostfinnmarken. Lappländische Studien.* Videnskabs-
            Selskabets Skrifter 2 Hist.-filos. klasse 7. Christiania: Dybwad.
SULIMIRSKI, TADEUSZ
    1970    *Prehistoric Russia: an outline.* London: Baker; New York: Humanities
            Press.
TROICKAJA, T. N., V. I. MOLODIN
    1971    "Raboty novosibirskoj ekspedicii," in *Arkheologicheskie otkrytija 1970
            goda.* Edited by B. A. Rybakov, 192–194. Moscow: Nauka.
VAJDA, LÁSZLÓ
    1968    *Untersuchungen zur Geschichte der Hirtenkulturen.* Veröffentlichungen
            des Osteuropa-Institutes München 31. Wiesbaden: Harrassowitz.
WATERBOLK, H. T.
    1968    Food production in prehistoric Europe. *Science* 162:1093–1102.
    1971    Working with radiocarbon dates. *Proceedings of the Prehistoric Society*
            37:15–33.
WATSON, WILLIAM
    1971    *Cultural frontiers in ancient East Asia.* Edinburgh: University Press.

PART TWO

*North Pacific and Bering Sea*

# Problems of the Origin of Ancient Sea Hunters' Cultures in the Northern Pacific

R. S. VASILIEVSKY

Some 3,000 years ago original cultures emerged in the northern part of the Pacific area with economies oriented toward sea animal hunting. At the end of the second and the beginning of the first millennium B.C., the west Alaskan coast was the scene of spreading Paleo-Eskimo cultures: Kachemak I, Choris, Norton, and Ipiutak. Those in the first centuries B.C. and A.D. made way for the Neo-Eskimo cultures of Okvik, ancient Bering Sea, and later Birnirk and Punuk. The Neo-Eskimo cultures also extended along the Chukotka coast. On the Aleutian Islands the culture of the ancient Aleutians emerged some 4,000 years ago. At the end of the second millennium B.C. the ancient Koryak culture appeared on the coast of the Okhotsk Sea, with the Okhotsk culture originating in North Hokkaido, Sakhalin, and the Kuril Islands.

In recent years Soviet scientists and those from other countries have established the main stages and local variants of these cultures and specific features of each and have elaborated a typological classification of harpoon heads. However, in the development of and relations between cultures of sea hunters there still are many issues that have to be resolved. Unsolved too is the problem of origin of the sea hunters' economy. Solving this problem is of vital importance toward understanding ethnogenetic processes in northeast Asia as well as cultural contacts between the inhabitants of the north Pacific coast.

Of key interest in this respect is the Anangula site on the Aleutians with radiocarbon dates ranging from 7660 ± 300 to 8425 ± 275 years ago. The topographical position and stone industry of Anangula suggest that its population was engaged in a coastal type of economy (Laughlin 1963).

As the earliest layer of coastal traditions in North America, the Anangula complex may be regarded as an important one, at least for the cultures of the Aleutian Islands and southwest Alaska. The Anangula complex contains new elements which differ considerably from everything previously known all over the arctic and subarctic districts of North America.

The Anangula microblades, for instance, look quite different from the tools of the Denbigh microlithic complex which represents an ancient culture whose people are believed to be the immediate ancestors of the Eskimo. These tools also differ from the implements of the so-called arctic tradition of small tools and from the microblades of the northwestern tradition which existed in the arctic areas some 7,000 years ago. This distinction has also been established by American researchers (Laughlin 1963).

On the whole the Anangula complex is Asian rather than American in appearance, and it is in this direction that the most clear-cut analogies to the Anangula artifacts are found. The closest analogies to the materials of Anangula are found in Kamchatka, in the fifth and sixth cultural layers of the Ushkovo site studied by Dikov (1967: 16–31). Resemblance to the Ushkovo finds is seen in the conical and cylindrical cores, microblades, end- and side-scrapers, and cleavers on blades found in Anangula. Significant, too, is the fact that these sites are comparable in time. Anangula dates 8,000 or even 10,000 years back, whereas the radiocarbon date of the sixth layer of the Ushkovo site is 10,675 ± 360 (Dikov 1961).

It is hardly possible to speak of the full identity of these complexes. In Anangula the blade industry was developed to a much greater extent; hence, the more intensive usage of different kinds of blades. Distinctions are also to be found in technical traditions. Yet the similarity of Anangula to the fifth and sixth layers of the Ushkovo site shows that complexes were definitely close. The explanation apparently lies in the more ancient Asian roots common to both. The explanation for distinctions can be found in the rather early regional isolation.

In this connection the question arises as to the initial culture on the basis of which the traditions of Anangula's blade industry could emerge and develop. This question has not been posed or studied either in Soviet or other literature. True, Laughlin has pointed out that the Anangula materials are similar to the microblades of the Sakkotsu stone industry in Hokkaido, of Araya in Honshu, and of the Budun site in Siberia (Laughlin 1963). Later the point was repeated by Fajnberg (1971: 6). Laughlin's observation deserves attention. The establishment of analogies, and hence ties, between Anangula and the cultures on the Asian continent will bring the solution of the problems posed much closer. There is, therefore, a need for a more detailed examination of the character of the coincidences established.

We shall begin with the areas deep inside Siberia, primarily because the materials of precisely the Paleolithic and Mesolithic cultures of the Baikal and Angara areas have in recent years increasingly attracted American and Japanese archaeologists attempting to find an explanation for the similarity of the stone implements of Alaska, Japan, and continental Asia. In this case we are interested in the complexes comparable to Anangula. The Budun site mentioned by Laughlin is on Olkhon Island in the center of Lake Baikal and was discovered by Khoroshikh during reconnaissance in 1927–1928. The materials have been partially published by Okladnikov (1950: 158, Figure 17).

The collections of the Budun site are represented mainly by surface finds. The collection is Mesolithic in appearance, consisting of different kinds of blades. Most of them are sharpened at the top and retouched just like the Anangula cleavers. The similarity can be seen also in retouch technique, which is abrupt with short facets, involving mainly the blade margin. Also of interest is the distribution of the retouching. As in several Anangula samples, it covered both sides of the tool. There also are blades with points formed by oblique-cutting microblades with marginal flaking, wedge-shaped cores, and end-scrapers. Similar articles are also found in the materials of Anangula.

At the same time, the Budun complex is linked to other preceramic complexes of Baikal-Kharilgai and Sarma which, in turn, may be compared to the Mesolithic relics of the Angara area, specifically of Ust-Belaya, Badai, Cheremushnik, and Mt. Verkholenskaya. The stone tools at those sites present a more complete assortment than at Budun. The earliest sites are those of Cheremushnik, Badai, and Peresheyek. Aksënov singled these out into a separate Badai culture dated at the primary stage of the Mesolithic period (Aksënov 1966: 37).

A comparison of the set of stone articles of these sites with the Anangula implements shows that on the whole these collections are quite different. Similarity can be traced only between individual forms of tools. These are pointed blades retouched at the front side and several types of wedge-shaped cores and chisels which in the Angara area are called the "Verkholensk type." The latter have stable shapes and are typical of the Upper Paleolithic and Mesolithic sites in east Siberia. Tracing the territorial distribution of these chisels, Aksënov finds analogical ones not only in the Trans-Baikal area and in Mongolia but also on the Japanese islands in the materials of the Araya site, where they are known as the "Araya chisels." He stresses that Verkholensk chisels invariably go together with "Gobi-type" cores. The latter demonstrate a variety of the wedge-shaped cores encountered in the Upper Paleolithic and Mesolithic sites of the Angara, the Trans-Baikal, the Aldan Amur, and Maritime areas, in northern China, Japan, Kamchatka, and Alaska.

Although in Kamchatka the finds of Gobi cores in the Mesolithic layers of the Ushkovo site do not include chisels, this is apparently a specific feature of regional development. Generally, the areas where the Verkholensk-type chisels and Gobi cores are found basically coincide.

Thus, the combination of Verkholensk-type chisels with Gobi cores may be regarded as an element linking a number of monuments scattered over an extensive territory, ranging from central Asia to Alaska. Yet in different places these relics possess distinctive features which apparently have not only a local but also a genetic character. Thus, for example, at the late Paleolithic and early Mesolithic sites of the Angara area, the finds of Verkholensk-type chisels and Gobi cores are usually augmented by chopper-like tools and big scrapers of the Siberian type, all forming a single complex. At Anangula and in general in Alaska, these tools are not found.

In the Mesolithic layers of the Ushkovo site in Kamchatka there are Gobi cores, scrapers, and knives broad-worked on both sides, similar to the late Paleolithic and early Mesolithic tools of the Angara area, but there are no chisels of the Verkholensk type. At the same time tools are encountered here that are not found among the relics of the Angara area. It must, therefore, be said that though the analogies noted indicate a certain unity in the stone-cutting technique and the types of stone industry in the Angara area, Kamchatka (the Ushkovo site), and Anangula, they do not provide sufficient grounds for pointing to a single center in the Angara area from which these common elements could have diffused. Analogies to the Anangula stone industry should be sought in another direction. Possibilities in this respect are offered by studies of the Japanese islands and areas of the Far East to which the Angara parallels point.

In Japan, the blade technique that may be compared to the technical principles of the Anangula stone industry was most developed in Hokkaido and northern Honshu in Mesolithic times or during a late period of preceramic cultures, some 13,000 to 10,000 years ago, according to Japanese archaeologists. The most expressive specimens of that period are currently regarded to be Shirataki 30 (3,000 years), Shirataki 32 (12,700), Sakkotsu (12,500), Tachikava I, Tovarubetsu (12,500), Tachikava II (9,900) in Hokkaido; and Araya (13,200 $\pm$ 350 years) in northern Honshu (Befu and Chard 1960; Larichev 1970). The tools at those sites were mostly made of blades constructed from prismatic-like, conical, and wedge-shaped cores and also from cores close in type to the Gobi ones.

In general, the form and character of the work on many samples of these artifacts are similar to the stone industry at Anangula. The analogy to Anangula is also most clearly seen in the materials of the Sakkotsu and Araya sites. There is the same assortment of micro- and mesoblades. The toolmaking technique is typical of the extensive usage of transverse or diagonal scraper-flaking which usually shaped the upper end of the tool, whereas the sides were covered with abrupt and small retouching. Similar to the Japanese specimens in this respect are the Anangula retouched blades with symmetrically or asymmetrically sharpened points. In Araya there are wedge-shaped cores made in Horoko techniques: chisels, end scrapers on blades, ski-like and marginal blades and retouched blades resembling the Anangula forms. Wedge-shaped cores, cores with bevel-striking platforms, symmetrical bifacially worked blades, and asymmetrical retouched points of Anangula have their counterparts in Sakkotsu. In the Sakkotsu complex there also are blade chips taken off the corner of cores and chips from already faceted striking platforms. All these correspond to the Anangula specimens. These chip finds show the similarity of technological operations in stone technique. The parallelism in the materials of these complexes is supplemented by the fact that both in Anangula and Sakkotsu most of the tools are made of obsidian. On the basis of this similarity, which in a number of cases extends to absolute identity, a conclusion might be drawn that the traditions of Anangula's stone industry emerged precisely in northern Japan, in Hokkaido, or Honshu, and from there extended to the Aleutian Islands via the Kurils and Kamchatka.

However, as the Japanese archaeologists themselves maintain, Japan is not the place where the blade culture originated. They feel that the blade techniques were brought in from the north of the Asian continent and that it was in Hokkaido where these developed to the greatest degree (Serizawa and Ikawa 1960). Serizawa and Ikawa presume, just as Okladnikov does, that the center of the immediate predecessors of blade-like points was somewhere on the plains of Asia. This idea was repeatedly stated by Okladnikov (1959, 1966), and has been more recently supported and developed by Derevjanko (1971). Of great importance in this connection is the discovery in recent years of Upper Paleolithic and Mesolithic monuments in the southern part of the Soviet Far East: Osinovka, the Geographic Society Cave, Osinovka Maihe I, and particularly Tadushi (Ustinovka) where blading technique was at its highest (Okladnikov 1959, 1966; Derevjanko 1971).

Okladnikov deals in detail in one of his works with the issue of similarity in the development of preceramic cultures on the Japanese islands and in the Maritime area (1966: 352–372). Examining the reasons for this similarity, he draws a comparison between the preceramic complexes in Japan and the finds at the Tadushi (Ustinovka) site. He feels that these complexes have "doubtless and direct conformities." These are seen in a number of common elements; for instance, the characteristic blade cores, the blanks and completed specimens of Gobi-type cores, long oval-pointed end scrapers, one-sided retouched points, and medium-type chisels (Okladnikov 1966: 362–363).

Morlan, when analyzing materials from the sites of the preceramic period in northern Japan, Alaska, Mongolia, Kamchatka, and the Maritime and Baikal areas, gives a typological characteristic of the wedge-shaped cores. He relates the cores of the Tadushi site which Okladnikov regards as Gobi to the wedge-shaped ones made in Horoka techniques, and compares them to the cores of the Japanese sites of Araya and the Fukui cave (fourth layer), where they are the leading forms (Morlan 1968). To this we must add that at the Tadushi site a big series of blanks for elongated Gobi cores identical to the Japanese "boot-type" tools has been found, also made by means of Horoka techniques. Many of these Tadushi elements common to the preceramic complexes of the Japanese islands also link Anangula to the Tadushi site. This connection is further supported by the fact that in the upper layer of the Tadushi site Okladnikov has discovered a semi-pit dwelling, close in type to Anangula.

It is very important that the finds of the Tadushi habitation be compared with the early preceramic complexes of Japan, in which big blades similar to those in the Maritime area are found, as well as the archaic blade-like cores of the epi-Levallois type, according to the terminology of Okladnikov (Okladnikov 1966: 363). On the basis of these epi-Levalloisian traditions, again according to Okladnikov, there emerged and developed the Paleolithic and Mesolithic cultures of the Japanese Islands and the Soviet Far East. They originated, to his mind, in the areas of inner Asia (Okladnikov 1966: 371). For instance, in the Here-Uul complex all the characteristic elements are concentrated, such as the Gobi cores, the ski-shaped and margined chips, chisels of the Araya type, chopper-like pebble cores, Siberian scrapers, and knives of the Verkholensk type, which in different combinations are found in the Baikal area, the Far East (Tadushi), Japan, Kamchatka (the Ushkovo site), and on the Aleutian Islands (Anangula).

This makes it possible to draw the conclusion that precisely the area of eastern Mongolia was the center from which cultural impulses went to the north and the east. Under the impact of these continental cultures there emerged and developed the blade-making technique of the Far East and, apparently, northern Japan which at the end of the Paleolithic period must have formed a unified culture area. Its borders coincided with the Pacific ethnocultural region singled out by Mochanov and included the Lower Amur and Maritime areas, Hokkaido, Sakhalin, and Kamchatka. In the intercontinental areas there emerged approximately at the same time and on the same technological basis a second local culture area, embracing parts of Mongolia, the Trans-Baikal, Angara, and Aldan River areas (Aksënov 1970: 46–48; Mochanov 1969: 83–84).

The typological analogies of the Anangula stone industry show that it is closest in character to the Pacific culture area. Significantly, all the similar finds on the Japanese islands and in the Maritime area either date back to an earlier time, or are synchronous. It is apparently in this area that the starting point has to be found from which the ancestors of the Anangula people moved northwards.

The northward spread of the blade-making culture began, apparently on the verge of Pleistocene and Holocene when the Japanese and the Kuril Islands were still linked with the continent, and when in the northeast there existed ancient Beringia, a stretch of land more than 1,000 miles wide, linking Asia with Alaska. St. Lawrence Island, Nunivak, and the Pribilov Islands were at the time elevations on the Bering platform; Umnak Island was a continuation of the Alaskan peninsula, its southwestern tip; while Anangula Island formed part of Umnak Island. The movement from the Pacific area northward could be effected either along the mainland, along the Okhotsk coast and then across Chukotka to Beringia, or across Hokkaido, then the Kurils and Kamchatka, and further rounding the Bering Sea along the southern edge of the Bering platform to the Aleutian Islands.

The Anangula parallels with the implements of the Sakkotsu site in Hokkaido, and also the morphological similarity between the protohistoric Aleutians and the population of Hokkaido, which has been pointed out by Laughlin (1963: 643–645), makes the second route more likely although the first cannot be ruled out. Movement along the route was not a mass one but gradual and in stages, by small groups which in time spread out along the entire itinerary from Hokkaido to Alaska. Traces can still be found, for instance, in Kamchatka in the fifth and sixth layers of the Ushkov site.

Individual groups of settlers managed 10,000 years ago to round the Bering Sea by moving along the southern edge of Beringia and heading down the edge of the platform to the Umnak-Anangula promontory. There, having encountered favorable geographic conditions and a rich animal world, they settled. The Anangula were, apparently, the first people to have reached that part of Alaska. At any rate, there are no indications pointing to more ancient traces of man's stay there.

Thus, the stone industry of Anangula has deep Asian roots. It was shaped on Asian soil. The intermediate regions during the course of its spread were the Kuril Islands and Kamchatka. Eventually on this basis there developed the ancient Aleutian culture with its clear-cut specialized maritime way of economic life. Proof of this is offered by the many layers of the Chaluka settlement on Umnak Island.

# REFERENCES

AKSËNOV, M. P.
  1966   Stojanka Cheremushnik [The Cheremushnik site]. *Sibirskij arkheo-logicheskij sbornik* 2. Novosibirsk.
  1970   Kompleks nizhnego kul'turnogo gorizonta stojanki Makhorovo na Lene [The complex of the lower culture horizon of the Makhorovo site on the Lena]. *Sibir' i eë sosedi v drevnosti.* Novosibirsk.
BEFU, H., C. S. CHARD
  1960   Preceramic cultures in Japan. *American Anthropologist* 62(5).
DEREVJANKO, A. P.
  1971   "Priamur'e v drevnosti [The Amur region in earliest times]." Unpublished doctoral dissertation. Novosibirsk.
DIKOV, N. N.
  1961   Otkrytie paleolita na Kamchatke i problema pervonachal'nogo zaselenija Ameriki [Discovery of the Paleolithic in Kamchatka and the problem of the original settlement of America]. *Trudy Severo-Vostochn. kompl. nauch.-issled. instituta* 17. Magadan.
FAJNBERG, L. A.
  1971   *Ocherki etnicheskoj istorii zarubezhnogo severa* [Essays on the ethnic history of the foreign north]. Moscow.
LARICHEV, V. E.
  1970   Paleolit i mezolit Japonii [Paleolithic and Mesolithic of Japan]. *Sibir' i eë sosedi v drevnosti.* Novosibirsk.
LAUGHLIN, W. S.
  1963   The earliest Aleuts. *Anthropological Papers of the University of Alaska* 10(2).
MOCHANOV, JU. A.
  1969   Drevnejshie etapy zaselenija Severo-Vostochnoj Azii i Aljaski [Earliest stages in the settlement of northeast Asia and Alaska]. *Sovetskaia etnografija* 1.
MORLAN, RICHARD
  1968   "Technological characteristics of some wedge-shaped cores in north-western North America and northeastern Asia." Paper presented at

the 33rd Annual Meetings of the Society for American Archaeology,
Santa Fe, New Mexico.

OKLADNIKOV, A. P.
   1950   *Nedit i bronzovyj vek Pribajkal'ja, I–II* [The Neolithic and Bronze Age
           of the Lake Baikal region, parts one and two]. Moscow, Leningrad.
   1959   *Dalëkoe proshloe Primor'ja* [Distant past of the Pacific Coast region].
           Vladivostok.
   1966   *Drevnee poselenie na r. Tadushi u der. Ustinovki i problema Dal'ne-
           vostochnogo mezolita. Chetvertichnyj period Sibiri* [The ancient settle-
           ment on the Tadushi River by the village of Ustinovka and the problem
           of the Far Eastern Mesolithic. The Siberian quaternary period].
           Moscow.

SERIZAWA, C., F. IKAWA
   1960   The oldest archaeological materials from Japan. *Asian Perspectives*
           2(2): 1–39.

# The Okhotsk Culture, a Maritime Culture of the Southern Okhotsk Sea Region

HARUO OHYI

Almost ten years ago Befu and Chard (1964) discussed a prehistoric maritime culture of the southern coast of the Sea of Okhotsk. This was the first publication on the so-called Okhotsk culture written by Western scholars.

Befu and Chard traced the specific material aspects of the Okhotsk culture, depending mainly on Japanese works. They paid special attention to the maritime adaptation of the Okhotsk people compared with that of the Aleut and Eskimo. In spite of the existence of some local components such as the local origin of the Okhotsk-type pottery, they tentatively suggested an Aleut-Eskimo derivation for the Okhotsk culture.

Although there remain some problems, it should be said that their article marked an important step in the history of research in this area. Their view of the Okhotsk culture in the wider context of the maritime cultures of the Okhotsk seacoast, North Pacific coast and Bering region, was needed for a complete understanding of the culture. Until today this article is the only comprehensive work on the Okhotsk culture. Thus, the article can be used as a starting point.

Subsequent to publication of the article many Japanese scholars, including the present author, have excavated a considerable number of Okhotsk sites in Hokkaidō and continued the investigation of the Okhotsk culture. There has been a remarkable increase in material and considerable progress in knowledge of the culture. Thus, in following up Befu and Chard's work, I will provide an outline of the Okhotsk culture based on the latest results, and will discuss the culture in the whole context of maritime cultures around the Sea of Okhotsk and those on the North Pacific coast and in the Bering region.

## CHRONOLOGY OF THE OKHOTSK CULTURE

As will be discussed later, the Okhotsk culture started in southern Sakhalin around the fifth century A.D., and flourished as long as 1,000 years on the southern coast of the Okhotsk Sea (Figure 1). We can easily suspect that the culture will have had some evolutional stages and regional developments owing to its long duration and wide distribution. Befu and Chard have already briefly discussed these chronological changes and regional differences within the Okhotsk culture. But in the light of the latest investigations, their discussion is now insufficient for an understanding of its detailed history. First of all, therefore, I will re-examine subdivisions of the Okhotsk culture and their chronology.

For the subdivision and chronology of the Okhotsk culture, the typology of the Okhotsk pottery seems to be most useful. The first detailed discussion on the Okhotsk type pottery was published by Itō (1943). He discussed the chronology of pottery found in southern Sakhalin, and established nine groups. Five of them, namely Towada type, Enoura A type, Enoura B type, Minami-kaizuka type and Higashi-taraika type, are classified as Okhotsk type pottery according to current knowledge. He reached the conclusion that, except for the last-named, they were serial and evolutional stages of one and the same tradition. On the other hand, Higashi-taraika type pottery was a regional facies on the east coast of Sakhalin correlated with Enoura A type and Minami-kaizuka type in the south. Though materials treated in the discussion were quite limited, and stratigraphic results were not so clear, his conclusion seems to be quite reasonable. As for the chronology of the Okhotsk type pottery in southern Sakhalin, we can certainly rely upon his work.[1]

In Hokkaidō, somewhat different groups of the Okhotsk type pottery have been known; these are the noodle appliqué potteries, which are not found in Sakhalin. It is widely believed that these are newer than the groups of pottery with short incised line decoration which bear some resemblances to Enoura B and A type in Sakhalin. But, probably because of the lack of stratigraphic results, the chronological discussion on the Okhotsk type pottery in Hokkaidō was delayed a little longer.

The outstanding work on the chronology of the Okhotsk type pottery in Hokkaidō is by Fujimoto (1965). He established five groups, namely, from A to E, from the materials found in pit houses and shell mounds as a unit. He has pointed out a related group pre-dating the Okhotsk type

[1]   Yoshizaki (1963) has discussed the archaeological succession including the Okhotsk groups in southern Sakhalin. He also has agreed to Itō's chronology and, except for the date of the Susuya type, te dates proposed by him are nearly consistent with my views.

Figure 1.  Distribution of the Okhotsk Culture

Sites mentioned in the article

1  Higashi-taraika shell mound
2  Raichishi site
3  Starodupskoe (Sakaehama) site
4  Enoura site
5  Susuya shell mound
6  Minami-kaizuka site
7  Towada site
8  Funadomari site
9  Kabukai site
10  Motochi site
11  Koetoi shell mound
12  Tomiiso shell mound
13  Onkoromanai sites
14  Omisaki site
15  Tomarinai site

16  Menashidomari site
17  Kawajiri-kita-chashi site
18  Sakae site
19  Kawanishi site
20  Sakaeura II site
21  Tokoro-chashi site
22  Moyoro shell mound
23  Motomachi site
24  Utoro sand-dune site
25  Aidomari site
26  Tobinitai site
27  Tsujinaka site
28  Bentenjima site
29  Tōsamuporo site
30  Shimo-tōbetsu site

pottery, the pottery found in Pit House I of the Tomarinai site which closely resembles the Towada type in Sakhalin, and a group of later date, the pottery found in Pit House II of the Tobinitai site. This shows some similarity to the Satsumon pottery in its typology. Though he misunderstands the chronological position of his A group, the rest of his chronology — the seriation from group B to group E — is sufficiently trustworthy.

From this chronological cataloguing of the Okhotsk type pottery, he concluded that the Okhotsk culture started in southern Sakhalin and northern Hokkaidō, then widened its distribution to eastern Hokkaidō and the Kuril Islands. He thought that the Okhotsk culture had moved its center slowly to the southeast, and that, as a result of these movements, the Okhotsk culture in southern Sakhalin terminated a little earlier than that of Hokkaidō. He also added that the pottery found at Pit House II of the Tobinitai site represented the last pottery-using people in Hokkaidō. Thus, he concluded, at least for eastern Hokkaidō and the Kuril Islands, that the people who had the Okhotsk type pottery were the direct ancestors of the Ainu in these regions.

Because of a scarcity of investigations in northern Hokkaidō, materials treated by Fujimoto are mainly those of eastern Hokkaidō. After his work, we of the Research Institute for Northern Cultures, Hokkaidō University, started a systematic investigation of the Okhotsk culture in 1966. Our work was mainly concentrated in northern Hokkaidō, to fill the gap in materials from that region. Fortunately, our excavations will reveal much important data, including some reliable stratigraphy of the series of Okhotsk type pottery and also some unknown regional groups (Ohyi 1972; Oba and Ohyi 1973). From the results of our investigation, Fujimoto's chronology should be revised at least partially. Here, we again discuss the problem of subdivision and chronology of the Okhotsk type pottery as a whole (Figure 2).

The oldest subdivision of the Okhotsk type pottery in Hokkaidō is the group found at Pit House I of the Tomarinai site (Tadao Sato, et al. 1964) and Pit House II of the Kawajiri-kita-chashi site (Oba, et al. 1972).[2] The group is characterized by a series of punctuations just below the rim. In addition, incised lines, short oblique incisions, and appliqué of broader bands or buttons are seen on the body. Sometimes there appears a varia-

---

[2] As already mentioned, Fujimoto has treated the Towada type as a different group from the Okhotsk type pottery. However, he has not explained thoroughly the reason for such a treatment. As will be noted below, recent excavations in northern Hokkaidō have clearly shown an undeniable affiliation of material cultures to the later stages of the Okhotsk culture. The culture complex was already completed. It is better to look upon the group as the first sign of the Okhotsk culture in Hokkaidō.

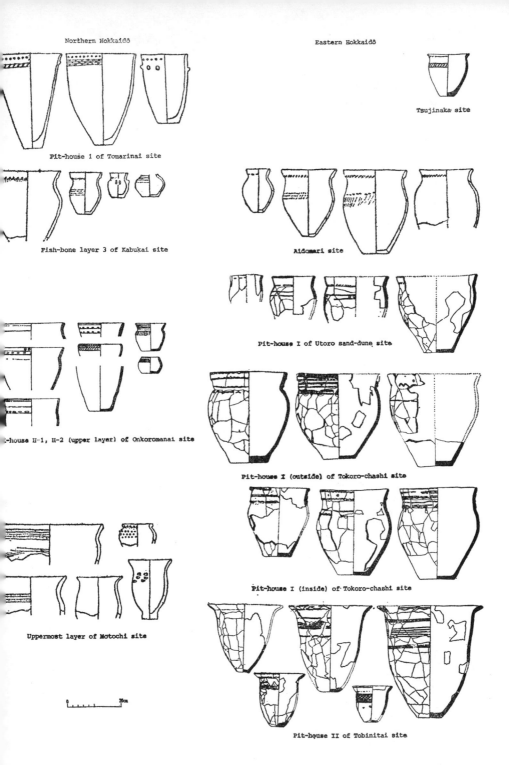

Northern Hokkaidō

Eastern Hokkaidō

Tsujinaka site

Pit-house 1 of Tomarinai site

Fish-bone layer 3 of Kabukai site

Aidomari site

Pit-house I of Utoro sand-dune site

-house II-1, II-2 (upper layer) of Onkoromanai site

Pit-house I (outside) of Tokoro-chashi site

Pit-house I (inside) of Tokoro-chashi site

Uppermost layer of Motochi site

Pit-house II of Tobinitai site

Figure 2. A tentative chronology of the Okhotsk type pottery in Hokkaidō

tion without punctuations or with punctuations from the inside. The form of pottery is usually a simple cylindrical or conical shape with flat base. There is no doubt that this group of pottery has the closest connection with the Towada type in southern Sakhalin; or perhaps it is better to say these two are the only similar groups.

The materials of this group are sporadically known in eastern Hokkaidō too; for example, pottery found at the Tsujinaka site (Onuma and Honda 1970) on Shiretoko Peninsula and in the Bentenjima Island shell mound (Hokuchi Bunka Kenkyū-kai 1968) in the Nemuro district can be classed with this group. Considering the relation to the last Post-Jōmon group and the first Satsumon group, which are decorated also by serial punctuations, and again the relation between the first Satsumon group and the group represented by Haji-ware in southern Hokkaidō and northern Honshū, the first subdivision of the Okhotsk type pottery can be dated around the eighth century A.D.

The second subdivision of the Okhotsk type pottery in Hokkaidō is the B group in Fujimoto's chronology represented by the pottery of the Tōsamuporo site (Kitakamae and Sumi 1953) in the Nemuro district and at the Aidomari site (Sawa, et al. 1971a) on Shiretoko Peninsula.[3] The pottery of this group is characterized by a decoration of short incisions by nail or spatula, which are applied seriately on the neck and the body of the vessels. Sometimes stamps from a comb-like instrument, or incised lines are added. The series of punctuations which were noted in the foregoing subdivisions are rare or completely extinct. Changes are also seen in the shape of the vessels. Wide-mouth jars with slightly contracted necks and flat bottoms are usual. The distribution of the group extends widely along the Okhotsk seacoast of Hokkaidō, from the northernmost part to the easternmost part. An example of the group in northern Hokkaidō is the material of the fish-bone Layer 3 of the Kabukai site on Rebun Island.[4]

[3]   The examples mentioned are materials from unstable layers, and no pit dwellings belonging to the group have as yet been excavated. Thus, there is some probability that they include some admixture from other groups of the Okhotsk type pottery. In spite of uncertainty as to the materials, judging from the whole context, there is sufficient possibility that the group is different from the other groups of the Okhotsk type pottery.

[4]   The Kabukai site was excavated by us (the Research Institute for Northern Cultures, Hokkaidō University), during the 1968, 1969, 1971, and 1972 field seasons. The condition of the cultural layers was quite good. We found six fish-bone layers lying one on the other with intervening sand layers. We also found five pit dwellings between these layers. They all contained extraordinarily rich materials of the Okhotsk culture. We now think that from these materials we can clearly trace the detailed succession of the Okhotsk culture in northern Hokkaidō. In addition, we found two pit houses belonging to the Satsumon phase above the layers of the Okhotsk phase, thus showing the stratigraphical relation of the two. We are now preparing a report on the excavations at the Kabukai site.

Enoura B type pottery in southern Sakhalin probably belongs to the same group or at least has close correlation with the second subdivision of Hokkaidō.

The uniformity in typology at the second subdivision of the Okhotsk type pottery seems to be broken in the following stage. Enoura A type in southern Sakhalin, which follows Enoura B type in the region, is not found in Hokkaidō. Then, in northern Hokkaidō, on one hand, the pottery found in the shell layer at the Tomiiso shell mound (Tadao Satō, et al. 1964) is thought to have nearly the same date. As for the decoration of pottery, serial short incisions which are characteristic in the foregoing group, parallel incised lines and so-called *masatsu-shiki fumon* (a group of parallel shallow broad lines making triangular sectioned ridges between them) increase notably. The shape of vessels is more or less similar to that of the foregoing subdivision.

In eastern Hokkaidō, on the other hand, the noodle appliqué variation of the Okhotsk type pottery started its own development. The group which follows the B group of Fujimoto's chronology in the region is known from Pit House I at the Utoro sand dune site (Komai 1964). This group of pottery is characterized by the appearance of noodle appliqué designs with incisions. However they are rather few in number, that being their major difference from the foregoing group. That is to say, the group is the intervening facies between the incised decoration pottery and the noodle appliqué pottery in eastern Hokkaidō. Usually, some examples with incised line decoration accompany the group. They probably show sporadic intercourse between the groups in northern and eastern Hokkaidō. The so-called Okhotsk type pottery in the northern Kurils (Baba 1939) seems to have some connection with these groups in Hokkaidō. If it is thought of as the derivative of the Okhotsk type pottery in Hokkaidō, the pottery should be classed with this subdivision.

Regional differences of the Okhotsk type pottery which started in the third subdivision become clear in the following stages: in northern Hokkaidō, the following subdivision is represented by pottery found in upper layers of two pit houses, H-1 and H-2, on the terrace behind the Onkoramanai shell mound (Izumi and Sono 1967). The group is characterized by predominating parallel-incised line decoration, sometimes combined with serial short incisions. Some variations with *masatsu-shiki fumon*, stamping and appliqué design accompany the group. In eastern Hokkaidō, by contrast, the noodle appliqué pottery flourished widely at the same stage. A considerable number of pit houses belonging to this phase have been excavated in eastern Hokkaidō, and Fujimoto has indicated two subdivisions of the group based on typologies of the pottery, namely his D and E groups. The vessels of these two groups are both decorated only by noodle appliqué designs. However, a slight difference can be seen between the two groups, such as simpler combinations in group D and somewhat more complicated ones in group E. Stratigraphic relations between the two are known at Pit House I of the Tokoro-chashi site (Komai 1964). Here, after abandonment of a larger pit house associated with the pottery of group D, a smaller pit house was rebuilt inside by the people who were represented by the pottery of group E.

The stratigraphy clearly shows that group D predates group E. The noodle appliqué pottery group is also known in the southern part of the Kuril Islands, i.e. Kunashiri and Etorofu (Iturup), but no pottery of the groups has been reported from the northern part of the islands. The circumstances in southern Sakhalin at that time are somewhat obscure.

It is probable that the Enoura A type was prolonged in the southern-most part, and on the eastern coast of Sakhalin, Higashi-taraika type pottery appeared at the same time. Of course there are marked similarities which would suggest a possible contemporaneity of these two groups; on the other hand, the two have undeniable differences in typologies. That is to say, we can recognize some local developments of the Okhotsk type pottery even in a limited area such as southern Sakhalin. In short, at these stages, the uniformity in typology of the Okhotsk type pottery has already been lost and, as a result of different indigenous developments, several local groups of the Okhotsk type pottery have appeared in each area of the distribution.

In southern Sakhalin, the last currently known group of the Okhotsk type pottery is the Minami-kaizuka type. On the other hand, it is quite probable that the Higashi-taraika type, or at least a part of it, existed on the eastern coast of Sakhalin at the same time, because the group has some features similar to the Minami-kaizuka type in its typology. It is supposed that the coexistence of these two groups is a characteristic of the last Okhotsk phase in southern Sakhalin. The situation in Hokkaidō at that time was somewhat different. By reason of the migration of the Satsumon people to northern and eastern Hokkaidō, Satsumon influences on the Okhotsk type pottery become clear in that region. An example in northern Hokkaidō is the pottery found in the uppermost layer of Motochi site, Rebun Island (Ohyi 1972). The group is characterized by a Satsumon-like shape of the pottery such as a slightly curved rim and a straight body with flat base. On the other hand, some traditional designs of the Okhotsk type are seen in the decoration, such as prevailing *masatsu-shiki fumon* and stampings, etc., which suggest a possible relation with the Minami-kaizuka type in southern Sakhalin.

A different local group is known in eastern Hokkaidō, probably a little later than the group mentioned above — i.e. the pottery found at Pit House II of the Tobinitai site (Komai 1964) on the Shiretoko Peninsula. The Satsumon-like shape of vessels is also seen in the group and, in this regard, it is more or less similar to the group from the Motochi site in northern Hokkaidō. Decoration of the vessel is mostly in noodle appliqué designs which are typical for the foregoing groups of the Okhotsk type pottery in the region. Sometimes incised geometric designs, usual for the Satsumon type pottery, are added.

Materials from the group are also reported from the southern part of the Kuril Islands, but not from the northern part. In these two groups, one in northern Hokkaidō and another in eastern Hokkaidō, the same pattern of change can be traced, i.e., Satsumon affinity in shape and traditional decorative motives of the Okhotsk type pottery in each region. There is no doubt that they show the processes of hybridization of the Okhotsk type pottery with the Satsumon type. These groups are the last Okhotsk type pottery in Hokkaidō and, as already discussed, they can be dated around the thirteenth century A.D.

After the extinction of the Okhotsk type pottery in Hokkaidō, the later groups of the Satsumon type pottery flourished widely in northern and eastern Hokkaidō. By contrast, the situation in Sakhalin seems to be quite different, because no site of the Satsumon group has been reported there. One of the sporadic finds of Minami-kaizuka type pottery in northern Hokkaidō accompanied the later group of Satsumon type pottery in a pit house (Satō 1972). If the data are trustworthy, we should conclude that, in southern Sakhalin, the Minami-kaizuka type, and probably the Migashi-tanaika type also, lasted a little longer than the last groups of the Okhotsk type pottery in Hokkaidō. The same is suspected in the southern Kurils, though materials are limited; there would be some groups in the tradition of the Okhotsk type pottery contemporary with the later groups of the Satsumon type pottery in Hokkaidō.

The subdivisions and their chronology which I have discussed are only those of the Okhotsk type pottery. However, the changes in this pottery must have been prompted by some changes which occurred in the groups of people and their culture complex. Thus, it can be said that the subdivisions and chronology of the Okhotsk type pottery have more or less reflected the developments and changes of the Okhotsk culture itself. In the following section I will trace the brief history of the Okhotsk culture on the basis of the subdivisions and chronology mentioned above.

## ORIGIN OF THE OKHOTSK CULTURE

In discussing the origin of the Okhotsk culture, one should first consider what constitutes this culture, or by what features one can determine if materials at a site belong to it.

The first Okhotsk site known in detail is the Moyoro shell mound (Yonemura 1950; Oba 1955, 1956, 1957; Komai, et al. 1964) in the Abashiri district. Even today, it is thought of as a typical site of the Okhotsk culture. In the site, numerous materials belonging to the Okhotsk phase were found: various kinds of pottery from the incised pottery to the noodle appliqué variation; relatively poor stone implements, such as projectile points including arrowheads and inset tip ends for a kind of harpoon, axes, grinding stones, grooved or holed net-sinkers, and so on; rich bone and antler implements elaborately made by metal tools such as points, arrowheads, various kinds of harpoon, spatulas, composite fishhooks, shovels, etc. In addition to these, needle cases, various kinds of ornaments, objects of unknown use with fine incised decoration or engraving, and some carved figurines were found.

Extraordinarily large pit houses, hexagonal in plan and with clay-paved floors, a hearth with a stone arrangement, heaps of animal bones on opposite ends of the floor, are characteristic for the structural remains of the Okhotsk phase in the site. Many graves in various styles were reported. It can be said that materials and structural remains of the Moyoro shell mound show the typical material culture of the Okhotsk people and, moreover, one can understand their mode of life by these materials and remains — e.g. their economic basis,[5] patterns of settlement, social structures, religious concepts, and so forth. Thus, I would like to explore the Okhotsk culture, not only the material culture but also the whole known culture complex.

In this exploration, the first representative of the Okhotsk culture in Hokkaidō is a group of the first subdivision of the Okhotsk type pottery. Pit House II of the Kawajiri-kita-chashi site has typical Okhotsk traits, being large in size and hexagonal in plan. The remains found in the

---

[5] There is no question that, to study the economic basis of the Okhotsk culture, an investigation of faunal remains of the site is of prime importance. Regrettably, the report of faunal remains found in the Moyoro shell mound is quite incomplete. Only the species of animals, birds, fishes, and mollusks are named; the number and ratio of each species are not reported. Thus, we can hardly discuss the economy of Okhotsk people at this shell mound in detail. However, considering data reported from other sites (such as Naora 1964; Kaneko 1972, 1973), the prevailing understanding that the economic basis of the Okhotsk culture lies chiefly in sea mammal hunting and fishing should be acceptable.

pit house, the pottery and shards and some stone implements, show the typical complex of the Okhotsk culture, though no bone and antler objects were found because of poor preservation of the layers (Figure 3a). The component of bone and antler objects of the group is known from the fish-bone Layers 5 and 6 at the Kabukai site, Rebun Island, where the pottery and shards are quite similar to those of Kawajiri-kita-chashi site.

In these layers, we have found a typical complex of bone and antler objects for the Okhotsk culture, such as points, arrowheads, two or three variations of harpoon, spatulas, composite fishhooks, etc. Also, faunal remains, fish bones and sea urchins, of which the layers themselves consist, are numerous. In addition to these, sea animals, including fur seals, sea lions, seals, whales, and land animals, including dogs and bears are found in the layers. Remains of sea animals are far more numerous than those of land animals. From the results mentioned above, there is no doubt that the group represented by the first subdivision of the Okhotsk type pottery was a typical complex of the Okhotsk culture.

Compared with the known groups which predate this group in northern Hokkaidō, namely, the group of post-Jōmon culture and the group represented by Susuya type pottery, they have almost no affiliation except for the serial punctuations just below the rim which are typical both for the Susuya type and the first group of Okhotsk type pottery. Therefore, we cannot suspect that the first Okhotsk group in northern Hokkaidō has some genetic sources in these groups. A better view is that the Okhotsk culture is not the derivative of foregoing groups in Hokkaidō but an exotic intrusive group from the north, namely southern Sakhalin, at that time.

The data on the group in Sakhalin are inadequate. Though the pottery, which is similar to the first group in Hokkaidō, is known, other components of the group are not at all clear. However, the total coincidence in typology of pottery between the two leads us to the assumption that the group represented by Towada type pottery had a more or less similar culture complex to that of the group in Hokkaidō. In other words, typical traits for the Okhotsk culture have already been completed in southern Sakhalin at that time. Anyone who wants to reveal the origin of the Okhotsk culture should seek the sources for the foregoing groups in Sakhalin.

According to Itō's chronology, the groups of pottery predating the Towada type are the Sōnin type, Enbuchi type, and Susuya type. For the groups represented by the first two, it is difficult to suppose any relationship with the previous Okhotsk culture. For the last-named,

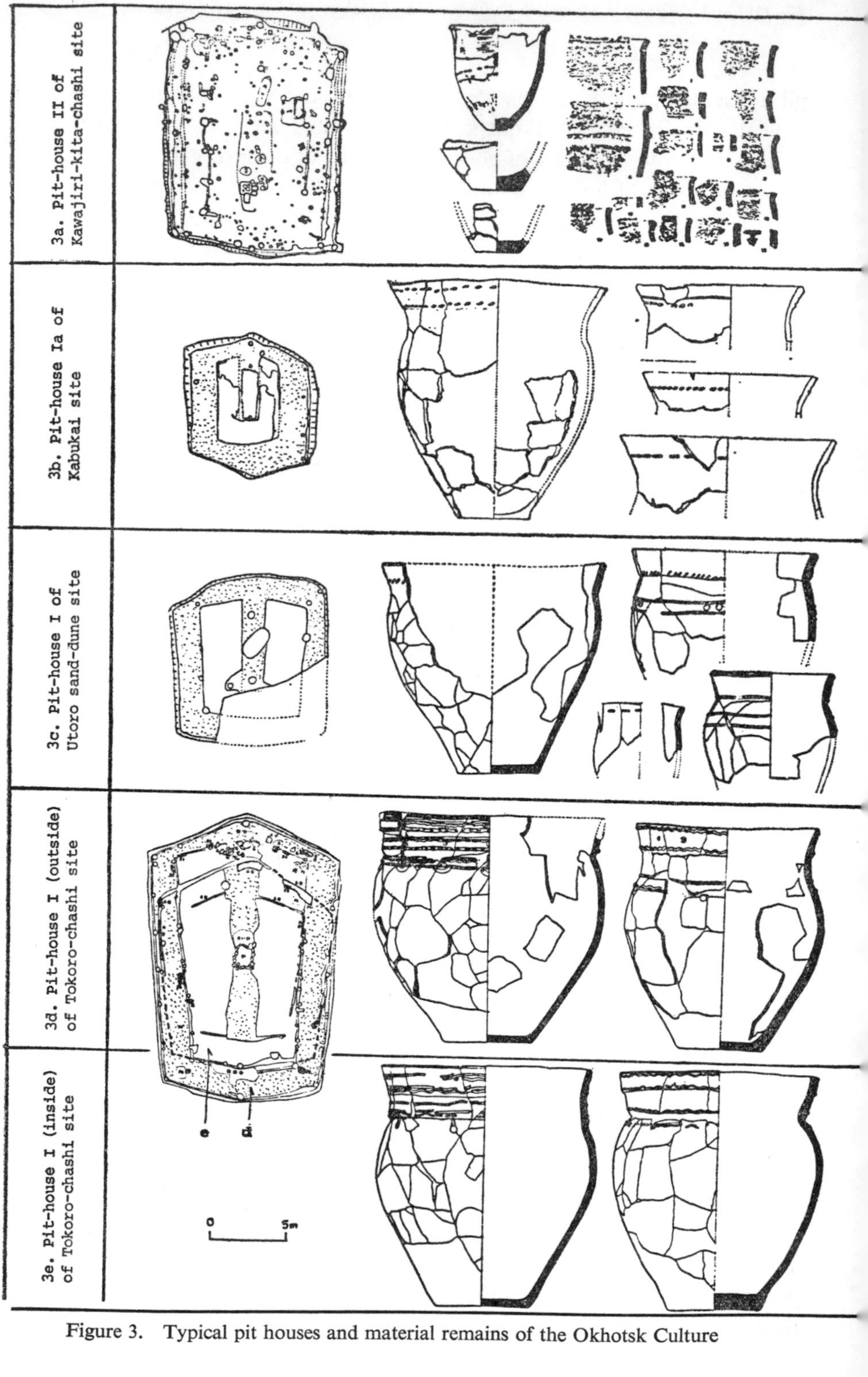
3a. Pit-house II of Kawajiri-kita-chashi site
3b. Pit-house Ia of Kabukai site
3c. Pit-house I of Utoro sand-dune site
3d. Pit-house I (outside) of Tokoro-chashi site
3e. Pit-house I (inside) of Tokoro-chashi site
e
d
0
5m

Figure 3. Typical pit houses and material remains of the Okhotsk Culture

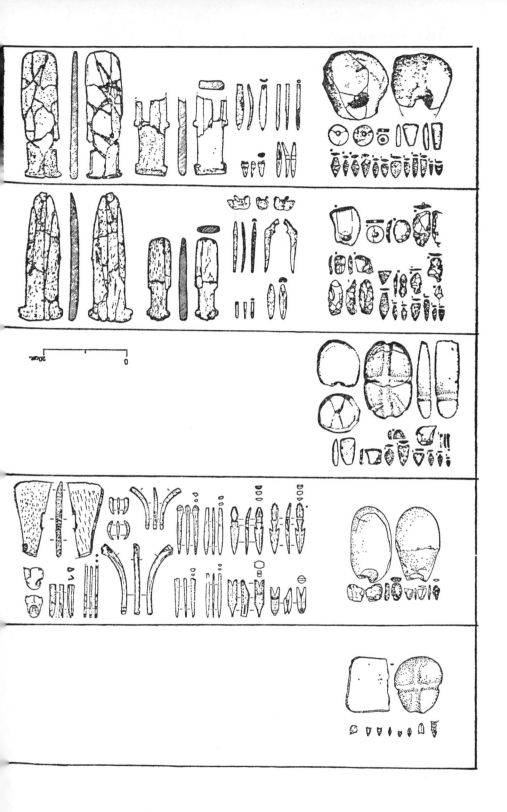

20cm.    0

namely the Susuya type, there remain some problems to be considered. Itō has already investigated the two variations of the so-called Susuya type pottery. One of them is the group of pottery with parallel cord impressions on the neck, distributed only in the southernmost part of Sakhalin, which is similar to the group in northern Hokkaidō. Another one is represented by the pottery found at the Raichishi site on the west coast of Sakhalin and distributed even farther north. The pottery is characterized by various stampings, for instance, with a comb-like instrument, making parallel lines on the neck. Sometimes vessels with incised decoration, a few horizontal short incisions arranged vertically, accompany the group. Though Itō has concluded that these two variations are one and the same group, because of the coexistence of them in the Susuya shell mound, it is possible to divide them into two different groups, because, accompanying the distributional differences, there are clear distinctions in technique of decoration between the two. For the first group of Susuya type vessels with parallel cord impressions, I doubt its affiliation with the Okhotsk type pottery due to the data in northern Hokkaidō. On the other hand, the second variation with stamped decoration seems to have some connection with the Okhotsk type pottery.

Pit House II of the Starodupskoe (Sakaehama) site probably belongs to the latter group (Kozyreva 1964). The pottery found in the pit house contains the variations with parallel cord impressions, stampings with a comb-like instrument, short incisions etc., and almost all the vessels have conical shapes with round bottoms, usual for Susuya type pottery. In the pit house, a good number of stone implements are also found, for example, projectile points including arrowheads, various kinds of scrapers, adzes, grinding stones etc., and also two stone rings. These stone implements show undeniable resemblances with those of the Okhotsk culture in Hokkaidō. Especially adzes with square cross-sections and stone rings seem to be typical components of the culture. Regrettably, no bone and antler implements were found in the pit house because of the bad condition of the layers. The pit house itself is nearly hexagonal in plan and very large in size with some narrow ditches on the floor. Here, we have a strict copy of Pit House II of the Kawajiri-kita-chashi site in Hokkaidō. The remains, strict coincidence of the pit houses and close relationships with accompanying material, suggest that the culture complex known from the remains of the Pit House II of the Starodupskoe site is in no way different from that of the Okhotsk culture in Hokkaidō. Judging from general resemblances in culture complex between the two, if the condition of the layers in the site allows, there should be a similar assemblage of bone and antler implements in the Okhotsk culture, which shows a specific maritime adaptation of the people. In conclusion, it can be said that in Sakhalin the entire complex of the Okhotsk culture was already completed at the group of the Starodupskoe site a little earlier than at the first Okhotsk group in Hokkaidō;[6] that is, it was the first representative of the Okhotsk culture in its entire area of distribution.

Probably, the components of the Okhotsk culture derived not from a single origin but from plural sources by complicated processes. As already stated, the pottery found in Pit House II of the Starodupskoe site includes two or three variations. Among them, on the one hand, those with cord line impressions can be traced in relation to Susuya type pottery and also the post-Jōmon group in Hokkaidō. On the other hand, those with stampings, including those made with a comb-like instrument, and incised decoration, seem to have their derivation in northern Sakhalin and also in the lower Amur region (Kozyreva 1967). The related group is also known in the Maritime Territory (Okladnikov 1963). On the contrary, the shape of the vessels, conical with round base, has no parallel in the surrounding areas at that time. It is likely that the feature is unique for the group and Susuya type.

Considering the circumstances, one can suppose that the shape is an indigenous tradition in southern Sakhalin. Anyhow, it is sure that the pottery found in Pit House II of the Starodupskoe site was not in any single tradition but a mixture of diverse elements from various traditions in and around the region. As for the stone component, the circumstances are nearly the same. Known stone implements of the group, especially flake tools, are not so different from those of the group represented by Susuya type pottery, for example, those reported from the Onkoromanai site in northern Hokkaidō, about which Okada (1967) has pointed out a resemblance to the stone implements of post-Jōmon culture. On the other hand, Kozyreva has investigated the relationships of stone objects of the group, for instance adzes with square cross-sections and stone rings, with the parallels in the Amur-Maritime Territory regions (Kozyreva 1967).

---

[6]  Kozyreva has dated Pit House II of the Starodupskoe site in the latter part of the second millennium or the beginning of the first millennium B.C. In comparison with sequences in Hokkaidō, the date seems to be much too early. The group of Susuya type pottery with cord impressions, which has undeniable relationships with the materials of the Pit House II in the Starodupskoe site, is distributed also in northern-most Hokkaidō (Izumi and Sono 1967). And in view of archaeological chronology in Hokkaidō, it should be thought to be in a parallel chronological position with the later group of the post-Jōmon culture and be dated around the fifth or sixth century A.D.

For the component of bone and antler objects, which is one of the most characteristic features of the Okhotsk culture, the circumstances are somewhat different. In northern and eastern Hokkaidō, there are no predated groups which had such a specific bone and antler assemblage. In northern Sakhalin, and also in the Amur-Maritime Territory regions, no groups were reported which show the certain maritime adaptation as is seen in the assemblage of bone and antler implements of the Okhotsk culture. In the Esan culture distributed in southern Hokkaidō, a variation of post-Jōmon culture, bone and antler implements which suggest a certain maritime adaptation of the group are known (Hokkaidō University 1963). But, though there are some parallels, such as a kind of harpoon, foreshaft, and so forth, the assemblage as a whole is not similar to that of the Okhotsk culture. Moreover, because of gaps in distribution and chronological position, there seems to be no possibility of affiliation between the two. That is to say, it is difficult to find any sources or derivations of bone and antler components of the Okhotsk culture in the surrounding areas. The only possible exception is that of the Ancient Koryak culture in the far north on the northern coast of the Okhotsk Sea (Vasilievsky 1969, 1971).

This culture, which is characterized by the hunting of sea mammals, is rich in bone and antler objects containing some implements related to the Okhotsk culture, such as kinds of harpoons,[7] needle cases decorated in similar design, shovels, and so on. Of course, the assemblages of bone and antler objects in these two groups are not the same, but general affinities of the component are adequate to establish a relationship between the two. But it is difficult to determine which one is the ancestor of the other — whether the bone and antler component of the Okhotsk culture was derived from the ancient Koryak culture, or vice versa; or whether there was an unknown ancestor common to both.

In addition, the possible domestication of pigs in the Okhotsk culture seems to have a special meaning. The remains of pigs are found not only in Sakhalin (Naora 1938) but also in Hokkaidō, namely at the Kabukai site, the Onkoromanai shell mound (Kaneko 1973) and the Sakaeura II site (Kaneko 1972). Because there are no wild boars in Sakhalin and Hokkaidō, the domesticated pigs are thought to have been introduced from an adjacent area. In this case, the derivation of pigs can be traced

[7]  Vasilievsky has indicated a certain similarity in two or three kinds of harpoon heads found in both of the two groups. However, at least for the Okhotsk culture in Hokkaidō, these kinds of harpoons are not known as yet; it is therefore difficult to say whether these are typical for the Okhotsk culture itself. It seems probable that these are intrusive elements found only in southern Sakhalin and the northern Kurils in its later stages.

to the Maritime Territory, where domestication of pigs can be traced back to the first millennium B.C.; for example, the remains found at the Peschani site near Vladivostok (Okladnikov 1963) belong to the Cidemi culture. Also in the first millennium A.D., there were people called Yi-lou, probably heirs of the Cidemi culture, who had domesticated pigs. Perhaps, the domestication of pigs in the Okhotsk culture had its origin in these groups.

As discussed above, determining the origin of the Okhotsk culture would not be simple. Thus, one can conclude that the Okhotsk culture developed as a mixture of plural components from plural sources by complicated processes. In the present state of knowledge, regrettably, these processes have not been defined. Even so, it seems clear that the culture complex of the Okhotsk culture was completed only in Sakhalin, not elsewhere.

Considering the date of the group represented by Towada type pottery, the date of the first representatives of the Okhotsk culture in Sakhalin, namely the group of Pit House II of the Starodupskoe site, might be thought to be in the fifth or sixth century A.D.. Shortly after that, around 700 A.D., the Okhotsk culture spread to the island of Hokkaidō. That is the first Okhotsk group in Hokkaidō, represented by Pit House I of the Tomarinai site and Pit House II of the Kawajiri-kita-chashi site. The distribution of the group was not confined to northern Hokkaidō. At least a part of the group sporadically arrived in eastern Hokkaidō sooner or later, as was seen by the sites in the Shiretoko Peninsula and the Nemuro district. The reason why the Okhotsk group was able to spread quickly is one of the most important questions we face. A plausible hypothesis is that completion of the Okhotsk culture complex, especially the introduction of sea mammal hunting and breeding of pigs, fortified the economic base of the group and, in consequence, the population of the group increased considerably in the area. Then, a part of the group started their immigration into Hokkaidō via La Perouse Strait from their native territory.

## DEVELOPMENTS IN THE OKHOTSK CULTURE

In the following stages, the Okhotsk culture continued its expansion. The group which followed the Towada type pottery in Sakhalin is represented by the Enoura B type. At least in the typology of pottery, the group was closely related to, or, it should be said, nearly the same as, the second subdivision of the Okhotsk type pottery in Hokkaidō, the

so-called incised pottery, which is distributed not only in northern Hokkaidō but also in eastern Hokkaidō and the southern Kurils.

Unfortunately, there has been no detailed investigation of the group in
Sakhalin until recently. Therefore, we do not have enough data to recon-
struct the whole culture complex of the group in Sakhalin. However, the
materials reported individually (Baba 1940) and the close resemblances
in types of pottery suggest that there are few differences in the culture
complex of the two groups — the one in southern Sakhalin and the other
in Hokkaidō.

In Hokkaidō, many sites belonging to the group are known along the
Okhotsk seacoast, and some of them have been partially investigated, but
the present state of knowledge of the group is far from satisfactory. The
results of the excavations in the Kabukai site should fill in the gap of
knowledge on the group. Pit House Ia of the site has shown, though
somewhat smaller in scale, a typical hexagonal plan, and is accompanied
by considerable quantities of pottery and shards, some stone implements,
and bone and antler objects (Figure 3b). It should be said that they show
the typical material culture of the Okhotsk culture at that stage. Perhaps
there would have been a certain number of such dwellings in the site,
making a more or less stationary village, one of the typical patterns of
settlement of the Okhotsk people.

On the border of Wakkanai city, the northernmost town of Hokkaidō,
we have seen a remarkable concentration of the Okhotsk sites which clearly contrast with the surrounding areas. In the group of sites, the Koetoi
shell mound, the westernmost of the group, is the largest in scale and has
some pit houses in the area. The features of the site are similar to those
of the *abukai* site mentioned before. By contrast, the rest of the group
including the Tomiiso shell mound and Onkoromanai shell mound are
limited in scale. Though a number of remains have been found, there are
no proper pit houses in the area. From these results, we hypothesize that
the group of sites as a whole would have shown a complete settlement
pattern of a regional community of the Okhotsk people (i.e. the former,
the Koetoi shell mound, would be the center of the community, and the
latter, the Tomiiso shell mound, Onkoromanai shell mound, and the
others, would be more or less temporary hunting-fishing camps. Of
course, the data related are far from satisfactory; however, the hypothesis
seems worthy of pursuit.

We are able to point out a considerable number of such groups of sites
along the Okhotsk seacoast of Hokkaidō, namely, from north to east,
that of the Rebun and Rishiri Islands including the Kabukai site; the
Wakkanai district already mentioned; around Esashi Town; the Abashiri

district including the Moyoro shell mound; the northern coast of Shiretoko Peninsula; the southern coast of the peninsula including the Aidomari site; and that of the Nemuro district including the Tōsamuporo site. Whether the hypothesis is plausible or not, this distribution of sites clearly shows that the Okhotsk culture remarkably widened its territory and established firm bases in eastern Hokkaidō, and even in the southern Kurils, at this stage.

At least from the known data, a striking homogeneity of materials is seen in these groups of sites, such as the pottery with incised decoration, relatively poor assemblages of stone implements, many bone and antler objects sometimes elaborately decorated, and so on. It seems that there was the same culture complex in the whole distributional area, and almost no noticeable regional differences existed between any groups in any of the regions. The only possible exception is the barbed harpoon with a line hole in its base, unknown in the sites in northern Hokkaidō, but found at some sites in eastern Hokkaidō, for instance the Moyoro shell mound (Oba 1955: Figure 1; Natori and Oba 1964; Figures 1–20, 3–16) and the Tōsamuporo site (Kitakamae and Sumi 1953: Figures 8–14, 15, 16, 17, 18, 19). Probably, at that time these harpoons were the intrusive element newly added to the Okhotsk culture complex only in eastern Hokkaidō.[8] The examples are also reported from the southern Kurils (Saigawa-kai 1933: Plates 41–10, 12 and 43, 2), and related remains, though not the same, are known from the northern Kurils (Baba 1939). (The problems related to these examples will be discussed later.)

Other factors that one cannot neglect are the somewhat different ecological environments in each region within the distribution, such as the differences in fauna: for example, fur seals abundant in Sakhalin and northern Hokkaidō are rare in eastern Hokkaidō; also deer are absent or rare in Sakhalin and northern Hokkaidō but abundant in eastern Hokkaidō. Despite general homogeneities in the material cultures, there is some probability that certain regional differences in their mode of life may have started already in each area of the distribution. The differences seem to be suggested in the faunal remains from the sites. It is said that the ratios of land animals to sea animals in faunal remains at the sites in eastern Hokkaidō are usually greater than those in northern Hokkaidō.[9]

---

[8] Because of incomplete descriptions of the sites, it is difficult to decide to what group or stage these barbed harpoons are to be attributed. However, at least for the Tōsamuporo site, almost all of the materials seem to belong to this stage; the appearance of this type of harpoon in the bone assemblage of the Okhotsk culture thus could be traced back to this stage.

[9] Personal communication from Hiromasa Kaneko. A detailed discussion has not yet been published.

These differences are possibly the predecessors of different regional developments of the Okhotsk culture in the following stages.

As already discussed in the previous section on chronology, the Okhotsk culture seems to be divided into three or four regional groups: there is the group in southern Sakhalin represented by Enoura A type, Minami-kaizuka type, and Higashi-taraika type pottery; the group in northern Hokkaidō represented by the materials from the Tomiiso shell mound and those found in the upper level of the pit houses in the Onkoromanai site; and the group in eastern Hokkaidō represented by so-called noodle appliqué pottery. Probably the group from the northern Kurils makes another one in nearly the same stage. In these groups, at least for the types of pottery, we can easily distinguish one from another, and so we can reasonably suspect that there were different indigenous developments of the Okhotsk people in each region. However we must ask whether the differences between these groups are limited only to the types of pottery or include differences in the other components, such as stone implements, bone and antler objects and, furthermore, their economics, their social structures, and so forth.

The data on the groups represented by Enoura A type pottery in southern Sakhalin are so limited that we cannot have a further discussion about the differences in pottery between them and the groups in Hokkaidō.

As for the sites of the group in northern Hokkaidō at similar stages, we can name the Motochi site and the Kabukai site, both on Rebun Island, Tomiiso shell mound and the Onkoromanai site in the city of Wakkanai, and the Menashidomari site in the town of Esashi.[10] Except for the changes in pottery type, the results from these sites are nearly the same as those of the foregoing groups in the area, regarding artificial remains, faunal remains, and settlement patterns. Thus, it can be said that there were almost no fundamental differences between the groups and the foregoing groups in the region.

By contrast, in eastern Hokkaidō, there is some probability that certain changes took place in the group at these stages. One of the most remarkable features for the groups in eastern Hokkaidō at these stages was the notable increase in sites, or, more accurately, in stationary sites with pit houses. For example, in the Abashiri district, where only one group is supposed to have been at the previous stage, we are able to name five sites with a definite number of pit houses, namely, from west to east: the Sakae site in the city of Monbetsu (Koyanagi and Inaba 1969), the

---

[10] The Research Institute for Northern Cultures has been excavating the site continuously since the 1967 field season. No report has as yet been published.

Kawanishi site in the Town of Yūbetsu (Yonemura 1961), the Sakaeura II site (Fujimoto, et al. 1972), the Tokoro-chashi site in the town of Tokoro, and then the Moyoro shell mound in the city of Abashiri. Probably one or two more sites will be added to the list of sites in the district. On the other hand, no sites without pit houses, (i.e. supposed hunting-fishing camps) belonging to these stages were found in the district. The similarities are seen everywhere in eastern Hokkaidō, on both the northern and eastern sides of the Shiretoko Peninsula and the Nemuro district. It is quite probable that these similarities show, on the one hand, a remarkable increase in the population of the Okhotsk people in the area and, on the other hand, that certain changes in their settlement pattern took place. That is to say, a relatively wide area for a group at the previous stage, where a stationary village and some hunting-fishing camps had been settled, was divided into several smaller territories belonging to different groups, in each of which only the stationary village was settled. These changes would be brought about chiefly by the changes in their mode of life; for instance, for the foregoing group in eastern Hokkaidō, their hunting was not limited to sea mammals, but also was widened to include land animals, such as bears, deer, and so on. Probably, the new mode of life made their economic base firm and, in consequence, let them increase in population and, at the same time, change their patterns of settlement.

As for the material cultures, however — except in the types of pottery — we are able to point out little change in the group compared with changes in the foregoing groups. A considerable number of pit houses belonging to these stages has been excavated and reported on in eastern Hokkaidō and, as already mentioned, Fujimoto has divided them into three groups, his groups C to E. The only example of his group C is Pit House I of the Utoro sand-dune site (Figure 3c). The pit house itself shows typical Okhotsk traits, such as a large-scale, hexagonal plan, and partial, clay-paved floor. The remains found in the pit house, though no bone and antler implements were found, are also said to be a good example of the material culture of the Okhotsk culture at that stage. As the representatives of his groups D and E, we can name the double Pit House I of the Tokoro-chashi site, where at first a large pit house had been settled at the stage of group D, then, after its destruction by a fire, a smaller pit house was rebuilt inside at the stage of group E (Figures 3d and 3e). The outer pit house belonging to group D is the largest one known thus far. Both pit houses show typical Okhotsk traits, also hexagonal in plan and partially paved by clay. In the pit houses, there are heaps of animal bones at both ends of the clay floor and a hearth surrounded by a stone arrangement, rectangular in shape, at the center.

There also are a considerable number of remains, such as pottery and shards, stone implements, bone and antler objects, and so forth. Though we cannot think of them as a complete assemblage, it can be said that they form one of the typical material cultures of the Okhotsk culture.

A fact that probably cannot be overlooked is the existence of the hearth with stone arrangement in Pit House I of the Tokoro-chashi site, which is unknown in the sites in northern Hokkaidō and southern Sakhalin, but, on the contrary, is usually known in the sites in eastern Hokkaidō, especially in the later stages, Fujimoto's groups C to E. (The example belonging to group C is reported at the lower stratum of Pit House X of the Moyoro shell mound; see Komai, et al. 1964: Figure 15). If this is so, we should think of the hearth as a new and intrusive element come from somewhere adjacent to eastern Hokkaidō. It is reported that the hearth surrounded by the stone arrangement in the pit house is characteristic of the so-called Okhotsk period in the northern Kurils. Under these circumstances, with the barbed harpoon already mentioned, we are able to suspect that in eastern Hokkaidō there were certain cultural currents, though limited, which came from the northern Kurils at that time.

For the Kuril Islands, the data known until today are quite limited compared with those from Hokkaidō. However, so far as the reported data have indicated, the Okhotsk culture in Kunashiri and Iturup (Eto-rofy) Islands seems to have nearly the same developmental stages as seen in eastern Hokkaidō (Hirakō 1929; Saitō 1933; Chubarova 1960). Accordingly, at least for the southernmost parts of the islands, the Okhotsk culture in the islands should be added to the same regional groups as those in eastern Hokkaidō. On the other hand, for the northern Kurils, where reliable data have been given only by Baba's excavations in the Shumshu and Paramushir islands, the circumstances are somewhat different. Baba (1939) has divided the sites in these islands into three groups and classified the oldest one as the regional group of the Okhotsk culture. But it is difficult to accept his definition of the group without comment. In his report, ten pit houses and nine shell mounds have been listed as sites belonging to the group. Among them, all of the pit houses are round or are square with rounded corners, and their diameters range from four to six meters. The shape and scale of these pit houses are by no means similar to typical Okhotsk pit houses in Hokkaidō. Probably, the fact that each of them usually has a hearth with a stone arrangement in it makes the only exception. As mentioned above, it should be thought of as a sign of a possible interrelation between the two regions, eastern Hokkaidō and the northern Kurils. At the same time, materials found in the sites (both pit houses and shell mounds), such as pottery and shards, stone implements, and abundant bone and antler objects, leads one to suspect the complicated character of the group. For example, on the one hand, the pottery and shards show a close relationship with the Okhotsk type pottery in Hokkaidō and, on the other hand, the bone and antler assemblage contains some types unfamiliar to the Okhotsk culture in Hokkaidō, such as barbed harpoons already mentioned, a kind of toggle harpoon, decorated round plates, combs, and so on. The stone lamps are also cited as a clue which suggests a derivation of the group other than the Okhotsk culture. As a result of the above arguments, one can safely conclude that it is difficult to see it as a regional group of the Okhotsk culture itself. Of course, the Okhotsk derivations in certain components — the pottery is one of them — are by no means negligible. Therefore, the group should be understood as a hybrid between the Okhotsk culture and some other group in the adjoining area. Kikuchi (1972) has suggested the relationship between the group and the Ancient Koryak culture by reason of certain similarities in types of bone and antler objects and also the common existence of stone lamps in both groups. In spite of some vacant spaces in the southern part of the Kamtchatka peninsula, it should be said his hypothesis is one of the most reasonable explanations for the group we have to date.

## DECLINE OF THE OKHOTSK CULTURE

Though there remains a slight diversity of opinion,[11] it is widely believed that while the Okhotsk culture flourished on the Okhotsk seacoast of Hokkaidō, there was another group of people in other parts of Hokkaidō: the bearers of the Satsumon culture who were successors to the tradition of the native post-Jōmon culture and were heavily acculturated by the Japanese culture introduced in the eighth or ninth century A.D.

According to present knowledge, the Satsumon culture can be divided into four succesive groups (Komai 1964). The first two are almost exclusively known from the southern and central parts of Hokkaidō, outside the territories of the Okhotsk culture. The Satsumon group then started their northern expansion. The first extensive contact between the Okhotsk

---

[11]  For instance, Tatsuo Satō has given a detailed chronology of the Satsumon type pottery in his article (1972), and in relation to that also has discussed the chronological situation of the Okhotsk type pottery as postdating the whole Satsumon succession. However, the stratigraphy of the Motochi site does not support his opinion (Ohyi 1972). His theory is by no means plausible.

group and the Satsumon group seems to have occurred in the latter half of the second stage of the Satsumon culture.

In the uppermost layer of the Motochi site on Rebun Island, which lies directly over the fish-bone layers containing a variation of the Okhotsk type pottery decorated by parallel incised lines — so to speak, belonging to the later stages of the Okhotsk culture in northern Hokkaidō — we have found certain examples of pottery and shards belonging to the second subdivision of the Satsumon type pottery. They have coexisted in the stratum with the kind of Okhotsk type pottery already mentioned in the previous section. The other remains found in the stratum, such as stone implements, bone and antler implements, and faunal remains, have revealed nearly the same culture complex of the group as in the foregoing Okhotsk groups. Furthermore, a pit house belonging to the group in the site has also shown typical Okhotsk traits, such as a large-scale, hexagonal plan, partial clay pavement on the floor, and an accumulation of sea mammal skulls at the end of the clay pavement. The finds in the uppermost layer of the Motochi site, as a whole, would indicate that there were some Satsumon influences on the indigenous Okhotsk group at that time. However, though there were doubtless certain changes, the influence was limited to the type of pottery or, it should be said, was a superficial one. The group represented by the remains of the uppermost layer of the Motochi site seem to have kept their traditional mode of life, as did the Okhotsk group.

The known distribution of the group is actually confined to Rebun Island. In northern Hokkaidō, though some sporadic finds are known, the remains of the group at the sites are usually quite poor. This is in clear contrast to the density of distribution of sites and the richness of remains in the sites belonging to the previous Okhotsk groups in the region. The distribution of the group leads us to believe that, as a result of the arrival of the Satsumon people, the Okhotsk people retired from the region, except for the group in Rebun Island and probably also in Rishiri Island, both some distance off the mainland of Hokkaidō. Then, at the end of the second subdivision of the Satsumon culture or the beginning of the third, these areas, even Rebun and Rishiri Islands, were exclusively occupied by the Satsumon people. In short, the northward expansion of the Satsumon group and the contact between them and the Okhotsk people in the area resulted in the complete retirement of the latter from the region. It may be that the Okhotsk people were driven from northern Hokkaidō to southern Sakhalin during the advance.

Some Satsumon immigrants, then, seem to have turned to the east. We can point out undeniable traces of the Satsumon group along the Okhotsk seacoast at that time, and again, as a matter of course, we can point out another contact between the two — the Satsumon immigrants and the indigenous Okhotsk group — in eastern Hokkaidō. However, the contact had a somewhat different result than in northern Hokkaidō. As a good example illustrating the contact, we can name Pit House I of the Moto-machi site, at the town of Memanbetsu (Oba and Okuda 1960), not far from the Moyoro shell mound. The pit house itself is nearly square in plan and some eight meters in diameter. It is clear that, except for a hearth surrounded by a stone arrangement at the center, the pit house has almost no resemblance to that of the typical Okhotsk group. In the pit house, two complete vessels have been found. One of them clearly is to be classed with the Satsumon type pottery and another has Satsumon-like features and also noodle appliqué designs typical for the Okhotsk type. The finds mentioned above, as a whole, doubtless show the mixed character of the group. Probably the group were the direct heirs of the previous Okhotsk group in the region and were heavily acculturated in the course of contact with the Satsumon immigrants.

A considerable number of the sites classed with the group have been excavated and reported on in the last decade. Actually, the sites of the group are distributed over the whole area in eastern Hokkaidō and probably also in the southern Kurils. The density of the sites and their distribution suggest that the population of the group was not small and therefore the appearance of the group was not a temporal or exceptional occurrence. For the same reasons, it is supposed that occupation by the group here had a certain duration. A fact one cannot overlook is that the distribution of sites of the group is not confined to the coastal areas, but is known also in inland areas far away from the sea (see Figure 1). This doubtless indicates that the group, or a part of it, underwent a some-what fundamental change at that time. For example, Pit House I of the Shimo-tōbetsu site, at the town of Teshikaga (Sawa, et al. 1971b), which is situated in a mountainous region, is clearly to be classed with the group. Thus, it could be thought that dwellers in the pit house sought their economic base in hunting land animals and possibly fishing on rivers instead of their traditional way of life, such as hunting and fishing on the sea. One can understand this as being a result of assimilation of the Okhotsk people into the Satsumon culture.

We can summarize matters as follows. The immigration of the Satsu-mon group into eastern Hokkaidō started at the end of their second stage or the beginning of the third and resulted in the gradual assimilation of the Okhotsk group into the Satsumon culture and the decline of the former in these areas. It is quite probable that, during the advance, a part of the

Okhotsk group were pushed out to the southern Kurils. However, most of the group stayed in the area, coexisting with the Satsumon immigrants. It should be noted that the group were the last Okhotsk people in Hokkaidō because, a little later than that, in the latter half of the third stage of the Satsumon culture, the areas were occupied only by Satsumon people, and the Okhotsk people had vanished from the area. That was the end of the Okhotsk culture in Hokkaidō.

As stated above, the decline of the Okhotsk culture in Hokkaidō, in both the eastern part and northern parts, might be explained in relation to the movements of the Satsumon group. On the other hand, in Sakhalin, where no Satsumon site has been reported thus far,[12] the decline of the Okhotsk culture could have happened under other circumstances or for other reasons. As already mentioned, the group which followed the one represented by Enoura A type pottery was represented by the Minami-kaizuka and the Higashi-taraika types. There is no doubt that these two groups, whether or not some changes occurred in some components in their culture complex, were still in the Okhotsk tradition. Unfortunately, the detailed reports on the sites belonging to the groups have not yet been published, so we cannot directly discuss in detail the Okhotsk culture in Sakhalin at that time. The only thing one can safely conclude is that no Satsumon immigrants passed across the La Perouse Strait, a barrier between Sakhalin and Hokkaidō, and that no other drastic disturbances occurred in Sakhalin at that date. Thus the Okhotsk culture, or at least its derivatives, lasted a little longer in Sakhalin than in Hokkaidō.

In addition to that, the report on faunal remains found in the Higashi-taraika shell mound by Naora has revealed an interesting feature of the group. His report (1938) says that the remains consisted of domestic animals, such as dogs, boars, and reindeer, with only a limited amount of wild game such as sea mammals (Naora 1938). If such remains were usual for the group, it should be said that there was a definite difference in the group's economic base compared with that of the foregoing groups and, as a matter of course, probably also in their whole culture complex. The importance of breeding animals in the group would be partly derived from indigenous development within the group, and, at the same time, partly brought to them as the influence of unknown groups in the north — northern Sakhalin or even the Amur region on the continent. Anyway,

---

[12]   A few Satsumon type potsherds were found in the southernmost part of Sakhalin, but there are no exact sites or layers belonging to this culture. The potsherds mentioned could be interpreted as signs of sporadic contacts between Satsumon and Okhotsk groups across La Perouse Strait.

there is enough probability that this was one of the typical features of the latest Okhotsk group in Sakhalin.

Recent written records, both Japanese and Chinese, have indicated that there were considerable numbers of the Ainu in Sakhalin in the seventeenth century A.D. Archaeologically they are represented by pit houses accompanied with Naiji pottery (the pottery with ears for handles inside, in imitation of the iron pan). Actually, Naiji pottery is the last type of archaeological material in Sakhalin and there are no materials intervening between it and the last Okhotsk groups represented by the Minami-kaizuka and Higashi-taraika types. Of course, there remains a slight possibility that some unknown materials which could indicate an intervening group will be found in a future investigation. But, according to latest results, it is difficult to suppose that there were any other groups of different tradition occurring between the two, the Okhotsk group and the Ainu. In the circumstances, the most plausible hypothesis is that the tradition of the Okhotsk culture, i.e. the groups represented by the Minami-kaizuka and the Higashi-taraika types themselves or their derivatives, lasted a little longer, until a time just before the immigration of the Ainu to Sakhalin. As already discussed in my previous article (1972), the Ainu immigration into Sakhalin, which was prompted by the Japanese expansion to northern and eastern Hokkaidō, can be dated in the sixteenth or even the beginning of the seventeenth century. Therefore, the end of the Okhotsk culture or the extinction of the Okhotsk tradition in Sakhalin should be thought to have occurred at that time.

A similar process also would seem likely in the Kuril Islands. As in Sakhalin, no Satsumon site is reported from the Kurils, and the only archaeological materials later than the Okhotsk group or of the Okhotsk tradition are some pit houses accompanied by Naiji pottery which is attributed to the Ainu. In consequence, we are easily led to the assumption, as for the Okhotsk group in Sakhalin, that in the Kuril Islands there would be some survival of the Okhotsk tradition later than that in Hokkaidō. Not only that, because no other immigration or cultural flows from the north are suggested at that date, the only possible reason for the extinction of the Okhotsk tradition could be the recent immigration of Ainu into the islands. Some Japanese records have shown that the Kuril Islands were the farthest point in all the Ainu territories from Japanese influence. Therefore, while the Ainu were for a time forced to migrate into the area under Japanese pressure, data shows the immigration of the Ainu into the Kuril Islands occurred at a somewhat later date than into Sakhalin. The Ainu probably started their immigration into the Kuril Islands at the beginning of the seventeenth century, and they arrived not only at the northernmost island of the Kurils (Baba 1939) but also at the southernmost part of the Kamchatka peninsula (Jochelson 1928) before the end of the seventeenth century, as suggested by Tatsuo Satō (1967). The Ainu immigration into the Kuril Islands mentioned above resulted in the complete destruction of the Okhotsk tradition in the area. Thus, it could be said that that was the exact end of the long history of the Okhotsk culture which covered the whole southern coast of the Sea of Okhotsk.

## SOME PROBLEMS REGARDING THE OKHOTSK CULTURE: TENTATIVE CONCLUSIONS

As may be seen in the previous discussions, the Okhotsk culture, though it had only a few developmental stages and regional differences, is revealed as a distinct unit clearly different from any other culture or group chronologically and geographically adjacent to it.

One of the important problems regarding the Okhotsk culture, about which there is no general agreement, relates to the ethnic make-up of the Okhotsk culture. In the early period of investigation, Kōno (1935) thought that the bearers of the Okhotsk culture were the ancestors of the so-called Sakhalin Ainu, and there are still some scholars who agree with his view (see Tatsuo Satō 1972). However, it is quite clear that there are almost no unmistakable similarities or undeniable linkages in the material cultures or any other cultural components between the Okhotsk culture and the recent Ainu culture,[13] so it is difficult to agree with Kōno's view without comment. Numerous archaeological materials belonging to the Okhotsk culture as a whole show unique and specific features of a distinct unit. There is, therefore, no doubt that these materials were made, used, and left by a single ethnic group different from the others adjacent to them, such as the bearers of the Satsumon culture or the ancestors of Hokkaidō Ainu.

The findings of physical anthropology should play an important role. As for human skeletal remains, materials found in the Moyoro shell mound (Kodama 1947), in the Omisaki site (Mitsuhashi and Yamaguchi 1961, 1962), in the Funadomari site (S. Itō and Kodama 1963), and in the

---

[13]    Okada (1960) has suggested that a type of harpoon of the recent Ainu culture would have its derivation not in the Satsumon culture but in the Okhotsk culture. However, it seems difficult to look for a parallel in the assemblage of the Okhotsk culture. It is better to seek the derivation among the harpoons of the Satsumon culture. Though little is known about the bone component of the Satsumon culture, some examples are reported from the Aonae shell mound in Okushiri Island off the west coast of Oshima Peninsula in southernmost Hokkaidō (Sakurai 1958).

Omkoromanai shell mound (Oba 1973) have been investigated and reported. These reports, except for the last basically agree in the conclusion that the bearers of the Okhotsk culture had specific common physical features markedly different from those of the Ainu or the ancestors of the Ainu.[14] It can be said that the conclusion shows strong accordance with the archaeological results stated before. In reality it should be said that this is the only definite conclusion on the Okhotsk culture and its bearers on which most scholars, both of physical anthropology and archaeology, agree.

Of course, there still remain some questions, such as to which racial group the bearers of the Okhotsk culture belong, or where they originated. As an answer Kodama (1947) has proposed a hypothesis: that they were a group of the Aleut who migrated by way of the Kuril Islands. However, the archaeological data does not support his hypothesis. That is to say, as already discussed, the so-called Okhotsk group in the northern Kurils should be thought of as a somewhat atypical or hybridized group and, in addition to that, as having a later date in the chronology of the Okhotsk culture. Thus, the hypothesis is by no means plausible. In opposition, if one agrees with the contention that southern Sakhalin is the only cradleland of the Okhotsk culture, as is proposed in the previous section, one should look for the ethnic origin of the culture in and around Sakhalin, probably in the north. Yamaguchi has suggested the possible ethnic relationships between the Okhotsk group and the Orochi in the Amur basin and the Maritime Territory.[15] Consulting the archaeological results which indicate a possible cross-tie between the Amur-Maritime Territory regions and southern Sakhalin, his suggestion seems to be quite interesting and plausible. However, the ethnic origin of the Okhotsk culture is still a difficult question left for future investigation.

Whatever the racial origin of the culture may be, the sites and materials show a close uniformity as being of one and the same culture. Of course, we can point out the unique features or unmistakable linkage throughout the chronology and distribution in every component of the culture, such

[14] Shōichi Itō (1948) has described the hybridization between the Okhotsk and Ainu people in skeletal remains found at the Moyoro shell mound. On the other hand, he also noted that the recent Kitami Ainu and the Sakhalin Ainu have shown somewhat similar features, and that they formed a distinctive group different from Ainu in the other regions. He concluded that this was the result of hybridizations of the Ainu with the Okhotsk peoples (1967). His conclusions coincide fairly well with my understanding of the later archaeological results. In this regard, Oba's identification in noting the similarity of the Onkoromanai shell mound dweller with the Sakhalin Ainu is not surprising.
[15] Oral report on the annual meeting of the Japan Association of Quarternary Research held at the Historical Museum of Hokkaidō on January 1973.

as type of pottery, stone industry, specific assemblage of bone and antler objects, large-sized hexagonal pit houses and so on, and each of them would not come out independently but appear in closest inter-dependence with the others. Nevertheless, as the most distinctive feature of the culture, we might point out the specific maritime adaptation re-presented by the prevailing sea mammal hunting and fishing, because this was the economic base for the bearers of the culture and, accord-ingly, would be more or less undeniably reflected in almost all materials, settlement patterns, social structures, and probably also religious con-cepts. Of course, there are some other elements in the Okhotsk culture, for instance, the breeding of dogs and boars in southern Sakhalin and northern Hokkaidō groups and also the partial land animal hunting seen in the eastern Hokkaidō groups. But these elements would never out-weigh the sea mammal hunting and fishing in their economy. Therefore, it would seem that these were at any rate additional ones for the groups and, in every case, the specific maritime adaptation was the only indisput-able characteristic of the Okhotsk culture throughout its duration and distribution.

Vasilievsky (1969, 1970) has repeatedly emphasized the striking simi-larities between the Ancient Koryak culture and the Okhotsk culture. The circumstance which led him to the hypothesis is first of all that the eco-nomy of the Okhotsk culture has a common base with the Ancient Koryak culture, and the two cultures flourished in the same period, apparently from 500 to 1700 A.D. It is certain that his hypothesis is by no means negligible; indeed it is a quite reasonable one. However, despite the general uniformity of the economic base or the culture complexes of these two cultures, there are some undeniable differences between the two, especially in types of materials, such as pottery, stone implements, bone and antler objects, and so forth. In fact, on detailed comparison of materials in both cultures, at least for the earlier stages of the Okhotsk culture, there seems to be almost an exact counterpart which indicates direct contacts or interrelations between the two.

Nevertheless, Vasilievsky's discussion has gone further. He has pointed out, as examples which show the close analogies with the Ancient Koryak culture, barbed harpoons and a kind of toggle harpoon in the northern Kurils and also two types of toggle harpoons in Sakhalin. Unfortunately, however, as already discussed, these harpoons seem to be not typical but additional components in the peripheral zone of distribution in the later stages of the Okhotsk culture. The same is thought regarding the hearths surrounded by stone arrangements at the center of pit houses found in the sites of eastern Hokkaidō. He has also noted fishhooks, needles, needle cases, shovels, and stone sinkers and lamps as common traits of the two cultures. Except for the latter, which are limited to the Kuril Islands and possibly eastern Hokkaidō too, surely they are the usual remains in the Okhotsk sites. But, it is a question whether or not they undoubtedly indicate contact or intercourse between the two. In short, there is no exact evidence which shows a deeper and undeniable coincidence between the Okhotsk culture and the Ancient Koryak culture.

Vasilievsky (1969) has sought the origin of the Ancient Koryak culture in the tradition of the local Neolithic culture in the upper reaches of the Koryma River, and, at the same time, regarded the group in the Maritime Territory as the accelerator in the crystallization of the maritime economy of the culture. More or less similar processes do occur, on the other hand, in the Okhotsk culture. As has already been discussed in the previous section, the Okhotsk culture crystallized in southern Sakhalin under the influences of groups in the Amur-Maritime Territory region. Thus, it can be said that there is, at least partly, a common derivation of the Ancient Koryak and the Okhotsk cultures in the same region. In spite of a similar process of the crystallization, the Ancient Koryak and Okhotsk cultures show somewhat different traits, especially in their earlier stages, and there is no irrefutable evidence of contact or interrelation between the two. The circumstances as a whole show no evidence of there being common ancestors of the two; in other words, the culture complex of the two derived not only from the groups in the Amur-Maritime Territory regions but also from the local traditions in the areas where they had crystallized.

Thus, we can conclude that the Ancient Koryak culture and the Okhotsk culture started independently on the basis of indigenous traditions in each region under similar influence from the same unknown group in the Amur-Maritime Territory region. Then, the development of the two progressed without any further contact or marked intercourse with each other. The first contact between the two occurred in the northern Kurils in a somewhat later period and resulted in the appearance of the hybrid. Though a few intrusive elements from the Ancient Koryak culture can be seen even in eastern Hokkaidō,[16] they are no more than minor additions to the whole material make-up of the Okhotsk culture.

---

[16]   Other intrusive elements are reported at the Higashi-taraika shell mound in southern Sakhalin (Baba 1940: Figure 16–1, 2, 4). They are two barbed harpoons and a toggle harpoon. They all have U-shaped slits and small round holes at the upper end for fixing metal blades, and they also have elaborately carved decorations on the back. These features suggest the late date of the specimens. Vasilievsky (1969) is looking for remnants of the Ancient Koryak culture; however, because of the long distance between

Through the discussions above, it will be seen that the general homogeneity of the economic base and material culture of the Ancient Koryak
and Okhotsk cultures should not be overlooked. Compared with the
sequences in the Bering region, Aleutian Islands and southwestern Alaska,
the resemblances between the two seem to indicate a closer relationship
than there exists among the cultures in the adjoining areas. With respect
to these problems, Vasilievsky (1970) has denied Eskimo influence on the
development of the Ancient Koryak culture on one hand, and, on the
other hand, he has emphasized close kinship between the Ancient Koryak
culture, the Okhotsk culture, and Paleo-Aleutian culture, especially in
their bone and antler objects. He is sure that there are certain similar
types of bone and antler implements, and also of stone objects, in the
latter group, but the resemblances between them are at any rate partial
ones in the whole material culture. In addition to that, his hypothesis does
not answer the question proposed by Chard (1956); for example, he does
not explain the complete absence of pottery in the Aleutian Islands in
clear contrast to the Okhotsk seacoast. At any rate, the linkages between
the cultures in the Aleutian Islands and on the Okhotsk sea coast, if any,
seem to be by no means comparable to those between the groups around
the Sea of Okhotsk. Thus, we can conclude that the Ancient Koryak and
Okhotsk peoples in the Sea of Okhotsk region, the former in the north
and the latter in the south, were developing a group of cultures different
from the other groups in the North Pacific and on the Arctic coast. The
appearances and developments of these two cultures were almost completely beyond the reach of Eskimo-Aleut influences.

## REFERENCES

BABA, OSAMU
　1939　Kokogaku-jo yori mitaru kita Chishima [The northern Kurils from
　　　　the viewpoint of archaeology]. *Jinruigaku Senshigaku Koza* 10, 11:1–
　　　　154. Tōkyō: Yuzan-kaku.
　1940　Karafuto no kōkogaku-teki gaikan [Archaeological outline of south-
　　　　ern Sakhalin]. *Jinruigaku Senshigaku Koza* 17:1–119. Tōkyō: Yuzan-
　　　　kaku.
BEFU, HARUMI, CHESTER S. CHARD
　1964　A prehistoric maritime culture of the Okhotsk Sea. *American
　　　　Antiquity* 30:1–18.

---

them and the lack of materials in the intervening areas, it is questionable whether or
not they indicate an interrelation of the two cultures. Anyhow, it is certain that
there also were certain cultural influences from some group in the north on the latest
group of the Okhotsk culture in southern Sakhalin.

CHARD, CHESTER S.
1956   Chronology and cultural succession in the northern Kuriles. *American Antiquity* 21:287–292.

CHUBAROVA, R, V.
1960   Neoliticheskie stianki na O. Iturup. *Sovetskaia Arkheologiia* 1960(2): 128–938.

FUJIMOTO, TSUYOSHI
1965   Ohōtsuku-doki ni tsuite [On the Okhotsk pottery]. *Kōkogaku Zasshi* 51(4):28–44.

FUJIMOTO, TSUYOSHI, *et al.*
1972   "Sakaeura daini iseki [The Sakaeura II site]," in *Tokoro.* Edited by the Institute of Archaeology, 265–399. Tokyō: Faculty of Letters, University of Tokyō.

HIRAKŌ, GOICHI
1929   *Chishima oyobi Bentenjima shutsudo doki-hahen ni tsuite* [On the potsherds found in the Kuril Islands and Bentenjima]. *Jinruigaku Zasshi* 44(4, 5, 7):131–143, 192–200, 384–389.

HOKKAIDŌ UNIVERSITY
1963   Koboro dokutsu iseki [The Koboro cave site]. Report of the Research team, Hokkaidō University School of Medicine. *Hoppō Bunka Kenkyū Hokoku* 18:179–285.

HOKUCHI BUNKA KENKYŪ-KAI
1968   Nemuro-shi Bentenjima mishi kaizuka chōsa gaihō [Report on the west shell mound at Bentenjima Island, city of Nemuro]. *Kōkogaku Zasshi* 54(2):49-64.

ITŌ, NOBUO
1943   "Karafuto senshi-jidai doki hennen shiron [Preliminary attempt at the establishment of a chronology of prehistoric pottery in Sakhalin]," in *Kokushi Ronshū.* Edited by Tōhoku Teikoku Daigaku Kokushigakkai, 19–28. Tokyō: Daitō-shokan.

ITŌ, SHŌICHI
1948   Moyoro Kaizuka-jin to Ainu tono konketsu ni tsuite [On the admixture of the Moyoro man and the Ainu]. *Shinrinshō* 3(2):1–6.
1967   Ainu zugai no chihō-teki sai [Local differences on Ainu skulls]. *Hoppō Bunka Kenkyū* 2:191–238.

ITŌ SHŌICHI, GEORGE KODAMA
1963   Hokkaidō Rebun-tō Funadomari-mura iseki ni oite hakkutsu shita jin-tōgai ni tsuite [On the human skulls excavated at the sites in Funadomari village, Rebun Island, Hokkaidō]. *Kaibōgaku Zasshi* 38(1):29.

IZUMI, SEIICHI, TOSHIHIKO SONO, *editors*
1967   *Onkoromanai.* Proceedings of the Department of Humanities, College of General Education, University of Tokyō, volume forty-two. Series on Cultural Anthropology 1, Tokyō: University of Tokyō Press.

JOCHELSON, WALDEMAR
1928   *Archaeological investigations in Kamchatka.* Washington D.C.: Carnegie Institution of Washington.

KANEKO, HIROMASA
1972   "Sakaeura daini iseki no dōbutsu-igai [Faunal remains of the

Sakaeura II site]," in *Tokoro*. Edited by the Institute of Archaeology, 505–535. Tokyō: Faculty of letters, University of Tokyō.

1973  "Onkoromanai Kaizuka no okeru Dōbutsu-igai [Faunal remains from the Onkoromanai shell mound]," in *Onkoromanai Kaizuka*. Edited by T. Oba and H. Ohyi, 187–246. Tokyō: University of Tokyō Press.

KIKUCHI, TOSHIHIKO
1972  Kita Chushima no Ohotsuku-bunka ni kansuru sho-mondai [Problems of the Okhotsk culture in the northern Kurils]. *Hokkaidō Kōkogaku* 8:73–85.

KITAKAMAE, YASUO
1940  Hokkaidō Wakkanai-chō fukin no senshi-jidai iseki chōsa hōkoku [Report on the prehistoric investigations in the town of Wakkanai, Hokkaidō]. *Jōdai Bunka* 17:32–49.

KITAKAMAE, YASUO, HIROSHI SUMI
1953  Hokkaidō Nemuro-hantō Tōsamuporo Ohotsuku iseki chōsa hōkoku [Report on the Okhotsk site at Tosamuporo in Nemuro, Hokkaidō]. *Jōdai Bunka* 24:31–48.

KODAMA, SAKUZAEMON
1947  Moyoro Kaizuka no minzoku ni tsuite [On the population of the Moyoro shell mound]. *Shin-rinshō* 2–3:1–7.

KOMAI, KAZUCHIKA, *editor*
1964  *Ohotsuku-kai engan, Shiretoko-hantō no iseki* [Archaeological sites on the Okhotsk sea coast and the Shiretoko Peninsula in Hokkaidō], volume two. Tokyō: Faculty of Letters, University of Tokyō.

KOMAI, KAZUCHIKA, *et al.*
1964  "Abashiri Moyoro kaizuka [The Moyoro shell mound in Abashiri]," in *Ohotsuku-kai engan, Shiretoko-hantō no iseki* [Archaeological sites on the Okhotsk sea coast and the Shiretoko Peninsula in Hokkaidō], volume two. Edited by K. Komai, 1–96. Tokyō: Faculty of Letters, University of Tokyō.

KŌNO, HIROMICHI
1935  Hokkaidō sekki-jidai gaiyō [An outline of the stone age in Hokkaidō]. *Dorumen* 4(6):114–122.

KOYANAGI, MASAO, KATSUO INABA
1969  Sakae iseki chōsa ryakuhō [Preliminary report of the excavation at Sakae site]. *Moupett* 1:3–15.

KOZYREVA, R. V.
1964  Neoliticheskoe poselenie Starodupskoe II na o. Sakhaline. *Drevniaia Sibiri* 1:49–72.
1967  *Drevnii Sakhalin*. Moscow: Akademiia Nauk SSSR.

MITSUHASHI, KŌHEI, BIN YAMAGUCHI
1961, 1962  Omisaki shutsudo jinkotsu no jinruigaku-teki kenkyū [Anthropological studies on the human remains from Omisaki, Hokkaidō]. *Sapporo Igaku Zasshi* 19:268–276; 21:23–32, 106–114.

NAORA, NOBUO
1938  Hoppō bunka-ken no jūkotsu [On the animal bones in the arctic cultural circle]. *Minzokugaku Kenkyū* 4(4):599–622.
1964  "Tokoro, Utoro, Tobinitai kaku-iseki hakkutsu no shizen-ibutsu

[Natural remains found in the sites of Tokoro, Utoro and Tobinitai]," in *Ohotsuku-kai engan. Shiretoko-hantō no iseki* [Archaeological sites on the Okhotsk sea coast and the Shiretoko Peninsula in Hokkaidō], volume two. Edited by K. Komai, 176–189. Tokyō: Faculty of Letters, University of Tokyō.

NATORI, TAKEMITSU, TOSHIO OBA
1964 "Moyoro Kaizuka shutsudo no bunka-ibutsu [Cultural remains found in the Moyoro shell mound]," in *Ohotsuku-kai engan, Shiretoko-hantō no iseki*. Edited by K. Komai, 42–63. Tokyō: Faculty of Letters, University of Tokyō.

OBA, TOSHIO
1955 Moyoro Kaizuka shutsudo no kokkaki [On the bone implements found in the Moyoro shell mound]. *Hoppō Bunka Kenkyū Hōkoku* 10:173–249.
1956 Moyoro Kaizuka shutsudo no Ohotsuku-shiki doki [On the Okhotsk type pottery found in the Moyoro shell mound]. *Hoppō Bunka Kenkyū Hōkoku* 11:187–256.
1957 Moyoro Kaizuka shutsudo no sekki [On the stone implement found in the Moyoro shell mound]. *Hoppō Bunka Kenkyū Hōkoku* 12:167–221.
1973 "1966nen oyobi 1967nendo chōsa no jinkotsu [Human skulls excavated in the 1966 and 1967 field seasons]," in *Onkoromanai Kaizuka*. Edited by T. Oba and H. Ohyi, 175–186. Tokyō: University of Tokyō Press.

OBA, TOSHIO, HARUO OHYI, *editors*
1973 *Onkoromanai Kaizuka* [The Onkoromanai shell mound] Tokyō: University of Tokyō Press.

OBA, TOSHIO, HIROSHI OKUDA
1960 *Memanbetsu iseki* [The sites in the town of Memanbetsu]. Memanbetsu, Hokkaido: Board of Education.

OBA, TOSHIO, *et al.*
1972 *Esashi-chō Kawajiri-chashi chōsa gaihō* [Preliminary report of the excavation in Kawajiri-chashi, town of Esashi]. Esashi, Hokkaidō: Board of Education.

OHYI, HARUO
1970 Satsumon bunka to Ohotsuku bunka no kankei ni tsuite [Relations between the Satsumon culture and the Okhotsk culture]. *Hoppō Bunka Kenkyū* 4:21–70.
1972 Rebun-tō Motochi iseki no Ohotsuku-shiki doki ni tsuite [On the Okhotsk type pottery found in Motochi site, Rebun Island]. *Hoppō Bunka Kenkyū* 6:1–36.

OKADA, HIROAKI
1960 Ainu bunka-shi ni kansuru ichi-kōsatsu [Some notes on the history of Ainu culture]. *Minzokugaku Kenkyū* 24:361–365.
1967 "Summary and comparison," in *Onkoromanai*. Edited by S. Izumi, and T. Sono, 72–82. Tokyō: University of Tokyō Press.

OKLADNIKOV, A. P.
1963 *Drevnee poselenie na poluostrove Peschanom u Bladivostoka.* (MNA. 112). Moscow: Akademiia Nauk SSSR.

ONUMA, TADAHARU, KATSUYO HONDA
1970   Rausu-chō shutsudo no Ohotsuku-shiki doki ni tsuite [On the Okhotsk type pottery of the sites in the town of Rausu]. *Hokkaidō Kōkogaku* 6:27–38.

SAIGAWAT, KAI
1933   *Hokkaidō genshi bunka shūei* [Corpus of the prehistoric remains in Hokkaidō]. Tokyō: Minzoku-kōgei Kenkyū-kai.

SAITŌ, TADASHI
1933   Chishima Etorofu-tō shutsudo no doki oyobi sekki [Potteries and stone implements found in the sites of Etorofu Islands, Kurils]. *Kōkogaku Zasshi* 23:333–344.

SAKURAI, KIYOHIKO
1958   Hokkaidō Okushiri-tō Aonae kaizuka ni tsuite [On the Aonae shell mound, Okushiri Island, Hokkaidō]. *Kodai* 27:1–8.

SATŌ, TADAO, *et al.*
1964   *Wakkanai, Sōya no iseki* [The prehistoric sites in the city of Wakkanai and the town of Sōya]. Wakkanai, Hokkaidō: Board of Education.

SATŌ, TATSUO
1967   Ryūki kō [On the Ryūki]. *Museum* 197:2–10.
1972   "Satsumon doki no hensen ni tsuite [On the chronological changes of the Satsumon pottery]," in *Tokoro*. Edited by the Institute of Archaeology, 462–488. Tokyō: Faculty of Letters, University of Tokyō.

SAWA, SHIRŌ, *et al.*
1971a   *Rausu.* Rausu, Hokkaidō: Board of Education.
1971b   *Teshikaga-chō Shimo-tōbetsu iseki bakkutsu hōkoku* [Report of the excavation at the Shimo-tōbetsu site in the town of Teshikaga]. Teshikaga, Hokkaidō: Board of Education.

VASILIEVSKY, R. S.
1969   The origin of the ancient Koryak culture on the northern Okhotsk coast. *Arctic Anthropology* 6(1):150–164.
1970   The problem of the North Pacific sea hunters' culture. *Proceedings of the Eighth International Congress of Anthropological and Ethnological Sciences*, 359–361. Tokyō: Science Council of Japan.
1971   *Proiskhozhdenie i drevniaia kul'tura Koriakov.* Novosibirsk: Akademi-ia Nauk SSSR.

YONEMURA, KIOE
1950   *Moyoro Kaizuka shiryō-shū* [The Moyoro shell mound]. Abashiri, Hokkaidō: Abashiri Municipal Museum.
1961   *Kawanishi iseki chōsa hōkoku* [Report of the excavation at the Kawanishi site]. Abashiri, Hokkaidō: Abashiri Municipal Museum.

YOSHIZAKI, MASAKAZU
1963   Prehistoric culture in southern Sakhalin in the light of Japanese research. *Arctic Anthropology* 1(2):131–158.

# Stability and Adaptability in the Evolution of Hunting Tools in Ancient Eskimo Cultures

S. ARUTIUNOV and D. SERGEEV

In this article we discuss the technical complex of the harpoon-hunting tools and related utensils the ancient Eskimos used in their economic activity. An overwhelming majority of these implements were made of walrus ivory and were richly ornamented.

This ornamentation undoubtedly possessed some religious-ritual-magic significance. However, the spiritual expression of any primitive people can never be reduced merely to religious ideas. Such behavior, as a matter of fact, shaped and conceptualized as religious, also serves to fulfill the basic needs of life, both social and emotional. This seems to be true where, especially among the Eskimos, we observe animal images engraved and carved on hunting tools, in the form either of representative sculpture or abstract ornament. It is quite possible that in a charade-like form they relate many important myths and legends.

Interesting from this point of view are the polyiconic images which from a certain angle represent, for instance, a pregnant woman, but from another can be viewed as a female walrus with her child, a walrus turned into a ram, or a wolf into a killer whale. These correspond to a group of myths with a common theme of transformation of a human being into a beast or vice versa, or of the transformation of one beast into another. In the materials from the Uelen and Ekven burial grounds there are many implements such as pendants, towing hooks, and so on, bearing such engraved or carved polyiconic images.

The polyiconic art of the ancient Eskimos somehow prolongs in plastic form the Upper Paleolithic artistic traditions. Parallels can be seen in the similarity of themes (women, animals) and in the styles and techniques of expression that are the most favored. Quite possibly, it is not a mere coincidence but a reflection of more complicated patterns of dependence. There may also be some elements of a genetic succession preserved in the sculptured compositions expressing certain ideas connected with the hunting way of life. In both the Eurasian Paleolithic paintings and sculptures and the Eskimo polyiconic sculpture similar concepts are reflected, born of the primitive hunters' thoughts. Besides these more or less obvious ways of reading the decoration of tools, there may also be other ways which thus far can be only very tentatively identified.

Both Old Bering Sea and Okvik ornamental styles are characterized by a single and sharp movement of the burin with only small punctations or indentations when the burin scratches or picks the bone's surface. During a graphic reproduction of these designs it became obvious that these indentations and punctations follow numerical and rhythmic patterns. It was evident that after frequent reproduction of the ornament the hand movements tend to become automatic and the artist's hand somehow feels this rhythm and forecasts how many points or indentations there must be in the next element of the ornamental composition. Thus, in the process of the work the engraving hand renders a rhythmic dance, kept in the kinetic memory. The ornament makes a record of the movement of the hand.

This implies that the ornament is built not quite voluntarily and arbitrarily but is both consciously and subconsciously subordinated to the kinetically memorized regularities. These, we believe, have guaranteed stability of design in the transfer from person to person, from generation to generation.

If we consider such relatively standardized and mass-produced items as harpoon heads it becomes obvious that though each head is to a certain degree unique and has its peculiar features, nonetheless in their ornamentation the heads can be classified into several types where certain elements of ornament are more or less regularly combined following a predetermined scheme.

This scheme is only partly conventional. It is also partly natural and unavoidable because it results automatically from the rhythmic character of the ornament. Since the form of an object is closely connected with its ornamentation, it means that not only the form of an object predetermines its ornamentation, but the stable ornament type, in turn, favors the stability and traditional succession of the form.

In some burials we have found unusual constructions of harpoon heads, obviously experimental; they were usually represented by only one sample and were rejected in the course of natural selection of the most rational forms. These experimental forms or mutations usually are typified by

either the absence of an ornament or the addition of an unusual ornament, while the common harpoon head types correspond to usual and
stable ornamental motives. Hence, we can see in the ornament still another
important role. It reflects the genotype of the object, its scheme, which
helps the craftsman memorize its construction, makes copying easier,
and safeguards the stability and succession of selected forms.

A formal typology of the large variety of heads enables us to recon-
struct the evolution of these hunting tools. For killing walruses ashore, the
Eskimos used long ivory pikes or lances with inserted small flint blades,
in keeping with a well-known and long-used Mesolithic and Upper Paleolithic tradition of microlithic insertion tools. A flat harpoon head with
side blades is a development of such a lance head, the number of blades
being reduced to two.

The next step in the evolution was placing the blades in the plane
parallel to that of the line hole, which makes the head's penetration into
the animal's body more sure. An occasionally broken basal spur might
have prompted the introduction of heads with an asymmetrical spur and
single line hole — they look almost exactly like a head of the preceding
series with a broken spur — and from here a transition can be marked to
the closed socket forms.

The introduction of the polished end points was probably done on an
analogy with darts; both types of points are nearly identical.

Another line of evolution ascends to the barbed forms of nontoggle
harpoon heads. A combination of the Old Bering Sea side-bladed head
with the principle of barbing produced the Birnirk type of heads (circa
600 A.D.).

It is worth noting that toggle harpoon heads of the northern Pacific are
mostly in use in those places where the sea is often covered by floating ice
but hunting from the boats is still possible. Where there is no floating ice,
e.g. adjacent to the Aleutians or Honshu, or where there are nearly
always large fields of packed ice and hunting is possible only at the
breathing holes, toggle harpoon heads are not so widespread, and either
simple, non-toggle forms or combination Birnirk forms prevail.

The use of the toggle harpoon head in the areas with floating ice or on
large areas of open water is due to the fact that in such places a wounded
animal seeks an escape under ice. In the case of a non-toggle head, its basal
part, with the bound line protruding from the animal's body, may be easily
broken by a sunken part of the ice. A toggle harpoon head with only the line
remaining on the body's surface is clearly preferable under such conditions.

The problem of assigning reasons for the long coexistence of a multi-
tude of various harpoon head forms can be solved by a statistical analysis

of their distribution. A total of 100 harpoon heads were found in our excavations at the Uelen and Ekven burial grounds.

To classify these harpoon heads we employ the same criteria that have been used by Collins in the classification of St. Lawrence finds, but instead of Collins' types, which are largely arbitrary, we prefer to designate the heads by formulas that are completely objective.

In these formulas the first number indicates the number of line holes — either 1 or 2; the following letter, the socket — A for open, B for closed; the next number, the number of lashing slots — 2, 1, or none; the capital letters X or Y indicate the end points — according to Collins' tradition, X when parallel in plane to the line holes and Y when perpendicular; the lower-case letters x and y, respectively, indicate the side blades; the following number 2 indicates their number if two; the letters M or P, respectively, a symmetric or asymmetric spur; the following number, the number of spur prongs when necessary; and paired final numbers, the number of barbs from each side, e.g. (0–1), (1–1), (2–2), etc.

All formulas and consequently the heads themselves are readily classed into four basic groups.

The first group is characterized by two line holes, an open socket, and symmetric spur. This group is typical for the early Old Bering Sea stage; the formula is 2A2–M.

The second group includes the heads with one line hole and closed socket — 1–BM. These heads are present at all known stages from Old Bering Sea to Modern, but they become a leading form only as late as Punuk.

The third group (rather intermediary between the first and the second) includes the heads with one line hole, open socket, and asymmetric spur — 1A–P. It is also present at all stages.

The fourth group, an offspring of the third one, is that of barbed Birnirk heads, 1A–P(0–1). Thus, we suppose the evolution line as beginning from the 2A2y2M, soon becoming 2A2x2M, and later also 2A2XM. Hence further 1A–P with all variations, including the Birnirk ramification of 1A–P(0–1), and at the end of the typological line (though present already at the Old Bering Sea stage) 1B–M.

The Ekven burial ground from which the majority of the analyzed harpoon heads comes, includes burials of all these cultures and stages. The finds in Ekven are very similar to the finds in the Uelen burial ground, where several cultures and stages are also represented. This is not surprising, because both Uelen and Ekven existed together as settlements for millennia, and the distance between them is no more than twenty-five kilometers by land or forty kilometers by sea.

But even though they were close together they show certain differences. The qualitative differences in the inventory are rare but more important are the quantitative ones. For instance, if we compare the correlation between the heads of the X and Y group, we can see that while in Uelen burials the X types prevail, in Ekven, on the contrary, the Y forms are more numerous.

The heads 1A1XP and 1A1YP are numerous both in Uelen (twenty-five pieces) and in Ekven (forty-two pieces) sites. There is usually one (seldom two) in a burial, combined with numerous heads of other types, chiefly 2A2–M and 1B–M series. In Ekven the type 1A2yP (forty-five pieces) is numerous, but in Uelen there are only a few occasional finds of this and related types, while in Ekven we find two or three, maybe even six heads in a burial also combined with other types.

The fourth group, a very small one, comprises the barbed heads of the Birnirk type of 1A — P(0–1) series. They are found with nonbarbed forms of 1A–P series but never with 2A–2M series.

All these facts of frequency, distribution, and compatibility of various types enable us to propose some hypotheses.

As to the correlation between x and y and especially between 2A2x2M and 2A2y2M, we have already mentioned that 2A2x2M possesses certain advantages, e.g. provides a surer penetration into the body. But the type 2A2y2M also has advantages of its own. Being broad and flat, knife-like, this head, even with a smaller effort of piercing, provides a sufficient attachment. This advantage was important for the inhabitants of ancient Ekven, where 2A2y2M are much more numerous than in Uelen. Uelen is situated on the northern shore of the peninsula; Ekven lies on the southern shore. Consequently, the ice and water surrounding the two differ. Large areas of ice-free, open water prevail around Ekven while Uelen is often surrounded by ice packs. Therefore, in Uelen there is greater need for heavier, so-called winter harpoons to which the 2A2x2 type head is better suited. As a whole, socket pieces in Uelen are more massive and heavier. In Ekven light socket pieces prevail, suited for lighter, so-called summer harpoons, which are thrown from a further distance.

With less throwing effort the broad knife-like head of the 2A2y2 series was preferable. Thus, even slight microclimatical nuances can explain a very strong contrast in the proportion of x and y series in two sites almost identical in other respects.

The coexistence in almost every burial of heads of different series finds its explanation when we notice that they were designed for hunting different animals. 1BYM heads, very suitable for hunting the thick-skinned walrus, are found in most burials, usually several pieces in each, which corresponds well to the leading role of walrus hunting in the Eskimo economy. Long and narrow heads of 1A2XP series usually are found with them but mostly only one per burial. They are designed for thin-skinned animals, like the beluga (white whale). They were of secondary importance and therefore not so many heads were needed.

The 1A2y2P series are found in Ekven very often, frequently several pieces per burial. They are small and obviously designed for hunting small seals. This animal was of importance secondary only to that of the walrus because before the spread of reindeer breeding, seal skins were the main material for clothing. The abundance of seal hunting heads in the Ekven burial can thus be easily explained. But it may seem strange that in the Uelen burials these forms are practically absent. The solution of this controversy lies again in the microclimate. In Uelen the ice packs stay much longer than in Ekven. On the other hand, there is a large lagoon abounding in seals. These conditions favor catching seals with nets instead of harpoon hunting, which was much in practice in Uelen before the mass introduction of rifles.

In Ekven, on the contrary, lagoons are too small for seals, and the ice-free period is longer; this handicaps the net-catch and favors harpoon hunting of seals, either from the ice-edge or from kayaks.

Especially interesting are unique types of which only one sample each has been found. They are 2A2xM3(1–0), 1A2M(1–1) and 2AXM2. The first two of these are found in the same burial (N42). Occasional finds, alongside the stable traditional types, of some singularly unusual heads can evidence constant operation of constructive thinking and the presence in ancient times of active experimenters seeking for new, more effective ways to make hunting tools.

In the Ekven shore there is also present a small series 2A2XP, which in Uelen is absent. From the point of view of construction they represent a synthesis between 2A2–M and 1A2–P and probably originated as an attempt to reinforce the latter series by a return to the double line hole. All these heads are large; they are found in nine burials, one piece in each. Judging from their size they were designed for whaling, and represent a search for a constructive form which would combine a deep penetration into the body and a complete turn of the head. The double line hole provided a supplementary result because in this case the loop kept the wound from closing and provoked more bleeding.

But these advantages were achieved at the cost of some disadvantages. The open socket was not as safe as the closed one, and the narrow cross-piece between two line holes could be easily broken by tension on the line. Therefore, all these whaling heads failed in the competition with the simultaneously evolving form 1B–M, which later became the only form of the harpoon head for all purposes.

To summarize, we can say that the mechanism of combining stability with adaptability, the adjustment and evolution of material culture, in some respects is similar to the genetic background of stability and evolution of a species. It is a complex of obligatory features, a kind of genotype of the objects and genofund of their class. It allows mutations, which can be preserved or rejected by natural selection. A well-balanced polymorphism of typological variations provides a great adaptability in their statistical correlations, through which an adjustment is achieved to the nuances of the ecological environment. On the contrary, a high specialization of a culture results in the loss of this polymorphism. The specialized culture is much more homogeneous. On the one hand this provides a higher productivity, but on the other hand it is dangerous for the survival of the culture if the environment changes considerably.

# Coastal Adaptation and Cultural Change in Alaskan Eskimo Prehistory

DON E. DUMOND

This paper is concerned with aspects of the prehistory of Alaskan Eskimos, which is taken here to begin with the earliest manifestation of the so-called Arctic Small Tool tradition, and to end with historic contact. The suggestion that sometime during this period there occurred a change toward the increased use of coastal resources has taken a number of different forms (e.g. Birket-Smith 1959: 199, with references). This paper will reiterate one version of that suggestion, and will briefly sketch the nature of some evidence for it; it will then attempt to set out both some dimensions along which certain related cultural changes occurred, and some apparent historical effects of those changes.

## INDICATIONS OF CHANGE

Archaeological evidence will be discussed as three major sequential traditions, termed here ARCTIC SMALL TOOL, NORTON, and THULE. These are represented over most of coastal Alaska, and the first and last are represented in arctic Canada and Greenland as well.

The Arctic Small Tool tradition has been defined (Irving 1962: 56) so as to include relatively early manifestations characterized by small bipointed end- and sideblades, microblades, retouched burins, and some other tools, to which is here added the definitional requirement that pottery be absent. In spite of the fact that collections commonly assigned to the Arctic Small Tool tradition are known widely through the Arctic north of the Alaska Peninsula, most of the sites in Alaska are apparently remains of temporary campsites, undistinguished by constructed habitations. Such is the case with the coastal sites at Cape Denbigh and at Cape

Krusenstern, as well as with most of the interior sites in the central Brooks Range. The remains of more substantial habitations, interpreted as relatively permanent dwellings, are now known in Alaska only from three locations — Onion Portage on the Kobuk River, Itivlik Lake near Howard Pass in the upper Noatak drainage, and Brooks River in the Naknek drainage. These locations lie between 40 and more than 150 miles from the coast, and the people represented in them have therefore been interpreted as being briefly seasonal sea mammal hunters, apparently relying most heavily upon caribou and, in many places at least, upon river fish (Dumond 1969a: with additional references; cf. Giddings 1964: 242). The organization of settlements would then have included some relatively permanent dwellings in interior locations suitable for land mammal hunting and possibly fishing, and temporary seasonal camps both in interior hunting and fishing locations, and in coastal sea mammal hunting locations.

Representatives of the tradition date from no earlier than 3000 B.C. in the Bering Strait region, appear on the Alaska Peninsula after about 1900 B.C., and in Canada and Greenland by 2000 B.C. In Alaska the tradition ends everywhere no later than 1000 B.C., and possibly earlier in some places.

The Norton tradition, as the term is used here, subsumes all manifestations of the material culture type first reported as Norton culture (Giddings 1964), and characterized by stone implements constructed primarily by chipping, the use of some at least rudimentarily ground slate, of oil lamps, and of a broad class of pottery commonly but not exclusively check-stamped and fiber-tempered (Dumond 1969b). Unlike their predecessors of the Arctic Small Tool tradition, the Norton people apparently did not occupy the central Brooks Range, even though their easternmost extension was as far east as the Firth River in extreme northwestern Canada (MacNeish 1959), where, it may be presumed, they arrived by transit along the coastline. Their constructed houses are known to be relatively abundant at locations on the Alaskan coast — Point Hope (Larsen and Rainey 1948), Wales (Giddings 1967), Cape Nome (Bockstoce and Rainey 1972), Cape Denbigh (Giddings 1964), Unalakleet (Lutz 1972), Nunivak Island (Nowak 1970, and personal communication), the Platinum vicinity (Ackerman 1964; Larsen 1950; Ross 1971), probably along the lower course of the Naknek River (Dumond 1971), and perhaps near Barrow (Stanford 1969). Additional temporary campsites also occur at locations along the coast (e.g. Giddings 1967: 197), as well as along some fishing streams in the interior (Dumond 1971, 1972b). The system of settlement, then, involves permanent habitations at or near the sea coast with temporary campsites both on the coast and at interior hunting and fishing stations. The Eskimo use of oil lamps, presumably burning sea mammal oil, begins in this period. At Point Hope whaling harpoons are known in deposits of Norton-related Near Ipiutak material, and in the few additional locations where organic artifacts have survived, smaller harpoons are common. That is to say, the location of the settlements, and the presence of abundant sea mammal hunting gear — whaling harpoons in particular — suggest the development of techniques for taking large sea mammals in open water.

Materials assigned to this tradition are first evident in the early Choris remains of around 700 B.C. (Giddings 1957), then as Norton culture proper by the middle of the first millennium B.C. They were spread through the area of their distribution by 200 B.C. North of Bering Strait the tradition may be definitionally stretched to include in its later aspects the somewhat intrusive but related Ipiutak variant (without ceramics and lamps), which lasted to the middle of the first millennium A.D. South of Bering Strait the tradition ends at the close of the first millennium A.D., after Norton culture has undergone a remarkably steady evolution over the course of more than a thousand years.

Given the differences in settlement distribution between them, it may be concluded that the transition from the Arctic Small Tool tradition to the Norton tradition involved a transition from an orientation toward the tundra strip adjacent to the Arctic coast to one directed more toward the resources of the coast itself. This notion has been developed at some length by more than one investigator (compare Dumond 1969a, 1972b; Giddings 1967), and appears to be defensible in spite of the unfortunate lack of adequate samples of food refuse from sites of either the Arctic Small Tool or of the Norton occupations.

The succeeding Thule tradition — in which are included all manifestations of the midden-depositing, polished-slate-using, lampburning, kayak- and umiak-paddling Eskimos of later times — evidences considerable variety in subsistence, and the patterns of settlement reflect that variety. Some people depended almost entirely upon sea mammals; a few of these, strategically located for the purpose, exploited whales as a major resource. Many more people maintained a balanced reliance upon sea resources and land resources. All of these people lived in substantial coastal villages, many of them making use also of dispersed seasonal camps, both interior and coastal, often characterized by a lack of permanent habitations. Other groups penetrated major watercourses, becoming residents of permanent river villages rather than of coastal ones, even though many of them periodically journeyed to the sea to hunt. Heavy use of sea mammals at all seasons characterized coastal dwellers; and although some people came to rely almost entirely upon river products — especially migrating fish — and others almost entirely upon land mammals — particularly caribou — all of them continued to make heavy use of sea mammal oil, obtained either by seasonal hunting trips or by trade.

This tradition appeared shortly after the beginning of the Christian era at Bering Strait (Okvik-Old Bering Sea); by shortly after the middle of the first millennium A.D. north of Bering Strait (Birnirk); by shortly before the end of the first millennium A.D. south of Bering Strait (Nukleet). It ends everywhere with the beginning of the period of European domination.

The transition that is of special interest here is that between the Arctic Small Tool and the Norton traditions, when there occurred the major shift in settlement pattern and apparently in resource use. The cause of the change is uncertain. It has been suggested that the general lowering of temperature during the first millennium B.C. forced a greater reliance upon ocean products (Dikov 1965), but evidence is poor. Whatever the initial cause, the position taken here is that the increased use of resources of the open sea coast by people of the Norton culture led to the florescence of techniques of sea hunting that in the vicinity of the Bering Strait brought about the development of the spectacular Old Bering Sea culture, and culminated in the later Thule tradition cultures of Alaska (cf. Larsen 1968).

## THE ORIGINS OF NORTON CULTURE

In considering the beginnings of the culture that was characteristic of the Norton tradition, several points must be considered.

a.   Important elements of Norton culture are Asian in derivation. These include especially the pottery, which seems clearly to owe its origin to somewhat earlier Asian manifestations (Griffin 1970).

b.   Important elements of Norton culture are apparently derived from the earlier Arctic Small Tool tradition. These include a portion of the stone technology — in which there are obvious typological continuities in polished adzes, bipointed projectile blades, and polished burin-like implements — as well as a certain house form (Dumond 1971).

c.   Important elements of Norton culture are apparently derived from the Pacific coastal area south of the Alaska Peninsula. These include the increased reliance upon polished slate and the use of oil lamps — both of which were characteristic of that area's Takli Birch phase and its related manifestations of 1500 B.C. and earlier (D. Clark 1966; G. Clark 1968;

Dumond 1971). Furthermore, hunting in open water, probably including some whaling, was already firmly established on the Pacific coast long before the Norton period brought the increased northern Eskimo use of the coastline (Dumond 1969a). It is possible that some southern elements might have been derived not from the New World but from southern areas in Asia, but it seems more economical, in view of the obvious Eskimo bias toward life in America, to hypothesize that all were derived from the neighborhood of the Pacific coast of the Alaska Peninsula, even though the specific avenue of transmission remains obscure for now (cf. Dumond 1968).

d.   In spite of these three indications of continuities of certain kinds, the direct antecedents of Norton culture are not known. The time following the disappearance of the Arctic Small Tool tradition is marked everywhere by a hiatus. North of Bering Strait, people of the Choris variant of Norton culture appeared on the coastline after this occupational gap (Giddings 1967: 275) and shortly before the advent of people of Norton culture proper, to whom they bequeathed the earliest form of Alaskan pottery. South of Bering Strait, where no Choris variant has been identified, people of recognizable Norton culture type followed directly after the period without known occupation (cf. Giddings 1964).[1]

Although it has not been identified south of Bering Strait, of importance to understanding the origins of the Norton culture type is the so-called Choris culture, which has been identified by a respectably large sample only on the Choris Peninsula, but is also believed on the basis of much smaller samples to be represented at Cape Krusenstern (Giddings 1957, 1967). According to the view here, it is an early aspect of Norton culture, of relatively restricted regional occurrence; it has an industry in which stone implements were made predominantly by chipping, together with some rudimentary use of polished or scratched slate, with oil lamps, and with pottery that is typologically indistinguishable from that of some Norton finds. Choris also represents one of the few deposits before the beginning of the Christian era that has yielded significant evidence of food habits in the form of surviving bone trash. More than half of the bone remains were from caribou, most of the remainder from sea mammals

[1]   The construction favored here includes the provision that people of Norton culture were descended rather directly from people of the Arctic Small Tool tradition, with certain outside influences as indicated above. It is possible that this is a misapprehension, for more than one sort of beginning for Norton culture can be hypothesized from the present evidence. In all such models, however, the transition from the Arctic Small Tool tradition to the Norton tradition is taken to involve some flow of ideas from the Pacific coast of Alaska. Intricacies of variant construction within this limit are not germane to this paper (cf. Dumond 1972c).

(Giddings 1967: 213). These, together with the permanent coastal houses of the Choris Peninsula, suggest that the transition to coastal resources must have been under way by 700 B.C., although substantial reliance was still placed upon caribou.

## DIMENSIONS OF CHANGE

But the change of interest to this paper is not only that of the use of resources. Rather, changes that were presumably related to one another in some systematic fashion occurred in what may for heuristic purposes be conceived of as four dimensions. These will be indicated briefly.

### Subsistence

This, of course, has been discussed, and is in effect the diagnostic attribute for the phenomena under consideration. Its listing here indicates that there is no necessary reason to feel that it is any more PRIMARY, in a causal sense, than the other dimensions distinguished. This idea has been previously outlined (Dumond 1972a), and will be reiterated briefly below.

### Technology

One of the major difficulties in dealing with the lengthy Arctic Small Tool period is the apparent stability of material culture. Thus, in the Naknek drainage in southwestern Alaska the initial analysis suggested that the 800 to 1000 years of Small Tool occupation could be divided into two cultural phases on the basis of technological change (Dumond 1963). But further research with a much larger sample indicates that the original distinction was based upon sampling error, and suggests that technological change during the time was in fact negligible. At Cape Krusenstern, where Giddings (1967) worked out a careful sequence based upon a progression of ocean-beach ridges, he discerned two stages of technological development within the period, and the same two may be represented at Onion Portage, although neither sequence has yet been published in sufficient detail to substantiate this. From no other area is there enough evidence to bear on the question.

Such stability does not characterize the later periods, for with the appearance of Norton culture there began a continuing evolution in tool forms. These changes have been hypothesized to involve a net increase in the amount of labor expended in subsistence tasks (Dumond 1972b), and they led through time to the bewildering variety of gadgets that characterize recent Eskimo material culture. New power resources were also devised, so that evidence of dog traction is plentiful by late Thule times. As is the case with the introduction of domestic animals in agriculture (e.g. Boserup 1965: 35ff.), one may expect that the addition to the household of animals (here, meat-eating dogs) would have increased the total human labor requirements for subsistence. Coupled with technological evolution were also certain social reorganizations for subsistence purposes — for example, the organization of whaling crews, an occurrence that must have followed upon the use of umiaks and toggling harpoons in the taking of whales. A similar crew organization was later transplanted for use in caribou hunting in the Brooks Range (Spencer 1959). All of these changes are obviously correlated with the shift in subsistence, although it is not possible to say that they either clearly preceded or clearly followed it.

## Settlement Stability

As a rule, Alaskan Eskimos have been transhumant. But it appears that with the beginnings of coastal villages in the Norton period their home bases became more permanent than they had been earlier. In later times much of the travel was by boat or dog sled, both of which permitted the transportation of a large kit over considerable distances. It seems likely then that the technological developments mentioned above relate not only to increasing use of open sea resources, but also to increased sedentism and the aggregation of population into larger and larger settlements, as it became possible for a group to control a larger hunting territory from a single center. In some cases the later transhumance involved movements from a home base not to temporary hunting camps, but to permanently established camps with privately-owned, permanent dwellings, the title to some of which might even be transmitted by inheritance (Lantis 1946; Oswalt 1963: 82).

## Population Size

The evidence for fluctuations in prehistoric Eskimo population size has been considered at some length elsewhere (Dumond 1972b). In brief, it was concluded that there is no evidence for significant change in population density during the Arctic Small Tool period, but that beginning with the Norton horizon and continuing steadily throughout the succeeding Thule period, there is evidence of increasing settlement density in coastal regions and elsewhere, and evidence of population movements into the interior that may be interpreted as expansion by a growing population into areas requiring specialization in subsistence practices ever greater than that of the more usual and more generalized Eskimo economy based upon a balance of use of both sea and land products.

*Conclusions*

From the data of Eskimo prehistory, changes along the four dimensions sketched here cannot be inferred to begin during the time of the Arctic Small Tool tradition, but can be thought to be initiated with the beginning of the succeeding Norton tradition, and to be visible throughout the rest of Eskimo prehistory. It is tempting to view the dimensions as functionally interrelated in some essential and more general way. For example, and to begin the heuristic circle of interconnected changes at random, it is possible to conceive that an increase in sedentation should be accompanied almost automatically by population expansion, which would necessitate changes in technology for intensified use of resources, which in turn should serve to increase the degree of sedentism.[2]

If this truly is the general case, then one should always find changes in those dimensions linked to one another. That is, evidence of change toward the intensified use of maritime resources should always be accompanied by evidence of changes in the other dimensions; a heavy use of maritime resources should be accompanied by a sedentary, relatively dense, and perhaps expanding population. Whether this is the case in Eskimo Alaska and nearby areas will be taken up in the succeeding sections.

## RESULTS OF CHANGE: POPULATION MOVEMENTS

Two cases of expansion by the prehistoric northern population have been suggested to have their cause in circumstances an important component of which was a strong dependence upon open-water sea mammal hunting.

---

[2] This circular chain of cause-effect relationships can easily be described in terms familiar to the general systems theorist (Dumond 1972a).

## Thule Migration

McGhee (1970) has argued persuasively that the movements of sea mammal hunting Thule people across the Arctic in the tenth century A.D. occurred in response to a change in climate that altered the polar pack ice and thereby the migration patterns of sea mammals, particularly whales, and expanded geographically the niche occupied by coastal people. A result was the disappearance of Dorset culture in the eastern Arctic, and so one must conclude that at that time the Thule lifeway conveyed a definite selective advantage to those people practicing it. Inasmuch as there seems no reason to think that the Dorset folk were as well attuned to the use of open sea resources as were their Thule successors, one or more of the correlates of maritime subsistence given above can be suspected of being instrumental in conveying this advantage. We may expect, at least, that the Thule people were more populous and better organized.[3]

## Eskimos to the Pacific

It has also been argued (Dumond 1969a) that the increase in communication across the Alaska Peninsula that is evidenced at about the same time as the Thule migration was owed to a similar situation; that is, Bering Sea people with a developing interest in the open sea coast and its food resources moved across the Aleutian Range and onto the North Pacific. The first archaeological evidence of this can be seen on the Pacific coast of the Alaska Peninsula shortly after the beginning of the Christian era, apparently reaching a climax around and after A.D. 1000 (Dumond 1971). Additional evidence for such a movement exists in the distribution of Eskimo speech (Dumond 1965, 1971); in the distribution of certain ethnographic characteristics, particularly in the area of ceremonialism (Lantis 1947); and in the nature of archaeological assemblages from Kodiak Island (D. Clark 1968). Recently, confirmatory evidence has also been recovered near the tip of the Alaska Peninsula, where for the first time a Bering Sea Eskimo-like assemblage, complete with pottery and polished slate, has been found to occur after A.D. 1000 (McCartney 1972).

---

[3] The same conditions may not have been effective in relation to the much earlier spread over much the same route by the Arctic Small Tool people. Evidence is less than clear in much of the area, but at least a portion of the area exploited by them in northern Greenland was made attractive by the availability not of sea mammals, but of musk oxen (Knuth 1966–1967).

None of the evidence indicates that there was achieved on the Pacific coast a total population replacement or complete cultural absorption, as seems to have been the fate of the Dorset people. Nevertheless, it seems clear that the northern influence was strong and in some cases dominant, so that the intrusive lifeway must here, too, have conveyed at least some advantage.

## LIMITS OF EXPLANATION

From some of the foregoing one might conclude that the historical effect of adaptation to the seacoast is easily discernible, offering a relatively complete explanation of the broad population readjustments referred to above. It is probably the case with the Thule migration toward Greenland, but reflection suggests that it is not the whole case with respect to the movement to the Pacific.

Evidence now suggests that an orientation toward coastal resources existed in the Aleutian Islands as early as about 6000 B.C., represented by the assemblage from Anangula (Aigner 1970). Certainly the earliest well-sampled and unmistakable Aleut remains, from Chaluka (Aigner 1966; Denniston 1966) early in the second millennium B.C., are those of people with a clear dependence upon the sea coast (Lippold 1966). It therefore seems evident that the Aleut adaptation to the open sea coast predates that of the northern Alaskan Eskimos by at least two, and perhaps as many as six, millennia.

It seems equally clear that the earliest people yet known from the Pacific coast of the Alaska Peninsula and from Kodiak Island were also oriented most strongly toward the sea. The earliest cultural manifestation from the Kodiak Island group, of the fourth millennium B.C., includes an apparent oil lamp (D. Clark 1966). For the period between 4000 and 1000 B.C., in abundant faunal remains from the major site on Takli Island just off the coast of the Alaska Peninsula (G. Clark 1968: Appendix 6), minimum individuals of sea mammals represented outnumber minimum individuals of all land mammals in a ratio of eight to one. But the same ratio of sea mammals to land mammals from the same coast during the period between A.D. 500 and A.D. 1500 — the time of strongest influence from the Bering Sea region, represented by the site at Kukak Bay (Dumond 1971, and unpublished data) — is only about eight to five. Because of imperfect control of seasonal settlement variation, and uncompleted analysis of data at hand, it would be premature to conclude that people of the earlier period in fact depended MORE heavily upon sea mammals than did their successors, but certainly one cannot conclude that they depended upon them any LESS.

What this amounts to, then, is that one can explain a movement of northern Alaskan Eskimos toward Greenland in the tenth century on the basis of subsistence techniques and climatic change; and one can probably explain their impact on the more land-loving Dorset settlers as being the result of their greater population density and superior organization, both concomitants of their use of sea resources. One can also explain the interest of the Bering Sea Eskimos in the Pacific coast by the attraction of open-water hunting, but one can in no sense account in any similarly simple way for the apparent impact of the northerners upon the people already resident on the Pacific coast at the time of the intrusion, for these Pacific coastal people had at least an equal, if not a more complete, reliance upon ocean resources than had the people of Bering Sea.

Does this imply that even though long adapted to maritime life the earlier inhabitants of the Pacific coast were not so populous nor so densely settled as people of the Bering Sea? Does it mean that the Pacific people (who, for instance, did not practice whaling by umiak crew with toggling harpoon) were less well organized than the northern intruders? Or does it merely mean that resource use and related phenomena have nothing to do with it?

It is impossible to answer these questions at this time, in large part because of a lack of data from the Pacific coast. But it must follow that the characteristics of Thule culture that apparently evolved with the shift to open-sea resources during Norton times, and that are here presumed to have conveyed some selective advantage over the lifeways of their neighbors, nevertheless cannot be said to be AUTOMATIC correlates of coastal subsistence.


## SUMMARY AND CONCLUSION

The following points have been presented.

a.   There was a significant shift in subsistence interest in coastal Alaska north of the Alaska Peninsula beginning in the first millennium B.C., when attention was devoted more strongly to coastal resources.

b.   Apparently correlated with this shift were developments toward increased stability of settlement, increased population, and diversified technology.

c.   These related changes may be taken to account for certain population movements apparently climaxing around the end of the first millennium

A.D. with the Thule migration and with a movement of northerners to the Pacific coast. They also may well provide an adequate explanation for the complete displacement of Dorset culture.

d. Whatever advantage their particular evolution upon a coastal subsistence pattern may have given the northern people so that they could leave such an unmistakable mark on the population already present on the Pacific coast, this advantageous development cannot have been an automatic correlate of coastal subsistence, for the earlier Pacific people possessed an orientation toward the sea at least as strong as that of the expanding northerners.

## REFERENCES

ACKERMAN, ROBERT E.
  1964  Prehistory in the Kuskokwim-Bristol Bay region, southwestern Alaska. Washington State University Laboratory of Anthropology, Report of Investigations, 26.
AIGNER, JEAN S.
  1966  Bone tools and decorative motifs from Chaluka, Umnak Island. Arctic Anthropology 3(2):57–83.
  1970  The unifacial, core and blade site on Anangula Island, Aleutians. Arctic Anthropology 7(2):59–88.
BIRKET-SMITH, KAJ
  1959  The Eskimos. London: Methuen.
BOCKSTOCE, JOHN R., FROELICH G. RAINEY
  1972  "The archaeology of Cape Nome." Unpublished report on excavations carried out under Antiquities Act Permit by the University Museum, University of Pennsylvania.
BOSERUP, ESTHER
  1965  The conditions of agricultural growth. Chicago: Aldine.
CLARK, DONALD W.
  1966  Perspectives in the prehistory of Kodiak Island, Alaska. American Antiquity 31:358–371.
  1968  "Koniag prehistory." Ph.D. thesis, University of Wisconsin. University Microfilms 68–17, 886.
CLARK, GERALD H.
  1968  "Archaeology of the Takli site, Katmai National Monument, Alaska." M. A. thesis, University of Oregon. University Microfilms M–1439.
DENNISTON, GLENDA B.
  1966  Cultural change at Chaluka, Umnak Island: stone artifacts and features. Arctic Anthropology 3(2):84–126.
DIKOV, N. N.
  1965  The stone age of Kamchatka and the Chukchi Peninsula in the light of new archaeological data. Arctic Anthropology 3(1):10–24.

DUMOND, D. E.
  1963   Two early phases from the Naknek drainage. *Arctic Anthropology* 1
         (2):93–104.
  1965   On Eskaleutian linguistics, archaeology, and prehistory. *American
         Anthropologist* 67:1231–1257.
  1968   On the presumed spread of slate grinding in Alaska. *Arctic Anthro-
         pology* 5(1):82–91.
  1969a  Prehistoric cultural contacts in Southwestern Alaska. *Science* 166:
         1108–1115.
  1969b  The prehistoric pottery of Southwestern Alaska. *Anthropological
         Papers of the University of Alaska* 14(2):18–42.
  1971   *A summary of archaeology in the Katmai region, Southwestern Alaska.*
         University of Oregon Anthropological Papers 2.
  1972a  "Population growth and political centralization," in *Population growth:
         anthropological implications.* Edited by Brian Spooner. Cambridge:
         M.I.T. Press.
  1972b  "Prehistoric population growth and subsistence change in Eskimo
         Alaska," in *Population growth: anthropological implications.* Edited by
         Brian Spooner. Cambridge: M.I.T. Press.
  1972c  "The Alaska Peninsula in Alaskan prehistory," in *For the chief: essays
         in honor of L. S. Cressman.* Edited by F. W. Voget and R. S. Stevenson.
         University of Oregon Anthropological Papers 4.

GIDDINGS, JAMES L., JR.
  1957   Round houses in the western Arctic. *American Antiquity* 23:121–135.
  1964   *The archaeology of Cape Denbigh.* Providence, Rhode Island: Brown
         University Press.
  1967   *Ancient men of the Arctic.* New York: Alfred A. Knopf.

GRIFFIN, JAMES B.
  1970   "Northeast Asian and northwestern American ceramics." *Proceedings
         of the Eighth International Congress of Anthropological and Ethnological
         Sciences, 1968,* 3:327–330. Tokyo: Science Council of Japan.

IRVING, WILLIAM N.
  1962   "A provisional comparison of some Alaskan and Asian stone in-
         dustries," in *Prehistoric cultural relations between the Arctic and
         temperate zones of North America.* Edited by John M. Campbell.
         Arctic Institute of North America, Technical Paper 11.

KNUTH, EIGIL
  1966–1967   The ruins of the musk-ox way. *Folk* 8–9:191–219.

LANTIS, MARGARET
  1946   The social culture of the Nunivak Eskimo. *Transactions of the American
         Philosophical Society* (n.s.), 35, part 3.
  1947   *Alaskan Eskimo ceremonialism.* American Ethnological Society Mo-
         nograph 11

LARSEN, HELGE
  1950   Archaeological investigations in Southwestern Alaska. *American
         Antiquity* 15:177–186.
  1968   Near Ipiutak and Uwelen-Okvik. *Folk* 10:81–90.

LARSEN, HELGE, FROELICH RAINEY
 1948   Ipiutak and the arctic whale hunting culture. *Anthropological Papers of the American Museum of Natural History*, 42.
LIPPOLD, LOIS K.
 1966   Chaluka: the economic base. *Arctic Anthropology* 3(2):125–131.
LUTZ, BRUCE J.
 1972   "A methodology for determining regional intracultural variation within the Norton, an Alaskan culture." Unpublished Ph.D. thesis, University of Pennsylvania.
MAC NEISH, RICHARD S.
 1959   Men out of Asia: as seen from the Northwest Yukon. *Anthropological Papers of the University of Alaska* 4:91–111.
MC CARTNEY, A. P.
 1972   "Prehistoric cultural integration along the Alaska Peninsula." Paper read at the 37th Annual Meeting of the Society for American Archaeology, Miami, Florida, May 4–6.
MC GHEE, R. J.
 1970   Speculations on climatic change and Thule culture development. *Folk* 11–12:173–184.
NOWAK, MICHAEL
 1970   A preliminary report on the archaeology of Nunivak Island, Alaska. *Anthropological Papers of the University of Alaska* 15(1):19–32.
OSWALT, WENDELL
 1963   *Napaskiak: an Alaskan Eskimo community*. Tucson: University of Arizona Press.
ROSS, RICHARD E.
 1971   "The cultural sequence at Chagvan Bay, Alaska: a matrix analysis." Unpublished Ph. D. thesis, Washington State University.
SPENCER, ROBERT F.
 1959   *North Alaskan Eskimo*. Bureau of American Ethnology, Bulletin 171.
STANFORD, DENNIS J.
 1969   "Recent excavations near Point Barrow, Alaska." Paper read at the 34th Annual Meeting of the Society for American Archaeology, Milwaukee, Wisconsin, May 1–3.

# Aleut Adaptation and Evolution

WILLIAM S. LAUGHLIN and JEAN S. AIGNER

We should like to deal here with the Aleutian ecosystem as it was defined by the Aleuts, the maritime and littoral components of that human adaptation and its history as it is revealed archaeologically, and the consequences of these for the structure, development, and evolution of the Aleut population system.

## ALEUTIAN ECOSYSTEM

The territory occupied by the Aleuts, exclusive to and wholly encompassing them, was concordant with natural geographic and zoogeographic provinces. Thus, the Aleuts may also be seen as one of the index mammals within the Aleutian ecosystem. In fact, like the collared lemming, they are a key terrestrial mammal, and have a known antiquity in the Aleutians of over 8,700 years.[1]

The distribution of the human population and the eastern boundary of the Aleutian ecosystem begins at Port Moller on the Bering Sea side of the Alaska Peninsula and the Shumagin Islands immediately south of the peninsula in the Pacific Ocean. The western boundary is the Near Islands, a linear distance of 1,250 miles. Uniquely, this chain of over seventy Aleutian islands is distributed both linearly and longitudinally, and, with the Peninsula, forms the border between the deep Pacific Ocean and the more shallow and colder Bering Sea.

---

[1] Lemmings are documented archaelogically at at least 5000 B.P. (at Sandy Beach Bay). They could have reached Umnak only in the earlier period, when Umnak was part of the Bering Land Bridge.

The portion of Aleut territory with the simplest and poorest coastline lies on the Alaska Peninsula, but the human population occupied the occasional habitat-rich localities on both the Pacific and Bering Sea coasts. Many more Aleuts lived along the complex coasts of the Shumagin Islands cluster; these were the only Aleuts confined to coasts of the Pacific Ocean.

The Pribilof Islands, 260 miles north of Umnak, and the Siberian Commander Islands, 180 miles west of Attu, were uninhabited in pre-Russian times. Thus, the only contact border the Aleuts had was in the east with Eskimos, and that border ran from Kupreanof Point on the south side to Port Moller on the north side of the Peninsula. The Aleuts were highly isolated geographically from other populations. Cultural barriers also existed, language being prominent among these.

The Aleutians, in general, have larger and more clustered islands in the east, somewhat smaller, more spaced and strung-out ones in the west. The Shumagin Islands, Alaska Peninsula, and Fox Islands form a larger territorial subgrouping historically linked as part of the Bering Land Bridge. Aleuts speaking the Fox Island dialect occupied these coasts and comprised some 65 percent of all Aleuts. After about 1826 the Islands of the Four Mountains were embraced by this dialect group; geographically these islands are separated from Umnak by Samalga Pass. Some sixteen miles across, this is the first deep pass — some 180 meters — westward along the chain, and it defined the terminus of the Pleistocene Bering Land Bridge in southwestern Alaska.

The next two island groups, the Andreanof and the Rat Islands, compose the territory of the Atka or central dialect speakers. The Near Islands are separated from the Rat Islands by 120 miles of open water broken only by Buldir Island midway between. Attuan speakers occupied the Near Islands of Attu and Agattu, but this western dialect is closer to the central than the central is to the eastern according to Bergsland (1959).

As a natural consequence of the linear, longitudinal distribution of the territory, the inventory of food and fabrication resources is generally similar throughout the Aleut domain. Differential concentrations occurred depending upon coastline complexity, amount of coastal lowland, degree of clustering of islands and islets, and other factors. Of the principal sea mammals, sea lion, hair seal, and sea otter were year-round residents while several of the whales and fur seals were migrants, the latter passing through the Aleutians twice a year on the way to and from the Pribilofs.

The principal fish included salmon, halibut, cod, and a number of shoal, bay, and deep-sea fish and trout. Birds are abundantly represented, especially in the migratory sea birds and waterfowl, which use the chain as part of their flyway. Cliff-dwelling forms such as puffins, cormorants, and murres are particularly common; and there are geese, ducks, swans, albatross, ptarmigan, and a large variety of songbirds.

Invertebrates were extremely common on the strandflats, a diagnostic geologic form and habitat used and especially well developed by Aleuts. In the Aleutian ecosystem the invertebrate life forms were of unusual importance, both within the energy-flow system and (for a number of the larger ones) directly to the Aleuts. The principal forms exploited by the humans were the sea urchins, mussels, limpets, chitons, octopuses, whelks, and clams. Absence of permanent winter ice favors maintenance of the rich intertidal fauna.

Plant foods used by the Aleuts were confined to the strandflats and adjacent coastal strip. These supplied perhaps 10 percent of the caloric intake and included both marine algae and flowering land plants such as Kamchatka lily, lupine, wild parsnip, angelica, and orchid. Rye grass provided a common and widely used material for basketry, mats, flooring, and roofing. A variety of woods was available as drift and composed a major fabricational resource for boats, utensils, and houses in particular.

In the Aleut territory, then, the distribution of utilized natural resources is most closely coincident with the coastline. While walrus are known in the extreme east where there is discontinuous winter ice, and terrestrial mammals such as bears, caribou, wolves, and wolverines extend west to Unimak but rarely beyond, these did not form a major economic focus for the Aleuts. In the eastern area there are more large islands with complex and habitable coastlines than in the central regions and still more than in the west (see maps in Kenyon 1969). The most meaningful measure of area for dealing with human exploitational patterns is habitat area or the zone about the island coast actually utilized by the Aleuts. This is employed below in our discussion.

*Historical-Geographical Sketch*

The climate which Aleuts have faced for some 10,000 years is moist, with low annual and diurnal temperature variation. Cool but not commonly freezing temperatures, high winds, and long periods of foggy and misty weather are constants. Vulcanism is another feature; the chain is composed largely of volcanic mountains of which some eighty are active. The lush, terrestrial lowlands fringing some coasts are best described as subarctic, maritime grasslands (Joan Hett 1971, personal communication) with more typically tundra plants found on higher elevations.

While the general climate and rich maritime environment have remained relatively unchanged and always favorable to humans over the last 12,000 years, significant geographic changes did occur which affected the humans directly and indirectly. These involved primarily absolute and relative changes in sea level and attendant erosional and depositional phenomena, uplift and volcanic eruption, and deglaciation. Directly affecting the Aleuts were sea-level changes due to absolute rise, those related to deglaciation and rebound, and those caused by tectonic activity. These changed the coastal configuration, size of islands, and clustering of islands (and concentration of habitats). Deglaciation after 12,000 B.P. gradually added the Pacific coast for human occupancy beginning in the west and continuing to the east in Holocene times. Extensive strandflats were key factors in maintaining the distinctive Aleut population structure (see below).

As nearly as we can tell from the oceanographic, geomorphic and glacial evidence, 12,000 to 10,000 B.P., the eastern Aleutians (Unimak, Unalaska, Umnak-Anangula) formed the southwestern extension of the Alaskan remnant of Beringia. The first pass between the Pacific Ocean and the Bering Sea lay between Umnak and the Islands of the Four Mountains. Samalga Pass is still the first deep pass (more than 100 meters) in the Aleutians and marks a true permanent upwelling system. Samalga Island as recently as 10,000 years ago did not exist, and the Islands of the Four Mountains were a single island.

With the relative rise in sea level during the early Holocene, resulting from the world-wide rise with deglaciation and influenced by rebound and uplift, the old elongated Peninsula was converted into over twenty-five islands. However, three major shallow passes were opened east of Umnak: Unimak Pass (55 meters); Unalga Pass (46 meters); and Umnak Pass (29 meters).

Continuing rise of sea level involved at least one major period of tectonic uplift. This resulted in coastal changes, causing both abandonment of villages and establishment of new ones, and in the emergence of strandflats.

## Maritime Hunting and Fishing

Throughout their Aleutian history the Aleuts have necessarily focused on maritime hunting. This emphasized the hunting of sea mammals from boats on the deep sea as well as of those hauled up or stranded along the coasts. It also included deep-sea line fishing from boats and line fishing from the shore. It is to be emphasized that for most Aleuts throughout most of their history in the Aleutians, ice-free hunting from boats was typical, characteristic, and the adaptive norm. Some birds were also taken at sea as well as on lakes, marshes and in cliff-nesting areas.

Based on eighteenth-century observations, all boat hunting, whether kayak or umiak, was performed by able-bodied males primarily between the ages of sixteen and fifty-five. Some of the sea mammal hunting, especially that of hair seals and of some sea otters, was performed by single hunters. Most bird hunting from kayaks was also undertaken by single males or a man and his partner. It, like hair seal and sea otter hunting, was generally done close to shore. Deep-sea fishing was done from both kayaks and umiaks; some line fishing, including inside bays and other protected waters, was done by aged men who could no longer be active open-sea hunters but who could procure halibut, cod, and other bottom fish from kayaks.

Male hunting partnerships have long been a major structural feature of Aleut society. Partners would commonly hunt, fish or trap together and partners would use the two-hatch kayak *(baidarka)* in either their hunting or travelling, including group hunting.

Many swimming sea lions were hunted by partners in a single double-hatch boat or each in his single-hatch boat. A great deal of time and energy was invested in scanning for free-swimming mammals. This cooperative partnership contrasts with the loosely structured group hunting that characterizes taking sea lions at their rookeries. Some hunters came overland or ashore to hunt while others remained at sea to harpoon from boats. Hunters were not usually in competition for the same animals but did compete with each other for the quality and number of sea lions they sought.

Whaling was ordinarily performed by especially skilled and recognized hunters and often functioned within a modified partnership arrangement. When two-hatch kayaks were used, an "apprentice" occupied the rear hatch and maneuvered the boat for the whaler in the forward hatch. It was also common for two partners to accompany each other in their single-hatch kayaks. It is known that when a school of whales passed a village, several whalers went out to lance them. A large village might have as many as four "top whalers," each with his apprentice. The possibility of mummification and a good deal of specialized and restricted training, including instruction in ritual and magic, attended the whalers.

Structurally the most complex hunting pattern is associated with the sea otter surround. Although smaller parties from a single village were the norm, as many as twenty-four men in twelve kayaks cooperated under the direction of a head man. Sometimes hunters from different but related villages were involved. The coordinated party commonly advanced in a straight line or with the end kayaks in forward position. Detection of a sea otter was signaled by a paddle held vertically and the other hunters automatically closed in a ring about the animal and harpooned it.

Ice-free conditions prevailed in most areas. Because kayak hunting was a year-round, economically important and demanding activity, it constituted a major focus which began with early childhood training for males. This focused on the lengthening of tendons and ligaments of the shoulder, back, and knee for throwing harpoons by throwing boards from a sitting position, legs extended fully, in the kayak. Other exercises and games contributed to general strengthening of the body. Handling the kayak and navigation out of sight of land were absolutely critical and vital skills having their own rigorous forms of instruction about which little detailed information remains.

We estimate that able-bodied males collecting and hunting sea mammals and birds and engaged in deep-sea fishing probably contributed 35 to 50 percent of the protein and fat intake for the entire village over the year. Protein and fat probably constituted 90 percent of the total caloric intake; vegetable carbohydrates made a minor contribution although the actual use of seaweeds and land plants may be underestimated in the lean seasons. Invertebrates, especially sea urchins, were a mainstay in the diet.

### Coastal Fishing and Collecting

Most of the old permanent villages including Sandy Beach Bay (4300–5600 B.P.; east of Cape Starr) were situated on or close to a protected body of water with a fresh-water lake drained by a stream, strandflats, offshore islets, and nearby cliffs (Table 1). Whereas open-sea hunting was, by its physical demands and cultural definition of sex roles, the monopoly of able-bodied men, many other rich habitats could be exploited significantly by other age and sex cohorts. Seasonal salmon fishing in bays and streams could be done by men and women. Handline fishing from the shore could be done by males and females ranging from children to very old persons. Seasonal egg collecting on the cliffs restricted the collectors to a younger and more agile group, but of both sexes. Collecting duck and sea gull eggs required less agility than collecting eggs of puffins and other cliff-nesters; if nesting areas were offshore, men paddled boats. Bolas hunting of ducks around the lake shores was usually done by men

Table 1.   Habitat keyed to population cohorts

| Inland | Lakes and Streams | Beach | Village | Reef | Bay | Off-shore islands | Cliffs | Open sea |
|--------|-------------------|-------|---------|------|-----|-------------------|--------|----------|
| + | + | + | Old infirm females | + | + | − | − | − |
| − | + | + | Old infirm males | + | + | − | − | − |
| (+) | − | (+) | Pregnant women | (+) | (+) | − | − | − |
| + | + | + | Children | + | + | (+) | (+) | − |
| + | (+) | + | Young to middle-aged females | + | + | + | + | − |
| (+) | + | + | Young to middle-aged males | + | + | + | + | + |
|   |   |   | *(Increasing mobility from top to bottom)* |   |   |   |   |   |

Beginning with the kinds of people, their use of the habitats is indicated by a plus sign. Parentheses indicate qualified use or special limitations. This chart provides no indication of the different methods of using the same area nor the different resources procured. Thus, old men hand-line fish the bay from boats, old women fish from the shore. Men collect driftwood suitable for manufacture of boat frames, women collect driftwood suitable only for fuel.

but of varied ages. Plant collecting was a near monopoly of women, with aged women prominent among them. Driftwood was collected by both sexes and was carried to the village or boated back by men.

*Littoral Exploitation*

An outstanding characteristic of the Aleut ecosystem and diagnostic of Aleut culture for at least 4,000 years (with procurement techniques and an understanding of the various resources developed far earlier) is the presence and use of the extensive and rich strandflats. Of the various invertebrate forms sea urchins were clearly the most extensively exploited. Those living on kelp were preferred for their "sweeter" flavor. In fact, the kelp-eating urchins do ingest manitol which gives them a different flavor from urchins living off different organisms in deeper waters. Urchins, along with the other invertebrates, were fairly easily collected by children as well as adults including the aged and infirm of both sexes. There is no doubt that these groups made a major dietary contribution which was often of crucial importance in the winter months. At the same time, the accessible littoral resources probably help account for the relatively large proportion of aged persons in this population (Figure 1).

The distinctive Aleut demographic profile probably developed after the emergence of the strandflats and a modern sea level. Good-sized

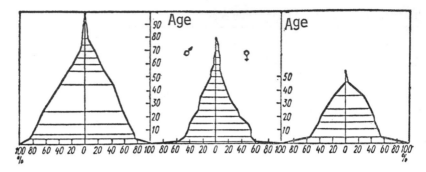

Figure 1.   Life-span in populations of Aleuts of the Fox Islands (Unalaska Island 1822–1836, data from Veniaminof 1840); Commander Islands (1902–1917), and of the Eskimos of Southampton Island in Hudson Bay (until 1903, data from Laughlin 1963). From Rychkov and Sheremetyeva (1972).

villages such as at Anangula Blade Site (8700 B.P.) and Sandy Beach Bay (4300–5600 B.P.) may indicate a relatively high population density.

## History of the Adaption

Of critical consequence for Aleut evolution has been the continuity in maritime adaptation documented in the eastern Aleutians for more than 8,700 years. Three major Aleut villages on southwestern Umnak Island — Anangula, Sandy Beach Bay, and Chaluka — provide rich archaeological verification of this economic pattern. They also show consistencies in village layout, house construction, activity zonation and definition of space in and around houses, and proximity of exploitable habitats which indicate strongly temporal coherence of the Aleut culture system for 8,700 years in this locale.

These three sequential sites in the same exploitational area (Map 1) maintain in their locations a strikingly coastal focus. The superior locations of all three have led to their repeated use by Aleut communities over thousands of years. At the time of its initial occupation some 8,700 years ago, Anangula (now on Anangula Island) was located on the northern arm of Nikolski Bay and overlooked both that bay and the Bering Sea. The location was a superior station for both bay fishing and for sighting sea mammals as they moved between the Pacific and Bering. On the same bay were two salmon streams (Sheep Creek and Umnak Lake Creek), limited strandflats, and bird cliffs. Offshore islets were also present.

The village called Sandy Beach Bay, at the time of its occupation 4300 to 5600 B.P., was located with access to the bay and strandflats (more

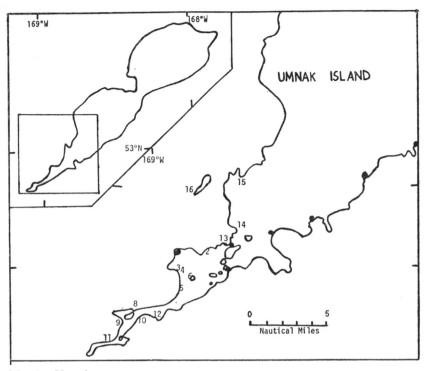

Map 1. Umnak

1. Anangula Island Village Site    7. Idaliuk West        12. Sheep Cabin Sites
2. Elbow Lake Sites               8. Idaliuk East         13. Chaluka
3. Sandy Beach                    9. Idaliuk Bay          14. Sheep Creek
4. Sandy Beach Bay               10. Chungsin            15. Okee Bay
5. Sand Dune Localities          11. Hook Lake           16. Blade Site
6. Salmon Lake

extensive than Anangula, perhaps not so rich as early Chaluka). Salmon streams, bird cliffs, offshore islets and islands, and sand beaches provided varied exploitable habitats in addition to those of the bay and deep sea. Varied raw materials for stone tools were abundantly available, and edible plants and usable grasses were well represented on the adjacent coastal plain. (Anangula imported more than half its lithic materials, from several kilometers to eighty kilometers away in the case of obsidian.)

Chaluka, like Sandy Beach Bay, has had continuous occupation, but beginning perhaps only 4,000 years ago. Located deep in Nikolski Bay and protected by Rudisell Reef, the site enjoyed easy access to a variety of habitats, most prominently a well-developed and economically rich strandflat. Two salmon streams, a large lake frequented by migratory waterfowl, bird cliffs, and offshore islets, in addition to the bay and deep water, were available for a base village. Chaluka preserves faunal deposits of sea mammals, birds, fish and invertebrates.

Common to all three sites, each of which was a base village (and possibly a periodic camp — seasonal multifamily — when an alternate base village was utilized) during much of its existence, is diverse habitat accessibility including easy access to the Pacific Ocean and coast as well as the Bering Sea. Similarities in exploitation and social patterns are reflected in details of the occupations (see above) in addition to locational strategy. There were many houses in each village, and these were structurally similar. Subrectangular in shape, these semisubterranean houses had only roof entryways. We infer from the uniformity of size, $2\frac{1}{2}$ to 3 meters by 5 to 6 meters, from the presence of but one lamp and image of deity, and from zonation and clustering of tools and workshops that these were probably single-family dwellings.

A combination of archaeological traits present from earliest times reflects deep-seated, complex, pervasive Aleut cultural patterns and interests. Prominent among these traits are lamps, bowls, images of the deity, and multifaceted red ochre grinders and pallets. Lamps, tended by women, were a primary source of heat and light. Each family unit maintained its lamp, carrying it with them to summer or winter camps and back. Carved stone dishes and bowls in addition to their obvious functions also provided an aesthetic outlet; Aleuts did not take over the practice of pottery manufacture.

The *Kaadaraadar* [image of the deity] was a household or family image through whom the deity was contacted. While the suspension girdle was the common element in these images a man expressed himself aesthetically and individually in its carving. Size, shape, and surface detail could vary within wide limits, and the material carved might be bone, stone, or ivory. Often a Mongoloid physiognomy is clearly depicted. Images were suspended from beams inside houses and carried with the family when residence was changed.

The use of ochre prepared with a faceted grinding stone on a pallet reflects several patterns and interests. It was used in tool and clothing decoration and in burial preparation. It was more than simply a coloring material; it had several meanings including blood (when used on throwing boards), danger, and protection — depending upon the referent (when used at the mouth of burial caves to repel entry, and on burials to protect the individual passing into the next world). It was applied to both male and female tools, ornaments, and burials. Again, the presence of this combination of traits in site context argues strongly for full development by 8,700 years ago of these ideas, and for their continuity.

The maintenance of cultural practices with a material component which are key or essential attributes in the Aleut culture system (we cited image of the deity, carved stone lamps, and others) and the overall maritime adaptation are clearly demonstrable archaeologically. At the same time, another characteristic we may define in terms of the Aleut system pertains to the kinds and amounts of individual expression and stylistic variation (inessential attributes). We have already noted that there is a wide range of variation in FORMAL attributes of the image of the deity through both time and space. However, their archaeologically demonstrable context and reticulation within the larger system appear not to vary. Harpoons and spears, functional attributes, occur in all Aleut assemblages and are basic to procurement techniques (and reflect the basic definition of resources made by Aleuts). The generation of style variants over time (with a basic suite of functional variants extant at any one time) is particularly obvious and is an expression of idiosyncratic variation. Variation in chipped-stone tools and in techniques for their production is even more marked than variation in bone tools, both synchronically and diachronically. This makes comparisons with non-Aleut systems very difficult or invalid.

In order to illustrate the aspects of persistence, continuity, and change we present a short list of key artifacts and contextual features of the Aleut culture system. This chart may appear to favor similarities at the expense of dissimilarities. A fuller account, not possible here, discusses the dissimilarities as well (Aigner 1970). However, the unique situation here is the conversion of a totally unifacial industry to a bifacial industry. The beginning industry has no parallel on the entire Bering Sea and automatically appears to be unrelated to any other Bering Sea cultures if this aspect is given primary rank. Obviously, statements concerning phenetic and phylogenetic similarity to Aleut remains or affinity based upon the traditional comparative approach will vary in their quality dependent upon the attributes considered. This last point is too often overlooked by prehistorians.

Using only objects which are identical (in formal identity, contextual features, and method of manufacture), there is an impressive number of persistences throughout these sites over an 8,700-year time span:

1. Stone bowls or dishes
2. Faceted ochre rubbing stones
3. Pallets for grinding ochre
4. Scoria abraders, grooved and ungrooved
5. Obsidian scrapers
6. Carved stone lamps

### 7.   Line weights

In regard to Table 2 we would reiterate that attributes which are information-laden and which elaborate and reticulate and integrate in the Aleut system are fairly constant over time and between base villages. The FORM of procurement and the manufacturing of tools made of stone does change to a noteworthy extent — noteworthy but not significant so far as phenetic and phylogenetic comparative studies are concerned. At the same time, all the available evidence indicates that their FUNCTIONAL attributes are intact to a large degree. They appear in the same clusterings and spatial arrays in each site, indicating that their "use" and "meaning" (reticulation) within the system context are probably also maintained.

The observation that these continuous and discontinuous trends and changes occur while the maritime focus, village, and house patterns, and key patterns reflected in images, ochre, lamps, and bowls persist is consonant with the model we have been developing regarding the original population entering the Aleutian Islands. Accumulating evidence tied into the geological history of Beringia, as well as the local geological history of southwestern Umnak and points east in the chain, strongly indicate the early arrival of a population with a fully developed culture system, elaborating and focusing upon a maritime adaptation based increasingly and finally, both characteristically and exclusively, upon year-round ice-free conditions. This presupposes a population which, when advantageous, could deploy itself into large-sized and stable village communities. Similarly, there was technological variability and latitude to permit the highly visible changes and diversity in lithic materials and basic tool styles.

## EVOLUTIONARY CONSEQUENCES OF ADAPTATION TO THE MARINE ECOSYSTEM

*Morphological Configuration and Its Geographic Variation*

The Aleuts are characterized by a distinctive combination of morphological traits. These include a large and low-vaulted head, with very large face and generally Mongoloid physiognomy. The trunk length is relatively long in proportion to the short legs and arms. The dentition displays the Mongoloid dental complex with shovel-shaped incisors, absent or redusen third molars, low frequency of Carabelli's cusp, relatively broad lateral incisors in proportion to median incisors, high frequency

Table 2. Artifacts and contextual features of the Aleut culture system selected for their archaeological expression[1]

| | 8700–7800 B.P. Anangula | 5600–4300 B.P. Sandy Beach Bay | 4000–3500 B.P.[3] Chaluka |
|---|---|---|---|
| **Technofacts[2]** | | | |
| Characteristics of the stone tool manufacturing system: | | | |
| Core and blade | + | ± | − |
| Core and flake | + | + | + |
| Prior shape alteration (e.g. rare shaping by secondary retouch) | + | − | − |
| Restricted shape alteration of some tool classes by retouch | | + | − |
| Common shape alteration in some categories of tools | | − | + |
| Unifacial, marginal retouch | + | + | + |
| Bifacial, marginal retouch | − | + | + |
| Unifacial, facial retouch | ? | + | + |
| Bifacial, facial retouch | − | + | + |
| Burinization technique | + | + | − |
| Typical Aleut clusterings of tools: | | | |
| Ochre-pounders, -lamps, -bowls | + | + | + |
| Core, blanks, anvil stones, chipping debris, pumice abraders | + | + | + |
| Specific categories of tools (excluding the above): | | | |
| Chipped stone adze bits | − | + | + |
| Ulus | + | + | + |
| Unstemmed, large, symmetrical knives | + | + | + |
| Stemmed, large, symmetrical knives | − | ± | + |
| Small, formalized projectiles for insertion into harpoons | − | ± | + |
| Evidence for spears and harpoons | + | + | + |
| Line weights | + | + | + |
| Formalized scrapers: "thumbnail" | + | + | + |
| Formalized scrapers: "burinized" | + | ± | − |
| Other: | | | |
| Burin spalls (rejuvenation flakes) | + | + | − |
| Utilization of burin spalls | − | − | ... |
| Core tablets or tablet flakes | + | + | + |
| Microblade sub-industry | − | − | − |
| **Sociofacts** | | | |
| Characteristics of settlement and house morphology: | | | |
| Houses 2–3 × 5–6 meters | + | + | + |
| Long axis parallel to water | + | + | + |
| Exclusive roof entry | + | + | + |
| Wood-and-bone superstructure for sodded walls and roof | + | + | + |
| Large stones for wall bracing or interior seating | + | + | + |

Table 2 (continued)

|  | 8700–7800 B.P. Anangula | 5600–4300 B.P. Sandy Beach Bay | 4000–3500 B.P.[3] Chaluka |
|---|---|---|---|
| Inside-coursed stones for wall support | — | — | + |
| Stone-lined interior floor storage pits | — | ? | + |
| United interior floor storage pits | + | + | + |
| Interior hearth (one only) | + | + | + |
| Exterior hearths, fireplaces | + | + | + |
| Stone lamp (one only) | + | + | + |
| Image of the Deity (one only)[4] | ± | ± | + |
| Ochre-stained floors | + | + | + |
| Clear delineation of interior fabricational loci | + | + | + |
| Activity loci: |  |  |  |
| Factory workshops associated with houses (one major per house) | + | + | + |
| Use of roof margins and area immediately adjacent for storage of (male) items | + | + | + |
| Use of area immediately adjacent to houses for processing and manufacture (exclusive of stone and bone factory locus) | + | + | + |
| Intense occupation: numerous houses | + | + | + |
| Individual sociofacts: |  |  |  |
| Ulus (women's knives) | + | + | + |
| Labrets (normally bone and ivory) | ... | ... | + |
| Image of the Deity (male) | + | + | + |
| Needles, awls (female)[5] | + | + | + |
| Factories (male) | + | + | + |
| Spears, harpoons[4] | + | + | + |
| Woodworking equipment — wedges or adze-bits or heads | ? | + | + |
| Stone lamps (one/family, tended by female) | + | + | + |
| Ideofacts |  |  |  |
| Red ochre, pounder/grinder complex for preparing paints | + | + | + |
| Image of the Deity | + | + | + |
| Lamps (to burn the oil of animal-beings) | + | + | + |
| Carved stone bowls | + | + | + |

± Indicates but very few examples.

[1] The listings are not exhaustive and the actual degree of reticulation has been reduced. For example, many of the individual sociofacts should also be listed with specific categories of tools under Technofacts.

[2] After Binford (1965:203–210).

[3] The time intercept is chosen for comparisons; Chaluka continues to be occupied by Aleuts today.

[4] Images mainly in bone and ivory so only the rare stone examples are preserved.

[5] Evidence at Anangula and Sandy Beach Bay based upon a study of diameters of shafts carved in grooved abrading stones.

of three-rooted first lower molars, paramolar occlusal tubercles, and both palatine and mandibular tori. The hair is straight, black, and scanty on all parts except the head. The complexion is variable but tends toward light and even ruddy, especially in the face.

The head form, brachycephalic in modern Aleuts, nevertheless displays an east-west difference with even broader heads in the east than in the west. Past populations in the west and much of the east were markedly dolichocephalic (see below). Several skeletal traits provide a characterization of the Aleut population and the basis for individual assignment to the group. These include the high frequency of separate neural arches, fossa hypotrochanterica on the femur, large deltoid tuberosity on the humerus, and marked temporal lines in association with an exceptionally large mandible. The last is also characterized by a very broad ascending ramus which is both low and inclined, and an auditory meatus that is round, tubular, and straight.

## Population Structure

LONGEVITY AND INFANT MORTALITY  The outstanding characteristic of the Aleut population as a whole is the achievement of considerable longevity by a high proportion of both males and females (Figure 1). On the basis of age at death for 411 persons in the period between 1824 and 1834, it can be seen that an exceptionally high proportion survived beyond the sixth decade and some individuals beyond the eighth. At the same time, infant mortality appears to be significantly lower than in comparable hunting populations.

To some extent these postcontact data are well supported by precontact and early-contact archaeological data. A high proportion of recovered skeletons are of aged individuals; several in their seventh and eighth decades. Burial practices included interment of infants and young children as well as adults, often in elaborate circumstances. The documented pattern of *umqan* burials in which many infant skeletal remains have been recovered supports the ethnographic observation that the Aleuts had a culturally patterned concern for reporting miscarriages and deaths of newborn to the community. *Umqan* burials studied during 1972 by Aigner have not been previously reported; they are, however, common and conspicuous near the precontact middens, where subsequent cultural activities have not obliterated their topographic expression.

*Umqan* consist of flexed burials placed in pits and associated with whalebone slabs approximately 1 meter in diameter and 1 meter deep. The pit is centered at the open end of a V-shaped feature. The V normally consists of trenched legs 7 to 15 meters long and less than 1 meter deep. Fill from the trench is mounded over the burial pit and the V interior generally, to a height of several meters in some cases. Before resodding, the mound is paved with lines of large flat boulders up to 1 meter long and over 220 kilos in weight. Very often *umqan* are visible on steep hillsides near villages; the V opens downward in all cases. Stone materials used in *umqan* burials have been carried long distances in many cases, and up steep cliffs and hillsides in most. This practice in which considerable time and great effort have gone into interment of community members of all age classes — stillborn, infant, and adult — suggests that the demographic data based on native reports of infant deaths may be more accurate than is usually the case.

ISOLATE INTEGRITY   Isolate integrity is marked between the three Aleut dialect groups, which also serve as breeding isolates. In the time of Veniaminof, the Atka people were considered separate from the Fox Islands Aleuts as well as the Attu people when the Russians relocated Aleuts to the Commander Islands in 1826. They preserved these groups by placing Atka Aleuts on Bering Island and Attuans on Medni Island. Administratively, the Russians recognized only two districts, the Atka District and the Fox Island District.

An examination of the residence and the place of birth of all Aleuts living within their dialect group confirms the strong tendency for Aleuts to select their mates within their dialect group (Laughlin 1972). Migration was clearly, then as now, more common among females than among males. The geographic difference in many physical traits between east and west Aleuts is firm evidence that isolate integrity has ancient roots. Exchange of mates with Koniag Eskimos was vigorously discouraged and the minor gene flow between Aleuts and Eskimos is again confirmed by the physical differences between them.

The numbers of Aleuts and their density in relation to the habitat area they actually exploited reflects both the distribution of resources in the Aleutians and the overall uniformity of the adaptation to this marine habitat (Laughlin 1973). The most important point is that density remained much the same in all three dialect groups, some three per square mile (calculated on basis of exploitational area), but the numbers differed by several magnitudes (Table 3). This had evolutionary consequences. The large population size of the eastern Aleuts, some 10,000, indicates an effective breeding size large enough for the influence of selection to operate. In contrast, the small size of the Attu population suggests that

Table 3.  Habitat area, numbers, and density for the three Aleut dialect groups

|  | Habitat area (square miles) | Number of Aleuts | Aleut density | Number of sea otter | Sea otter density (mean estimate) |
|---|---|---|---|---|---|
| West | 326 | 1000 | 3.0 | 4150 | 12.73 |
| Central | 1236 | 5000 | 4.0 | 15500 | 12.54 |
| East | 3370 | 10000 | 3.0 | 42100 | 12.49 |
|  | 4932 | 16000 | 3.2 | 61750 | 12.52 |

these Aleuts were likely more affected by genetic drift. The evolution of the Neo-Aleut vault form in the eastern area reflects this prerequisite component of population size.

The large site of the eastern population also served as an inhibiting barrier to gene flow from the much less numerous Koniag Eskimos occupying the contiguous portion of the Alaska Peninsula.

*Evolutionary Trends*

Tangible evolutionary changes have taken place in the Aleut population. These are seen directly in the evolution of the Neo-Aleut vault form without corresponding changes in other traits. They are confirmed by the geographic gradient in vault form running from east to west.

The population termed Paleo-Aleut (in place of Hrdlička's pre-Aleut) is characterized by a low vault but is narrow and dolichocranic, with indices ranging from seventy to seventy-six. The temporal lines reflect the large temporalis muscle appropriate to the large mandible. They are high on the vault, approximate each other relatively closely, and accent a scaphoid keel or sagittal elevation. Viewed from the base and in profile the great post-condylar length of the occipital bone, often assuming a bun shape, forms a relatively constant feature. They are found in Port Moller at the eastern boundary of the Aleut domain.

The Neo-Aleut vault form is also low, but is very broad, with indices ranging from seventy to eighty-nine; though the mandible is also large, the temporal lines are much farther apart owing to the great breadth of the vault. A keel or sagittal elevation is rarely developed. The occipital bone is shorter and the frontal bone shows even less profile elevation than in the Paleo-Aleut form. Neo-Aleut are clearly part of a postcontact re-location-migration at Chaluka. The only precontact Neo-Aleut skeletons known, as we predicted from density and size of effective breeding population, are in the east on Akun Island (1300 B.P.) according to Turner and Turner (1972).

Common to both Paleo- and Neo-Aleuts are many features including large cranial size, large face and mandible, especially large ascending rami, high frequency of mandibular and palatine tori, three-rooted first lower molars, reduced or peg-shaped or missing third molars, very large deltoid tuberosity of the humerus, marked gluteal lines and hypotrochanteric fossa on the femur, and separate neural arches in the lumbar vertebrae.

Present evidence suggests that the vault form of the Aleuts has changed significantly from a narrow to a very broad transverse diameter. There does not appear to be a significant change in other traits of the skull or postcranial skeleton. Therefore, it is most likely that a developmental change with a genetic basis has taken place within this population system.

There is some evidence in the geographic distribution of physical traits that confirm the evolutionary succession in vault form and also points to the predicted eastern Aleutian geographic center for the change. The living western Aleuts are more narrow-headed than the eastern Aleuts. The difference is approximately two index units in cephalic index. There are other differences as well, particularly in the frequency of discontinuous traits. The mandibular torus, for example, is more frequent in the eastern Aleuts than in the western Aleuts. Even though the difference between eastern and western Aleuts over the total distance of 1,250 miles is considerable, and is greater than the differences between northern and southern Greenlandic Eskimos, or greater than those between Eskimos and Chukchee, the Aleut isolates maintain a single breeding population. The variation is between isolates within a linearly distributed single population, not between two or more different populations. This variation therefore provides a valuable measure of how much a single population can differentiate internally.

Two kinds of factors generate this geographic variation. One factor is simply the automatic differentiation that arises from the inability of a long, linear population to maintain random breeding over such a distance. The other has to do more with the content of the traits which vary. Thus, the broadheadedness of the easterners appears to be the manifestation of their historical change, a response to selection, whereas the narrowheadedness of the westerners appears to be the reflection of the earlier Paleo-Aleut form surviving in the absence of sufficient migration from the east to replace the genetic constitution of the earlier population.

The center of change is in the eastern Aleutians, between Unalaska and the Shumagin Islands. As recently as 1764 Paleo-Aleuts inhabited Umnak Island, and probably continued to a somewhat later date. The one Aleut skeleton found with the Russian Cossack party of Dennis Medvedeff was a Paleo-Aleut. The Neo-Aleut skeletons of Chaluka date to times later than 1764. Presumably the appearance of the Neo-Aleut vault form is earlier at Unalaska and other eastern dialect area islands. A paucity of radiocarbon dates and well-documented stratigraphy does not now permit more precision in the dating of the change in vault form.

It is relevant to recall that the change in vault form is obviously more expectable in the eastern area of large population size, where the population of some 10,000 provided an adequate base for the operation of selection and population pressure for migration to the west.

The period of Russian occupation (1741–1867) introduced many changes, particularly in the size and the distribution of the population. Early reduction of the population was achieved through disease and killing. The massacres by Solovioff and others seriously reduced the number of Aleuts and simultaneously required relocation of villages for administrative purposes and for access by sailing ships. As a consequence, a relatively sharp interface between the two vault forms may appear where immigration from one dialect group into the territory of another dialect group has been encouraged.

Also instructive in this problem is the Ship Rock mummy cave. Ship Rock was used for burial by the Aleuts of Tuliskoe, a large village located on Umnak Island immediately opposite the southwesternmost extension of Unalaska Island. The cultural materials associated with the mummies belong to the last few centuries and the Neo-Aleut vault form is present.

At this time it is not yet possible to determine whether the eastern dialect had already moved across from Unalaska to the adjacent shore of Umnak Island prior to the Russian occupation of Umnak in 1759 although we think it unlikely. It is clear that at least at Chaluka the Neo-Aleuts represent eastern-dialect speakers and that here and at Sandy Beach the local interface is relatively distinct.

## SUMMARY

The Aleuts occupied and defined an Aleutian ecosystem over 2,000 kilometers in length. A marine adapted community is first visible to us on the coast of Anangula (8700 B.P.) at the western terminus of the earlier Bering Land Bridge. The succeeding village sites of Sandy Beach Bay and Chaluka continue this major adaptive configuration.

Persistence and continuity are seen in key artifacts and features: large coastal villages. small semisubterranean houses with roof entry;

lamps; bowls; images of the deity; faceted ochre rubbing stones and pallets; scoria abraders; obsidian scrapers; line weights; and unifacial tools. Archaeologically derived artifacts, faunal remains, and human skeletons extend the ethnographic picture of intensive exploitation of rich marine resources and fluid population deployment corresponding to an optimal exploitational strategy. A consequence of the maritime adaptational system is an extended length of life, frequently beyond age seventy-five. Furthermore, the diversity of tools, the features and the zonation patterning and structure already present in Anangula (8700 B.P.) indicate that this complex marine adaptation must antedate the submergence of Beringia.

The Aleuts present a unique combination of physical traits recognizable in the earliest skeletons and in the living people. These traits include large and low heads, high frequencies of tori, supernumerary dental roots and cusps, separate neural arches and blood group $A_1$, and low frequencies of group B. This anatomical distinctiveness of the Aleuts is congruent with several thousands of years of relatively independent evolution with minimal external contact. An evolutionary change in cranial vault morphology from narrow to broad recorded in the archaeological sites suggests the effect of selection in the more numerous, but not more densely settled, eastern Aleut isolate.

# REFERENCES

AIGNER, JEAN S.
   1970   "Configuration, continuity and time depth in Aleut culture." Paper presented at the American Association for the Advancement of Science Symposium, Aleutian Ecosystem, Chicago.
BERGSLAND, KNUT
   1959   Aleut dialects of Atka and Attu. *Transactions of the American Philosophical Society*, n.s. 49 (part 3).
BINFORD, L. R.
   1965   Archaeological systematics and the study of culture process. *American Antiquity* 31 (2, part 1):203–210.
KENYON, KARL W.
   1969   *The sea otter in the eastern Pacific Ocean.* U.S. Fish and Wildlife Service, North American Fauna 68. Washington, D.C.
LAUGHLIN, W. S.
   1972   "Ecology and population structure in the Arctic," in *The structure of human populations.* Edited by G. A. Harrison and A. J. Boyce, 379–392. Oxford: Clarendon Press.

1973   "Holocene history of Nikolski Bay, Alaska, and Aleut evolution," in *The Bering Land Bridge and its role for the history of Holarctic floras and faunas in the Late Cenozoic: theses of the reports of the All-Union Symposium.* Edited by the Academy of Sciences of the U.S.S.R. Far-Eastern Scientific Centre, 211–215. Khabarovsk.

RYCHKOV, Y. G., V. A. SHEREMETYEVA
1972   Population genetics of the Aleuts of the Commander Islands (in connection with the problems of the history of the peoples and the adaptation of the population of ancient Beringia). *Voprosi Antropologii* 40:45–70. (In Russian.)

TURNER, CHRISTY G. II, J. A. TURNER
1972   "Report of the 1972 evolutionary anthropology field investigations on Akun and Akutan Islands, eastern Aleutians, Alaska." Unpublished manuscript.

## ADDENDUM

The major points of this article have been substantially enhanced by the cooperative field studies of a joint USA–USSR team under the direction of W. S. Laughlin and A. P. Okladnikov. In the summer of 1974 we excavated in the Anangula Unifacial Blade site and in the Anangula Village site. We discovered a new transition culture which continued the older core, blade and burin industry with the addition of small stemmed projectile points, a highly torqued bifacial blade ("propeller blade"), and seal bones. This transition culture fills in the period between approximately 7,800 and 5,600 years ago. Its higher elevation, about twenty-two meters, indicates that the people of the lower and older blade site, about sixteen meters, moved uphill to a higher and more protected position in response to the rise of sea level which made the lower tail of the island untenable for year-round occupation. The Asiatic nature of the Anangula industry was established and several Siberian and Mongolian parallels were identified. The Soviet party included Academician A. P. Okladnikov, Dr. A. P. Derevyanko, Dr. V. E. Larichev, Dr. R. S. Vasilievsky, and Mr. S. Konopatskij.

# Technological Continuity and Change Within a Persistent Maritime Adaptation: Kodiak Island, Alaska

DONALD W. CLARK

This study describes and interprets continuity and change within a relatively persistent maritime adaptation found in an area where environmental and ecological factors have virtually excluded any alternate pattern for a noncomplex society. Both cultural and technological continuity are given equal consideration in this study, but cultural continuity and change are inferred here from technical continuity and change; technology includes exploitative techniques as well as fabrication processes.

The locality is not only one of a single practical ecosystem but occurs in a milieu of geographic and ecologic isolation. Although a high degree of mobility was achieved, almost exclusively by small boats, in order to operate within the system or pattern, it did not allow assumption of a significantly different pattern or adaptation. Also, trade with adjacent areas was essentially for luxury items only. The Kodiak example, with nearly 6,000 years of time depth, may be of special interest because of two particular factors. First, Kodiak, including adjacent islands, is in a pivotal geographic position as is part of the Alaskan Peninsula at the intersection or "four corners" of the Aleut, Eskimo, Subarctic Athabaskan, and Northwest Coast ethnic and culture areas (Eskimo and Aleut together are Arctic area). These areas now have an established time depth on the order of 8,000 to 10,500 years, although ethnic or racial correlations for the earliest periods may be different from the historic pattern. Second, there is evidence that there was a succession of peoples or cultures on Kodiak while the same adaptive pattern was maintained.

The Kodiak case provides an example of the communication and development of common adjustments to an ecosystem, although the persisting adaptive pattern, which may be extended to include adjacent groups, does not constitute a tradition in the generic sense.


## THE ECOSYSTEM

Kodiak is a relatively isolated, northern north temperate maritime area with abundant marine resources toward which its economy is oriented, but with few land-based resources. This section provides a qualitative description based upon twenty-five years' residence in the area. It will not be statistically documented.

The term "isolation" used in the introduction requires explication. Certainly the twenty miles of Shelikof Strait which, at its narrowest point separate Kodiak from the Alaska Peninsula, were only a minor barrier to proficient boatmen like those of the North Pacific coast who have traveled several hundred miles in a single trip. This strait and the wider water expanses separating Kodiak from other parts of the mainland would, however, likely be significant obstacles to people who were not proficient on the sea, i.e. who had not achieved a maritime adaptation. More significant than the fact of separation from the mainland is isolation from other areas offering the potential for a different lifeway. Thus, departure to the south side of the Alaska Peninsula or to the outer Kenai Peninsula does not materially change positions in terms of exploitative potential or ecosystems, although some caribou and a further varied fauna absent on Kodiak are available. The larger caribou herds, moose, rabbits, and the very important freshwater fish stocks which form the core of interior Athabaskan and riverine Eskimo economy are essentially outside the reach of the inhabitants of Kodiak.

The indigenous mammalian land fauna of Kodiak is very limited, being restricted essentially to brown bear, foxes, river otter, and some smaller species such as voles and local ground squirrels (W. Clark 1958; cf. Manville and Young 1965, for taxonomic terms). Ungulates of all kinds — caribou, black-tail deer, elk, moose, and mountain sheep — were lacking prior to modern introduction, along with black bear and some of the smaller animals utilized for game and fur elsewhere in Alaska, such as muskrat, beaver, porcupine, marmot and lynx.

The principal inland game species of avifauna is the ptarmigan, but it is not established that it was utilized aboriginally to any significant degree. Ducks, geese and swans also are available during migration. Waterfowl were used extensively but exploitation of fowl, including egg collecting, was oriented towards the saltwater habitat and coast line.

One of the main resources of the region is the salmon, of which there are two prolific species, the humpback or pink salmon *(Oncorhynchus gorbuscha)* and the red salmon *(O. nerka)*, as well as three additional species locally of lesser importance. This resource is highly seasonal, however, being limited essentially to the summer months, although during former years of abundance early running red salmon appeared by the beginning of May and late running silver or coho salmon *(O. kisutch)* could be taken from the spawning streams in the fall. Other fresh water fish of potential significance are limited to trout and char but, exclusive of the sea run component, these represent a relatively small biomass. Lacking are the several species of whitefish and iconnu or shee, pike, suckers, losh or ling cod, blackfish, grayling, and the large lake trout which are important to the maintenance of subarctic populations. Though salmon is considered a marine resource, its travels to spawn take it many hundred miles up the major rivers where it becomes accessible to inland populations. On Kodiak, due to the intricate but small-scale topography and proximity to the sea, the fishery still is marine patterned, although aboriginally salmon might not have been taken at sea. The area lacks any large rivers, but it has hundreds of streams and creeks that formerly carried runs of approximately 1,000 to 10,000,000 salmon. This distribution over a large number of relatively small short units — small in terms of both the size of the run and the size of the water body to which a particular fishing technique has to be applied — has resulted in the salmon fishery being oriented primarily towards the stream mouths along the coast, which actually are the most convenient places for fishing camps. Other aspects of the marine ecosystem could thereby be exploited at the same time. There are, however, a few outstanding exceptions that have not been investigated by archaeologists. These are the inland camps or settlements located on the Karluk and Red (Ayakulik) river systems, the two largest stream systems on Kodiak.

The saltwater fishery, which may have been as important as the salmon fishery, concentrated on sculpin, cod, and halibut (Hewes 1947). In addition, the littoral zone was extensively utilized for shellfish. Clams of several species, periwinkles and whelks, blue mussels, and sea urchins are the principal components of Kodiak shell middens. Little use appears to have been made of the several species of crabs, shrimp, and scallops which are important in the commercial fishery of the region, possibly because of inadequately developed exploitative techniques. Herring roe, seaweed, and other nutrient sources could have been harvested, although they are not mentioned in ethnographic accounts. The bird species exploited are principally those associated with saltwater and sea cliff habitats, although the range of species taken is extensive (Heizer 1956: 26).

The maritime orientation is seen most strongly in the sea mammal hunting complex which includes ceremonialism and utilization practices as well as hunting techniques. Although few species were available, including harbor seals, sea lions, fur seals, sea otter, and several species of whales and porpoise, these were good providers of meat, animal fat or oil, and hides or furs. It can be surmised that the sea mammals were a relatively reliable and stable economic base even though they were in part seasonal.

Prehistoric economy on Kodiak focused on the sea mammal hunt, salt water fishery, salmon fishery, and on littoral gathering. Land resources were not neglected. They simply were inadequate and overshadowed by products of the sea. Brown bear, river otter, foxes, and ground squirrels, where available, were utilized as was the domesticated dog, probably for dietary purposes and fur. Simple minimum individual counts show, exclusive of the domestic dog and large whales, land to sea mammal proportions respectively of 18/36, 22/37, 2/33, 8/26, and 5/35 for five sites (D. Clark 1968). The lower proportions are from three relatively late Koniag phase sites and are due principally to a decreased incidence of fox bones. The main component lacking in these statistics is caribou and other ungulates although, incidentally, they do include three deer or caribou bones which must represent imports.

Resources are referred to as belonging to the land or to the sea, but it is inappropriate to think of any inland or hinterland zone, inasmuch as the intricate embayment of the area has made all parts of the Kodiak group accessible from the coast through distances not exceeding at the very most 14 miles. Furthermore, outside of the southwestern part of the island much of the land is so mountainous and brushy that penetration away from the coast is difficult (Capps 1937). The intricate coastline of approximately 1,000 miles for a land area of about 5,000 square miles has enhanced the potential of the area as a habitat for marine species, including maritime oriented man. No attempt is being made here to offer any biological assessment of the merits of an intricate coastline versus a simple one. Nevertheless, the following factors bear consideration: (1) greatly increased length of the littoral zone; (2) a probable concomitant increase in the animal populations, including fish and birds that depend directly or indirectly upon the littoral zone for food and reproduction; (3) semi-protected embayments in which to carry out hunting and fishing activities; (4) features which tend to localize whale herds and which are particularly suited for the lance method of whaling in which the whale is allowed to die and drift ashore; and (5) probable correlates in settlement pattern.

Regional geography, terrain, and ecology have been considered thus far. Climate is an additional factor likely to have had a major effect on the exploitative pattern. The climate is maritime insofar as that term denotes moderated temperature extremes and a large number of overcast and rainy days with frequent stormy periods. Its temperature characteristics are northern north temperate. Thus, winter extremes infrequently go below zero degrees Fahrenheit; the summer maximum is seldom above eighty degrees; and diurnal variation is small. During winter, late fall, and early spring the temperature often hovers near freezing and at almost any time the snow may change to rain or the rain to snow. The ground usually is covered with snow from sometime in December until April, but often there is a false spring or warm period in February or March, commonly the worst months of the year, during which low altitude snow disappears. Kodiak is not icebound at any time, but thick ice does form at the heads of protected bays where freshwater streams enter. Although the climate is in a temperate range, inclement weather often accompanied by gale storms is a factor that profoundly affects living conditions and industry there today as it undoubtedly did in the past. Rainfall is not over sixty inches, but it is distributed over a large number of drizzly days punctuated by lashing gales. One weather summary lists 191 days with 0.01 inch or more precipitation including snow, and to that precipitation-free, gloomy days may be added (Rieger and Wunderlich 1960: Table 1). Morale, living conditions, and food preservation suffer, and it is difficult to hunt, fish, and travel. Less frequently the reverse happens — a prolonged redeeming period of dry, clear weather. Such weather "spells," good and bad, tend to override the seasonal pattern, which in addition to winter and summer in a more or less conventional sense are characterized also by powerful equinoctial storms and high tides.

Livestock is raised commercially on Kodiak today and some crops can be grown, although presently there is no commercial horticulture. Animal husbandry and horticulture are not considered as potential alternate economic patterns inasmuch as their successful maintenance is difficult; the area is poorly suited for the development of domesticates, and earlier there was no contact with any areas from which domesticates might have been introduced.

Because technological change and continuity will be viewed diachronically it is essential that similar consideration be given to the environment and ecosystem. This is not an easy task inasmuch as the definitive studies available deal only with flora and, indirectly, climate (Heusser 1960; also Heusser 1963). The climatic changes delineated by Heusser, however, may not have been significant to human occupation. Also, these are given in relative terms and it is difficult to formulate precisely their quantified equivalents. It is doubtful if any amount of change experienced was sufficient to cause the coast around Kodiak to become icebound or to cause the salmon streams to dry up or change in critical spawning temperature. Thus, the marine ecosystem probably was not, for purposes under consideration, significantly affected by post-glacial climatic change. What happened on the land is of less significance; there were no crops to harvest or herds of animals whose range might be affected. These assumptions, however, require eventual critical examination. For instance, the question of sea temperature, currents, and the distribution of important fish stocks and associated components of the food chain should be considered. Interestingly, the spruce forest has spread over the northern half of Kodiak only during recent millennia (Heusser 1960). The advance of the forest is only approximately dated, and it has not been tied into the archaeological sequence. In the north the spruce forest probably appeared during the span of the Kachemak tradition (see section below), but it has not yet reached the southern half of Kodiak. Poplar and Kenai birch are available in some localities that lack spruce, and it is probable that the native inhabitants utilized driftwood more than they did standing timber.


## CULTURAL SEQUENCE

The archaeological sequence for Kodiak is first described and in the ensuing discussion reconsidered in terms of continuity and change. Particular attention is given to technological and exploitative elements and also to the evidence for ethnic or group continuity and discontinuity.


*Ocean Bay I*

Ocean Bay I, the earliest known prehistoric culture on Kodiak and adjacent islands, is represented by test excavations at Ocean Bay (D. Clark 1966) and at the mouth of the Afognak River (D. Clark 1971, 1972). It is very similar to the Takli Alder phase of the adjacent Alaska Peninsula (G. Clark 1968; Dumond 1971). Radiocarbon dating at all three locations indicates an antiquity starting 5,900–5,500 radiocarbon years ago.

The salient feature of Ocean Bay I is an overwhelming reliance on flaked stone in contrast to the emphasis on ground slate found throughout the rest of the Kodiak sequence. Otherwise, the lithic inventory is not particularly complex. It consists principally of rough bifaced blades and a few smaller, thin bifaced blades, stemmed and leaf-shaped projectile points and knives, and at the Afognak site crude microcores, "wedges" or *pièces esquillées*, and the occasional boulder flake. Small quantities of chipped slate and ground slate, sometimes sawed, also were present. A stone lamp was found at the base of the Ocean Bay site. Precise delineation of the Ocean Bay I phase is compromised by the presence in higher levels at Ocean Bay of the sequent Ocean Bay II component and at Afognak likewise in the upper levels by a component of transitional configuration. Thus, artifacts displaced or eroded out of the sites could belong to either component, and it can be argued that some artifacts in the lower levels originated from the upper components. This reasoning might be applied to the very few pieces of slate found in the original Ocean Bay I component. The question actually is not whether slate grinding is an Ocean Bay I trait inasmuch as ground slate also has been found at the very base of the Afognak site, but it pertains to specific attributes of slate working. Thus, while the Sitkalidak site slate from the lower component at Ocean Bay, which must be labeled equivocal because of its rarity, displays the scraping and sawing techniques, these slate-working techniques do not appear in the lowest three levels of the Afognak site which are the only Ocean Bay I levels there that do not display a transitional character. The earliest Afognak slate consists simply of beach-rolled bars and rods that have been retouched by grinding. Slate work does not become abundant until the appearance of sawed, scraped, and ground pieces along with chipped slate specimens which effect a transitional appearance probably late in the Ocean Bay I phase.

Ecological data for Ocean Bay I is largely inferential, particularly because there is no organic preservation. The Ocean Bay site on Sitkalidak Island is situated near but not on a multispecies salmon stream. The embayment here extended farther inland in the past, but it remains likely that a salmon spawning area had formed here by Ocean Bay I times. The location of this site toward the open ocean suggests a maritime hunting economy, including whaling, and, interestingly, a Koniag whaling village was located at Ocean Bay during the contact period. There may have been some littoral gathering, but presently the sand beach is poor for this purpose. It is, however, easy to communicate overland from Ocean Bay to more protected rocky embayments around Sitkalidak Island.

The site at the mouth of the Afognak River appears to have been located there primarily for the purpose of exploiting salmon runs which, as at Ocean Bay, include the early running red salmon and the late running silver salmon as well as, in between, the prolific pink salmon. Presently, the site is located on salt water at the head of Afognak Bay, but prior to subsidence during the 1964 earthquake it was situated on the tidal estuary of the Afognak River. Probably land hunting and littoral gathering were practiced too, but in the brackish water invertebrate fauna of economic significance in the littoral zone would be limited largely to blue mussels and some clams. It is, however, easy to reach the waters of Afognak Bay and Marmot Bay beyond for sea mammal hunting and whaling. The high frequency of projectile tips in the Ocean Bay I assemblage at Afognak emphatically suggests that hunting as well as fishing was undertaken from this site. Bone harpoon dart heads have been recovered from the related Takli Alder phase (G. Clark 1968: Plate 7) where also a faunal assemblage strongly emphasizing seal, porpoise, sea otter, and sea lion has been recovered (G. Clark 1968: 196, Table 41). Because of the sheet of ice which forms where the river enters Afognak Bay, it is very doubtful that the Afognak site was occupied during winter and early spring; and this fact may be taken as evidence of a structured annual cycle with seasonal settlements.

*Ocean Bay II*

Sequent upon Ocean Bay I at the Sitkalidak Island or Ocean Bay site and also found on Afognak, at a site located across the river from the one to which reference has been made, is Ocean Bay II. The two Afognak sites (Afo–106 and Afo–109) will be distinguished hereafter as the chert site and the slate site. Ocean Bay II, in the strict sense, is characterized by the near total eclipse of stone flaking and by its apparent replacement by slate working. By stone flaking reference is made to the working of flinty materials, particularly poor grade cherts and basalt, and not to the production of simple heavy items such as boulder flakes or to the production of blanks to be finished later through grinding. Ocean Bay II begins about 4,200 years ago, but a transition of I and II characteristics is earlier, and it lasts only a few centuries.

Flaking is almost completely absent in the upper Ocean Bay II levels at the Sitkalidak site while flaked artifacts are more common, but still a minor element, at the Afognak slate site. In addition to this shift in technology, one of the main characteristics of Ocean Bay II is its constellation of slate working attributes. Least distinctive is the final stage of finishing a slate object, rubbing or honing, which is not different from that found in later cultures of the region. Whetstones of varied texture found in Ocean Bay II undoubtedly were used to finish slate and possibly other materials. Blanks were reduced sometimes through coarse grinding but most frequently they were scraped to form. The latter technique, scraping, is peculiar to Ocean Bay II and, as far as is known, occurs elsewhere only in the unrelated Choris culture (Giddings 1957). The implement used to scrape slate has not been isolated. At one time it was considered to be a chert flake, either retouched or unretouched, but too few possible implements of this kind have been recovered. Experiments will be made to determine if boulderflakes and hard sandstone slabs could have been used for this purpose. The initial blank was formed either by sawing a slate sheet into straight-sided strips or tablets or by flaking. The flaking technique was used only occasionally, while Ocean Bay II deposits are littered with sawn slate fragments. By contrast, most later blanks up to the time of historic contact were chipped, and only the occasional find shows that the same sawing technique was still known. Opposing saw cuts were made and the piece was then snapped through the remaining septum. The instrument for sawing appears to have been a boulder flake or sandstone tablet, numerous examples of which have been recovered. Ocean Bay II may exemplify the transferral of bone-working techniques to slate but this hypothesis cannot be tested without recovery of organic material. The sawing technique noted here was, however, later used on Kodiak for bone.

Ocean Bay II slate work emphasizes pointed implements including numerous spear or lance points on the order of twenty centimeters long. Large, broad, stemmed and unstemmed double-edged knives are also common while single-edged knives comparable to the Eskimo ulu are rare. Wood-working tools, particularly adzes, are also rare. Notched pebbles and cobbles which probably were used as line and net weights are present but are uncommon compared to their incidence in later phases and may in fact appear late in Ocean Bay II. Slightly modified cobble mauls are found here as well as in later phases. Elliptical stone lamps were used throughout the Kodiak sequence. End scrapers are absent in Ocean Bay II and later phases and other scrapers of any recognized format, aside from boulder flakes, are rare. Retouched flakes are found in Ocean Bay I, but only poorly defined or equivocal end scrapers have been recognized. Thus, few tool and implement types are represented.

Differences in lithic technology notwithstanding, Ocean Bay I and II industries are similar in scope. This consideration, along with the fact that one was found physically overlying the other, suggests that they are sequent phases of a single culture. Transitional between Ocean Bay I and II is a period characterized by elements of both phases, especially by a strong emphasis on both slate work and flaked stone. At Ocean Bay such characteristics are found through a limited interval of the site deposit and, in part, could be due to physical intermixture at what otherwise could have been a sharper interface. The slate site on Afognak, to interject an interpretation, has changed completely to Ocean Bay II characteristics while the upper half of the chert site is seemingly transitional. Additional time should have elapsed between the abandonment of one site and occupation of the other to allow for the shift from flaked stone to ground slate.

A simple, straight-line development of this nature does not, however, fit the radiocarbon dates which indicate that on Afognak the transitional aspect and Ocean Bay II proper are contemporary. Either the single radiocarbon date applicable to the transitional material, 4200 B.P., is to be rejected as being too late, thus allowing the model of unilineal development to be retained, or the Ocean Bay tradition should be considered as bifurcating into two parts. In one branch slate working almost excluded chert flaking, while the other branch simply added slate technology to stone flaking. The unilineal model is most acceptable on the basis of simplicity, but the transitional aspect or branch of the bifurcation model does appear to approximate best the Takli Birch phase of the mainland opposite which is sequent upon Ocean Bay I (G. Clark 1968; Dumond 1971). In the mainland case Takli Birch is not transitional to Ocean Bay II but is simply non-Ocean Bay II. This discussion involves uncertainties in our present knowledge and, except to indicate that there are two possible *in situ* bases for the development of subsequent cultures on Kodiak, further consideration must be held in abeyance.

Ecologic interpretation of Ocean Bay II, including any transitional stage and aspect, is essentially the same as that offered for Ocean Bay I. In part the same sites are involved, and at Afognak the slate site and the chert site are located in close proximity, the former being on the opposite side of the river estuary and slightly farther upstream. Situational evidence, as earlier discussed, suggests a primary focus on salmon fishing at the river mouth on Afognak. The upriver displacement of the site could be an adjustment to subsidence at some prehistoric date and, as such, it reiterates the focus on the stream and its salmon fishery. The appearance of notched pebbles may be indicative of netting or line fishing in deep water while cobble mauls could have been used to drive trap stakes along the tidal reaches of the stream. As noted earlier, it is doubtful that there was year-round occupation due to ice conditions at the river mouth.

Debris from slate working reaches such proportions at the Afognak slate site as to suggest that slate was processed there to be utilized elsewhere. The numerous large bayonet points and fragments found in Ocean Bay II sites suggest an emphasis on large mammals, possibly including whales. The large slate tips might also be thrust into a brown bear or human intruders. Use of slate weapons may, however, be more feasible for marine hunting than for hunting on land inasmuch as a cast that misses its mark and plunges into the water is less likely to result in a broken point than a deviant cast on land. No bone artifacts are preserved in any Ocean Bay II sites, but harpoon dart heads were probably made in styles similar to those of the Takli Birch phase (G. Clark 1968) which are not appreciably different from some later harpoon heads from the Kachemak-Kodiak-Aleutian region.

*Kachemak Tradition*

Succeeding the Ocean Bay phases or tradition on Kodiak, and also found in the outer Cook Inlet area, is a developmental series of stages or phases called the Kachemak tradition. Various components have been radiocarbon dated from 1300 B.C. to A.D. 900, and it is estimated that the tradition spans an additional 200-year period at each end of this time range. This tradition was first investigated and periodized by de Laguna's work at Kachemak Bay (1934). The Uyak "Pre-Koniag" lower levels (Heizer 1956; Hrdlička 1944) and the Crag Point site (D. Clark 1970) contain both early and late Kachemak tradition components, while the Three Saints site (D. Clark 1970) is relatively late, largely spanning the first millennium A.D. The Old Kiavak site (D. Clark 1966a) is early — first to second millennium B.C. Some surface collections from the Afognak River also belong to this tradition (Workman 1972). For our present purposes only certain characteristics of the Kachemak tradition need to be discussed.

Through two-and-a-half millennia the Kachemak tradition became progressively more elaborate, but the early impoverishment is in part only an appearance due to limited organic preservation. The earliest Kachemak people had a simple implement kit. They flaked and ground stone, but not in the Ocean Bay II slate-working technique and styles; they wore labrets and lighted their dwellings with oil lamps. Among their distinctive implements are a plummet-style stone weight grooved about one end and an archaic appearing toggle harpoon head (de Laguna 1934: Plate 38, Numbers 11–16).

Through time, in Kachemak II (Cook Inlet sequence), including the Old Kiavak phase of Kodiak, material culture became more complex, but still there was little elaboration of implements and art. The active Kachemak fishermen now produced, probably for fish net weights, large numbers of notched pebbles and, more likely, for line and seal net weights, several varieties of grooved stones. An occasional implement might be flaked from chert now and throughout the rest of the Kachemak tradition, but ground slate predominated. Slate was also flaked.

The first millennium A.D. was the zenith of the Kachemak tradition. The distinctiveness of late Kachemak culture is seen best when it is contrasted with the succeeding Koniag culture. Although there is considerable continuity in the types of implements used, late Kachemak produced better finished implements and hunting equipment. Furthermore, many stylistic attributes change, generally, to simpler ones in the Koniag phase. Late Kachemak people were appreciative of personal adornment and art which are represented by their beads, pendants, figurines, labrets, designs incised on ground slate points, and massive, pecked-stone lamps with human and animal figures on the exterior or carved in the bowl in high relief. Occupation sites and refuse deposits are replete with evidence for varied practices with the dead, including cut and drilled human bones, artificial eyes, and probable cannibalism.

Ecologic data for the Kachemak tradition is good due to improved preservation of refuse and bone artifacts at several midden sites. The data cannot be discussed here, but are available in the publications cited earlier in this section. There is an all-pervasive emphasis on maritime hunting and fishing and seasonal exploitation of salmon streams with extensive use of birds and harvesting of the littoral zone. This is what was inferred for the Ocean Bay tradition but can now be better substantiated.

At the Afognak River, Kachemak tradition sites are located a short distance upriver from the two Ocean Bay tradition sites, the apparent earliest Kachemak site (Workman 1972) being nearly opposite the Ocean Bay II slate site; and, thus, they continue the upriver shift noted earlier. A damaged, late Kachemak site was observed close to the edge of the beach at Ocean Bay in a situation analagous, in many aspects, to that of the Ocean Bay tradition site there. The majority of Kachemak tradition sites are distributed along the coast in precisely the same manner as succeeding Koniag culture sites and, in fact, many midden sites up to fifteen feet deep present more than one Kachemak tradition stage and are further overlain, with or without an occupational hiatus, by Koniag culture, and even by historic deposits. A similar settlement pattern, and probably exploitative pattern, thus is indicated for all cultural traditions on Kodiak.

*Koniag Culture*

The last culture to be described for the Kodiak area is one which has been traced to the contact horizon of the Koniags. The Koniag Eskimos have been described by several late eighteenth and early nineteenth century explorers, principally Lisianski (1814) but also by Davidov (1810–1812), Merck (in Jacobi 1937), Gedeon (in Valaam Monastry 1894), and others. Excavations on the southeastern side of Kodiak further document Koniag culture at the time of contact and during the centuries immediately preceding (D. Clark 1966b, 1968). Koniag phase sites also have been excavated elsewhere on Kodiak (Hrdlička 1944; Heizer 1956; D. Clark, unpublished manuscripts). Those on the southeastern side and southwestern half of Kodiak present a complexion differing from that of other Koniag phase sites. This southwestern or ceramic variant probably owes its distinctiveness to two principal factors. The first is that, through a somewhat different history or different lines of communication, cultural attributes and preferences differed between the geographic ends of the Koniag distribution; the second is that the southwestern sites represent, on the average, a later period, largely after A.D. 1500. Nevertheless, the oldest Koniag radiocarbon date comes from a ceramic component (P–1041; D. Clark 1966b). The question of regional and temporal variation within the Koniag phase has been discussed elsewhere (D. Clark 1968, Chapter 10). The paramount archaeological trait involved in this differentiation is pottery of a Bering Sea type which is limited essentially to the southwestern Koniags. The implement list of the Koniags is very much like that of the Kachemak tradition except, as noted, for variation at the attribute level. Some differences of a more absolute nature include, in the functional category, the use of ceramics, notched stones or cobbles, and heavy wood-working tools, particularly adzes, while social significance may be attached to Koniag sweatbathing and incised figurine production (D. Clark 1964). These traits are discussed further in the context of cultural continuity and discontinuity.

A large body of ethnographic description complements our knowledge of the Koniag phase, but at the same time it is hardly equivalent to the strictly archaeologic data for earlier cultures.

Koniag ecology has been described elsewhere on the basis of ethnological and archaeological data (D. Clark 1968). The earlier discussion of ecological factors is also appropriate here. Except for some possible differences in fishing techniques and a varied emphasis on certain mammals, particularly less use of fox and at the time of contact, more emphasis on fur seal, Koniag ecology does not appear to have differed greatly from that of the Kachemak tradition.

## CONTINUITY, CHANGE, AND DISCONTINUITY IN THE CULTURAL SEQUENCE

*Discussion*

At the risk of confusing fact with interpretation, the two are integrated in the paragraphs to follow. The discussion also supplements that of the cultural sequence, although regrettably there is some redundancy.

It can be assumed that Ocean Bay I is a continuity from an as yet undiscovered base on Kodiak or the adjacent mainland. The Aleutian site, Anangula, dated at about 8,000 years B.P. (Laughlin 1967; Aigner 1970), does not appear to be related to Ocean Bay I, but it and sites along the coast of British Columbia (Fladmark 1970, and verbal communications to the author, 1971) and southeastern Alaska (Ackerman 1968) show that some kind of North Pacific maritime occupation or adaptation had been achieved before Ocean Bay I time. This, of course, is a prerequisite to the pattern found on Kodiak.

The striking difference in technology between Ocean Bay I and II, which includes not only the adoption of slate working, but also a concomitant and extreme decrease in stone flaking in Ocean Bay II proper, invites speculation regarding the processes involved. The choice between chert flaking and slate working is a cultural one, and apparently was not forced by the lack or availability of raw material even though much of the chert utilized is of a poor quality. However, some factors in the environment, such as hunting on a water medium, may have facilitated the practical employment of slate. Presently, it is not established that Ocean Bay II could not have developed separately from Ocean Bay I, later to become fused with it to form an apparent transitional stage; it is more likely a simple lineal development from Ocean Bay I. Ocean Bay I and II are similar in the general scope of implement classes, probably implying an overall similarity in lifeways. A single historical tradition is seen here as enveloping marked technological changes, including, in addition to the factors already discussed, the loss of microblade and core technology early within the time span of Ocean Bay I.

The question of continuity between the Ocean Bay tradition and the Kachemak tradition is presently unresolved. On the Pacific side of the Alaska Peninsula, continuity is seen during the pertinent period, about 1800–1300 B.C. (Dumond 1971); but the Peninsula and Kodiak phases now are not closely equivalent, and the Kachemak tradition as narrowly defined for Kodiak and outer Cook Inlet may not be appropriate to the nearby shores of the Alaska Peninsula. Continuity is less apparent on Kodiak.

That such continuity is found a few miles away on the mainland could mean that it is present but not recognized on Kodiak due to insufficient investigation there. Otherwise, the moderate divergence in regional phases at this time could indicate that the course of history on Kodiak was different and that there is a distinct cultural break between Ocean Bay II and early Kachemak. The synchronic similarities between early-middle Kachemak on Kodiak and late Takli Birch on the Pacific side of the Alaska Peninsula would be due to extensive borrowing between or among cultures existing in close spatial or temporal proximity and adjusting to an exploitative pattern common to the greater region.

We do not intend to go through a trait-by-trait recounting of points of continuity and discontinuity between Ocean Bay II and early-middle stages of the Kachemak tradition in order to document these remarks. Certain technological aspects, however, should be mentioned, particularly points of departure, omitting from consideration the several traits which do continue from Ocean Bay II. Although ground slate is well represented, flaked stone is more common in early-middle Kachemak sites than it is in either Ocean Bay II or in the later Kachemak and Koniag phases. *Vis-à-vis* Ocean Bay II proper, this situation represents a partial resurgence of flaking, but it could be seen as a smooth development out of any I–II transitional aspect of Ocean Bay culture. Less uncertainty exists in the complete cessation of Ocean Bay slate scraping technology, common to both Ocean Bay II proper and any I–II transitional aspect, and, in a marked decrease in the incidence of stone sawing prior to or at the inception of the Kachemak tradition. Also, the large Ocean Bay II bayonet points, which frequently have diminutive barbs and cut lines, are not found in the Kachemak tradition. Unfortunately, bone recovery is poor in Ocean Bay tradition sites; therefore, toggle harpoon heads can only provisionally be considered as absent. Toggling harpoons appear very early in the Kachemak tradition at Cook Inlet. Numerous grooved stones and exceedingly abundant notched pebbles suggest that the Kachemak people made much greater use of net fishing and line fishing than their predecessors, although a few notched pebbles were used in Ocean Bay II. The shift in slate-working technology and styles is seen as indicating a change in people or ethnic groups while the congruities with the earlier culture developed in the manner proposed in the preceding paragraph.

In addition to the elaboration that developed during the Kachemak tradition, stone drilling was adopted part way through, particularly to facilitate hafting slate knives of the double-edged flensing blade and single-edged ulu types. The latter, which are represented only by possible fragments in Ocean Bay II, are at first small and uncommon, but following a trend that continues through the Koniag phase, they become larger and more numerous, while wide double-edged knives, which were never very common, become rare. The ulu was the ethnographic fish-processing and skinning tool; therefore, inasmuch as it is doubtful that the fisheries came into prominence only during the last two or three millennia, other tools were used at one time for splitting fish. Perhaps the boulder flake, which is well represented through the Kodiak sequence except in Ocean Bay I where it is rare, was used (Workman 1972). Boulder flakes were tremendously popular during the Kachemak tradition, but they were usually blunted, probably for scraping hides. It is obvious, however, that the boulder chip is not a single trait. Thus, in Ocean Bay II, but rarely at any other time, at one site there are numerous smooth-edged specimens that had been used as saws. In addition to the blunted scrapers, there are for all periods sharp-edged specimens which heretofore have been considered as rejects or nonutilized pieces, but which might be reconsidered as knives and fish scalers.

De Laguna's outline of Kachemak Bay culture (1934: 121–131), while only partially applicable to Kodiak, indicates in general the development involved. The distinctiveness and later elaboration of this tradition is seen in the local geographic and time perspective; thus, in a different context, it might not be particularly outstanding. Essentially, the same conclusion as that offered in the case of the Ocean Bay-Kachemak succession was reached from a much larger data base in a detailed consideration of the Koniag succession which occurred about A.D. 1000–1100 (D. Clark 1968). That is, there is no total break, but the degree of continuity is overshadowed by the amount of change. Events leading to the formation of Koniag culture — positive accretions, modifications, and deletions from the pre-existing base — probably occurred over a period of several centuries. Unfortunately, however, our present undetailed knowledge of the period A.D. 1000–1300 on Kodiak has hindered attaining a thorough understanding of the transition between Kachemak and Koniag cultures. The changes which took place approximately between A.D. 800 and A.D. 1300 appear to be too extensive to be explained simply as the result of ongoing change and development. A reworking of cultural values, probable strong influence from outside, and some population movement appear to have been involved. Influences and new settlers came from the adjacent Alaska Peninsula or from the Bering Sea across the Peninsula and also from other parts of the mainland, particularly from the south central region. This activity appears to have had its inception during the

Kachemak tradition and continued throughout the Koniag phase.

The Koniag are a Yupik-speaking Eskimo group, and, as known ethnographically, their culture is in many aspects typically Eskimo while at the same time it has a particular northern North Pacific cast which is shared with its Aleut and non-Eskimo neighbors. The linguistic affiliation of the Kachemak tradition has not been established with certainty (Dumond 1965, 1971, and elsewhere), but is has generally been assumed to be Eskimo. A dialect probably has existed with its present form and relationships for only a limited period, but it can be put into progressively larger and more encompassing linguistic groups for progressively remoter periods. Thus, the appropriate question to ask is: Was the Koniag succession also a linguistic succession; and if so, did the change cross language, language family, or language stock and presumably major racial boundaries? The last, Esk-Aleutian replacing an Indian stock, is very unlikely while the other alternatives have been the topic of considerable discussion which does not, in the writer's estimation, lead to any firm conclusion. Although linguistic or ethnic identification is of critical import to some problems in prehistory such as that of the origin of Eskimos and their maritime adaptation, the present discussion will sidestep this issue.

Technological changes occurring between the Kachemak tradition and the Koniag culture, to consider now some of the data upon which the foregoing discussion was based, include a possible greater emphasis on heavy wood working as represented by considerably more numerous planing adzes and a new trait, the common heavy grooved splitting adze, and also by larger bone wedges. The type of stone drill used on slate changed later in the Koniag phase to one which produced a less regular and often canted hole. Small notched pebbles no longer are produced while larger notched and grooved cobbles are common. Such larger weights would likely have been used for line fishing in the sea and on sea mammal nets, and thus from the absence of small pebbles, a change in fishing techniques away from nets may be indicated. Also, the disappearance of barbs on almost all but the largest slate points may indicate a modification in weapons. In the southwestern area, the Koniags boiled food in earthenware pots placed over or adjacent to the fire while evidence of such direct boiling is unusual for the Kachemak tradition.

Aside from the question of Koniag-Kachemak comparisons, long, slender slate bayonet points for whaling spear-darts (Heizer 1956: Plate 62) and also sea otter harpoon arrowheads and foreshafts are poorly represented archaeologically. In the case of the whaling projectiles it is probable that at an earlier time the same darting technique, not harpooning, was employed since it also is well established in the Aleutian Islands (Heizer 1943). But, as in the Aleutian case, a shorter stone tip could have been inserted into a long bone point. In the absence of the distinctive whaling points prior to the contact horizon, evidence for whaling is of a less direct nature, consisting of faunal remains in the sites and representational art found in the Kachemak tradition as well as in the Koniag phase. Interestingly, the long bayonet points of Ocean Bay II are very suggestive of late Koniag whaling points.

The scarcity of sea otter harpoon arrow foreshafts and heads may indicate simply that prior to contact most sea otter were taken with the similarly modeled but heavier harpoon dart. On the other hand, it correlates very well with the extreme rarity of sea otter remains in both Kachemak tradition and Koniag sites. This matter is open to further interpretation, however, because the lack of sea otter could be due to special disposal practices instead of a low level of utilization, although in adjacent Prince William Sound sea otter remains are common in a first millennium A.D. midden (de Laguna 1956). The Pacific Eskimo had a well-delineated sea otter hunting complex involving the cooperative water-surround method of hunting (Lisianski 1814: 203–205), bows and harpoon arrows or sometimes the harpoon dart, hunting hats, and amulet boxes. This is similar to the Aleut sea otter hunt (Heizer 1960). It is perplexing, then, to find the highly developed sea otter hunting complex so poorly represented in the archaeologic record.

### Recapitulation of Continuity and Change or Discontinuity

The adoption or innovation of slate working during Ocean Bay times was a major technological change. Ground slate present in low frequency increased to a moderate frequency during a transitional stage, then there was a marked shift away from stone flaking in Ocean Bay II proper with a concomitant surge in slate working. Between the Ocean Bay and Kachemak traditions there is again change involving the specific technology and styles of slate working. There also may have been a change in fishing techniques. Further technological change during the Kachemak tradition is seen principally as part of an ongoing development. Much of the differentiation between the Kachemak tradition and the Koniag phase is nontechnologic or is of a minor technological nature. Altogether, however, the differences are such that a period of moderate technological change, coincident with other cultural changes, is represented. The Koniag phase underwent continuing development.

After Ocean Bay I, slate grinding remained the major stone-working technique along with, at all times, rough chipping of slate and graywacke and stone pecking as used to produce stone lamps. The economy is seen as being essentially the same during the entire recorded occupation of Kodiak. Unfortunately, this assessment has had to be based in part upon *a priori* judgment from the broader situational context and settlement pattern, inasmuch as the evidence of faunal remains and bone projectile components is largely lacking for the Ocean Bay tradition. There may have been changes in exploitative techniques, probably in fishing. Differences which have occurred in the size and barbing of stone points are not necessarily very informative unless the whole weapons system is taken into consideration because a stone point might be part of a complex weapon head. The large bayonet points in Ocean Bay II do present a challenge for an explanation. If not used for whaling, they might have been used to lance harpooned animals. Trends with continuity over more than one tradition involve single-edged slate knives or ulus, adzes, and possibly other implement classes.

Ocean Bay II is seen as developmental from Ocean Bay I without any marked cultural discontinuity that might indicate population replacement. On the contrary, although several elements of continuity are present, the Kachemak tradition provisionally is seen as involving new people; but more needs to be learned about the period 1800–1400 B.C. before a firm statement is made. The Koniag phase was at one time seen as representing invaders who supplanted their pre-Koniag predecessors (Hrdlička 1944), but now it can best be characterized in a single word as an amalgamation of peoples and cultural elements. Accordingly, in the Kodiak sequence certain technologic traditions persisted through changes in cultural traditions, and, inversely, technological change does not necessarily indicate a change in peoples or tribal groups. This appraisal is admittedly highly interpretive — almost intuitive.

## CULTURAL MILIEU AND SIGNIFICANCE FOR PREHISTORIC INTERPRETATION

This section presents a brief comparison of Kodiak and adjacent regions and offers conclusions which take into account these comparisons and the previous discussion of technical and cultural continuity and change.

Ocean Bay I is found on the Pacific coast of the Alaska Peninsula in the form of the Takli Alder phase (Dumond 1971; G. Clark 1968). After Takli Alder, the Pacific coast becomes more or less divergent from Kodiak, although at the time of historic contact both areas were occupied by Koniags. The last three centuries there before contact have as yet to be represented by significant archaeologic investigations, and, when they are, it will be instructive to observe the variation or divergence that exists within a single-named ethnographic and dialect group. In outer Cook Inlet, the Kachemak Bay sequence (de Laguna 1934) is an expression of the Kachemak tradition. There is some question as to the nature of the outer Cook Inlet sequence prior to and following the Kachemak tradition due to insufficient exploration, but there is tentative evidence for a Pacific Eskimo occupation related to the Koniag phase. In much of the outer Inlet area this was succeeded recently by Athabaskan Indian occupation. A moderate degree of relationship is seen between Kodiak and outer Cook inlet on the one hand and the incomplete Prince William Sound sequence on the other hand (de Laguna 1956). All these areas indicated were occupied by Pacific Eskimo at the time of contact late in the eighteenth century and can be considered, with reservations, as a single entity.

Other archaeologic and ethnographic cultures of adjacent parts of the North Pacific arc include several phases of Aleut culture, the Tanaina Athabaskans which figuratively are intrusive into Pacific Eskimo territory, the Eyak to the immediate eastern flank of the Chugach section of the Pacific Eskimo, and farther east, but crowding the Eyak, the northern Tlingit.

Most of these groups occupy ecosystems — situations of terrain, environment, and resource potential — which are at least approximately comparable to Kodiak. The most divergent are those of the Tanaina (Osgood 1937) and the Eyak Indians (Birket-Smith and de Laguna 1938) for whom the economic orientation and lifeways were directed more towards riverine, estuarine, and inland lake and forest pursuits. The Tanaina expansion to outer Cook Inlet and into former Eskimo territory may, however, be relatively recent (Dumond and Mace 1968; D. Clark, unpublished research). Thus, while the outer inlet or Kenai and Kachemak Bay Tanaina groups share a very specific maritime hunting complex with their Eskimo neighbors from whom it probably was adopted, the interior or nonmaritime complexion of Tanaina culture would predominate even more if it were moved back a few centuries in time and space before historic contact. This case, nevertheless, may illustrate the formulation of a maritime adaptation through diffusion of equipment and techniques from others who had previously made such adjustments. Also, it may in part be a development of the historic fur trade era. These problems invite further research. The Eyak, in contrast to the Tanaina, may have become more constricted in their distribution after contact due to northern Tlingit expansion (de Laguna et al. 1964); and at one time, even though they are closely related linguistically to the Athabaskans, they may have been more distinctively a maritime hunting and fishing people.

Exploitative techniques and concomitant paraphernalia, and, to a considerable extent the associated lifeways, are nearly the same among the Aleuts and the Pacific Eskimo, particularly the Koniag (cf. ethnographic excerpts in Hrdlička 1944; 1945). Linguistic evidence indicates, however, that two distinctive groups are involved, the differentiation being at the language or language-family level (Dumond 1965). Distinctive differences between the two areas likewise appear in the archaeologic sequence, although there are also some very specific correspondences. Overall or gross similarity indicates like economic endeavors. The degree of dissimilarity between Pacific Eskimo and Aleut archaeology actually varies considerably according to the period involved and the regional phases being compared. In adjacent subareas there is further merging or convergence so that it becomes more difficult to tell eastern Aleut and western Pacific Eskimo sites apart (McCartney 1972; Workman 1969).

Probably late Eyak and northern Tlingit archaeology likewise show many correspondences with Pacific Eskimo archaeology, although the mainland sites are less rich, and numerous differences are seen at the attribute or stylistic level and in the presence or absence of a particular implement, e.g. the lack of stone lamps among the Tlingit (de Laguna et al. 1964; de Laguna 1960; Ackerman 1968). From ethnographic examples it is known in this case, however, that at least during the late prehistoric period these groups have stood in marked contrast to the Koniag in language stock, social organization, and in some major aspects of art and technology. Faunal remains indicate a very strong reliance on sea mammal hunting along with fishing and shellfish gathering (de Laguna 1960: 91–94; de Laguna et al. 1964), although the range of land mammals occasionally taken is much wider than it is on Kodiak. The same applies to the ecology of the mainland phases for which near identity with Kodiak has been indicated. De Laguna (1934) does not provide quantification for the impressive array of land mammals found in Kachemak tradition sites on Cook Inlet, but only the marmot or woodchuck (*Marmota caligata*) is reported as common or numerous. The marmot is also the principal land mammal taken, in terms of numbers, at Prince William Sound (de Laguna 1956: 52) and an analogous form, the arctic ground squirrel (*Citellus parryi*), was sought at selected localities on Kodiak. It hardly need be said that in the Aleutian Islands, excepting the eastern Aleut territory principally on the Alaska Peninsula, the mammalian land fauna is even more impoverished than it is on Kodiak.

Although the several maritime hunting and fishing people noted here can be traced archaeologically, there is some question as to the feasibility of the direct historic approach in remoter periods. Looking at the pre-historic eastern Aleut, central Aleut, Peninsula Aleut, Koniag, Chugach, Eyak, northern Tlingit continuum, one wonders how we would view this series if there were only archaeologic evidence to aid interpretation. Would it be possible to draw the known major ethnic or racial, linguistic, and ethnographic boundaries across what might appear to be regional phases of a single pattern? This discussion could be taken to mean that the writer is cautioning the use of the direct historic approach, but the point presently intended is subtly different. Specifically, concern is with the pro-cess of cultural succession and its recognition in a local sequence. The primarily synchronic situation just noted can, in a sense, be turned on end, e.g. interpretive problems involving regional variations and the re-cognition of prehistoric tribal and linguistic groups also arise in the analy-sis of temporal change or variation within a single regional sequence.


## CONCLUSION

For a maritime ecosystem that is semi-isolated in a region that offers no feasible alternate economic pattern or ecosystems to exploit, it is surmised that any succeeding culture will have made maritime adjustments largely the same as those of its predecessor from which it may have, in fact, taken on many adaptive elements. This is assuming that the latter had made, at the minimum, a satisfactory adjustment. Most of the techniques of the maritime hunting and fishing pattern would come from the technology common to a broad northern North Pacific area which, through diffusion at a relatively early date, can no longer be considered as characteristic of any one local culture. Overall, the environmental limitations and oppor-tunities on Kodiak act as a filter, mold, and stimulus. This being the case, the cultures of the area tend to take on the same configuration through time, particularly with regard to economic techniques, regardless of whether there is a direct generic relationship or whether there has been a succession of tribal groups. In order then to distinguish the kind of change seen in sequent developmental stages from change that occurs through population replacement, partial or complete, the one might be expected to show continuity of trends, particularly minor trends, which are broken in the other situation. There are, nevertheless, practical problems in isola-ting such trends from incomplete archaeologic data, and it even appears that many trends transcend the regional or tribal group and possibly cir-cumscribe an interaction area.

The prehistory of Kodiak Island is only one case in point. Other cases of cultural succession may also involve groups each so adapted to the same ecologic base that in the archaeologic record the passing or shifting from one to the other leaves only minor changes in implement attributes and categories and presents a problem in distinguishing between cultural succession and *in situ* development.


# REFERENCES

ACKERMAN, ROBERT E.
   1968   *The archaeology of the Glacier Bay region, southeastern Alaska.*
         Washington State University Laboratory of Anthropology, Report of
         Investigations 44. Pullman, Washington. D.C.

AIGNER, JEAN S.
   1970   The unifacial, core and blade site on Anangula Island, Aleutians.
         *Arctic Anthropology* 7(2):59–88.

BIRKET-SMITH, K., F. DE LAGUNA
   1938   *The Eyak Indians of the Copper River Delta, Alaska.* Copenhagen.

CAPPS, STEPHEN R.
   1937   *Kodiak and adjacent islands, Alaska.* United States Geological Survey
         Bulletin 880-C. Washington, D.C. Government Printing Office.

CLARK, DONALD W.
   1964   Incised figurine tablets from Kodiak, Alaska. *Arctic Anthropology*
         2(1):118–134.
   1966a  Two late prehistoric pottery-bearing sites on Kodiak Island, Alaska.
         *Arctic Anthropology* 3(3):157–184.
   1966b  Perspectives in the prehistory of Kodiak Island, Alaska. *American
         Antiquity* 31(3):358–371.
   1968   "Koniag prehistory." Unpublished Ph.D. dissertation, University of
         Wisconsin, Madison.
   1970   The late Kachemak tradition at Three Saints and Crag Point, Kodiak
         Island, Alaska. *Arctic Anthropology* 6(2):73–111.
   1971   "1971 Field work." Manuscript report, Archaeological Survey of
         Canada.
   1972   "The earliest prehistoric cultures of Kodiak Island, Alaska." Paper
         presented at the Thirty-seventh Annual Meeting of the Society for
         American Archaeology, Miami, Florida, May 4–6, 1972.

CLARK, GERALD H.
   1968   "Archaeology of the Takli Site, Katman National Monument,
         Alaska." Unpublished Master of Arts thesis. University of Oregon,
         Eugene.

CLARK, WEBSTER K.
   1958   The land mammals of the Kodiak Islands. *Journal of Mammalogy*
         39(4):574–577.

DAVIDOV, GAVRILA I.
1810–1812   *Dvukratnoie putieshestviye v Ameriku* [Two voyages to America], two volumes. St. Petersburg. (Translated excerpts published 1944 in *The anthropology of Kodiak Island* by A. H. Hrdlička.)

DE LAGUNA, FREDERICA
1934   *The archaeology of Cook Inlet, Alaska.* Philadelphia: The University Museum.
1956   *Chugach prehistory.* University of Washington Publications in Anthropology, volume 13. Seattle: University of Washington Press.
1960   *The story of a Tlingit community.* Bureau of American Ethnology Bulletin 172. Washington, D.C.

DE LAGUNA, F., F. A. RIDDELL, D. F. MC GEEIN, D. S. LANE, J. A. FREED, C. OSBORNE
1964   *Archaeology of the Yakutat Bay area, Alaska.* Bureau of American Ethnology Bulletin 192. Washington, D.C.

DUMOND, D. E.
1965   On Eskaleutian linguistics, archaeology, and prehistory. *American Anthropologist* 57:1231–1257.
1971   *A summary of archaeology in the Katmai region, southwestern Alaska.* University of Oregon Anthropological Papers 2. Eugene: University of Oregon Press.

DUMOND, D. E., ROBERT L. MACE
1968   An archaeological survey along Knik Arm. *Anthropological Papers of the University of Alaska* 14(1):1–22.

FLADMARK, KNUT R.
1970   "Preliminary report on the archaeology of the Queen Charlotte Islands," in *BC Studies* 6–7, special issue. Edited by Roy L. Carlson, 18–45. Vancouver.

GEDEON (See Valaam Monastery.)

GIDDINGS, JAMES L.
1957   Round houses in the American Arctic. *American Antiquity* 23(2):121–135.

HEIZER, ROBERT F.
1943   *Aconite poison whaling in Asia and America: an Aleutian transfer to the New World.* Bureau of American Ethnology Bulletin 133:415–468 and Plates 18–23A (Anthropological Papers 24). Washington, D.C.
1956   Archaeology of the Uyak Site, Kodiak Island, Alaska. *University of California Anthropological Records* 17(1). Berkeley.

HEIZER, ROBERT F., editor
1960   The Aleut sea otter hunt in the late nineteenth century. *Anthropological Papers of the University of Alaska* 8(2):131–135.

HEUSSER, CALVIN J.
1960   *Late-Pleistocene environments of North Pacific North America.* American Geographical Society, Special Publication 35. New York.
1963   Postglacial palynology and archaeology in the Naknek River drainage area, Alaska. *American Antiquity* 29(1):74–81.

HEWES, GORDON
1947   "Aboriginal use of fishery resources in northwestern North America." Unpublished Ph.D. dissertation. University of California, Berkeley.

HRDLIČKA, ALES H.
1944   *The anthropology of Kodiak Island.* Philadelphia: Wistar Institute of
       Anatomy and Biology.
1945   *The Aleutian and Commander Islands.* Philadelphia: Wistar Institute of
       Anatomy and Biology.

JACOBI, A.
1937   Carl Heinrich Mercks ethnographische Beobachtungen über die
       Völker des Beringsmeers 1789–1791. *Baessler-Archiv* 20:113–137.

LAUGHLIN, WILLIAM
1967   "Human migration and permanent occupation in the Bering Sea
       area" in *The Bering Land Bridge.* Edited by David M. Hopkins,
       409–450. Stanford: Stanford University Press.

LISIANSKI, YURI
1814   *A voyage round the world in the years 1803, 1804, 1805, and 1806.*
       London: John Booth.

MC CARTNEY, A. P.
1972   "Prehistoric cultural integration along the Alaska Peninsula." Paper
       presented at the Thirty-seventh Annual Meeting of the Society for
       American Archaeology, Miami, Florida, May 4–6.

MANVILLE, R. H., S. P. YOUNG
1965   *Distribution of Alaskan mammals.* United States Department of the
       Interior, Fish and Wildlife Service, Bureau of Sport Fisheries and
       Wildlife Circular 211. Washington, D.C.: Government Printing Office.

MERCK, CARL HEINRICH (See Jacobi, A.)

OSGOOD, CORNELIUS
1937   *The ethnography of the Tanaina.* Yale University Publication in
       Anthropology 16. New Haven: Yale University Press.

RIEGER, S., R. WUNDERLICH
1960   *Soil survey and vegetation of northeastern Kodiak Island area, Alaska.*
       Soil Survey Series 1956, 17. Washington: Government Printing Office.

VALAAM MONASTERY
1894   *Ocherk iz istorii amerikanskoi pravoslavnoi dukhovnoi missii, Kodiak-
       skoi missii 1794–1837 gg.* [One hundredth anniversary of orthodoxy in
       America 1794–1894: sketches from the history of the American
       orthodox ecclesiastical mission, Kodiak mission 1794–1837]. St.
       Petersburg.

WORKMAN, WILLIAM B.
1969   "Contributions to the prehistory of Chirikof Island, Southwestern
       Alaska." Unpublished M.A. thesis, University of Wisconsin, Madison.
1972   "A descriptive catalog of 1971 archaeological collections bearing on
       the later prehistory of the Afognak River estuary, Kodiak Island
       group, Alaska." Mimeographed report to the National Forest Service,
       Anchorage. Department of Anthropology, Alaska Methodist Uni-
       versity.

# Marine Transgressions and Cultural Adaptation: Preliminary Tests of an Environmental Model

G. F. GRABERT and C. E. LARSEN

The geographic region discussed in this paper is termed the Fraser Lowlands (Holland 1964: 36–37), and specifically that portion that lies in Washington State (Map 1). Physiographically the Fraser Lowlands can be traced to the southern limit of Bellingham Bay where the Chuckanut Mountain ridges rise sharply from the water. At historic contact, the coastal mainland in the southern part of the region and the islands adjacent were occupied by the Lummi Indians. To the north, from approximately Cherry Point beyond the international boundary was the territory of the Semiahmoo, while the Nooksack River drainage above Ferndale was the habitat of the Nooksack people. In the vicinity of the present town of Sumas the Sumas group is reported.

Ice masses of the Fraser Glaciation sculptured the Whatcom County landscape, with subsequent alluviation and erosion by melt water. Post-Pleistocene activity of the Nooksack River and numerous smaller streams has created the present drainage system and enlarged the major stream's flood plain (Easterbrook 1966). Land forms encountered in this study are alluvial plains, low uplands, beaches, and wave cut cliffs of glaciomarine drift. Surveys in this study cover an area from the Cascade foothills to the east, the Chuckanut mountains to the south, and the international

The studies described here are the results of many collaborative efforts. To Puget Sound Power and Light Company, Birch Bay Village, Incorporated, Mr. Harry Smith, Mr. Robert G. Smith, and Mr. Walter Gischer we extend our appreciation for permission to conduct excavations on their respective properties. Dr. Maurice Schwartz collaborated in the studies of coastal processes. His labors and advice, and the services of the Department of Geology at Western Washington State College are gratefully acknowledged. The students in field classes and those who volunteered their services in many other ways are no less due our thanks.

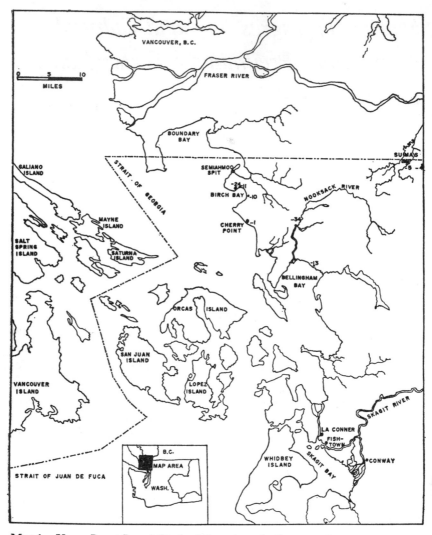

Map 1.  Upper Puget Sound, Strait of Georgia and adjacent mainland. Inset shows map area

Boundary on the north. Relief of the region is modest and rarely over 65 meters.

Insular and coastal environments of Northern Puget Sound and the Strait of Georgia are by no means uniform. Gradations between oak forest-grassland and river delta-flood plain cedar swamp can be found. Rainfall varies from 750 to approximately 1250 millimeters per year, so that floral cover is locally variant from that of the Coast Forest Biotic Area (Munro and Cowan 1947: 32). West and southwest exposures of the

Gulf and San Juan Islands possess an oak parkland environment in which the Garry oak (*Quercus garryana* Douglas) and the madrona (*Arbutus Menziesii* Pursh) are the prominent species of the arboreal flora. Conifer stands also occur where rainfall and edaphic conditions permit. The Washington coast to the east of the Gulf and Northern San Juan Islands lies in a zone of somewhat higher precipitation, where a gradation to Krajina's coastal Douglas Fir Zone occurs (Krajina 1965:4–7). This and several other areas of the United States San Juan Islands are thus divergent from the usually considered Northwest Coast environments. It is possible that the drier areas may have been more extensive in the Hypsithermal Interval. Greater extent of grassland and parkland prior to about 4,000 to 5,000 years ago has led to some workers assuming an earlier prehistoric hunting subsistence as predominant prior to emergence of the littoral-riverine cultures of the more recent past.

For the historic and late prehistoric Indians of the region both salt water and riverine fishing constituted a major food resource. Marine mammals were hunted, and, though there is little evidence for whaling in the area, seals of several species were taken. Bottom fishing also seems to have been practiced. The intertidal zone furnished a supplementary food supply — clams, the native oyster, blue mussel, cockles, marine gastropods, and limpets were available over much of the year. A short way inland were river bottoms with their cedar swamps and deciduous gallery growth. Berry patches covered old burns and provided many of the plants used as supplemental food sources and for medicinal purposes. Burns and grasslands provided graze and browse for elk and deer, and the bog lakes in the flood plain and near level alluvial "prairies" were another habitat for migratory waterfowl. In and above the foothills were found mountain sheep and goat, and the summer feeding grounds for elk and deer. Meat and sources of wool for the Salish weavers were found in this biotic province.

Anthropologists have made much of the food and domestic resource abundance of the historic Northwest Coast peoples. Even though Kroeber (1939: 30) considers the territory of the northern maritime tribes (Tlingit, Haida, Tsimshian) the cultural climax area he also admits the possibility of an earlier climax around the mouth of the Fraser River and the nearby islands of the Georgia Strait. This earlier climax may have occurred in the first millennium B.C. Were one seeking causal factors for the shift of climax areas, calling upon the model of Carneiro (1970) may provide a working hypothesis. The northern maritime cultures territory generally fulfills Carneiro's criteria for resource circumscription, territorial circumscription, and social constriction. Given his model, the development of the formalized ranking, wealth-oriented, and other more complex institutions of these northerly peoples is "explainable." It is not so much that there was less abundance in the north, simply that the resources tended to concentrate in more limited areas. Whether the seasonal and widely dispersed resources of the coast Salish area differ significantly from the northern part of the Northwest Coast is an area that needs further study.

Descriptive and interpretive archaeology of the Fraser Lowlands and adjacent islands is somewhat limited. Borden (1962, 1970), Calvert (1970), Carlson (1970b), and Mitchell (1971) have published most recently. Borden's pioneering research in the Fraser Delta and the Fraser Canyon raised the problems of Northwest Coast culture origins and provided a chronological framework for later phases. The apparently sudden appearance of a maritime oriented tradition in the area suggested migration as the processual agent (Borden 1962) and raised anew the questions posed by Drucker (1943) and Kroeber (1939). Borden's work provided both an impetus and substance with which further research could work. Work of the other scholars noted has shown by the supplementary materials, stratification, and fleshing-out of the radiocarbon chronology that there was a much longer continuum of cultures in the region than formerly supposed, and that migration models are not entirely satisfactory as explanatory constructs for the processes of peopling, adaptation, and the nature of the earlier regional cultures. Mitchell (1971) adds the best documented data for environmental factors operating in the Gulf Islands. He attempts to show a correlation between the amelioration of climate during the Neothermal period and the burgeoning of populations in that part of the region. This paper attempts to add further to substantive data and to show correlations with geomorphic changes during the Recent Period, and thus to supplement the climatic change models that have been proposed. We further suggest that there was no sudden shift to coastal-marine resources but a gradual transition that occurred as a correlate of coastal stabilization. Nor do the faunal remains from either coastal or inland sites suggest land mammal hunting was superseded.

The authors feel that climatic changes are important, but that these need to be considered in terms of other factors. Both inland and coastal-insular sites require treatment — it is likewise with changing landforms, stream regimes and their effects on the biota, as well as climate and its effects. All these factors contribute to forms of man-land relationships and to the potential for new modes of subsistence. Perhaps ultimately ideas are modified to accord. Kroeber proposed that while Northwest Coast peoples received numerous ideas and stimuli from other areas during their prehistory, these ideas were interpreted in the local frame of reference, and adapted to the subsistence patterns and resources, their seasonality and potential (1939: 30–31).

This paper attempts, then, to add to the substantive data and chronology, and to propose some working hypotheses regarding maritime orientation and its supposed sudden appearance on the scene some three millennia ago around the mouth of the Fraser River. To this end we treat both inland and coastal sites as forming complementary aspects of similar cultures, as task-specific variants of the same. We deal mainly with the relation of the prehistoric cultures to changing land-forms and their eventual stabilization in the late Holocene. While we neglect much of the paleo-climatic data for the locality, this is because it is still imperfectly understood, except for the works of Hansen (1947) and Heusser (1960). To the extent their data can be brought to bear on the problems, it is considered; otherwise we feel that there is a strong need for local elaboration of these useful and pioneering works.

There has been some feeling that inland cultures west of the Cascade Range were mainly "poor relations" of the coastal communities. However, little useful ethnography of these up-river peoples has been done, and even less archaeology dealing with their prehistoric settlements. This must apply to work in Washington State, since Borden's work in the Fraser Canyon has set the example and provided the model for similar explorations to the south of the border. To this end we include data from several inland sites: 45-WH-34 at Ferndale, 45-WH-5 at Sumas, and 45-WH-4 farther to the east near the base of Vedder Mountain. In Whatcom County, at least, the inland sites have proven as productive as the coastal ones.

## THE HYPOTHESES

Post-Pleistocene time in the subject region saw the operation of several environmental processes. Prominent among these was sea-level rise triggered by the release of vast amounts of water from glacial recession. In areas overridden by glacial ice, isostatic rebound was also prominent as a geological process. The Strait of Georgia-Puget Sound region was such a glaciated area. A somewhat less important process in this region was the climatic deterioration of the Hypsithermal Interval. Except for localities already poised on the edge of semiaridity in the Strait-Sound region, such as islands in the rain shadows of larger island and mountain masses, there was limited climatic and vegetational change in mid-post-Pleistocene time (Hansen 1947; Heusser 1960). However, recent work by Mitchell (1971: 7–14) suggests that the Canadian Gulf islands, lying in the rain shadow of Vancouver Island, underwent a more pronounced dessication.

There seems to be less conclusive evidence for pronounced altithermal aridity on the adjacent Washington and British Columbia clearings to have formed and maintained itself where exposure, edaphic conditions, and burns contributed to and allowed the expansion of grassy and brushy floral cover. This still remains to be fully demonstrated.

Affecting the visibility of such areas and archaeological sites in these micro-environments is the factor of relative sea-level rise. Those coastal sites situated on beaches and estuaries during the lower levels or minima of possible oscillations would have been inundated by rising water (cf. Duff 1963). Where isostasy prevailed over eustasy such sites would lie at considerably higher elevations today.

Recent works of several geologists (Easterbrook 1966; Matthews, Fyles, and Nasmith 1970) suggested that a fruitful approach to the location of archaeological sites would be to project broad sea-level changes onto the local topography, while assuming a degree of coastal orientation for early prehistoric peoples of the region. As did Giddings (1964: 256), we used a raised beach chronological model as a first approximation. Using topographic maps we projected two major sea-level periods. On the earlier level period, representing sea level as suggested by Mörner (1969) the junior author superimposed the rebound rate derived by Broecker (1966). This rate is approximately a 700 year "half-life." This model provides only a first approximation to a geochronology of raised beaches of the region, however. Revision as more data become available is clearly needed. For geological studies by Easterbrook have further suggested that differential isostasy and eustasy resulted in a relative sea level some 150 meters above the present level during the late Everson Interstade (ca. 10,500 B.P.). The relative sea level dropped to 12 meters above present following the Sumas ice re-advance about 9,500 years ago.

The junior author's calculation indicates that relative sea level falls below that of the present by as much as 10 meters during the 9000 to 4500 years B.P. interval. It is likely that this relative drop was noticeable throughout the Puget Sound-Strait of Georgia region and thus affected coast line morphology rather measurably.

While the geochronology remains to be fully worked out, and the model we are using must remain provisional, there are growing data suggesting correlations of site usages and locations with raised beaches and terraces. The submerged terraces at Birch Bay and possibly elsewhere in the area may be locations of archaeological sites falling within the time range 9,000 to 4,500 years ago — a time range that is as yet poorly represented or documented in the region.

These tendencies suggested two working hypotheses. The first assumes a generalized hunting/food-collecting economic base for early regional cultures. These peoples would have utilized coastal resources to the degree available, and to the limitations of their technical apparatus. It also assumes that with the sea-level changes as projected, the effective length of coastal and estuarine coast line was considerably longer than it is today. Location of low uplands in the Fraser Lowlands physiographic region (Holland 1964: 36–37) suggests that these uplands would have been an eastern extension of the San Juan Islands that emerged above the waters of the Strait of Georgia relatively rapidly.

The first hypothesis posits a much larger insular environment in early Recent time. It also assumes that a small population of hunter-gathering peoples lived in the region, possibly people already adapted to salmon fishing, the catching of migratory waterfowl, and perhaps molluscan resources in addition to land mammal hunting (cf. Borden 1962). Borden's studies of the Fraser Canyon site, DjRi-3, and Cressman's exhaustive report on The Dalles sites of the Columbia (1960), show that by 9,000 years ago communities existed in these two localities. The working assumption, in short, is that these people were not alone and that the Puget and Fraser Lowlands, foothills, and coastal sites were already utilized, as well as the two more favored localities these workers have investigated.

The second hypothesis deals with the beginnings of a maritime orientation which Borden has so ably documented (1970), and which has been documented further in the Gulf Islands by Mitchell (1971) and earlier workers. Wilson Duff proposed a "Gulf Islands Complex" as the originators and major producers of carved stone figurines and vessels (1956), and it should be noted too that it was Duff whom we believe to have first suggested that sea-level variations played a strong role in early Northwest Coast prehistory (Duff 1963). We propose that the maritime orientation of the Fraser Delta aspect of Northwest Coast maritime orientation (as well as that manifested throughout Puget Sound and the Gulf and Vancouver Islands) may have been given its impetus by the stabilization of local sea levels about 5,000–6,000 years ago. By perhaps 5,000 years ago stabilization of sea level would have left the coastal configuration much as it is seen today. Perhaps more importantly, the establishment of stable and possibly larger, intertidal environments capable of bearing larger molluscan populations would have removed one limitation to human populations using these resources. It may be significant to this hypothesis that an early date from the base of the St. Mungo Cannery site shell midden is approximately 2,300 years B.C. (Calvert 1970).

Study of the isostatic and eustatic processes affecting the mouth and delta of the Fraser River (Matthews, Fyles, and Nasmith 1970: Figure 4) indicated a date of approximately 5,600 years ago for stabilization or at least a sharp reduction in rate of change. The junior author, working independently of these studies in the Birch Bay (Plate 1, Map 2) locality, arrived at approximately the same time period on the basis of raised beaches, rates of sand spit accumulation (Larsen 1971), and the maximum age of a shell midden of Marpole Phase character on the active beach. This and other evidence collected in excavations and analysis of the Whatcom County subregion and environs is presented as a test of the utility of these working models.

In summary, the working model uses two hypotheses: the first proposes people with a cultural tradition of generalized hunting and food gathering, including some use of riverine and coastal resources, occupying a region with a much larger coast line during the early Holocene period. The second hypothesis suggests that coastal stabilization played a role in allowing larger and more accessible marine and intertidal food resources, with the possibility of larger human populations exploiting them. The second hypothesis has a corollary; given the reduction in coast line length, the concentration of intertidal and estuarine resources would also tend to concentrate communities, even if only on a seasonal basis. Such concentration of populations, although only temporarily, was a recurrent thing, and could become an agent in creating new patterns of cooperation, and determining, though only roughly at first, the limits of community territories.

Discussion and description of the archaeological sites and the geological evidence is given in the following section.

## THE ARCHAEOLOGICAL SITES

Five site localities are discussed in this section. There are four relatively unexplored sites which will be discussed as to environment and content. Two of the site localities, Semiahmoo Spit and Birch Bay, possess sites located on active or recently stabilized beaches. The latter has been shown to be of log-spiral configuration and growth process (Larsen 1971), and bears on an active spit system a shell midden (45-WH-11) yielding harpoons, chipped stone projectile points (rare), ground stone celts, and

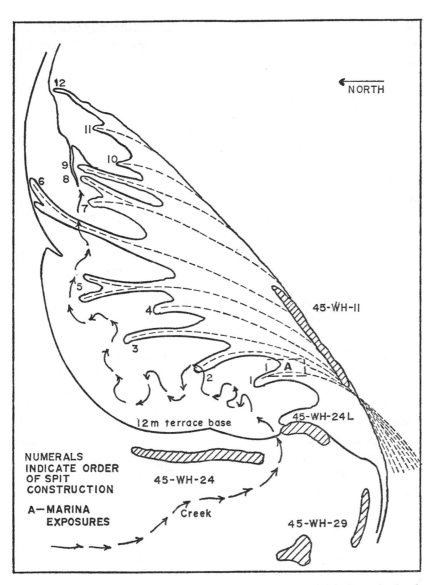

Map 2. Sand spit construction at Birch Bay. Source material is from the head-land, Birch Point (Larsen 1971). Site locations may be compared with Plate 1

bone objects of typically Marpole Phase characteristics (Plate 3). More recent occupation, perhaps to the historic contact period, is likely, although historical Euro-American trade goods were not found.

Birch Bay is bordered with both small and larger shell middens, most badly damaged by construction and road building in the resort community of Birch Bay. The bay is almost entirely tidal flat of sandy construction, dropping off gradually to the 6–7 meter submarine contour. This contour, incidentally, also closely follows the log-spiral now occupied by the Birch Bay Village resort development. Nine well-defined site localities are known, with 45-WH-11 on the currently active spit being the largest exposure. It was originally nearly one-half mile in length. Tests have been made at four of these sites — 45-WH-10, -11, -24, and -24L. Surface collections were made at 45-WH-29, which occupies the headland (Map 2) immediately to the west of 45-WH-11, and the camp site components exposed by the boat harbor excavations. The headland has been the major source of constructional material for the spit below.

Birch Bay locality topography has been partially described. The active spit beach and its berm are now occupied by recreational homes. Behind this area and an intervening filled salt marsh is a terrace at an average elevation of ten meters. To the southeast, about midway of the bay, an entrant estuarine channel, now partly marsh, extends inland for several miles. Where hills rise to elevations of forty and more meters farther inland a few traces of raised beaches can be seen. These were first noticed from the ground, and later corroborated by black-and-white and color aerial photographs. Examinations of sections in road cuts suggest that these beaches were of short duration. Walking of cleared portions of the area yielded a few pebble tools, but these lack any dense clustering. Evidence for early post-Pleistocene occupation of these land features is fairly clear, but still sparse, except in one or two localities.

The headland site, 45-WH-29, is one of the latter. It was discovered during clearing for new homes. Collectors followed the bulldozers, and much information about content was lost. The site appears to have two components; one is relatively recent shell midden occupying some one hundred meters along the headland. Somewhat overlapping was a non-shell area that yielded approximately one hundred pebble and flake implements. Density and clustering of the pebble implements approaches that of 45-WH-24, to be described. Elevation of this component ranges between 30 and 35 meters.

Another pebble-tool component lay on the 10–12 meter terrace. This site, 45-WH-24, lay on the terrace adjacent to the creek delta (Plate 1). More than 140 cobble and pebble implements and a few flakes were collected from the surface and in six test cuts located here. A few small patches of well-decayed shell were located, and a small hearth area. A radiocarbon assay of the charcoal contained gave the rather disappointing result of 1,580±120 radiocarbon years, A.D. 370 (RL-149). The date is hardly acceptable for several reasons. First, the only artifacts are pebble and flake implements. And regionally, while these objects do occur in shell midden contexts, they rarely show the kind of wear nor the choice of stone (quartzite) found in shell remains. There is also a high probability of fairly recent forest fire contamination by smoldering tree roots. Soils here are typically of the coniferous forest type, with thin and poorly developed A-horizons. The soil contains few pebbles of any size, nor does the till-weathering surface below contain many pebbles adequate for tools.

On the creek delta some 200 meters south of the above sites lies 45-WH-24-L. It is situated near the base of the 10–12 meter terrace, and lies three to four meters above the main level of the spit. Creek down-cutting has dissected the terrace to an elevation of 3–6 meters at this point. Two cuts here yielded historic objects from the turf level. Deeper levels encountered well-compacted silt and clay with scatters of fire-broken rocks, large basalt waste flakes, two burins, and pebble tools (Plate 2). Near the bottom of one cut a well-cemented gravel ridge was encountered. This ridge is interpreted as an old beach berm, formed at an early stage of spit construction. Its location against the lower edge of the terrace suggests that it may have been the first of the berms to form after sea level stabilization. This berm also contained a few tools in the form of flakes and choppers. The active portion of the spit now lies some 150 meters southeast and is the site of 45-WH-11, whose earlier deposits can be correlated to the Marpole Phase of the Fraser Delta.

Between 45-WH-24L and 45-WH-11, some 125 meters to the southeast of the former, excavation of a marina disclosed some significant deposits. A series of salt marsh peat, clay, and beach gravels helped the junior author define his sand spit and bay formation sequence (Larsen 1971). More important to this paper, seven hearths were revealed in the walls exposed by marina excavation. These hearths occupied the surfaces of earlier beaches, and were eventually overlaid by salt marsh deposits and silts borne out from the former creek delta where 45-WH-24L is situated.

Artifacts were limited to simple cobble tools, some flake implements, and one broken projectile point of probable lanceolate outline. The point was found in a hearth area that is presently submerged for several hours of the high tide period (Plate 3C). Hearths contained no evident charcoal and were manifest only by loose clusters of fire split rocks. These stood out clearly against the beach matrix of sand, gravel, and larger pebbles.

The Birch Bay Village site complex contains five sites distributed at various elevations from almost sea level to approximately 30 meters above it. In addition, there is evidence to suggest that each of the 11 or more sequential phases of spit construction was used by human communities.

It is likely that the late prehistoric shell middens represent a brief off-season use of the site by segments of a larger community.

Semiahmoo Spit some two miles north of Birch Bay is also a stabilized sand spit with some constructional and destructional activity at the seaward end. The base of this spit is the location of a large shell midden site, designated 45-WH-17. Deposits reach a depth of seven meters in places. Several outlying midden areas mark the locations of late prehistoric and historic Indian plank houses. Excavations so far have been limited. Amateur groups have worked in limited areas, and a still unanalyzed season was carried on in 1973. Artifacts tend to be limited to recent prehistoric types, consisting of bone and antler harpoons, points and awls, although a sizeable chipped stone assemblage was encountered in one area of the site. Stemmed and lanceolate points with some bipoints were found. One area of the site has yielded some 75 quartz crystal microblades and cores.

Observations on the stratification and geomorphology (Schwartz and Grabert 1972) indicate that the earliest cultural strata lie on an early phase of spit construction at or near the present water table. This early occupation occurred soon after the spit had begun to form at the base of a till cliff of Vashon glaciation age. A single radiocarbon assay on charcoal from the deepest cultural horizon gave a result of $4,100\pm500$ years (WWSC department of geology lab.). This date is another in the series from the region that place littoral habitation sites in the range of early first to late third millennium B.C. dates. This date range can be traced in a number of reports contained in this volume, around the perimeter of the Northwest Coast to the Aleutian chain. It should be observed that with formation of Semiahmoo Spit, as with that at Birch Bay, new and enlarged habitats for marine molluscan forms were created.

Cherry Point is located some seven miles south of Birch Bay. It is a wave-cut terrace overlooking the Strait of Georgia (Map 1). The habitation site located there is one of the more intensively tested of the region. Site elevation varies from about one meter to some ten meters above the mean high tide line. About 200 meters to the southeast of the major shell midden there is a small unnamed creek. Before most of the forest cover was removed this stream was probably perennial, and springs still flow between the creek and the site. About 125 meters from the beach and higher by 12 to 18 meters, faint traces of old strand lines may be traced. Testing of one of these small berms yielded only a small sand deposit, and no artifacts. Short duration of the higher beaches is assumed.

The most obvious feature of the site is a shell midden some 200 meters long roughly paralleling the wave-cut bank. Maximum midden width was probably little more than 40 meters even before the bank caved away some of the cultural deposits. Sketches of the site made in 1954 and extrapolation of midden strata indicate that as much as two meters of fill has been removed in the interim. This was evidently used for road ballast.

The shell layers did not compose the only cultural deposits, however. A deeper zone up to one meter thick lacks shell entirely, and contains a distinct lithic assemblage and little bone or antler. Overall, total deposit depth here still reaches as much as two meters.

The Cherry Point site seems to have been task specific. Its latter phases saw the gathering of abundant shell fish and salmon fishing with sea and land mammal hunting a less important activity. The deeper deposits show only remnants of fishing activity. Trap and near shore fishing is suggested for the earlier period. The later components yielded spears and leisters, and harpoon fragments of the composite type. Bones of deer, elk, dog, beaver, and seal were frequent in the order given.

The deeper, shell-free zone has been designated Cherry Point A. The stratum consists of a dark brown to locally black earth with numerous firepits, stone pavements, and occasional remains of stakes and other wood fragments (Figure 1). Five classes of artifacts make up the bulk of the assemblage from this horizon.

Approximately 600 of the 1600 recovered artifacts came from the A zone. It yielded more than 150 pebble tools, some 60 percent with well-battered edges (Plate 2), chipped slate knives or blanks for fish preparation, drilled net and line sinkers (approximately 80), and numerous elongate pebble hammers used in perforating the sinkers. Fourteen large cobble to boulder size rocks showed perforations, and are either canoe or breastline anchors for reef netting. The twenty or so other artifacts consist of two ground slate points resemblant of Locarno Beach forms (Borden 1962), a few flake tools, and a handful of ground slate and steatite objects resembling the carved pendant Borden also assigns to Locarno Beach (Borden 1962: Plate 5j). These objects conform to the "Gulf Island Complex" forms (Duff 1956: 93–94). One edge-chipped spall implement with a dentate edge was found with pebble tools in the subgravel zone near the east end of the site.

The shell midden layers produced artifacts fitting neatly into Borden's Fraser Delta sequence (1962, 1970). Ground serpentine adzes and their antler hafts, unilaterally barbed harpoons and fish leisters, composite harpoons, an abundance of herring rake teeth, harpoon arming points, and a few chipped stone projectile points compose the majority of the objects. A few quartz crystal microblades, and an exhausted core help

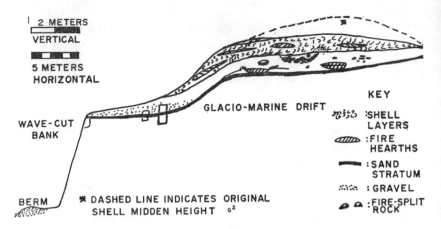

Figure 1.   Idealized section at Cherry Point site 45-WH-1. Rectangular outlines on the lower terrace represent late prehistoric structural remains believed to be a plank house. Basal shell layers were laid down about 2,300 years ago at the central part of the site, circa 1,600 years ago at the east end, with the western part dated to about 1,300 years ago. The lower cultural level has not been satisfactorily dated

place the chronological order. Wedges of antler and broken ground stone mauls attest to woodworking.

Bellingham glaciomarine drift on which the site lies has been dated to $11,800 \pm 400$ to $10,370 \pm 400$ years ago (Easterbrook 1966). Stream cutting formed the embayment and eroded the slope that grades down to the tide line. Evidence for isostatic and eustatic processes is found in the deposition of a thin sand layer atop the till weathering surface (Figure 1). The simplest explanation of the beach sand deposit is that early postglacial emergence of land by rapid isostasy created the beach. When rebound slowed, erosion assumed the dominant role and the wave cut bank appeared as the source for construction of the present beach. While Cherry Point A deposits begin immediately on the surface of the sand, mixing and down-migration of objects may have created the impression of a very brief interlude before human occupation. Processes forming the beach were probably only operative early in postglacial time — the cultural layers appear to date no earlier than the late second millennium B.C.

There is evidence for a brief marine transgression about 500–100 B.C. This has been found at the lowest part of the site where a 20–35 centimeter thick gravel zone intrudes into Marpole Phase deposits. At least some part of the site appears to have been inundated late in the first millennium B.C. Such sterile gravel layers appear also at the bottom of the 45-WH-11 midden at Birch Bay at about the same elevation above modern mean high tide line (ca. 1.25 to 1.5 meters A.S.L.). Unequivocal evidence for a transgression of similar age has not yet been noted at Semiahmoo Spit.

Cultural layers at Cherry Point have been placed in a fairly adequate chronology. A suite of five radiocarbon dates is now in hand. Four are within the expected range and a fifth is qualifiedly accepted. It may well have been badly contaminated. This sample gave results of $960 \pm 200$ years, A.D. 1000 (no WWSC laboratory number assigned), and came from a deeper portion of the Cherry Point A zone. Three samples from the base of the shell midden layers gave the following results: sample 633 $2,340 \pm 200$ years, 390 B.C. (no WWSC number); sample 1149 from an intrusive firepit some 16 meters southwest of 633 yielded a date of $1,300 \pm 200$ years, A.D. 650 (no WWSC number); while a cut near the east end of the site gave results of $1,640 \pm 200$ years, A.D. 350 (no WWSC number). These dates indicate Marpole, Whalen II and Pre-Stselax$^w$ contemporaneity (Borden 1970: Figure 29). There is reasonably good agreement in artifact associations. Cherry Point A later yielded a date of $2,630 \pm 240$ years (RL-272) which is a reasonable mid-range date for the earlier horizon.

West of the City of Bellingham, on Bellingham Bay, a rather unusual site was tested, and artifacts collected from there by the owner have been analyzed. This site yielded some 250 artifacts consisting mainly of basalt bipoints and stemmed points of lanceolate form. In addition a small number of ground slate points and knives as well as ground serpentine celts were recovered. The deepest cultural horizon at this site was also deposited on a much thicker beach and alluvial sand than that found at Cherry Point.

A provisional interpretation is that the sand also represents a beach deposit formed when sea level was relatively higher than 20 meters above the present level. The half mile wide embayment in which the site lies may be partially the result of erosion by run off water, although the creek's watershed is small and the gradient is slight. Again, the sand must have been deposited about the same time as that at Cherry Point for a slightly developed fossil soil horizon is also present at the Smith Garden site. At its western end the embayment bears a shell midden, also of Marpole affinities. Little shell appeared at the Smith Garden site, 45-WH-13.

Chipped stone projectile points and flake tools from the site display no similarity to Cherry Point, but are known from a number of inland sites of the region. The latter contexts are still undated. Some similarities to Marpole and earlier Fraser Delta and Gulf Islands sites (probably of Mayne Phase) are seen in the limited number of ground slate, serpentine, and smaller chipped stone objects (Carlson 1970a: 115, Figure 34).

Bellingham Bay sites investigated to date also indicate two kinds of subsistence activities which seem noncontemporaneous. Smith Garden materials indicate mammal hunting, and possibly fishing with very limited use of molluscs; and extensive intertidal zone resources must have existed since before the Christian era, judging by the shell midden site (45-WH-14) to the west of Smith Garden and its similarities to the artifact assemblages of the later Fraser Delta sites. Some part of the Smith Garden artifacts of the chipped stone group appear transitional to Locarno Beach Phase forms.

Looking inland, a site of interest is located at the town of Sumas (45-WH-5, Map 1). It is located at the edge of the town on the small Sumas River, which flows north to empty in the Fraser a few miles north. It lies on a bend of the river, occupying an area greater than 125 by 60 meters. The site is now occupied by a barn, house, and several outbuildings. The soil appears to be based on alluvial sand with up to 1.8 meters of cultural deposits.

The locale is one of low relief with elevations at the highest point less than six meters above sea level. A somewhat higher outwash ridge of the Sumas glacial stade (Easterbrook 1966) and terminal moraine and re-advance of ice probably established the drainage division between the Nooksack River to the south and the Sumas River. Elevation is still so low that a late nineteenth-century flood mingled waters of the Nooksack and Fraser. Early in the Holocene this low area was a shallow part of the Fraser mouth.

Once separation of the two drainage systems had occurred, the intervening area was occupied by shallow marshy lakes with sandy outwash ridges and meandering channels of several creeks draining from Vedder Mountain to the east. Lake margins and dune ridges are still traceable. Much of the marshy area north of the international boundary was drained in the later ninteteenth and early twentieth centuries. Prehistorically this area was a haven for migratory waterfowl and a salmon spawning area. That the locality was intensively used is evidenced by this and several other known sites.

Artifacts from this site are mainly of Marpole similarities, although a small assemblage of chipped stone appears distinct from the Marpole forms, resembling those of Smith Garden and a site to be described below. Seven zoomorphic bowls are known from the site as well as several score pieces of sawed serpentine, sandstone saws, more than two dozen celts, and ground slate implements. The number of zoomorphic vessels is unusual, unless this were a trade and manufacturing seat. Most such vessels have been isolated finds.

This site lies on a direct route to the interior via the Fraser Canyon. It could only have been inhabited after stabilization of sea level allowed it and relatively modern environments were established. Nearby terraces on Sumas Mountain and those on Vedder Mountain have only been cursorily searched with few positive results, although a few scattered pebble tools are known.

About seven miles upstream from the mouth of the Nooksack River a small, intensively used site was tested in 1972. Materials have not yet been completely analyzed, but some provisional statements can be made.

The site lies on an older levee ridge of the river, some forty meters behind the active levee. (Map 1). It was designated 45-WH-34. This part of the flood plain is still active. The site now lies at an elevation above sea level of 9.3 meters. Immediately to the north an older terrace at the 13–14 meter contour parallels the river.

Dense occupation debris occupies an area of about 30 by 40 meters. It was first seen in blue mussel shell among roots of a windfall. Testing by some 45 square meters of test cuts revealed several shell strata extending to depths of 140 centimeters in intrusive pits. Normal shell deposits did not exceed 65 centimeters. One of the two deep pits is a firepit. The second is apparently a pit dwelling of which several are known about 6–8 miles away. Four deeper cultural strata have been identified to depths of 120 centimeters in spots. These lack shell in quantity, with only small pieces of blue mussel shell found.

Artifact content of the shell zones can be paralleled in Marpole and later phases. Some Locarno Beach similarities are also posited. Most importantly, the deeper layers yielded only flake tools, a few pebble implements and some 30 of the 40 chipped stone projectile points. Some of the latter were of course, found in spoil cast up from digging the dwelling and firepits (Plate 3). One fine example of Marpole-like harpoon and three fragments were found (cf. Borden 1970: Figure 31k).

This site provided more evidence for sea-level and stream gradient stabilization. A fossil soil horizon was found at depths from 90 to 130 centimeters. Human use of the location began soon after the soil began to form, as seen in the charcoal stained bands bearing artifacts. An abrupt change in grain size of the alluvium is quite apparent. The base of the fossil soil lies on a very coarse sand lacking larger pebbles, while the matrix of the soil and subsequent occupation strata is fine sand and silt.

One of the deeper occupation strata has yielded charcoal dated at $4,180 \pm 120$ years ago (RL-273). This date is again in agreement with the one from Semiahmoo Spit, and both post-date the estimate of the junior author for a stabilization of major sea-level changes about 5,000–5,500 years ago. It may also be related to one of the earlier habitation levels at Cherry Point, but the most applicable early date from there is a millennium later. The Smith Garden site was first occupied on a much earlier land form, if elevation is any criterion, and if one may assume some constant function for rebound of land and eustasy.

## SUMMARY AND CONCLUSIONS

Two groups of sites can be discerned by comparison of artifacts. One is typical of the Fraser River mouth-Strait of Georgia region. Tool assemblages and food residue show a continuum from at least as early as the Marpole Phase (Borden 1962) to the recent prehistoric settlements. In addition, there are several sites and components which yield a variant artifact set — these can be equated with Locarno Beach and Mayne Phase manifestations of the Fraser and Gulf Islands. The lower horizon at Cherry Point distinctly denotes a fishing and processing station, with later use for a greater variety of resources. The frequency of worn cobble implements in the Cherry Point A horizon shows strong continuity from deep components at Birch Bay and at several other locations in the county. At the latter sites there are almost exclusively cobble and flake tools. This assemblage constitutes the content of the second group. These sites tend to lie on terraces above the ten-meter level and extend to elevations of 40 meters or more on old river, estuarine, and coastal terraces. They seem not to be associated with strongly developed fossil soil horizons. Also, some components show much higher frequency of chipped stone projectile points, as at the Smith Garden Ferndale sites.

Where well developed fossil beaches occur, as at Smith Garden and Cherry Point localities, there is still no definite indication that human occupancy occurred immediately upon emergence. This evidence is so far limited to Birch Bay. Given that the isostatic rebound rate had become small in relation to eustasy by perhaps five to six thousand years ago, beach construction was probably in progress early in the Holocene Period. That the Smith Garden embayment now lies at an approximate elevation of 21–22 meters strengthens the assumption. Cherry Point, on the other hand, has only a thin (5 to 18–20 centimeter) beach sand zone underlying the early horizon. Its formation probably postdates that on Bellingham Bay.

Birch Bay provides us with the best, albeit incompletely explored, series of geomorphic features with variant cultural components. The shell midden on the present line is certainly of Marpole affinities, giving a terminal date for the appearance of the present beach sometime early in the first millennium B.C. This leaves the series of camp sites on the buried beach sequence floating earlier in time. We need also to note the significance of the high tide floodings of the deeper of the beach ridge-fire hearth associations. It will probably be impossible to ever determine the number and dispersal of camp sites on these buried beaches. Suffice to say that they exist, and may be of an age contemporaneous with positive oscillations of sea level or final stages of stabilization.

The method of searching for sites associated with land forms related to old river terraces, sand spit formation, and raised beaches has proven effective. While there is some correlation of chronological age of the artifact associations with postulated ages of these land forms, it is by no means perfect. Further site sampling and accumulation of a larger number of geographically dispersed samples should demonstrate whether the assumed long-standing riverine-estuarine-coastal tradition is correct. There is one definite result — Marpole-type, and later prehistoric culture phases are by no means limited to coastal and river mouth sites in the study area. They also appear at 45-WH-34 and on the Sumas River. The assemblage in the lower horizon at Cherry Point also indicates a strong marine-fishing tradition prior to about 2,400 years ago. This local population seems to have practiced reef net fishing as did some of the historic peoples, if the artifact association is any criterion.

There are numerous inland stations now known which show a variety of lanceolate stemmed, bipointed, and even basally notched projectile point forms. Simple flake tools are abundant and occur in association with stone vessels and some other ground stone objects. To date, this association has most often been found in sites on or below the ten-meter elevation. Yet other sites lacking the ground stone aspect are more numerous now, after searching of terraces and slopes well above this elevation.

The preliminary radiocarbon date on materials from the base of 45-WH-17 on Semiahmoo Spit suggests an early occupation of this feature, probably soon after it became stabilized. Even so, there is still a cultural hiatus between ca. 2500 B.C. to around 5000–6000 B.C., when one considers both inland and coastal sites of the region. The presence of a submerged terrace at Birch Bay at the 6–8 meter level suggests that coastal occupation, if present during the period for which there are no presently known archaeological remains, may lie beneath the present intertidal zone. Reports of fire-broken rocks recovered from about the same depth at Garrison Bay on San Juan Island seem to support this idea (Roderick Sprague, personal communication). The next phase of exploration should include examination of submerged terraces in bays and near creek mouths. We feel that this exploration should yield positive results, even though much evidence may have been lost by wave action.

It is probably too simplistic to postulate a land hunting orientation of the early Holocene being replaced by a maritime orientation in the first to second millennium B.C. There is good evidence, as at 45-WH-34 and other inland sites, for task-specific kinds of sites. Cherry Point A is one such manifestation. Basing judgment on the artifact assemblage alone would lead one to suppose that a technologically simple community occupied the area for over a thousand years. Mitchell's (1971) evidence for habitation of the Gulf Islands clearly points to a long-standing tradition of hunting AND littoral-insular fishing and collecting. Contemporary communities on the mainland seem now to have followed the same trajectory.

We have observed in several sites that the ubiquitous blue mussel (*Mytilus edulis*) is a major component of molluscan remains in the earlier strata in shell middens of the region. Although the data are still incompletely analyzed, this may suggest that the species was a pioneering one when intertidal biomes reached relative stability. These were soon followed by extension and enlargement of populations of other and more desirable molluscs and gastropods. It could be argued that cultural selectivity operated, and ease of collection would support this argument. But at the same time the evidence also points to much of the Fraser Delta-Whatcom region being insular or inundated prior to about 5,000 years ago. Thus an entirely different series of habitats prevailed prior to this time. Human populations also would have been differently distributed and would necessarily have followed different patterns of resource collection. Borden's Fraser Canyon site and those of The Dalles of the Columbia lend support to an inference of sparsely distributed early populations west of the Cascade range.

Dancey (personal communication, August 1973) suggests that population pressures in the Fraser Delta region about A.D. 1 led to increasing community fission rates because of pressure on localized resources. Such a model may also obtain for the period before sea level stabilization, when much of the present land area was insular. At the end of the Hypsithermal Interval, stabilization of sea level, with extension of pioneering flora and fauna on newly emerged land, would have allowed human communities to grow and expand into new territories. But with the establishment of climax coniferous forests and environmental and human pressures on the reduced grazing game fauna, coincident with the enlargement of marine and intertidal habitats as well as new salmon spawning areas, greater human emphasis on maritime resources would come as no surprise. This is especially so if many techniques for marine resource acquisition and preparation were already available to the populace. At this point one could expect local cultural climaxes to occur as seen in Locarno Beach and Marpole Phases of the Fraser Delta region, followed by the north-ward shift to the state seen in the ethnographic present of the Northwest Coast cultures.

We must, for the present, label much of this speculation. Yet we wish to point out the multi-factored aspects of the early environmental rela-tions of man in this region. Among the factors, we may suggest these: growth in the human populations; coast-line and sea-level changes; the imperfectly understood effects of the Hypsithermal Interval; changes in marine and intertidal biota; the local floral successions which depended in large measure on sea level, soil formation, and rainfall regimes; and, last but not least, the socio-cultural relationships with peoples of the interior, the northern coast, and the southern areas of the West Coast. There is little doubt that regional insular environments of the past were more extensive than today. The effects upon the early residents are not fully known.

Continued use of the proposed model and the working hypotheses should provide some clues to the demographic and social aspects of the formative Northwest Coast cultures. There has been no conclusive test of the hypotheses as yet. Results at this time suggest that they have some explanatory power. At the very least the model has been effective in locating sites; the chronology and relationships among these regional sites have yet to be fully demonstrated.

## REFERENCES

BORDEN, CHARLES E.
  1962   "West Coast crossties with Alaska," in *Prehistoric cultural rela-tions between the arctic and temperate zones of North America.* Edited by John M. Campbell, 9–19. Arctic Institute of North America, Technical Paper 11. Montreal.
  1970   Culture history of the Fraser delta region: an outline. *B.C. Studies* 6–7:95–112.
BROECKER, W. S.
  1966   Glacial rebound and the deformation of the shorelines of pro-glacial lakes. *Journal of Geophysical Research* 71.
CALVERT, GAY
  1970   The St. Mungo Cannery site: a preliminary report. *B.C. Studies* 6–7.

CARLSON, ROY L.
  1970a  Archaeology in British Columbia. *B.C. Studies* 6–7:7–17.
  1970b  Excavations at Helen Point on Mayne Island. *B.C. Studies* 6–7:
         113–123.

CARNEIRO, R. L.
  1970  A theory of the origin of the state. *Science* 169:733–738.

CRESSMAN, L. S.
  1960  Cultural sequences at the Dalles, Oregon. *Transactions of the
        American Philosophical Society,* n.s. 50(10).

DRUCKER, PHILIP
  1943  *Archaeological surveys on the northern Northwest Coast.* Bureau
        of American Ethnology Bulletin 133:17–132.

DUFF, WILSON
  1956  Prehistoric stone sculpture of the Fraser River and the Gulf of
        Georgia. *Anthropology in British Columbia* 5:15–151.
  1963  "Sea levels and archaeology on the northwest coast." Paper pre-
        sented at the Sixteenth Annual Meeting of the Northwestern An-
        thropological Conference.

EASTERBROOK, DON J.
  1966  "Glaciomarine environments and the Fraser glaciation in north-
        west Washington." Guidebook for first annual conference, Paci-
        fic coast section, Friends of the Pleistocene, Bellingham, Wash-
        ington.

EMMONS, R. V.
  1952  An archaeological survey in the lower Nooksack River valley.
        *Anthropology in British Columbia* 3:49–56.

GIDDINGS, J. L.
  1964  *The archaeology of Cape Denbigh.* Providence: Brown University
        Press.

HANSEN, HENRY P.
  1947  Postglacial forest succession, climate and chronology in the Pa-
        cific Northwest. *Transactions of the American Philosophical So-
        ciety,* n.s. 37(1).

HEUSSER, CALVIN J.
  1960  *Late Pleistocene environments of north Pacific North America.*
        American Geographical Society Special Publication 35. New
        York.

HOLLAND, STUART S.
  1964  *Landforms of British Columbia: a physiographic outline.* British
        Columbia Department of Mines and Petroleum Resources Bulle-
        tin 48.

KRAJINA, V. J.
  1965  Biogeoclimatic zones and classification of British Columbia. *Eco-
        logy of western North America* 1:17.

KROEBER, A. L.
  1939  *Cultural and natural areas of native North America.* Berkeley:
        University of California Press.

LARSEN, CURTIS E.
1971  "An investigation into the relationship of change in relative sea level to social change in the prehistory of Birch Bay, Washington." Unpublished master's thesis, Western Washington State College.

MATTHEWS, W. H., J. G. FYLES, H. W. NASMITH
1970  Postglacial crustal movements in southwestern British Columbia and adjacent Washington State. *Canadian Journal of Earth Science* 7(4):690–702.

MITCHELL, DONALD H.
1971  Archaeology of the Gulf of Georgia area: a natural region and its culture types. *Syesis* 4, supplement 1.

MÖRNER, NILS-AXEL
1969  Eustatic and climatic changes during the last 15,000 years. *Geologie en Mijnbouw* 48.

MUNRO, J. A., I. MCT. COWAN
1947  *A review of the bird fauna of British Columbia.* Victoria: B.C. Provincial Museum.

SCHWARTZ, MAURICE L., GARLAND F. GRABERT
1972  "Coastal processes and prehistoric maritime cultures." Unpublished manuscript, Western Washington State College.

# PART THREE

*Northwest Atlantic*

# Maritime Adaptation on the Northwestern Atlantic Coast

JAMES A. TUCK

The group of Archaic hunters occupying the northwestern Atlantic coast during parts of the second and third millennia B.C. who are considered here were known originally as the Red Paint People of Maine and New Brunswick, and later called by Byers (1959) Coastal Archaic or Coastal Boreal Archaic. Most sites pertaining to the cultural manifestation discussed here were the "great boneless cemeteries" excavated by Willoughby (1898, 1935), Moorehead (1916, 1922), and others. These contained spectacular and seemingly homogeneous grave offerings (in fact, no one has yet successfully seriated the material from these cemeteries), including ground slate spears, lances, and "bayonets"; adzes, axes, and distinctive gouge forms; stemmed, or more rarely notched, projectile points of chipped stone, not infrequently the distinctive so-called Labrador Stone; pecked and ground plummets; and occasional perforated whetstones ("Passadumkaeg Problematicals") and carved stone effigies, usually depicting marine mammals.

Prior to World War II, Byers and Johnson excavated the Nevin site at Blue Hill, Maine, and recovered a small series of human skeletons, associated stone artifacts of the same Red Paint or Moorehead Complex affiliation, and, most important, a series of "bone tools, including a variety of barbed forms, worked beaver incisors ... and implements made from [swordfish] swords" that Byers saw as "evidence of development of a maritime aspect of the culture" (Byers 1959: 250).

Our subsequent discoveries at Port au Choix, Newfoundland (Tuck 1970, 1971a, i.p.), in northern Labrador at Saglek Bay (Tuck 1971b), Fitzhugh's excavations (especially 1972) on the central Labrador coast and along the north shore of Lake Melville, and the work of Snow (1969),

Sanger (1971), and Bourque (1971), among others, in the Maritime Provinces and northern New England have added new temporal, geographical, and cultural perspectives to this early "cemetery complex" of the Red Paint People.

The temporal and geographic dimensions have been expanded by the following radiocarbon-dated complexes, all showing clear affinities with previously discovered materials (dates are unadjusted and subtracted from A.D. 1950):

*Saglek Bay, northern Labrador*
Site Q, Band 7A, early Maritime Archaic      2580 ± 105 B.C.
Site Q, Band 4A, terminal Maritime Archaic      1940 ± 110 B.C.

*Groswater Bay, central Labrador coast* (Fitzhugh 1972)
Sandy Cove 4, early Maritime Archaic      2860 ± 115 B.C.
Rattlers Bight 1, late Maritime Archaic      2070 ± 150 B.C.
     1880 ± 140 B.C.

*Port au Choix, Newfoundland*
Locus II — Maritime Archaic      2340 ± 110 B.C.
     1970 ± 130 B.C.
     1820 ± 80 B.C.
Locus I — late Maritime Archaic      1740 ± 90 B.C.
Locus IV — terminal Maritime Archaic      1460 ± 100 B.C.
     1280 ± 220 B.C.

*Curtis Site, Twillingate, Newfoundland* (McLeod, personal communication)
contemporaneous with Locus I, Port au Choix      1770 ± 130 B.C.
     1610 ± 140 B.C.
     1250 ± 90 B.C.

*Cow Point, New Brunswick* (Sanger, personal communication)
late Maritime Archaic cemetery      1885 ± 115 B.C.
     1680 ± 135 B.C.

*Hathaway site, Passadumkaeg, Maine* (Snow 1969)
Maritime Archaic cemetery      3050 ± 140 B.C.

*Ellsworth Falls, Maine* (Byers 1959)
early Maritime Archaic component      2009 ± 310 B.C.
late Maritime Archaic component      1400 ± 400 B.C.

Finally, Harp's early dates from the Labrador shore of the Strait of Belle Isle — 4319 ± 76 B.C., 4223 ± 77 B.C., 3611 ± 60 B.C. (Harp and Hughes 1968: 44) — may pertain to a still earlier and as yet poorly known Maritime Archaic manifestation.

It is not my intention to argue the validity of the Maritime Archaic concept. I have presented evidence for unity in the technological, settlement, economic, aesthetic, and other systems of the complexes mentioned above (Tuck 1970, 1971a, i.p.) and newly accumulating evidence seems to strengthen these earlier conclusions. Modifications may become necessary as more is learned about the origin and demise of these coastal people, but as a unifying concept for the Late Archaic of the northwest Atlantic seaboard, the Maritime Archaic Tradition "seems likely to be a most useful designation" (Fitzhugh 1972: 3).

## SUBSISTENCE

A certain portion of the life of these people involved exploitation of resources not directly connected with the sea — terrestrial mammals and lithic raw materials, for instance — but in every instance there seems to have been a heavy commitment to the exploitation of marine resources.

We have not been blessed with good bone preservation at most Maritime Archaic sites, but several stations have produced bone or ivory artifacts or food remains that can be attributed to the marine or littoral species shown in Table 1.

Other species, especially beaver, caribou, bear, moose in the south, and other terrestrial mammals were also represented, but those listed above are of most concern here. Also, because many species are represented by grave offerings or were utilized as raw materials, it might be suspected that they did not serve as food. However, that would deny ethnographic analogy for all peoples of the northeastern littoral who took the birds, mammals, and fish listed above and used them as food (PERHAPS with the exception of sharks or skates); it seems certain that these early people did so as well.

To this list we may add several other species that were present in the area in aboriginal times but are not as yet represented in the archaeological record. These include harbor, grey, hood, ringed, and bearded seals in various regions; Atlantic salmon, eels, and numerous additional fishes; and many shorebirds, to name but a few.

Apparently lacking from most stations are the various species of shellfish that seem to have constituted a significant portion of the diet of later

Table 1.   Species whose remains have been found at Maritime Archaic sites

| | | |
|---|---|---|
| **Port au Choix** | | |
| *mammals* | | |
| seal (harp and others?) | whale (killer whale?) | |
| walrus | whale (large baleen whales) | |
| polar bear | | |
| | | |
| *birds* | | |
| black guillemot | gannet | merganser |
| Canada goose | great auk | murre, common |
| cormorant | gull | murre, thick-billed |
| curlew | harlequin duck | puffin |
| dovekie | loon, common | shearwater |
| eider duck | loon, red-throated | swan (trumpeter?) |
| tern | | |
| | | |
| *fish* | | |
| shark (mackerel shark?) | cod (otoliths only) | |
| skate (barn door skate?) | | |

| | |
|---|---|
| **Rattlers Bight, Labrador (Fitzhugh 1972)** | |
| *mammals* | *birds* |
| seal | goldeneye duck |

| | |
|---|---|
| **Nevin Site, Maine (Tuck)** | |
| *mammals* | *fish* |
| seal | swordfish |
| porpoise | skate (barn door skate?; same as Port au Choix specimens) |

| |
|---|
| **Taft's Point, Maine** |
| *fish* |
| swordfish |

| | |
|---|---|
| **The Basin, Maine (Bourque 1971)** | |
| *mammals* | *shellfish* |
| blackfish | blue mussel |
| porpoise | sea urchin |

| |
|---|
| **Goddard Site, Maine (Bourque 1971)** |
| *fish* |
| shark |

peoples. Indeed, Snow (1972) has suggested that the absence of shellfish remains in Archaic sites indicates a lack of knowledge of coastal resources on the part of the Archaic inhabitants of Maine. This hypothesis seems doubtful, however, in view of the evidence of fishing and especially of marine mammal and swordfish hunting which clearly indicates a thorough knowledge of the sea and how to exploit its resources. In fact, at least some coastal peoples eschew shellfish as an undesirable food source and turn to them in times of shortage of red meat, fish, or other "more desirable" food.

## TECHNOLOGY

With this reliance upon sea mammals, birds, and fish we might expect that some specialized devices for their capture would have developed on the northeast coast during the third and second millennia B.C. Our excavations at Port au Choix, those of Byers and Johnson at the Nevin site, and to a lesser extent those of Bourque and others have revealed evidence of a technology well adapted to the pursuit of marine mammals, birds, and fish.

Most outstanding in this respect is a series of toggling harpoons, found in some numbers at Port au Choix and represented by at least one specimen from the Nevin site. Our unadjusted dates in the early second millennium B.C. place these specimens among the oldest such weapons yet known from archaeological deposits in the world: they are exceeded in antiquity only by dates from the Mitimatalik site (Mary-Roussellière 1973) and the Closure site (Maxwell 1973), both on Baffin Island, and from Kaleruserk (Medlgaard, personal communication) at Igloolik, all of early pre-Dorset cultural provenience. Moreover, all these dates are suspect because of inconsistencies with typological dating and because they are derived from sea mammal remains (cf. McGhee and Tuck 1973) and might be reduced and adjusted to postdate the Port au Choix artifacts by some centuries. Also, of course, there are Maritime Archaic dates from Labrador that are close to (or before) 3000 B.C. If the people associated with these early dates were using toggling harpoons, the question of Indian-Eskimo contacts might be revived.

The Port au Choix harpoons of antler are self-pointed and have an open socket. The basal edge is beveled about forty-five degrees, often has a small spur, and is usually grooved for attachment to a bone or antler foreshaft. The gouged line hole is offset to facilitate toggling and often has the trailing edge thinned or grooved to allow easier penetration. Several foreshafts were recovered, and a harpoon and foreshaft are shown in Figure 1.

Barbed harpoons are even more plentiful. They are single-, double-, and triple-barbed, almost always unilaterally, and have a gouged line hole similar to that on the toggling harpoons. The base is tapered and designed to fit a socket on the thrusting shaft from which it probably detached after impact. No foreshafts that fitted these specimens were recovered.

Seals, walrus, and perhaps porpoises and small whales were taken with these weapons by the people of Port au Choix. The same is also true for the inhabitants of the Nevin site in Maine and perhaps the Taft's Point and Waterside shell heaps as well. In addition, the latter three stations

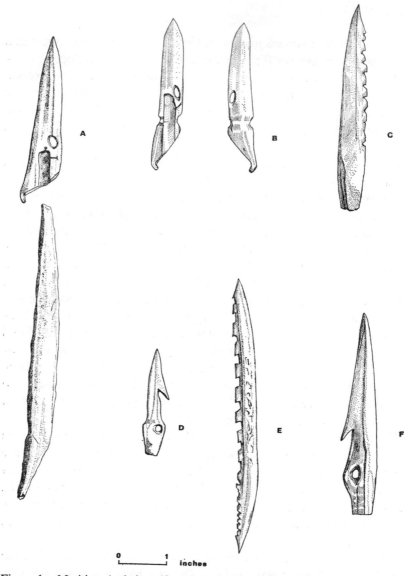

Figure 1.   Maritime Archaic artifacts from Port au Choix, Newfoundland
A, toggling harpoon and foreshaft; B, toggling harpoon; C, sawtooth bone point;
D and F, barbed harpoons; E, square-barbed leister point

produced ample evidence of the presence of swordfish, and I suspect that they were harpooned by the same technique and with the same implements as were sea mammals.

These species may have been dispatched with slate and bone spears and "bayonets," although the use of these weapons was probably not confined to sea mammals. Nonetheless, they seem to have figured prominently in the hunter's equipment among the Maritime Archaic people and among several other disparate coastally adapted people as well. The unusual slotted and lipped foreshafts of whale bone, antler, and, in the south, of swordfish bills may also have formed part of the pelagic hunter's equipment, but as yet we are unable to assign a particular function to these unusual artifacts.

We know that sea birds were taken in fair numbers, and at least some would seem to have been killed when they were not MOULTING or otherwise incapacitated. I have suggested that a series of sawtooth bone points were employed for this purpose. There is no evidence that they were hafted on the sides of a dart shaft as in contemporary Eskimo culture, but they may have been. What does seem certain is that they did not detach and that they were most likely thrown over water, probably at swimming birds, as to throw them around the rocky coasts of Maine or Newfoundland would clearly have resulted in an inordinate amount of breakage.

Fishing gear is perhaps better, or at least more clearly, represented than the proposed bird darts. Hook-and-line fishing is not positively indicated, although it has been suggested that plummets may have served as fishing-line weights. No hooks, or parts thereof, have yet been recovered from Maritime Archaic contexts, however, and from all indications fishing was done by means of spears or leisters.

A large number of square-barbed bone or antler fish-spear or leister points were recovered during our excavations at Port au Choix, and nearly identical specimens have been reported by Fitzhugh (1972: 101, Plate 79A) from Rattlers Bight 1 and from the Nevin site cemetery in Maine (Byers, personal communication). Size is extremely variable and there are some variations in the precise type of barb, but square barbs of the type shown in Figure 1 are most common.

Save a few skate teeth and codfish ossicles, there is presently no direct evidence of what species of fish were taken with these implements. But because Atlantic salmon were found in all areas, I suspect that they figured prominently in the summer diet of the Maritime Archaic Indians.

The above are practically the only directly marine-related tools and weapons recovered from Maritime Archaic contexts to date. We may be sure, of course, that boats were made and used, probably by skilled aboriginal boatsmen. Both dugout boats and skin boats may have been made by Maritime Archaic peoples, but no evidence of either survives. In the north there seems to have been no timber suitable for dugout manufacture, and perhaps the decrease in frequency of stone gouges in the Labrador and Newfoundland expressions of this cultural tradition is also significant. In Maine and the Maritimes, however, there were plenty of trees suitable for the manufacture of dugout boats; there are more gouges known; and if swordfishing was as important as it seems, the possibly more cumbersome (but considerably less susceptible to piscatorial perforation) dugout boat may have had some significant adaptive advantage.

Much more could be said, mostly of a speculative nature, concerning the technological adaptations of these Maritime Archaic peoples of the northwestern Atlantic. The brief statements above clearly indicate the importance of maritime products in the subsistence and technological systems of these Archaic people.

## SETTLEMENT SYSTEMS

The settlement system of these people, insofar as it can presently be reconstructed, suggests a major portion of the seasonal round was spent at or near the coast, where most of the species mentioned above can be found. I have suggested that the months from February to November or December were spent at the coast by the Newfoundland Maritime Archaic people (Tuck 1970, 1971a, i.p.). Fitzhugh (1972: 165) suggests an Interior-Maritime adaptation for the central Labrador coast that would involve "intensified summer coastal adaptation with large, stable sites" as the "culmination of Indian marine specialization." Bourque (1971: 237) suggests that among related groups in Maine "sites along the coast were occupied during the warmer months of the year and at least occasionally at other times."

The total picture from these three areas, then, is essentially one of strong seasonal coastal adaptation with occasional winter(?) hunting forays or journeys of several months into the interior of the Atlantic Provinces and northern New England. The precise species hunted varied somewhat in each area, but the overall exploitive patterns seem to have been remarkably homogeneous over the entire area.

## AESTHETICS, MAGIC, AND RELIGION

Although the economic, technological, and subsistence systems of the Maritime Archaic people all indicate a high degree of adjustment to coastal resources, it is the rarely indicated aesthetic and belief systems of these aboriginal people that most clearly bespeak their commitment to a life in a maritime environment. I have discussed these aspects of Maritime Archaic culture at some length previously and will not belabor the point here. However, mention should be made of the feet, bills, wings, and skulls of various sea birds, the bone and antler effigies of the same species that surmount pins, pendants, and combs; the teeth, claw cores, and other elements of seals, whales, porpoises, and at least one polar bear; the carved-stone killer whales and other marine species; and many other charms, fetishes, and decorative objects that all speak eloquently to me of a people whose entire lives were influenced by the sea.

## COMPARISONS

Comparisons of this whole cultural pattern with other maritime peoples, both in the northeast and elsewhere, provide some interesting and sometimes surprising results.

North of the St. Lawrence we see that many of the subsequent inhabitants of Newfoundland, Labrador, and the *côte nord* of Quebec had settlements, subsistence, and technological systems very similar to those of their Maritime Archaic predecessors.

Arctic Small Tool Tradition peoples, both earlier variants and the later Dorset Eskimos, seem to have occupied the same or similar site locations as Maritime Archaic peoples at Saglek Bay, on the central and southern Labrador coast, and on the Island of Newfoundland. What evidence we have also points to essentially similar extractive patterns, although the probable Archaic interior adaptation has yet to be demonstrated for Eskimo peoples in these areas. Interior Paleo-Eskimo stations have, however, been reported from Ungava, and may some day be found elsewhere.

The now extinct Beothuk Indians of Newfoundland, on the other hand, clearly had at least a brief winter interior phase to their seasonal round. Historical and archaeological sources coincide in indicating this, and recent excavations in the Exploits Valley (Raymond LeBlanc, personal communication) have revealed winter camps of both Beothuk and Maritime Archaic cultures in the same location; on the coast the same situation seems to obtain.

Other Indian groups in the Atlantic Provinces and northern New England appear to have had settlement and economic systems that differed significantly from those of the Maritime Archaic Indians. The Naskapi Indians of Labrador and to an even greater extent the Montagnais seem to have had an interior boreal forest adaptation that was far more significant than either their own coastal orientation or the interior orientation of the Maritime Archaic people.

The Algonkian peoples south of the St. Lawrence also show significant differences from the Maritime Archaic culture, although these groups clearly had at least seasonal, and perhaps in some places and at certain times, year-round littoral settlements. From what we know of the economies of these southern successors to the Maritime Archaic people, they seem to have depended to a much greater extent upon shellfish than had the earlier Archaic people, although significant numbers of fish, seals, and probably other sea mammals continued to be taken.

Significant differences in technology parallel and support these somewhat ephemeral settlement and subsistence pattern differences. For instance, whereas the Maritime Archaic, pre-Dorset, Dorset, and apparently even the Beothuk Indians all utilized toggling harpoons in the pursuit of sea mammals, the Naskapi, Montagnais, and northern New England Algonkian spearers did not. Barbed forms were probably utilized by all groups, although the broad distribution of these forms throughout North America seemingly makes them of somewhat less diagnostic value than the more specialized toggling forms.

Other distinctions and similarities within and between these two groups of "Far Northeastern" peoples could be pointed out and in all likelihood still others will emerge as new data become available. What seems apparent at this point is that the Paleo-Eskimos and perhaps Newfoundland's Beothuk Indians had whole ways of life very like that of the Maritime Archaic people, whereas the Naskapi, Montagnais, and Algonkians of the Maritimes and Maine show some significant distinctions between their ways of life and those of the Maritime Archaic people.

If we extend our comparisons to include maritime-adapted peoples from other areas of the northern hemisphere, some even more striking and provocative similarities at once become apparent.

Comparisons of our Port au Choix material with that from such areas as Prince William Sound, Alaska (de Laguna 1956), the Fraser Delta, British Columbia (cf. Borden 1962), and northern Scandinavia (Fitzhugh, this volume) display such remarkable similarities that it is no wonder that the idea of an ancient circumboreal culture persistently reappears (Spaulding n.d.; Gjessing 1944). Certain elements, of course, evoke no great surprise — it is not hard to understand the parallel developments of barbed bone fish spears, of detachable barbed harpoon heads, of the various forms of toggle-type harpoons that these peoples employed, and even of the aesthetic, magic, and religious systems as constructed by archaeologists specializing in these areas, for each has a clear adaptive advantage when dealing with the sea and its resources.

Somewhat more misunderstood is the presence of virtually identical ground slate spears, knives, and lances or "bayonets." These have frequently been cited as evidence of some historical connections among these (and other) groups, and their presence in the cultural congeries of widespread maritime-adapted peoples has been the source of considerable confusion and consternation. I am convinced that there is no historical connection among these various peoples, that the similarities among the ground slate artifacts and their bone counterparts are somehow functionally divided, and that the likenesses in form are the result of the same sorts of cultural convergence as resulted in the development of leisters, barbed bone points, and barbed and toggling harpoons. Misunderstanding about these artifacts results because the functional significance and adaptive advantage of these ground slate implements are not easily recognizable, as they are in the cases of the various harpoons and barbed bone point forms. I cannot offer any suggestions as to what the adaptive significance of these slate artifacts might be, but someone, Fitzhugh I think, has suggested that their ability to penetrate the thick skins and fat layers of sea mammals may have something to do with their appearance in disparate regions at various times in world prehistory. This may not be the answer, but I suspect that it is somehow rather closer to the truth than we have seen in previous considerations of historical connections among these ground slate tools.

To summarize briefly, during the third and second millennia B.C. the "Far Northeastern" coast supported a group of fully maritime-adjusted peoples whose ways of life were remarkably similar to those of other maritime peoples scattered throughout at least the northern hemisphere. These similarities in economy, aesthetics and religion, and even very particular technological elements are a result of cultural convergence rather than of historical connections among these far-flung maritime cultures.

## REFERENCES

BORDEN, CHARLES E.
    1962   "West Coast crossties with Alaska," in *Prehistoric cultural relations between the arctic and temperate zones of North America.* Edited by John M. Campbell, 9–19. Arctic Institute of North America, Technical Paper 11. Montreal.

BOURQUE, BRUCE J.
1971 "Prehistory of the central Maine coast." Unpublished thesis, Harvard University, Cambridge, Massachusetts.

BYERS, DOUGLAS S.
1959 The eastern Archaic: some problems and hypotheses. *American Antiquity* 24(3):233–256.

DE LAGUNA, FREDERICA
1956 *Chugach prehistory.* University of Washington Publications in Anthropology 13. Seattle.

FITZHUGH, WILLIAM W.
1972 *Environmental archaeology and cultural systems in Hamilton Inlet, Labrador.* Smithsonian Contributions to Anthropology 16. Washington, D.C.

GJESSING, G.
1944 Circumpolar Stone Age. *Acta Arctica* 2.

HARP, ELMER, JR., DAVID HUGHES
1968 Five prehistoric burials from Port au Choix, Newfoundland. *Polar Notes* 8:1–47.

MARY-ROUSSELIÈRE, GUY, O.M.I.
1973 "Dorset and pre-Dorset sites in the Pond Inlet Region." Paper presented at the School of American Research Advanced Seminar on the Palaeo-Eskimo, February, 1973, Santa Fe.

MAXWELL, MOREAU S.
1973 "Pre-Dorset and Dorset: the view from Lake Harbour." Paper presented at the School of American Research Advanced Seminar on the Palaeo-Eskimo, February, 1973, Santa Fe.

MC GHEE, ROBERT J., JAMES A. TUCK
1973 "Un-dating the Canadian Arctic." Paper presented at the School of American Research Advanced Seminar on the Palaeo-Eskimo, February, 1973, Santa Fe.

MOOREHEAD, WARREN K.
1916 The problem of the Red Paint People. *Holmes Anniversary Volume,* 359–365. Washington.
1922 *A report on the archaeology of Maine.* Andover: Department of Archaeology, Phillips Academy.

SANGER, DAVID
1971 Preliminary report on excavations at Cow Point, New Brunswick. *Man in the Northeast* 1:34–47.

SNOW, DEAN R.
1969 *A summary of excavations at the Hathaway site in Passadumkeag, Maine 1912, 1947, and 1968.* Orono: Department of Anthropology, University of Maine.
1972 Rising sea level and prehistoric cultural ecology in northern New England. *American Antiquity* 37(2):211–221.

SPAULDING, ALBERT C.
n.d. "Notes on the archaeology of the boreal forest zone." Unpublished doctoral dissertation, Columbia University, New York.

TUCK, JAMES A.

1970 An Archaic Indian cemetery in Newfoundland. *Scientific American* 22:112–121.

1971a An Archaic Indian cemetery at Port au Choix, Newfoundland. *American Antiquity* 36(3):343–358.

1971b "The archaeology of Saglek Bay, Labrador: an interior report." Paper read at the Annual Meeting of the Society for American Archaeology, Norman, Oklahoma, 1971. (Abstracted in *Man in the Northeast* 3:56–58.)

i.p. *Ancient people of Port au Choix.* St. John's: Newfoundland Social and Economic Research Papers, ISER, Memorial University of Newfoundland.

WILLOUGHBY, CHARLES C.

1898 *Prehistoric burial place in Maine.* Archaeological and Ethnological Papers of the Peabody Museum, Harvard University 1(6).

1935 *Antiquities of the New England Indians.* Cambridge: Peabody Museum of American Archaeology and Ethnology, Harvard University.

# Demography and Adaptations of Eighteenth-Century Eskimo Groups in Northern Labrador and Ungava

J. GARTH TAYLOR

## POPULATION DISTRIBUTION

The populations of the Eskimo groups on the coast of Labrador have been estimated for the period immediately prior to 1773 (Taylor 1968: 44). These estimates, which are used in this study, are based mainly on the accounts of the Moravian missionary, Jens Haven (1773a), and of Lieutenant Roger Curtis of the Royal Navy (1774), both of whom traveled along the north coast in the summer of 1773. While Lieutenant Curtis traveled only as far as Kivertlok, Haven reached Naghvakh, 120 miles farther to the north. Thus, most of Haven's information on the Labrador coast is based on personal observations.

Although there are no comparable population figures for the Ungava Bay and Hudson Strait groups at this early period, Haven refers to these groups in a separate account (1773b) and gives the number of dwellings in each of the places from Killinek to Stupart Bay. This information will be used here in order to estimate the size of local populations in the northern Ungava area.

It appears that much of Haven's information was obtained from the Eskimo pilot who guided him from Saglekh to Naghvakh (Haven 1773a:

The main sources of data used in the present paper are the unpublished reports of Jens Haven (1773a, 1773b). Additional information, particularly with regard to the location of places mentioned by Haven and with regard to ecological conditions, was gathered in the field. Information on the coast of Labrador was obtained during two field trips (May 25–August 3, 1966 and June 28–July 23, 1968), both of which were sponsored by the National Museum of Canada. Information on the northern Ungava region was gathered during a trip to Fort Chimo (May 14–June 7, 1968), sponsored by the Royal Ontario Museum.

August 27). The pilot was from Ungava Bay and had traveled extensively in that area and in some parts of Hudson Strait at least as far as the Stupart Bay area (Haven 1773b). Another informant was an old woman whom Haven met at Saglekh. She was also from Ungava Bay and "related to me much of her country farther north, which served to explain to me many things the pilot had told me" (1773a: August 29).

From the information he had received Haven concluded that beyond Naghvakh there were "10 more places," and he estimated the total population of these ten places to have been about 1,660. In his account he refers to the "10 places" in order from east to west, spelling out the names as follows: Killinek, Kangivak, Tessiugak, Aukpaluk, Ungava, Tuak, Aiviktok, Nuvongok, Iglurarsome, and Ittibime.

Most of these names represent reasonable phonemic approximations of names still used, or used within living memory, for places in the northern Ungava region. "Killinek" is still used on maps, "Kangivak" refers to the east coast of Ungava Bay between Abloviak Fiord and George River,[1] "Tessiugak" is undoubtedly Leaf Bay (Tasiuyak), "Aukpaluk" is Hopes Advance Bay (Aupaluk), "Ungava" was formerly the area north of Payne River, and "Aiviktok" probably refers to Aivertok,[2] a place near Stupart Bay (see Map 1).

The place name "Tuak" is no longer in use, but in view of the fact that Haven gave all the other names in order of location from east to west, the position of "Tuak" between Ungava and Aivertok makes it probable that it refers to Diana Bay.[3] This probability is heightened by the fact that Haven said it was "at the west side of the great bay [Ungava Bay]."

The last place on Haven's list, referred to as "Ittibime," was described as "the last dwelling place of the Eskimo" and it was reported that "a little way off the Land Indians begin." It seems highly likely, in view of this reference to the boundary between the Eskimos and Indians, that "Ittibime" refers to the east coast of Hudson Bay. The ethnologist Lucien Turner referred to the people of that area as "Itivimiut ... the people of the other side" (1894: 179).

---

[1]  Although Kangiva has been used in a general sense to indicate most of the east coast of Ungava Bay (Weiz 1888), it also refers to a specific location at the mouth of Abloviak Fiord (Joshua Makiuk, personal communication). Place names are spelled according to the R.G.S. II system, as presented by Wheeler (1953).

[2]  Aivertok is a cape located in latitude 61° 26′, longitude 71° 35′, approximately ten miles south of Stupart Bay. According to Saladin d'Anglure (1962: 34) there are the remains of semi-subterranean houses at this site. The site was used as an Eskimo winter camp as late as 1958 (1962: 38).

[3]  The traditional name of the Diana Bay region is "Tuvaaluk" (Saladin d'Anglure 1967: 3). "Tuak" may simply represent contraction of this form.

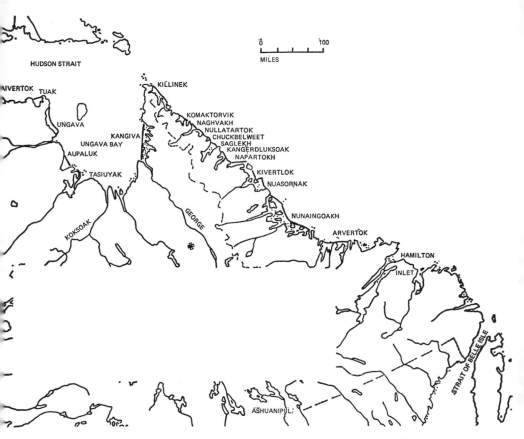

Map 1. Eskimo settlement areas in the Eastern Labrador-Ungava peninsula during the late eighteenth century.
(Dark line indicates minimum extension of the *sina* in each area)

In giving the number of dwellings in each locality, Haven distinguished between "winter houses" and "snow houses." The former were the semi-permanent sod-stone houses that were used on the coast of Labrador (Taylor 1968: 193). At Killinek, there were five winter houses and at Kangiva only one winter house and twenty snow houses. To the west of Kangiva snow houses were the only type of winter dwelling in use at the time of Haven's account. He reported there were twenty snow houses each at Tasiuyak, Aupaluk, and Ungava, ten snow houses at "Tuak," and thirty at Aivertok. He did not report the number of snow houses in the regions west of Stupart Bay, which was the farthest point his informant had traveled.

In order to make population estimates on the basis of these data each winter house will be considered as containing twenty persons, which was the average number of inhabitants in Labrador winter houses at this time (Taylor 1968: 195–196). Haven did not make an estimate of the number of people who dwelled in snow houses in the northern Ungava area. However, informant recall data and the observation of Stupart (1886: 102) suggest that the average number of inhabitants per snow house during the second half of the nineteenth century was at least ten persons. This figure will be used in estimating the populations of those areas where snow houses were in use.

Although Haven's information on the number of dwellings provides the only basis for estimating the population of most of these northern areas, some supplementary information in the Nain diary makes it possible to cross-check the estimate for Aupaluk. The population of this region, based on Haven's estimate of twenty snow houses, would be 200 persons. An Ungava Eskimo informed the missionaries at Nain that in "Aukpalluk" there were "fewer people than in Okak, Kivalek and Uivak together" (Nain diary: February 18, 1781). The population of these three settlements at the end of 1780 was 122, 48, and 39 respectively (Okak diary: December 31, 1780), making a total population of 209.

In addition, the visitor said there were ten boats in the Aupaluk area. Data from the coast of Labrador at this time indicate that the average number of people traveling in an umiak was about nineteen (Taylor 1968: 111). This suggests a population of approximately 190. Both of these population estimates are reasonably close to the estimate of 200 which is based on the number of dwellings.

## POPULATION DENSITY

It is impossible to calculate population densities on the basis of land area because the extent of territory exploited throughout the annual cycle is known for only a very few of the eighteen local groups. Although such information would in itself be interesting, it is doubtful whether relationship to the amount of land is the most significant way of expressing the population densities of maritime-adapted groups. This point has already been made by Kroeber (1963: 157), who suggests that Eskimo population densities should be calculated on the basis of the number of shore miles held by each group.

Although information is also lacking on the exact number of shore miles held by each group, it is suggested that a reasonable approximation can be obtained by measuring the length of the coastal strip of fast ice in each area. Detailed observations on the seasonal location of settlements in the Arvertok-Kivertlok areas (Taylor 1968: 143–166) indicate that almost the entire annual cycle was spent within an area that was covered during the winter season with relatively permanent fast ice.[4] The distribution of the remainder of the population groups under study here indicates that they too were located only in areas which had substantial expanses of fast ice during the winter season. The importance of fast ice to Central Eskimo populations was already noted by Boas (1888: 417), on the basis of his studies in Baffinland.

The area of the fast ice in any region varies constantly as the *sina* [ice edge] grows out toward open water in cold calm weather and is broken up again by the action of wind, current, and tide. However, in every area it is possible to define a minimum extension of the *sina*, inside of which fast ice can be expected to occur even under relatively adverse conditions. When the width of the fast ice is at its minimum extent, the *sina* is usually terminated at both ends by headlands which jut out into exposed stretches of open water.

Because it represents a reasonable boundary for the extent of fast ice of a relatively permanent nature, and because its limits are fairly easy to define, the length of the *sina* at its minimum extent will be used here to represent the length of the coastal strip of fast ice. The locations of the *sina* in each area were drawn on topographical maps by informants who were familiar with ice conditions in that particular area.[5] The lengths, measured from these maps, together with the population densities based on them, are presented in Table 1.

## DEMOGRAPHY AND ADAPTATION

Data presented in the table indicate that population densities of local groups varied widely, from two to ten persons per mile of shore line. The extent to which this variation can be related to variations in adaptation is briefly considered below.

Information from the coast of Labrador (Taylor 1968: 150) indicates

---

[4] Although some people hunted caribou in the interior this activity was restricted mainly to the late summer period and was done to obtain furs for winter clothing. Inland hunting is discussed more fully later.

[5] Most of the information on local ice conditions was provided by George Dicker, Ama Harris, and Joshua Obed of Nain; Nathan Friede of Hopedale; and George Kauki, Jimmy Kooktook, and Joshua Makiuk of Fort Chimo.

Table 1.   Shoreline population densities in northern Labrador and Ungava: 1773

| Area | Total population | Miles of shoreline* | Persons per mile |
|---|---|---|---|
| Arvertok | 270 | 52 | 5.2 |
| Nunaingoakh | 250 | 100 | 2.5 |
| Nuasornak | 140 | 32 | 4.4 |
| Kivertlok | 160 | 16 | 10.0 |
| Napartokh | 140 | 35 | 4.0 |
| Kangerdluksoak | 120 | 12 | 10.0 |
| Saglekh | 100 | 15 | 6.6 |
| "Chuckbelweet"** | 40 | 10 | 4.0 |
| Nullatartok | 30 | 10 | 3.0 |
| Naghvakh | 80 | 10 | 8.0 |
| Komaktorvik | 30 | 15 | 2.0 |
| Killinek | 100 | 50 | 2.0 |
| Kangiva | 170 | 65 | 2.6 |
| Tasiuyak | 200 | 35 | 5.7 |
| Aupaluk | 200 | 20 | 10.0 |
| Ungava | 200 | 50 | 4.0 |
| "Tuak"*** | 100 | 20 | 5.0 |
| Aivertok | 300 | 30 | 10.0 |

\*     Shoreline measurement taken at minimum extension of the *sina* (see text).
\*\*    Probably Bears Gut.
\*\*\*   Probably Diana Bay.

that winter was the hardest season for survival, and therefore it seems likely that winter adaptations were most crucial with regard to the limiting of population density. At this time of year many settlements relied almost exclusively on seals for their survival. However, in some areas a substantial addition to the winter food and fuel supply came from the stored meat and blubber of the Greenland whale (*Balaena mysticetus*), which was hunted during its southward migration during the month of November (1968: 145). People who lived in whaling areas experienced considerable hardship during the winter if the fall whaling was unsuccessful (1968: 69).

Moravian records indicate that the Greenland whale was captured regularly in the Kangerdluksoak, Naghvakh, Kivertlok, Saglekh, and Arvertok areas (Taylor 1968: 96).[6] These sources (1968: 92–96) indicate that between 1771 and 1784 at least forty-one whales were captured on the coast of Labrador. Since whaling records were only available for eleven years during this period, this suggests an average annual kill of at least 3.7 whales. Whaling success seems to have declined in the early years of the nineteenth century and after 1821 the Periodical Accounts of the Moravians contain no more references to the killing of whales.

[6]   Although whaling success in the Arvertok region seems to have declined after 1780 (Taylor 1968: 97), whales appear to have been captured fairly regularly prior to this date.

The information on the capture of whales in the remainder of the Labrador-Ungava peninsula is less detailed. However, Haven (1773b) mentioned that there were "many large whales" at "Tuak" and Aivertok. He referred to the latter as "the most famous place in all Labrador for whales" and said that the Eskimos gathered there in summer "probably to get the large joints of the whales which they use in their sledges."

On the other hand large whales were probably not available in the areas within Ungava Bay. Haven reported that there were no whales at Killinek, Kangiva, and Ungava and only "small whales" and "small whales without fins (baleen)" at Tasiuyak and Aupaluk. The latter may have been specimens of Minke whale (*Balaenoptera acutorostrata*). These are much faster than Greenland whales and there is no evidence that they were ever hunted. However, they were probably utilized whenever they were found stranded by tidal action or sudden ice formation, as was the case on the Labrador coast (Taylor 1968: 93). Informants state that within living memory large whales have not entered Ungava Bay and attribute this to the shallowness and relative freshness of the water.[7]

Data in Table 1 indicate that those areas where successful whaling was undertaken tend to have the highest population densities. This applies to the two favorable whaling locations in Hudson Strait as well as to the five on the coast of Labrador. The population densities in these seven regions range from five to ten persons per mile of shore line, suggesting that a successful whaling adaptation was consistently associated with high population density.

Of the remaining eleven places there are only two that have population densities that fall within this range. These are Tasiuyak and Aupaluk, with densities of 5.7 and 10 persons per mile of shore line. The other ten have very low densities, ranging from 2 to 4.4.

The unusually high densities in the Tasiuyak and Aupaluk regions suggest that there may have been pursuits other than whaling which could support dense populations. Brief references to former adaptations in these localities suggest two possibilities, both of which should be considered.

One possibility is an adaptation based on extensive hunting of the beluga or white whale (*Delphinapterus leucas*). Both informant recall and early records suggest that beluga were formerly very plentiful on the west coast of Ungava Bay, as well as being particularly easy to catch because of the shallow water and high tides characteristic of this area. One of the most highly successful of traditional hunting techniques was for several

---

[7]   The "freshness" of the water is attributed to the large output of fresh water from the many large rivers of the Labrador–Ungava peninsula. True salt water is only found in the northern half of the bay.

men in kayaks to drive a herd of beluga into a bay and then to harpoon them in the shallow water at low tide.

In 1831 Nicol Finlayson (Davies 1963: 143) reported from the new Hudson's Bay Company post at Fort Chimo that beluga were especially plentiful in the bay of "Hopes Advance" (Aupaluk). The Hudson's Bay Company later carried out intensive netting of beluga at Leaf Bay (Tasiuyak) and Whale River, and in the early years of this century their numbers became greatly diminished (Elton 1942: 345). In view of the fact that beluga, like Greenland whale, were frequently kept for winter use (Haven 1773a, August 10; Davies 1963: 154), it seems reasonable to assume that highly productive beluga hunting could account for high population densities on the lower west coast of Ungava Bay.

The high population densities in the Tasiuyak and Aupaluk regions may also result from a heavier reliance on inland resources, particularly caribou. On the coast of Labrador the most important caribou hunt took place during the autumn migration when the animals could be speared from kayaks while swimming across lakes and ponds (Taylor 1969: 146). The caribou hunters usually came back to the coast during the first weeks of October, just in time to move into their winter houses (Taylor 1968: 143). Although there are a few references to people remaining inland to consume stored caribou meat, the records suggest that this was a relatively infrequent occurrence and that it involved only very small numbers of people (1968: 148–149). Moreover, the route inland from the coast of Labrador was usually so difficult that it was frequently impossible to bring supplies of caribou meat out to the coast (1968: 153).

An early reference in the Nain diary suggests that the practice of remaining inland to live on stored caribou was much more common on the west coast of Ungava Bay, and indeed may even have been a regular occurrence. This information was given to the Nain missionaries by a visitor from Aupaluk, who said that when his people went inland in the summer, "They catch many [caribou] and many of them remain there over the winter for that reason, and live on caribou flesh" (Nain diary: February 18, 1781). The informant stated that the inland journey took several days by umiak and was so far inland that his people often met and camped beside Eskimos from Hudson Bay. This makes it probable that they were traveling inland from Tasiuyak by way of the Leaf River, a route which is navigable by umiak as far as Lake Minto (Low 1903: 11d). Since it was possible to navigate the umiaks to the caribou hunting grounds, it was probably also possible to bring large quantities of caribou meat back to the coast.

CONCLUSION

Population estimates of eighteen different Eskimo groups have been presented, and an effort has been made to calculate meaningful population densities from these figures. In view of the marked tendency for most seasonal settlements to locate in an area which is covered by fast ice during the winter months, the shore line population density of each area is calculated on the basis of the number of miles of relatively permanent fast ice in that area.

It appears that population densities obtained in this manner show a very significant degree of relationship to modes of adaptation. Very high densities were noted in all those areas which had a successful whaling adaptation. In most of the nonwhaling areas, where the bulk of the winter supply of food and fuel was derived from seals, the population densities fell well below those in the whaling areas.

Only two nonwhaling areas had population densities which fell within the range displayed in the whaling areas. Both of these were located on the lower west coast of Ungava Bay. It is suggested that the high density in these regions may indicate a type of adaptation in which stored beluga and/or caribou played a much greater role in the winter diet than was usually the case on the Labrador coast.

REFERENCES

BOAS, F.
    1888    *The Central Eskimo.* Sixth Annual Report of the Bureau of Ethnology, 1884–1885. Washington, D.C.: Smithsonian Institution.
CURTIS, R.
    1774    *Particulars of the country of Labrador. Extracted from the papers of Lieutenant Roger Curtis, of His Majesty's Ship "Otter," with a plane chart of the coast.* Philosophical Transactions of the Royal Society of London 64: 2.
DAVIES, K. G.
    1963    *Northern Quebec and Labrador journals and correspondence, 1819–1835.* Hudson Bay Record Society 24.
ELTON, CHARLES
    1942    *Voles, mice and lemmings: problems of population dynamics.* Oxford: Clarendon Press.
HAVEN, JENS
    1773a    "Extract of the voyage of the sloop George to reconnoitre the northern part of Labrador in the months of August and September 1773." Unpublished manuscript. London: Moravian Archives.

1773b  "A brief account of the dwelling places of the Eskimos to the north of Naghvakh." Unpublished manuscript. London: Moravian Archives.

KROEBER, A. L.
1963   *Cultural and natural areas of native North America.* Berkeley: University of California Press.

LOW, A. P.
1903   *Report on an exploration of the east coast of Hudson Bay from Cape Wolstenhome to the south end of Yarnes Bay.* Annual Report of the Geological Survey of Canada 13 (1900). Ottawa.

NAIN DIARY
n.d.   Manuscript copy of the diary of the Moravian Mission at Nain. London: Moravian Archives.

OKAK DIARY
n.d.   Manuscript copy of the diary of the Moravian Mission at Okak. London: Moravian Archives.

SALADIN D'ANGLURE, B.
1962   Découverte de Pétroglyphes à Qayartalik sur l'île de Qikertaaluk. *North* (November and December): 34–39.

1967   *L'Organisation Sociale Traditionnelle des Esquimaux de Kangirsujuaaq (Nouveau Québec).* Travaux Divers 17. Québec: Université Laval, Centre d'Etudes Nordiques.

STUPART, R. F.
1886   The Eskimo of Stupart Bay. *Proceedings of the Canadian Institute,* series 3, vol. 4: 95–114. Toronto.

TAYLOR, J. G.
1968   "An analysis of the size of Eskimo settlements on the coast of Labrador during the early contact period." Unpublished doctoral dissertation. University of Toronto.

TAYLOR, J. G., editor
1969   William Turner's journeys to the Caribou country with the Labrador Eskimos in 1780. *Ethnohistory* 16 (2):141–164.

TURNER, L. M.
1894   *Ethnology of the Ungava district.* Eleventh Annual Report of the Bureau of American Ethnology. Washington: Smithsonian Institution.

WEIZ, SAMUEL
1888   Nordspitze von Labrador, 1868. *Science* 11.

WHEELER, E. P.
1953   *List of Labrador Eskimo place names.* Bulletin of the Natural Museum of Canada 131. Ottawa.

# PART FOUR

*Comparative Studies*

# Maritime Adaptations in Cold Archipelagoes: An Analysis of Environment and Culture in the Aleutian and Other Island Chains

A. P. McCARTNEY

Occupants of marine island groups all share in some obvious common conditions. They are surrounded by water which (1) isolates them from occupants of other islands or mainlands, (2) requires some mode of water transportation and navigation, (3) offers relatively cornucopian marine resources, and (4) dictates the major weather affecting such islanders. However, a condition less obvious at first glance is that resource alternatives available to native occupants are more limited than on continents in the same geographic zone. This resource limitation is due to a depauperized or essentially nonexistent terrestrial fauna. Or to state the situation in a more biologically stringent fashion, if aboriginal human groups occupy archipelagoes, they must adapt to an almost total dependence on marine-related resources unless cultivation is known. This dependence is not one of choice but of necessity. If we consider the decrease of edible plant foods with the increase in latitude, then cold ocean islanders have even fewer resource alternatives than warm ocean counterparts.

My thesis is that cold ocean archipelagoes share in similar climatic, floral, and faunal characteristics which require similar prerequisite technologies for long-term human occupancy. In short, hunters and gatherers adapted to archipelago living should exhibit some cultural convergence unrelated to close genetic contact.

In studying Aleutian Islanders who occupy one of the most outstanding archipelagoes, I have been impressed with the similarity of the Fuegian

I wish to thank William M. Schneider for reading and commenting on this paper in draft. Nancy G. McCartney also provided helpful criticisms and pertinent biological information included in Tables 1 and 2. These commentators are absolved. of course, from the opinions and interpretations presented.

and Kurilean technology to that of the Aleuts. The Fuegian instance could only suggest convergence by Indians and Eskimoids at opposite ends of the New World. The Kuril Islands, however, are almost adjacent to the Aleutians in the North Pacific and on the basis of geographic proximity, cultures of one might have had direct and significant contact with the other. I have not addressed myself to this culture-history problem here but rather have attempted to demonstrate (1) the specific ways in which Aleutian Islanders are maritime-oriented, (2) the nature of adaptive alternatives made available by the physical and biological environment, and (3) how generalizations about this archipelago apply to other cold ocean examples, especially the Fuegian region.

## ARCHAEOLOGICAL CONDITIONS AND IMPLICATIONS

Prior to developing arguments for maritime adaptations in archipelagoes, a statement of intent and conditions is in order. Treating environmental-cultural interaction in anthropology today is hazardous because of possible misinterpretation in the active debate over systemic, processual, and deterministic approaches. Here we are offering an hypothesis to be considered and tested by future archaeological investigation; a demonstration of a particular theoretical position is not intended.

The subsistence alternatives possible for cold archipelago peoples are explored and no attempt is made to expand these adaptive implications to other cultural or social aspects. The prime reason for assuming a conservative "culture core" stance is that technological/subsistence spheres may be best analyzed with extant archeological knowledge from such archipelagoes. Archaeological endeavors in the Aleutians — the example emphasized here — have not been directed toward ascertaining cultural systems other than technological/subsistence ones. Only a handful of prehistoric Aleut house structures have been tested (Cook et al. 1972; McCartney n.d.). Only incomplete site inventories are available (McCartney 1972). Typical midden sites have confused stratigraphies with few recognizable living floors or surfaces.

In short, the stuff with which settlement pattern, social system, and processual analyses deal is not yet available. Therefore, while espousing the desirability of holistic approaches (e.g. Steward 1955; Heider 1972), I pragmatically accept Trigger's conclusion (1971:329–332) that (1) archaeologists cannot always treat whole cultural systems, (2) that archaeologists should address themselves to problems which can be handled by the archaeological evidence, and (3) that "the main contributions that prehistoric archaeology is likely to make in the near future will concern the manner in which specific economic, social, and demographic variables interact with one another in specified environmental settings over long periods of time."

Further, because of the relatively rich ethnohistoric sources available for the Aleutian area, I have combined eighteenth- and nineteenth-century cultural descriptions with archaeological data to synthesize a "typical" Aleutian lifeway. I make note that within this archipelago and others, adaptive variation occurred and that monolithic generalizations are subject to exceptions. However, a direct historical approach is especially appropriate here because what archaeological details are known suggest that there was strong cultural continuity over several millennia.

The most stimulating exposition of the ecological approach remains that of Steward (1955); the discussion here of how Aleut and other subsistence systems adjust to the environment follows Steward's dictum:

The problem is to ascertain whether the adjustments of human societies to their environments require particular modes of behavior or whether they permit latitude for a certain range of possible behavior patterns (36).

I seek the "cultural core — the constellation of features which are most closely related to subsistence activities and economic arrangements" (37) for cold archipelago peoples. The empirical charge to "determine whether similar adjustments occur in similar environments" (42) through the method of cultural ecology seems unencumbered with presumptions and suitable for establishing cultural regularities.

Finally, caution should be expressed prior to assuming determinisms of any sort. Because environmental factors and the way man has adapted to them are treated together, this does not lead to environmental causality of total culture. It does mean in the case of archipelago dwellers that the degree of latitude for existence is severely limited. Or positively stated, archipelago occupation "necessitates a distinctive mode of life" (Hawley, in Steward 1955: 34).

Seen as a matter of degree and not all-or-nothing causality, I suggest the probability is exceedingly low of humans surviving in archipelagoes such as the Aleutians without a maritime adaptation. While within a maritime ecosystem some latitude of staples is found, the particular species and their cyclical movements will restrict natives in the way those food resources are utilized and therefore, utilization behavior is highly predictable. In this regard, I propose, contrary to Trigger's admonition (1971: 329), that archipelago cultures, as "primitive" cultures, are more strictly limited in adaptive responses to the environment than are more complex cultures. Further, Trigger (327) states:

Most ecological explanations of ethnographic data are ad hoc, in the sense that they adduce plausible reasons to account for what is observed, but are unable to demonstrate that, given the same set of conditions, alternative solutions would be either impossible or highly unlikely.

Given the extreme nature of cold archipelago environments, I believe that such a demonstration is possible.

Sahlins (1972) contradicts the popular notion that hunters and gatherers suffer from almost constant deprivation. Specifically, Lee's study of Bushmen (1968) adequately deflates the notion that this hunting and gathering group is backed into an adaptive corner. But to use the bountifulness of Bushman life as indicative of all human cultural adaptations at the hunting/gathering level would be equally fallacious. Lee (1968: 40) does note that the Eskimo have "the most precarious human adaptation on earth" because plants are lacking as a resource complex and because the arctic fauna is cyclically variable in population and range. My contention is that the Aleut, as a variant of the Eskimoid adaptation, have a MARITIME specialization which is only slightly less precarious than that of mainland Eskimos.

Beyond the subsistence sphere, I make no claim about the types of social organization, religious systems, aesthetic developments, etc. which would result as a function of environmental adaptation.

## THE NATURE OF ARCHIPELAGOES

In scanning the world, one finds few large archipelagoes which are water-isolated year around and occupied by human groups. Nor does one find many continental coastal zones sufficiently isolated by geographic features to be treated as true archipelagoes. But what few pseudo- and true archipelagoes are known point to the fact THAT TERRESTRIAL FAUNA GENERALLY, AND LAND MAMMALS SPECIFICALLY, ARE SEVERELY LIMITED. Lacking cultivation, archipelago dwellers are limited to sole dependence on maritime resources.

### Faunal Limitations

There are few areas of the world which do not support a terrestrial mammalian fauna of some diversity. Even harsh deserts, high alpine plateaus, and arctic regions have some specially adapted species. Yet water-isolated islands have drastically fewer indigenous land mammals to be exploited by human groups. The terrestrial fauna are almost always less diverse the farther one moves from the originating mainland into an island chain.

Two major distributional situations are responsible for land mammals ever becoming established on marine islands. One is colonization from surrounding continental coasts or already populated islands themselves adjacent to continental edges. Ice or tree rafting are specific ways by which terrestrial game can occasionally spread across water barriers. The other is maintenance of old animal populations which existed prior to the formation of islands by rising sea water. Obviously the geologic origin of the islands is crucial to establishing which of these alternatives, or both, occurred.

Whatever the source of land mammals, their population equilibrium is delicate at best and especially subject to population crashes due to starvation, disease, or overhunting by man. Because island populations are isolated rather than being small but contiguous segments of a larger continental distribution, natural restocking may be sporadic at best. Darlington (1960: 666) refers directly to the relationship between climate and limited space and diversity:

Besides its special effects on different plants and animals, climate has a more general effect: cold, seasonal climate limits the total size (number of species) of floras and faunas. Limitation of area has the same effect: the smaller the area, the fewer the species that occur together in it. This effect is greatest in the case of large animals, which need large areas to maintain permanent populations, and this may be one reason why (small) invertebrates persist for long periods in small ... temperate areas while (larger) vertebrates do not.

Marine animals and birds are, by their nature, contiguous with a larger population, and a local gap left by a species extinction can easily be filled with identical or similar species. But for proof of the nonsuccess of land mammals in archipelagoes, one only need survey the extant marine islands for such fauna.

Island biogeography is treated in detail by MacArthur and Wilson (1967), but their discussion centers on nonmammalian species and is less applicable here.

## Comparative Archipelagoes

In the far north we find few major archipelagoes. The Aleutians and Kurils are the two largest subarctic examples of the New and Old World respectively. The Canadian archipelago is excluded because it is not isolated by year-round open water. And the Greenlandic coastal zone, as a pseudo-archipelago with its linear configuration between the ocean and interior ice cap, is not comparable because it, too, supported a set of land mammals during the prehistoric period. Musk ox, caribou, and lesser game all reached Greenland via the frozen islands of the Canadian archipelago.

Major archipelagoes in the tropical zone are also few. The major Oceanic or Pacific island groups and the Bahamas and Antilles are the best examples.

The southern hemisphere is almost devoid of major archipelagoes inhabited by prehistoric man. The Chilean archipelago along the southwestern and southern parts of that country does serve as an example made up of marine islands and an inhospitable mainland coast.

Brief inspection of these major archipelagoes verifies the conclusion that they support very few land mammals which could serve as major human resources. The Aleutians support only foxes and lemmings and, on very few islands, weasels and shrews (see below). The Kuril Islands support much the same variety of land mammals. The Oceanian archipelago considered as a whole, but excluding New Guinea, supports only tree-dwelling opossums in Melanesia, closest to the Asiatic mainland, and bats and rats in the remaining islands. Rats probably only spread to Micronesia and Polynesia with human colonists as they did in the Aleutians. A few land snakes and crocodiles reached Palau near the Philippines (Forde 1963: 175; Oliver 1961: 10; Mason 1968: 279). The Bahamas-Antilles have a recent mammalian fauna of bats, ground and arboreal rodents, insectivores, plus lizards and land mollusks (Sauer 1950: 361–362). The Fuegian region has isolated deer, guanaco, land otter, and bats in highly restricted zones (see below).

If we visualize three geographical macrohabitats — inland, coastal, and island, then obviously islanders have more restricted resources. Inland hunters/gatherers can exploit large and small land mammals as well as riverine fish and shellfish and terrestrial flora. Coastal dwellers on continental edges may add marine resources to all that inland dwellers have. But islanders lack important species of land mammals, usually have a poorer freshwater fish supply, and therefore must exploit the sea.

As an ethnographic comparison, we find that even classically marginal hunters and gatherers living on coasts outside the Arctic have more latitude in subsistence than do archipelago occupants. The following groups, for example, relied partially on terrestrial fauna and flora as well as on marine resources: Seri — mule deer, hares, cactus fruit, mesquite beans, seeds; Andamanese — wild pigs, civet cats, reptiles, roots, fruit, honey; Ingura — wallaby, goanna, bandicoots, yams, fruit, nuts, honey;

Tiwi — kangaroo, yams, nuts, other vegetables; and Tasmanians — kangaroos, wallaby, opossum, platypus, roots (Oswalt 1973; Hart and Pilling 1960).

## Cold Archipelagoes

Being interested in archipelagoes similar to the Aleutians, I will concentrate on those found in similar cold water regions. The subarctic Kurils and the subantarctic Fuegian region are perhaps the most environmentally analagous, falling above 45° North and below 45° South. By leaving out warm water archipelagoes between 30° North–30° South, we of course diminish the importance of plants as major food alternatives. Tropical archipelagoes such as the Bahamas, Antilles, and the Pacific Islands all have tropical vegetation which can greatly augment fishing and sea collecting. The fact that Micronesia and Polynesia were not colonized by human argonauts until a Neolithic level of cultivation had been mastered obviated any need for only collecting native foods.

But moving into cold, high-latitude environments brings about a reduction of plant diversity, which means essentially no plants provide edible nuts, plantains, large tubers, or abundant grain. And what plants were utilized could only be collected during the summer growing season. A few berries, roots, and stalks were utilized but because of the very low caloric yield per unit, such plants were primarily used for dietary diversity rather than stability. Thus, in a restrictive, cold environment, native plant utilization is not an alternative to land mammal utilization whether on islands or on continental masses.

Further, in none of the three cold archipelagoes treated here were domesticated crops ever successfully introduced. Cool summer growing seasons precluded the spread of temperate crops south into the Fuegian area, and North American Indian crops obviously never spread to the Alaska Peninsula to be introduced into the Aleutians.

Food is even a more limiting characteristic in cold regions than in warm because the caloric need is greatly increased for body warmth (see, for example, Newman 1962). As discussed below, fat is especially critical to survival and no plants in the Aleutians or other cold archipelagoes provide a vegetable source for food oil.

To reiterate, inhabitants of cold archipelagoes cannot depend on large or small land mammals for food and raw resources. Nor can they depend on high-quantity and/or high-quality plant foods for any significant part of the diet. Therefore, only marine resources are available to be exploited and the occurrence of people in such archipelagoes presumes an adequate cultural adaptation to these regional exigencies.

## ALEUT MARITIME ORGANIZATION

### The Aleuts as Unique Eskimos

Our topic is prehistoric maritime adaptations in circumpolar zones and Aleuts serve as an important example of Eskimoids dependent on sea life for survival. The following sections suggest not only HOW the Aleuts were maritime but also WHY.

The string of over 100 small-to-large Aleutian Islands stretching into the North Pacific is unique in shape and length. No other archipelago approaches this one in curved, linear configuration or in total extension out and away from a continental mass for 1,050 miles. It is the uniqueness of this island chain which makes it a valuable cultural laboratory. Conversely, it suffers from distinctiveness in that there are few other geographically analagous regions with which to compare cultural phenomena observed there.

The uniqueness of the archipelago is paralleled in the native inhabitants. Aleuts are the most westerly of Eskimoid groups and vie with Labrador Eskimos as the most southerly. Geographic isolation in this island *cul-de-sac* has brought about genetic and linguistic distinctiveness over several millennia. And coping in a different environment from that utilized by more northerly arctic peoples has produced a special emphasis on maritime subsistence. The involvement of Aleuts with the ocean environment was complete; they lived beside, traveled over, ate from, and often died in the surrounding Bering and Pacific waters. But whether considered marginal due to their peripheral location or because of their minority subsistence pattern in the Arctic, the success of Aleuts in adapting is attested by the large population size and multi-millennial time depth evidenced.

Past Aleuts were unlike mainland Eskimos (1) in occupying an archipelago of relatively small islands rather than the mainland coast or interior, or larger islands of the Canadian archipelago; (2) in lacking high-latitude cold temperatures and resulting marine ice and ice-edge or hole hunting; (3) in occupying a stormy, Pacific sea habitat in which high winds and precipitation dominate the weather conditions; (4) in lacking dog traction as a means of transportation; and (5) in lacking terrestrial food resources such as caribou and smaller game. Lack of winter sea ice adjacent to the coast prohibited sled transportation. Aleuts traveled via skin boats rather than with dog traction during the winter. Further, the steep, mountainous terrain would effectively prevent sled travel on most islands.

Whereas dog traction is a result of arctic adaptation, the lack of terrestrial food resources is a causative environmental element in directing adaptation. Beyond Unimak Island, the first large island adjacent to the Alaska Peninsula, the islands form a relatively uniform group. Minor climatic, topographic, floral, and faunal differences occur between the Fox, Four Mountains, Andreanof, Delarof, Rat, and Near Island groups comprising the chain's length. But these differences are below the level of general analysis offered here. Unimak is excluded because it is more similar vegetationally to the Alaska Peninsula and shares a mainland terrestrial fauna which extends no further west.

But it is precisely because this rich terrestrial fauna does not blanket the chain that we note a significant difference between the Aleutians and other Eskimo territories. Almost all the remaining coastal regions occupied by Eskimos offered a terrestrial fauna complementing a marine fauna. From earliest evidence of man in the Alaskan, Canadian, and Greenlandic Arctic, we note utilization of caribou, musk ox, and smaller and more scattered land mammals during some part of the annual cycle (Taylor 1968). As noted above, the Canadian archipelago is here considered an extension of mainland Canada and Greenland because during most of the year wandering caribou and musk ox herds and smaller game crossed from island to island on intervening ice.

Note that the distinction here is not between coastal versus inland adaptations. Taylor (1968) has discussed with insight the fallacy of originating Eskimo cultures from either extreme adaptation. Rather, he summarizes strong evidence for most arctic cultures, past and present, being dependent on both terrestrial and marine resources. Taylor stresses "omnivorous flexibility" in an arctic or subarctic environment as an overriding characteristic of Eskimo economies. Groups such as the Aleut are considered to be anomalous to this sea-land pattern:

The preceding review of archaeological and ethnological evidence of Eskimo economies does suggest, however, a mixed caribou-sea mammal economy with wide local variation in each major prehistoric and historic group, with few exceptions. These exceptions, pure inland and pure sea mammal economies, are sufficiently rare that they might be better considered as ECOLOGICAL ANOMALIES, explainable as special cases rather than as polarities from which to derive synthesis regarding the nature or origins of Eskimo economy and culture (15; emphasis added).

Kroeber (1939: 22) had earlier called attention to the nonuniformity of Eskimo groups:

What emerges from the total array of [Steensby's] succinctly analyzed data is not the primacy or priority of one particular economic adaptation, but a picture of the totality of Eskimo culture as a unit, modified by emphasis or reduction of its traits in direct response to local exigencies. Here seals are the important food, there whales, or walrus, or caribou, or birds, or salmon, while others are as good as unavailable.

Taylor cites not only Aleuts but also ethnographically known St. Lawrence Islanders and Ammassalik Eskimos as being purely maritime in dependence. Geist and Rainey (1936) and Murie (1936) report arctic foxes, mice, lemmings, ground squirrels, and occasional polar bears on St. Lawrence which evidently have some antiquity. Possible caribou antler tools were also found in the large Kukulik midden but it is impossible to state whether caribou lived on St. Lawrence or were hunted on the Siberian shores. Reindeer have been successfully stocked on the island in modern times. St. Lawrence Islanders, therefore, did have access to an inconsequential, but not totally absent, land fauna. The Ammassalik, on the other hand, did utilize caribou, musk ox, and hares in precontact times (Oswalt 1973: 135) and are therefore excluded from being solely maritime dependent.

Land-oriented counterparts to these maritime exceptions would be the caribou-dependent Nunamiut and Caribou Eskimos.

In sum, a major point to be stressed is that the Aleuts, while omnivorous like "typical" Eskimos, lacked the dual utilization of marine and terrestrial fauna. Marginal and anomalous the Aleuts may be to the remainder of the New World arctic region, but their degree of cultural success demands our fullest attention. About one-third of all the aboriginal Eskimoid population of Alaska were Aleuts (i.e. approximately 12,000 of 38,000; Lantis 1970: 172–179; Oswalt 1967: 24–25). They occupied approximately one-third of the total Alaskan coastal zone. They have persisted *in situ* and have shown strong cultural continuity for at least 4,000 years and perhaps as much as 8,000 years. No other subgroup of Eskimoids can parallel their spread, duration, or population success.

*Aleutian Faunal Restrictions*

Present faunal distributions are taken to approximate those for most of the postglacial period. We have no archaeological or ethnohistoric information which contradicts these general ranges although obviously minor population and areal shifts have occurred over time.

Whereas Unimak and the Alaska Peninsula have caribou, brown bear, arctic hare, wolf, wolverine, mink, weasel, least weasel, ground squirrel, porcupine, lynx, and land otter which might be considered as food and raw material utilization (Murie 1959), none of these animals occurs farther west in the chain. Historic alterations of fauna include fox stocking on many of the islands throughout the chain, reindeer stocking on Umnak and Atka, caribou stocking on Adak (Jones 1966), and sheep ranching on Unalaska and Umnak. Dogs accompanied prehistoric man into the chain but were not used for sledding (Hrdlička 1945).

The Aleutians, as mentioned above, show evidence for both land mammal colonization and, presumably, maintenance of older animal populations. At the end of the Pleistocene glacial period, the eastern Aleutians formed an extension of the current Alaska Peninsula. Sea level was approximately 22 meters below present, and inter-island passes in the Fox Islands were presumably above water. This longer peninsula extended to southwestern Umnak Island where Samalga Pass presented a water barrier to terrestrial animals including man (Laughlin 1967; McCartney and Turner 1966). The only ancient site known on that peninsula extension is on present Ananiuliak or Anangula Island, off southwestern Umnak. Dated to about 8,000 years ago, the site may have harbored a population partially living on caribou and lesser land mammals. Only a few charred bones have been located at the Anangula site and these give an inadequate faunal picture when compared to rich midden sites of the last 4,000 years. Taking as our model the linear mammalian ranges of the present Alaska Peninsula in which populations have spread to their terrestrial limits and beyond to Unimak, we may safely assume that longer continuous space 8,000 to 10,000 years ago was similarly occupied from the northeast.

As sea level rose, isolating the old peninsula into individual islands, extant populations would be discontinuously spaced in the Fox Islands. The fact that during the last several millennia traced by archaeological deposits we find almost no evidence of land mammal fauna save some foxes and lemmings is consistent with the view that either natural or human factors caused the demise of such populations during the post-glacial period. Turner and Turner (1972: 52) have archaeologically located several caribou and bear bones on Akun Island, the first large island west of Unimak. These bones date older than A.D. 800. Rather than presuming this to be evidence for a remnant local caribou or bear population, these may be seen as evidence of Akun hunters visiting

Unimak across Unimak Pass and returning with carcasses from the latter island.

There is a similar case of caribou bone distribution in the northern Kurils where carcasses from the southern end of the Kamchatka peninsula were carried into the islands (Chard 1956: 290). Maintenance of land mammals which are now limited to Unimak and the Alaska Peninsula is presumed to have occurred for only a short period following eustatic adjustment in the Fox Islands. If ever other Anangula-age sites are found, we may locate preserved faunal evidence to corroborate this view.

As evidence of land mammal colonization, we see that the remaining islands west of the Fox Islands are isolated by deep-water passes in excess of 110 fathoms, the approximate lowest sea level during the last 100,000 years (Müller-Beck 1967: 378). Foxes, probably red foxes, are known prehistorically from the islands of the same name and these may be relic populations derived from Pleistocene ancestors. Or these may be due to island-hopping from the northeast. But the fact that arctic foxes are known in the western part of the chain suggests colonization by island-hopping from Asia via the Commander Islands (Jochelson 1933: 35; Murie 1959: 292). Present distribution data of arctic foxes is completely misleading because of twentieth-century stocking of most islands for fox-trapping purposes.

The fact that foxes survive as the largest and almost sole remaining land mammal throughout the chain suggests they were not suitable food animals and were not depleted by past Aleut populations. Fox bone artifacts have been recovered from archaeological sites in the Fox Islands (McCartney 1967: 351) and thus were used. But the great number of foxes taken by early Russian trappers (Murie 1959: 294) and the relatively infrequent occurrence in ancient sites point toward their being a less than tasty resource. Perhaps they were trapped when starvation was imminent, just as dogs were probably killed, but they do not appear to be a dietary staple.

In sum, prehistoric Aleuts were compelled to subsist almost entirely on food sources other than land mammals. No prolific ground squirrels or caribou herds were available and island-based birds were insignificant. The Aleuts, therefore, created a hunting/gathering lifeway designed to maximize sea resources.

## ALEUT SUBSISTENCE

As we focus on what the prehistoric Aleuts DID eat rather than what they did not, we find archaeological and ethnographic evidence for six principal food and resource categories exploited: sea mammals, fish, marine invertebrates, marine algae, sea birds, and terrestrial flora. The first four are marine organisms, the fifth is directly dependent on the sea, and even the sixth is dominated by marine climate. I hasten to add that these categories were not equally important but, conversely, it is difficult to approximately quantify their relative significance in the annual diet at different locations along the chain.

Due to incomplete site preservation, the fact that butchery often occurred away from permanent settlements, and the fact that food resources often cannot be distinguished from raw material resources, about our only recourse is to specify what is found archaeologically or what, assuming a uniformitarian approach, is suggested in the ethnographic and ethnohistoric literature. Quantification and analysis of faunal remains are rare for the Aleutians (see Lippold 1966, 1972; Turner and Turner 1972) and little is known of the importance of particular foods prehistorically. But as will be argued below, successful Aleut adaptations allowed for few resource alternatives. Following Taylor's suggestion of omnivorousness, we may surmise that most of the potentially usable flora and fauna offering significant food value were actually utilized at some time during the seasonal cycle.

Besides detailing the hunting, fishing, and collecting systems developed, a brief sketch of available food resources, nutritional requirements, food cycles, and other pertinent limitations is offered.

*Food Resources*

The general categories of animals and plants important to the Aleut diet are well known but their relative importance varies by region and seasons. Whereas most major species are pan-Aleutian in distribution, their density and abundance differs from island to island and from one local habitat to another. Because of an inter-island pass, coastal configuration, mountain, underwater trench, or other feature, one island will have sea otters, another will not. One island will have abundant clams, another will not. Birds will be plentiful on one islet and not on another. Seasonality of distribution for many species also necessitates some consideration of relative abundance during different months.

Ethnographic sources reveal different notions of what species were primary in the diet. For the above reasons, food staples vary from author to author. Coxe (1787), citing several sources, tells us that:

The inhabitants live upon roots which grow wild, and sea animals; they do not employ themselves in catching fish, although the rivers abound with all kinds of salmon, and the sea with turbot (50; Near Islands).

Their principal food is the flesh of sea animals, which they harpoon with their bone-lances; they also feed upon several species of roots and berries (62; Near Islands).

The natives chiefly subsist upon dried fish and other sea animals (82; Kanaga).

The quantity of provisions which they procure by hunting and fishing being far too small for their wants, the greatest part of their food consists of sea-wrack and shell-fish, which they find on the shore (178; Fox Islands).

Their principal nourishment is fish and whale fat, which they commonly eat raw (213; Unalaska).

Their principal food is fish, which they catch with bone hooks (215; Unalaska).

Cook (1784, in Hrdlička 1945: 91) states that:

Fish and other sea animals, birds, roots and berries, and even seaweed, compose their food (91; Unalaska).

Langsdorf (1814, in Hrdlička 1945: 92) states that:

The principal food of these islanders consists of fish, sea-dogs and the flesh of whales (92; Unalaska).

These selections give early historic period estimates of important foods. As we cannot control further for principal species known either ethnographically or archaeologically, one must assume that most food animals and plants available in sizable units and/or amounts were used.

The larger and more rewarding the food item, the greater the probability it was used. For instance, almost all sea mammals were hunted, a notable exception being the killer whale. Large or abundant fish were used but many marine fishes were excluded because of taste or difficulty of catching. Many birds were excluded also because of taste, scarcity, or difficulty in catching. As the least rewarding in terms of return rate, some edible plants were overlooked. There is no definite evidence that foxes were ever used for food. According to Ransom (1946: 615), dogs were never killed for food but this may reflect a modern and not an aboriginal trend.

What is clear from the ethnographic sources is that there was a preferential ranking in the minds of the natives as to yield of food per amount of effort and time expended to catch or collect and process it.

And taste is probably a consideration as well. Coxe (1787) reports, for instance, that:

They catch cod and turbot with bone-hooks, and eat them raw. As they never collect a store of provision, they suffer greatly from hunger in stormy weather, when they cannot go out for fish; at which time they are reduced to live upon small shell-fish and sea-wrack, which they pick up upon the beach and eat raw (86–87; Atka).

According to Langsdorf (1814, in Hrdlička 1945: 92):

Vegetable food is either not much esteemed by them, or else they do not like the trouble of procuring it.

It appears that sea mammal meat, blubber and blood, and fish were considered more satisfying and probably more scrumptious than seaweed, invertebrates, and plants, with birds falling between the two extremes. Fish and sea mammals appear to be the primary staples if any food can be so designated.

Detailed faunal analyses have yet to be published for any Aleutian site but even if such data were available, there is much latitude for interpretation of excavated samples without ethnographic and biologic assistance. For instance, because sea urchin spines comprise the greatest mass of midden debris, is it safe to assume that urchins were the most important species in the diet? Were periwinkles collected during only one season or throughout the year? Because salmon bones are relatively scarce even in middens beside fine salmon streams, do we presume the streams did not always have salmon or are there other preservation factors to explain their absence? Because whales are usually evidenced only by occasional mandible and rib fragments, do we surmise that whales were unimportant in the total diet? Probably the safest way out of such interpretive dilemmas is to maximize the ethnographic and independent ecological information which may help explain faunal remains.

*Food and Resource Procurement Systems*

Food is stressed in this paper as the primary limiting factor for Aleutian survival. Outlined here are the different ways in which Aleuts fed themselves; the problems of finding alternative foods are discussed in a following section. Animals which provided the most food also provided most of the raw manufacturing material. But, given the hunting/gathering level of Aleut existence, it was the lack of food and not tools which caused periodic starvation and thus secondary animal use for satisfying nonfood needs is not considered.

HABITATS   Aleuts subsisted in three major habitats — offshore, littoral, and terrestrial. The last-named habitat produced little potential food for Aleuts, and it was the marine-related ones that were crucial. From the steep cliffs and hillsides overlooking the sea where sea birds colonize in great numbers, down across the beach and inter-tidal zone to the open, unprotected sea surface, Aleuts concentrated on food provided by this marine environment.

These habitats were versatile in several ways. The three mentioned are to a degree continuous because the prime animals sought — sea mammals, fish, and birds — moved from one to another and could be procured accordingly. These animals were not strictly habitat-specific. Salmon moved up streams, sea mammals hauled up on shore rocks, and birds congregated on the ocean surface. By traveling only several hundred yards, hunters could exploit all three of these habitats. Travel in skin boats brought a large amount of coast within the range of an Aleut's search for food. Besides the exploitive value of boats, the use of kayaks and umiaks also circumvented the arduous and sometimes treacherous crossing on foot of cobble beaches, tussock-hummock vegetation, and precipitous cliffs.

FOOD WEB   Figure 1 graphically expresses the relationships between animals in a simple trophic hierarchy. Major species comprising these food categories are listed in Table 1. Figure 1 schematically indicates the approximate importance of these food categories to man at the top of the web; the proportional amounts of flow are liberally interpreted from ethnographic references as those cited above. Estimates of nonfood raw materials from the various categories are not illustrated.

Because birds are almost totally dependent on marine resources, they are included with marine rather than terrestrial organisms.

Clearly, man depends most heavily on Level 3 animals and less, in order, on Level 2 and 1 consumers and producers. As man seasonally shifts from Level 3 to Level 2 and 1 foods, greater quantities of the latter must be consumed to provide a minimum caloric intake. The dominant dependence of Aleuts on marine resources is also obvious. Marine mammals and fish provide primary support, birds secondary support, and invertebrates, algae, and land plants tertiary support.

PROCUREMENT SYSTEMS   By combining the various Aleutian habitats, major organisms exploited, and tools and techniques utilized, we arrive at a set of eight food and resource procurement systems thought to have been used for a long period. "System" is here used as "an intercommuni-

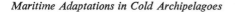

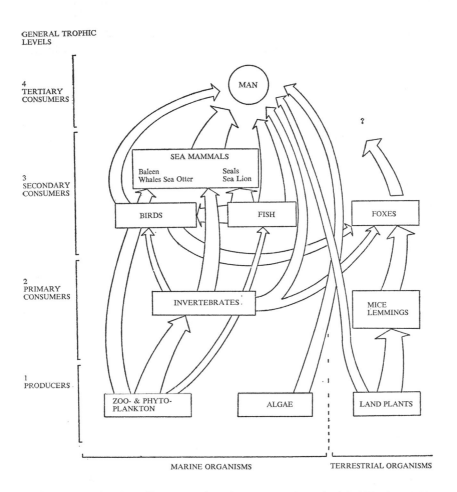

GENERAL TROPHIC
LEVELS

4
TERTIARY
CONSUMERS

3
SECONDARY
CONSUMERS

2
PRIMARY
CONSUMERS

1
PRODUCERS

MAN

SEA MAMMALS

Baleen          Seals
Whales Sea Otter   Sea Lion

BIRDS          FISH          FOXES

INVERTEBRATES.          MICE
LEMMINGS

ZOO- & PHYTO-          ALGAE          LAND PLANTS
PLANKTON

?

MARINE ORGANISMS          TERRESTRIAL ORGANISMS

cating network of attributes … forming a complex whole" (Clarke 1968: 42). Viewing all the variables in an integrated whole provides us with a better functional understanding of the attributes as well as a more realistic portrayal of Aleut subsistence. By reducing procurement to meaningful activity units, we recognize that the eight systems are abstractions from multiple and continuous facets of human behavior. As abstractions, they are open to various interpretations and future modification in order to better describe their respective activities.

Oswalt (1973: 28–30) integrates subsistence technology and utilization spheres by creating "associations" or groups of natural, anatomical, and artifactual "aids" directed toward a particular subsistence activity. Associations are roughly equated to what I accept as procurement systems. Comparative associations for the Yahgan will be reviewed in the following section.

Traditionally, major subsistence rubrics include hunting, fishing, and gathering. Following Lee (1968: 41–42), these are broken down in this manner:

a.   hunting — pursuit of all land and sea mammals, including trapping and fowling,

b.   fishing — pursuit of all fish, and

c.   gathering — collection of shellfish and other marine and land invertebrates and plants.

While the Aleutian systems are ordered by these traditional categories, I find no particular logic to these categories because they do not correspond to divisions based on (1) mobile versus immobile organisms, (2) marine versus terrestrial organisms, (3) sought-after (unpredictable) versus harvestable (predictable) organisms, or other relevant dimensions. Rather, sea lions may be predictably "collected" at an established rookery or octopi may be "hunted" on intertidal reefs. Also, no technologic common denominator is found where all "fishing" animals, for instance, are retrieved with one class of implements distinct from those used in either "gathering" or "hunting."

*Hunting*

1.   Sea Mammal Hunting Offshore:   Kayaks and, secondarily, umiaks used in locating, stalking, approaching, and surrounding one or more sea mammals (e.g. seals, sea lions, sea otter, small and large whales, and rarely dolphins and porpoises); cooperative hunting most successful in tiring diving sea mammals but individual boat hunting possible; animals wounded with harpoons or darts (and throwing boards) and killed with lances; wounded or dead animals linked by line to floats or harpoon shafts; all but whales retrieved immediately but whales left to die and wash ashore; possible poison used with whale harpooning (Veniaminof 1840; Jochelson 1933)

2.   Sea Mammal Hunting Onshore:   Seals, sea otter, sea lions, and walrus caught and hauled out at rookery localities on offshore islets or isolated coastal areas of islands; seals, sea lions, and walrus regularly haul up on rocky or cobble beaches but sea otter do so only rarely or during storms; hunters' approach is by foot or by boats; animals killed with harpoons, darts, or lances on land or from boats, or surrounded, driven up away from the water's edge, and clubbed to death (Veniaminof 1840; Jochelson 1933)

3.   Bird Hunting on Water:   Seasonal waterfowl and other marine

birds killed with bird leister darts and possibly bow and arrows from boats on open sea (Coxe 1787; Jochelson 1933)

4.  Bird Hunting at Nesting Sites:   Birds such as puffins and murres snared at nests with baleen nooses; cormorants and probably other species of colony birds caught on nests at night and killed by twisting necks (Jochelson 1933)

*Fishing*

5.  Fishing Offshore:   Fishing from boats with seaweed lines up to 150 fathoms long; cod, halibut and other fish caught with hook and line or sometimes speared with leisters; fishing as much as ten to fifteen miles offshore (Coxe 1787; Jochelson 1933)

6.  Fishing Onshore:   Salmon caught during runs at stream mouths with hands, dip nets, fish leisters; fish weirs and dams used; nets used in pre-Russian times for flounder, herring, and other fish; hook and line used for fish from shore; cod and halibut in shallow water during summer; salmon streams sometimes rare or nonexistent on many smaller islands; hook and line for freshwater lake trout (Jochelson 1933; Hrdlička 1945; Ransom 1946)

*Gathering*

7.  Intertidal and Beach Collecting:   Shellfish and other marine in-vertebrates collected at low tide on rocks or intertidal reefs with sticks or prying utensils and collecting baskets; marine algae or kelp collected; stranded dead animals collected when hunting impossible from boats due to weather; dead whales utilized after beaching; driftwood collected as raw material (Veniaminof 1840; Jochelson 1933)

8.  Onshore Collecting:   Edible berries, roots, and stalks collected in season; matting, basketry, and thatching grass also collected; eggs collected in rookeries in season; foxes possibly trapped in prehistoric period; nonfood resources collected at specific sites: obsidian, chert, greenstone, basalt, etc. for flaked stone artifacts; volcanic stone for carved bowls and lamps, scoria and pumice bombs for abraders; ocher and other minerals for paint, etc. (Veniaminof 1840; Jochelson 1933).

Not all of the implements utilized in these eight systems are listed. Major items such as harpoons, leisters, and fishhooks are ingeniously made to be used with a particular animal while other tools and weapons are easily transferred from one system to another. Any particular system is not defined by a particular tool type but rather by the combination of technology, habitat, animal, and human behavior which, *in toto*, makes one distinctive from another.

FAT REQUIREMENTS   As has long been recognized (see Stefansson 1962: 143–144; Sinclair 1953), large quantities of fat aboriginally known in the form of blubber or rendered oil are necessary for human survival in the arctic. Fat provides twice the caloric yield in humans as protein and supplies most of the body energy demands under cold stress. In the Aleutians proper, Veniaminof (1840, in Hrdlička 1945: 93) notes that:

The principal food of the Aleuts, is constituted by fat, from whatever animal. No matter how much fish, fresh or dried, there may be, the Aleut needs the addition of fat. He ate fat with everything, and some of the things were only thus edible. This applies even to the vegetables and berries.

Or:

Fat, from any animal whatever, except the sperm whale, is the principal food of the Aleuts. No matter how great a supply of fish the Aleut may have, if he does not have fat at the same time, one can positively state that he will incur the consequences of illness, if not of genuine hunger, because the *iukola*, dried fish, when eaten over a long period of time without fat results in diarrhea, and even fresh fish without it is not so nourishing. On the other hand, even if the Aleut does not have a single *iukola*, but has enough fat, he will not feel hunger, because with fat he can use everything for food: roots and marine cabbage, (these, especially the latter, are extremely harmful without fat), shell-fish, and the driest *iukola* and leather straps, in a word, everything that the stomach will digest (Veniaminof 1840: 231–232).

Eskimos living on or near the mainland coast have two alternatives for procuring fat — sea mammals and caribou. Large sea mammals provide more fat per animal than do caribou, but caribou in fall and winter have thick back fat suitable for food and fuel (Harper 1955: 60, 113–114). Because caribou are not an alternative available to Aleuts, hunting sea mammals of some form for fat was a necessity, not a choice.

Like other arctic occupants who ingest very little vegetable material, Aleuts received all the essential vitamins and trace elements from the varied animal diet consumed.

*Storage Capabilities*

Given the cyclical nature of animal resources (see below), a major survival prerequisite is food preservation. Food must be leveled out over the year so that surpluses are carried over for use during periods of scarcity. The Aleutian area, unlike the true Arctic, has an annual minimum mean temperature above freezing. Thus, the Eskimo practice of caching meat and fish in subfreezing temperature is not successful here. With no knowledge of smoking and having no salt, the Aleuts could preserve food only by drying. Apparently only fish were dried as we have no references to meat being so processed (Jochelson 1933: 11). Oil was kept in gut bags, and berries and roots were kept for winter food.

Because of wet weather conditions, fish drying was sometimes unsuccessful. Such failures were critical for winter and early spring survival:

They dry quantities of fish during the summer, which they lay up in small huts for their use in winter; and, probably, they preserve berries and roots for this same reason of scarcity (Cook 1784, in Hrdlička 1945: 91–92).

Although sea fish are abundant in many places, they cannot lay up a large supply because of lack of means and circumstances, for the preparation of fish here can only be done by seasoning [drying] them, but the weather very frequently hinders this process. In the winter the fish go out to the deep and the strong and ceaseless winds do not permit excursions on the sea after them (Veniaminof 1840: 230).

But if the weather should continue cloudy, damp, and raining, the fish cannot dry but instead mildew and mold, so that they have to be thrown away (text of Umnak priest, quoted by Ransom 1946: 618).

Absent to my knowledge in the Aleutians are clay-lined fish storage pits referred to as *chekalinas* and found on the Alaska Peninsula (Weyer 1930: 274; Workman 1966: 136), on Kodiak (Heizer 1956: 30), and on the mainland. Small stone-lined boxes and circular depressions are known from inside Aleutian houses (Denniston 1966: 88–89; McCartney n.d.: 11) but these are relatively small, are not in special storage huts or caches, and therefore are probably not variants of such clay-lined pits. According to Heizer (1956: 30), salmon were allowed to decay in these pits and then to freeze once in order to kill the maggots before being eaten. If freezing is in fact a critical aspect of such food storage, then the general lack, or at least inconsistency, or freezing temperatures in the Aleutians would preclude such a storage process.

*Food Cycles*

The following citations suggest that the cyclical faunal/floral availability caused seasonal food stress for the Aleuts:

In winter, when the digging of roots is impossible, the stormy sea prevents hunting and supplies are wanting, they are threatened by famine. Then they go with their wives and children to the shore, gather seaweed and every kind of shells, and are glad when they find a stranded whale or some other sea-mammal. And under such poor conditions their lives are passed (Jochelson 1933: 11).

The quantity of provisions which they procure by hunting and fishing being far too small, the greatest part of their food consists of seawrack and shellfish, which they find on shore (Coxe 1787: 178).

It is because the Aleuts never had large supplies of food against the time of unsuccessful hunting, they therefore almost annually suffer a scarcity of food during the first months of the year. The very designation of the month of March, *Kisagounak*, i.e. when they gnaw on straps, demonstrates that during this time, they were not wealthy in food. Therefore, it is obvious that during this time and as a result of the least misfortune, there could very easily arise the frightful consequences of hunger. But what could and must have been the lot of those women and children left behind in a village from which all the men had perished in some way? This was frequently the case in former times (Veniaminof 1840: 196–197).

This extensive list of productions may at first glance give the impression that the inhabitants of these localities have ample means for their sustenance, even to the point of luxury. But in point of fact, their diet is extremely limited and even meager because in general it depends upon circumstances and accidents incomparably more inconsistent than those of the dwellers on *terra firma*. They have nothing that could be, so to speak, their fundamental and steady food except water and air (Veniaminof 1840: 230).

From these references we learn that the cycle of summer plenty but winter scarcity pared down the population in part because of poor winter weather and lack of food preservation know-how. During late winter-early spring stress, Aleuts apparently starved often enough to merit regular references to the fact. Whether or not food deprivation usually included death is not known. Evidentally, some depopulation can be traced either to a combination of adverse winter weather and insufficient stored fish and oil, or to slain men leaving their families without providers.

The Aleut-Eskimo subsistence is an excellent variation on Liebig's Law, the law of the minimum, to the effect that population growth rate and equilibrium are dependent on the required nutrient present in the minimum quantity (Odum 1963: 65–66). Annual survival depended on the littoral species with perhaps some birds added, and to that degree, the most lowly urchin is equally important as the largest sea mammal. Bartholomew and Birdsell (1953: 490) express the limitations of minimum necessary resources as follows:

In some cases, the size of a population will be determined not by the availability of an abundance of food during ten months of the year but by a regular seasonal scarcity in the remaining two months.

The "Aleut year" of twelve "moons" is recorded by Veniaminof (1840: 256; also in Petroff 1884: 160 and Jochelson 1933: 85). Beginning in March, the month names reflect the subsistence activities for each of the twelve units. March and April are the "hunger" months, following February as the "month of last stored food" and coming before May, the month of flowers, and seal and sea lion hunting. Because seasonality is blurred at prehistoric midden sites, any notion of cyclical food unevenness must come from ethnographic records and modern information about plant and animal occurrence.

Table 1 lists major animal and plant species utilized for food and raw resources in the islands. The animal species are known, for the most part, both archaeologically and ethnographically whereas plant remains from middens are rare.

The gross Aleutian diet is as follows. However, by grouping the major resources by quarterly divisions, the amount of food and its availability is masked and food shortage is not reflected in such a scheme. Words emphasized indicate primary foods for each season (see Berreman 1953: Table 1).

Summer — WHALES, SEA OTTER; fresh SALMON, cod, halibut, and other fish; eggs; roots, leaves, and stalks.
Fall — SEA LIONS, FUR SEAL, fresh SALMON; migratory WATERFOWL; berries, and stored roots.
Winter — SEA LIONS, HARBOR SEAL; stored SALMON, fresh halibut, cod, trout; cormorants; stored berries, and roots.
Spring — FUR SEAL; SEA OTTER, SEA LIONS; cod, halibut, and other fish; URCHINS, and other invertebrates; kelp.

These major marine resources are presumed to have been consistently available for most if not all of the prehistoric period. The Aleutian climate has changed slightly over the past several millennia as world-wide climate has changed. But because this subarctic area is well south of modern winter sea ice distribution, open seas prevailed during the prehistoric period and we have no evidence to suggest that sea mammal distributions were affected by drift or pack ice.

Stone and mineral resources are fixed and driftwood is also consistently available on Aleutian beaches. These commodities were therefore available throughout the year.

Table 1.   Native food and raw material resources

| Animals | References | Utilization |
| --- | --- | --- |
| Sea otter (*Enhydra lutris*) | Murie 1959; Ransom 1946; Hrdlička 1945 Jochelson 1925; Coxe 1787 | Hunt late spring, early summer; women's and children's parkas; food |
| Steller's sea lion (*Eumetopias jubata*) | Desautels et al. 1971; Murie 1959; Ransom 1946; Hrdlička 1945; Collins 1945; Eyerdam 1936; Jochelson 1925; Coxe 1787 | Hunt late spring, main hunting in fall; meat, blubber, blood, liver eaten; skins and gut for boat covers, clothing; whiskers for decoration, etc. |
| Harbor seal (*Phoca vitulina*) | Desautels et al. 1971; Murie 1959; Ransom 1946; Eyerdam 1936 | Meat, blubber, blood eaten; skins used |
| Northern fur seal (*Callorhinus ursinus*) | Desautels et al. 1971; Murie 1959; Hrdlička 1945; Ransom 1946; Veniaminof 1840 | Hunt late spring, fall; food and raw materials |
| Pacific walrus (*Odobenus rosmarus*) | Hrdlička 1945; Ransom 1946; Veniaminof 1840 | Rare; occur during bad winters when they move south with drift ice; occasional food source |
| Sea cow (*Hydrodamalis gigas*) | Murie 1959 | Possibly found in pre-Russian times in the Near Islands; presumably used if they occurred there |
| Pacific right whale (*Eubalaena sieboldi*) | Murie 1959; Jochelson 1925 | Present in summer; used for blubber and meat |
| Bowhead whale (*Balaena mysticetus*) | Murie 1959; Jochelson 1925 | Summer migrants; used for blubber and meat |
| Gray whale (*Eschrictius glaucus*) | Murie 1959; Pike 1956 | Present in spring and winter when migrating; used for blubber and meat |
| Finback whale (*Balaenoptera physalus*) | Murie 1959; Pike 1956; Nishiwaki 1966; Eyerdam 1936; Jochelson 1925 | Found in summer; most numerous of all baleen whales |
| Sei whale (*Balaenoptera borealis*) | Nishiwaki 1966; Murie 1959; Pike 1956 | Present in early spring and fall |
| Blue whale (*Sibbaldus musculus*) | Nishiwaki 1966; Murie 1959; Hrdlička 1945 | Concentrated on Pacific coastal side recently |
| Humpback whale (*Megaptera novaeangliae*) | Nishiwaki 1966; Murie 1959; Clark 1945; Eyerdam 1936 | Summer; found throughout chain in ancient times |
| Sperm whale (*Physeter catodon*) | Nishiwaki 1966; Murie 1959; Veniaminof 1840 | According to Veniaminof, not eaten but used for blubber, etc. |
| Cuvier beaked whale (*Ziphius cavirostris*) | Murie 1959; Jochelson 1925 | Found archaeologically |

| Species | References | Notes |
|---|---|---|
| Pacific harbor porpoise (*Phocoena vomerina*) | Murie 1959; Hrdlička 1945; Eyerdam 1936 | Commonly seen near the coast in bays and inlets |
| Striped porpoise (*Lagenorhynchus obliquidens*) | Murie 1959 | Possibly used by Aleuts |
| Bearded seal (*Erignathus barbatus*) | Clark 1945; Murie 1959 | Reported to be common in the chain in the past (?) |
| Red fox (*Vulpes fulva*) | Murie 1959; Veniaminof 1840 | Found in the eastern islands; known archaeologically |
| Blue fox (*Alopex lagopus*) | Murie 1959; Veniaminof 1840 | Arctic fox restricted to the Near Islands |
| Weasel (*Mustela erminea*) | Murie 1959; Coxe 1787 | Reported on Unalaska and possibly surrounding eastern islands |
| Lemming (*Dicrostonyx* sp.) | Murie 1959 | Lemmings common in the eastern Aleutians; minor use by man |
| Dog (*Canis familiaris*) | Ransom 1946 | According to Ransom, dogs not eaten |
| King salmon (*Oncorhynchus tschawytscha*) | Scheffer 1959; Ransom 1946; Hrdlička 1945 | Caught in great numbers in late spring, early summer |
| Dog salmon (*Oncorhynchus keta*) | Scheffer 1959; Ransom 1946 | Less abundant than other species; summer |
| Silver salmon (*Oncorhynchus kisutch*) | Scheffer 1959; Ransom 1946 | Late summer arrival |
| Humpback salmon (*Oncorhynchus gorbuscha*) | Scheffer 1959; Ransom 1946 | Late summer, early fall |
| Red salmon (*Oncorhynchus nerka*) | Scheffer 1959; Turner 1886 | Run in summer in streams to lakes with mountain runoff |
| Pacific halibut (*Hippoglossus stenolepis*) | Scheffer 1959; Ransom 1946; Hrdlička 1945; Jochelson 1925, 1933 | This important food resource is found in deep water in winter, shallow water in spring, summer |
| Pacific cod (*Gadus macrocephalus*) | Scheffer 1959; Desautels et al. 1971; Hrdlička 1945; Ransom 1946; Coxe 1787 | A principal food source caught by line and hook |
| Great sculpin (*Myoxocephalus polyacanthocephalus*) | Desautels et al. 1971; Collins 1945; Clark 1945 | Caught with hook and line |
| Red Irish lord (*Hemilepidotus hemilepidotus*) | Desautels et al. 1971; Turner 1886 | Considered an excellent food |
| Atka mackerel (*Pleurogrammus monopterygius*) | Desautels et al. 1971; Collins 1945; Clark 1945 | Caught with gaffs and spears |

Table 1. (Continued)

| Animals | References | Utilization |
| --- | --- | --- |
| Rock greenling (*Hexagrammos lagocephalus*) | Desautels et al. 1971; Scheffer 1959; Jochelson 1925 | Same as *terpug*, as commonly referred to in Russian sources |
| Flounder (*Platichthys stellatus*) | Scheffer 1959; Jochelson 1933 | Caught with hook and line |
| Pogie (*Lebius superciliosus*) | Scheffer 1959 | Eaten |
| Flounder (*Atheresthes stomias*) | Scheffer 1959 | Thought to be the turbot commonly referred to in Russian sources |
| Herring (*Clupea pallasi*) | Scheffer 1959; Collins 1945; Clark 1945 | Summer; caught with nets and dried in great numbers |
| Dolly Varden trout (*Salvelinus malma spectabilis*) | Scheffer 1959; Jochelson 1933 | Commonly caught in nets and by hook and line |
| Capelin/smelt (*Mallotus* sp.) | Collins 1945; Clark 1945 | Abundant; caught in nets |
| Rainbow (?) trout (*Salmo* sp.) | Scheffer 1959; Ransom 1946 | Freshwater lake trout reported caught during winter |
| Tufted puffin (*Lunda cirrhata*) | Murie 1959; Ransom 1946; Hrdlička 1945; Jochelson 1925, 1933 | Eggs eaten; skins used for clothing |
| Horned puffin (*Fratercula corniculata*) | Murie 1959; Hrdlička 1945; Clark 1945; Jochelson 1933; Turner 1886 | Eggs presumably eaten; skins very commonly used for clothing |
| Whiskered auklet (*Aethia pygmaea*) | Murie 1959; Hrdlička 1945 | Found archaeologically; probably also utilized but not specifically cited were the other auklets found in great flocks throughout the chain: least, crested and parakeet auklets |
| Common murre (*Uria aalge*) | Murie 1959; Hrdlička 1945; Collins 1945; Jochelson 1933 | Eaten; used for parkas |
| Thick-billed murre (*Uria lomvia*) | Murie 1959; Jochelson 1933 | Possibly eaten; used for clothing |
| Black-legged kittiwake (*Rissa tridactyla*) | Murie 1959; Jochelson 1933 | Jochelson cites this bird or the red-legged species as being important to Aleuts; found in great flocks along the chain |
| Short-tailed albatross (*Diomedea albatrus*) | Murie 1959; Hrdlička 1945; Jochelson 1925; Turner 1886 | Sinew, feathers, beak, etc. used variously by Aleuts; common in archaeological sites |
| Slender-billed shearwater (*Puffinus tenuirostris*) | Murie 1959; Hrdlička 1945 | Known archaeologically |

| Species | References | Notes |
|---|---|---|
| Pelagic cormorant (*Phalacrocorax pelagicus*) | Murie 1959; Hrdlička 1945; Collins 1945 | Eaten; possibly used for clothes |
| Red-faced cormorant (*Phalacrocorax urile*) | Murie 1959; Ransom 1946; Collins 1945; Jochelson 1925, 1933 | Eggs eaten; bird eaten; skins used for clothes |
| Pigeon guillemot (*Cepphus columba*) | Murie 1959; Collins 1945; Jochelson 1925 | Skins used for parkas |
| White-winged scoter (*Melanitta deglandi*) | Murie 1959; Jochelson 1925 | Known archaeologically |
| Canada goose (*Branta canadensis*) | Murie 1959; Ransom 1946; Hrdlička 1945; Clark 1945 | Commonly eaten |
| Emperor goose (*Philacte canagica*) | Murie 1959; Ransom 1946; Jochelson 1933 | Eaten according to Ransom but poor food according to other authors; available in winter |
| Whistling swan (*Olor columbianus*) | Murie 1959; Jochelson 1933 | Eaten |
| Common teal (*Anas crecca*) | Murie 1959; Jochelson 1933 | Presumably eaten |
| Green-winged teal (*Anas carolinensis*) | Murie 1959; Ransom 1946 | Eaten |
| Common merganser (*Mergus merganser*) | Murie 1959; Ransom 1946; Jochelson 1933 | Eaten |
| Red-breasted merganser (*Mergus serrator*) | Murie 1959; Clark 1945 | Presumably eaten |
| King eider (*Somateria spectabilis*) | Murie 1959; Ransom 1946; Hrdlička 1945; Jochelson 1933 | Eaten |
| Common eider (*Somateria mollissima*) | Murie 1959; Hrdlička 1945; Jochelson 1933 | Known archaeologically |
| Pacific harlequin (*Histrionicus histrionicus pacificus*) | Murie 1959; Turner 1886 | Eaten |
| Mallard (*Anas platyrhynchos*) | Murie 1959; Ransom 1946; Clark 1945 | Eaten |
| Common loon (*Gavia immer*) | Murie 1959; Collins 1945 | Eaten |
| Glaucous-winged gull (*Larus glaucescens*) | Murie 1959; Ransom 1946; Hrdlička 1945; Jochelson 1925, 1933; Veniaminof 1840 | Eggs and meat eaten |
| Common raven (*Corvus corax*) | Murie 1959; Ransom 1946; Hrdlička 1945 | According to Ransom, this bird never eaten but known from archaeological sites |
| Bald eagle (*Haliaeetus leucocephalus*) | Murie 1959; Collins 1945; Hrdlička 1945 | Used for children's clothes |
| Rock ptarmigan (*Lagopus mutus*) | Murie 1959; Jochelson 1933; Veniaminof 1840 | Eaten |
| Green sea urchin (*Strongylocentrotus drobachiensis*) | Scheffer 1959; Ransom 1946; Hrdlička 1945; Desautels et al. 1971 | Eaten year-round |
| Blue mussel (*Mytilus edulis*) | Scheffer 1959; Ransom 1946; Hrdlička 1945; Collins 1945; Jochelson 1925; Veniaminof 1840; Desautels et al. 1971 | Eaten; important food mollusk |

Table 1. (Continued)

| Animals | References | Utilization |
|---|---|---|
| Razor clam (*Siliqua patula*) | Scheffer 1959 | Eaten where available |
| Butter clam (*Saxidomus giganteus*) | Scheffer 1959; Jochelson 1925 | Eaten; known archaeologically |
| Limpets (*Acmaea* sp.) | Scheffer 1959; Desautels et al. 1971; Hrdlička 1945; Jochelson 1925 | Eaten; known archaeologically |
| Periwinkles (*Littorina* sp.) | Scheffer 1959; Desautels et al. 1971; Hrdlička 1945; Jochelson 1925 | Eaten; known archaeologically |
| Chiton/black katy | Scheffer 1959; Desautels et al. 1971; Jochelson 1925 | Eaten; known archaeologically |
| Island scallop (*Chlamys islandicus*) | Scheffer 1959; Desautels et al. 1971 | Known archaeologically |
| Rock oyster/pearly monia (*Pododesmus macrochisma*) | Desautels et al. 1971; Clark 1945 | Eaten |
| Giant cockle (*Clinocardium nuttalli*) | Scheffer 1959 | Eaten |
| Channeled dogwinkle (*Thais canaliculata*) | Desautels et al. 1971 | Presumably eaten; known archaeologically |
| Hairy triton (*Fusitriton oregonensis*) | Desautels et al. 1971; Scheffer 1959 | Presumably eaten; known archaeologically |
| Octopus (*Octopus apollyon*) | Scheffer 1959; Collins 1945; Clark 1945 | Eaten; caught with spears on reefs |
| Barnacles (*Balanus* sp.) | Scheffer 1959; Desautels et al. 1971; Ransom 1946 | Eaten, especially when starving |
| Sea cucumbers (?) | Collins 1945 | Eaten |
| Crab (*Cancer magister*) | Scheffer 1959 | Eaten |

| Plants | References | Utilization |
|---|---|---|
| Algae — *Alaria* *Fucus* *Ulva* | Scheffer 1959; Walker 1945; Ransom 1946; Veniaminof 1840 | These thought to be the main edible kelp resources |
| Cloud berry (*Rubus chamaemorus*) | Hulten 1968; Coxe 1787 | Berries excellent to eat; no fruit in years of heavy frost |
| Crow berry (*Empetrum nigrum*) | Hulten 1968; Collins 1945; Jochelson 1933; Veniaminof 1840; Coxe 1787 | Berries used especially, also stems and leaves as fuel |

| | | |
|---|---|---|
| Dwarf bramble (*Rubus arcticus*) | Hrdlička 1945 | Berries eaten |
| Great bilberry (*Vaccinium uliginosum*) | Hulten 1968; Hrdlička 1945; Jochelson 1933; Turner 1886 | Berries eaten in great quantities; probably what Collins (1945) refers to as blueberries |
| Cranberry (*Oxycoccus microcarpus*) | Hulten 1968; Hrdlička 1945 | Berries eaten |
| Guelder-rose (*Viburnum edule*) | Hulten 1968; Hrdlička 1945 | Langsdorf (in Hrdlička) notes these berries present but Hulten does not indicate their presence in the Aleutians proper |
| Salmon berry (*Rubus spectabilis*) | Collins 1945 | Berries eaten |
| *Vaccinium ovalifolium* | Hulten 1968 | This is an edible berry with good flavor; this is thought to be the raspberry reported by Veniaminof |
| Alpine bear berry (*Arctostaphylos alpina*) | Hulten 1968 | Berries eaten |
| Strawberry (*Fragaria chiloensis*) | Hulten 1968 | Berries eaten |
| Clasping leaved twisted-stalk (*Streptopus amplexifolius*) | Hulten 1968 | Berries edible; young shoots edible |
| Cowslip (*Caltha palustris*) | Walker 1945 | Greens eaten |
| Monkshood (*Aconitum maximum*) | Walker 1945; Hulten 1968 | Roots supposedly produce poison used for whaling |
| Beach rye (*Elymus arenarius*) | Collins 1945; Walker 1945; Jochelson 1933 | One of the chief basketry grasses |
| Lupine (*Lupinus nootkatensis*) | Collins 1945; Walker 1945; Turner 1886 | Roots eaten |
| Anemone (*Anemone narcissiflora*) | Hulten 1968; Collins 1945; Walker 1945 | Roots and greens eaten |
| Wild parsnip (*Angelica lucida*) | Hulten 1968; Collins 1945; Walker 1945; Jochelson 1933 | Stalks eaten as "wild celery" |
| Cow parsnip (*Heracleum lanatum*) | Hrdlička 1945; Jochelson 1933; Turner 1886 | Stalks especially eaten |
| Kamchatka lily (*Fritillaria camschatcensis*) | Hulten 1968; Walker 1945; Collins 1945; Jochelson 1933; Turner 1886 | Roots of this plant eaten; called *sarana* in early historic literature |
| Willow (*Salix pallasii*) | Turner 1886 | Use unknown beyond firewood; not listed by Hulten 1968 |

Table 1. (Continued)

| Plants | References | Utilization |
|--------|-----------|-------------|
| Burnet (*Sanguisorba stipulata*) | Coxe 1787 | Use unknown |
| Scurvy grass (*Cochlearia officinalis*) | Hulten 1968; Walker 1945 | Greens eaten |
| Sea beach sandwort (*Honckenya peploides*) | Walker 1945 | Greens eaten |
| Beach pea (*Lathyrus maritima*) | Jochelson 1933 | Grass for weaving |
| Lousewort (*Pedicularis kanei*) | Hulten 1968 | Edible root |
| Beach lovage (*Ligusticum scoticum*) | Hulten 1968 | Young stems and leaves eaten |
| Broad-leaved willow herb (*Epilobium latifolium*) | Hulten 1968 | Young leaves eaten |
| Lyre-leafed rock cress (*Arabis lyrata*) | Hulten 1968 | Young leaves eaten |
| Horned winter cress (*Barbarea orthoceras*) | Hulten 1968 | Young leaves eaten |
| Spring beauty (*Claytonia siberica*) | Hulten 1968 | Young leaves eaten |
| Key flower (*Dactylorhiza aristata*) | Jochelson 1933 | Roots eaten |
| Northern bog orchid (*Platanthera hyperborea*) | Jochelson 1933 | Roots eaten |

*Alternative Food Resources*

Checking Kroeber's map of native population densities (1939: Map 18, facing 134), we note that the Aleutians supported thirty to seventy-five persons per 100 square kilometers. I have translated our population figures to mean that approximately four persons per coastal mile lived here aboriginally. The entire Pacific coast of North America is relatively high in density, reflecting the abundance of combined sea and terrestrial resources along this coastal zone. Given this high absolute population in a comparatively small space, we must judge that the Aleut were adaptively successful. And we have no reason to believe that the population size at the time of Russian contact was very different from that of several millennia ago.

To stress the point, as we have above, that Aleut subsistence was precarious would seem to be a contradiction to these population figures. To accommodate a precariously successful hypothesis, I suggest that food failures were local in extent and were not pan-Aleutian. The 1,050-mile expanse allows for enough variation to assume no complete climatic or faunal uniformity. Therefore, the net effect has been stable support of a large population, but at the village level, survival was not inevitable. This same pattern is typical of arctic Eskimos (Balikci 1968: 84). Further, high population need not necessarily require a broad-based versus a more specialized hunting/gathering subsistence. If the few species depended upon were abundant, then close adaptation to them would be productive.

In stressing Aleut specialization, I want to avoid the suggestion that these subarctic dwellers were more delicately balanced biologically than middle- and high-arctic Eskimos. Several comparative comments about Aleuts and Eskimos are in order at a gross level of abstraction.

a.  Both groups always suffered food shortage problems during late winter and early spring within their respective maritime versus maritime/ terrestrial adaptations. Whereas the weather is ultimately causal, the Aleutian effect is seen in storms and high winds which prevent access to marine animals. Aleuts were stranded on shore with little to eat and with their primary food species at sea. Eskimos suffered due to freezing conditions — blizzards and shifting sea ice — which prevented them from locating marine or terrestrial prey (Damas 1968: 83).

b.  Both Aleuts and arctic Eskimos are dependent on several primary food species in a seasonal cycle. It is impossible to categorically state which group would be more restricted in food alternatives during the year because whereas Eskimos exploit more major categories of food, Aleuts had larger numbers of animals to hunt and collect. Both had special foods critical to survival during the late winter and early spring before the new subsistence cycle began. Aleuts ate seaweed and invertebrates and Eskimos ate such species as ptarmigan and fish (Birket-Smith 1929: 134–135). Eskimos had a depauperate littoral zone due to cold water temperatures and it was usually frozen over and inaccessible besides. Conversely, Aleuts had a rich intertidal zone which was only iced over rarely for short periods and in limited spots.

c.   The Aleutian carrying capacity is greater than that of the middle and high Arctic as seen in greater population density in the former than in the latter. But even though local or regional starvation might eliminate proportionately the same number of natives in each area (large villages in the Subarctic and small bands in the Arctic), the population rebound will differ according to the carrying capacity. Surviving populations in the Aleutians with more abundant late spring, summer, and fall food resources would tend to rebound at a faster rate than would arctic Eskimos with less abundant resources.

d.   Because most Eskimos operate inland as well as along coasts, they operate in larger territories than do coastal-oriented Aleuts. This requires greater seasonal wandering to maximize resources. As winter weather varied, so wandering patterns in search of food over land and adjacent frozen seas also varied. Winter encampments in Canada and Greenland, anyway, tended to be less permanent than in the Aleutians. In the latter area, year-round open water and relatively few suitable topographic areas for villages consistently defined habitation areas. Villages were reused annually and great accumulations of cultural and faunal debris attest to such successive use. Aleut winter food stores were concentrated at the village and not at caches strategically located along a migratory route. Their total food reserves were more concentrated at the sea edge than were those of Eskimos, especially when caribou is included as a food staple. Therefore, concentrated winter food supplies made possible the permanent village settlement pattern.

To study the Aleutian subsistence adjustment in another way, we might begin afresh with no archaeological and ethnographic preconceptions and try to speculate on what MIGHT constitute the bulk of Aleutian food. This exercise stimulates our inquiry and presses us to see variables in different and creative ways. But the obvious danger is to speculate beyond the real world into a "theoretically possible" series of conclusions which simply do not describe what actual potential was available to maritime specialists at the hunting and gathering level.

Alternatives here include, at a minimum, (1) alternative food sources or species, (2) alternative procuring systems, (3) alternative food preservation methods, and (4) alternative energy expediture ratios. These characters interdigitate with each other and one can nullify another. These are briefly explored to suggest their inherent limitations on man.

Plants and animals must be edible, nutritious, and tasteful but they must have the additional qualities of being available and dependable in order to be considered as foods. Fish or invertebrates which cannot be caught or rare Asiatic birds only seldom found in the chain will likely not become food resources. Some animals and plants are available only during specific periods of the year. Some which are present year-round might be edible only during part of the year, as some shellfish. Although any particular organism may provide little nutritional value, the combined diet must meet the minimum requirements for survival and good health.

Animal procurement systems, as outlined previously, are based on the behavior, density, size, and agility of the animal sought. To successfully kill or catch a creature requires minimum implements, knowledge of the animal's behavior, and skill. The harpoon, fishhook, or snare is fitted to the animal pursued. The procedure of stalking, approaching, and killing or catching is designed as a function of the animal's characteristic behavior and its capability of rapid escape. Single animals may be pursued in a different manner than groups of animals. Hunters' success depends greatly on their ability as primitive ethologists to predict an animal's behavior given certain circumstances. As such, hunting information and skill is highly adaptive.

To soften the effects of lean periods, food preservation methods are developed to carry over food from periods of plenty. Animals undergo rapid decay unless somehow preserved. Various states of putrefaction and attending production of bacterial food poisons such as botulism in dead animals prevent them from being nutritious or safe.

Finally, high caloric intake necessitated by constant cold stress requires that the yield of food energy per man-hour spent acquiring it be relatively high. For survival value alone, animals or plants offering the greatest return would be expected to be pursued. Conversely, there is little survival value in gathering small units of food energy unless the density is sufficient to make the effort worthwhile.

Keeping these factors in mind while inspecting the Aleutian flora and fauna, we would predict that species available to Aleuts through a particular technology and which were seasonally dependable were high on their food list. Thus fish provided either a continuous availability in cod, halibut, and trout or a seasonal availability in salmon. Sea mammals following predictable migratory or other behavioral patterns would also be likely food sources. Such characteristics would apply to other birds, invertebrates, and marine and terrestrial plant species. And some foods more than others would perhaps provide vital nutrients and energy without which normal health would not be achieved. Oil has been cited above as an essential food necessary no matter what other foods were available.

Secondly, evidence that organisms ranging from urchins to whales were successfully killed shows that procurement systems spread to almost all available animals. Adequate technological innovations brought all the major sea mammals, fish, many birds, and other lesser species within man's reach. Degree of dependence also played a role in the exploitation of various habitats by procurement systems. If a bird colony were too zealously exploited, the bird population might well drop in size and no longer offer sustained bird and egg production. The fact that Aleut population was presumably stable over a long period suggests that the procurement systems were in equilibrium with food species and their habitats.

Thirdly, food preservation by smoking or salting might have produced a much greater bulk of storable food which in turn would have increased the human population. But, evidently smoking or salting were not understood and that potential was not realized.

Finally, some edible plants and animals were overlooked because, among other reasons, they provided too little return for the effort spent collecting them. Berries could never have provided much more than dietary variety; berries provide too little food energy per collection time for groups to depend heavily on them for any long period.

When comparing this ideal set of determinants against what foods were actually utilized, we find a fairly close correspondence. Foxes might be an exception in the sense that they were not reported as significant in the diet. Killer whales are also exceptions unless perhaps washed up on a beach. Sperm whales, according to Veniaminof (1840: 229), were also not used. Many other animals and plants indigenous to Aleutian waters and shores were also unavailable for man's utilization due to the above reasons.

In answer to the question of what food alternatives existed for the Aleuts we learn that there were few major alternatives. They consumed all that could profitably be consumed. It is because they lacked a food "cushion" that the Aleuts may be considered, along with the Eskimos, as being easily subject to depopulation from any shortages.

*Summary*

To review the above discussion about Aleut food, we have found that (1) only marine-related animals can be considered as staples; (2) of these, sea mammals, fish, and birds provide the most abundant portion of the animal diet; (3) few of the major food species are consistently available throughout the year and thus abundance is seasonal; (4) "crisis" foods were critical to support the population during late winter and early spring; (5) food storage was often inadequate; (6) a large amount of oil was required in response to cold stress; and (7) a relatively complete utilization of existing animals and plants by various procurement systems gives evidence of full habitat dependency.

The Aleut adaptation is considered as specialized in the sense that it is marine oriented with little possibility of utilizing land animals and plants. Most of the diet derives from sea mammals, fish, and birds. However, when considering the possible availability of food species, then the Aleut are broad-based in gleaning food from all six food categories described above. They capitalize on any and all species meeting the minimal limitations outlined above.

If the Aleutian subsistence pattern outlined here is to be considered typical of those found in cold archipelagoes, then we must compare it with other cold archipelago patterns to illustrate consistency. The Stewardian approach would be to predict that on the assumption of similar cultures arising in similar environments, another cold archipelago subsistence pattern should appear similar to the Aleutian example. In stressing the temporal dimension, we would expect to find a similar development in two like situations such that multilineal evolution would be demonstrated. To the degree that culture responds and adjusts to an environmental setting, then that cultural response should be predictable. The thesis above is that cold archipelago environments permit few alternative subsistence responses and as a result, the culture core should be more predictable than if it occurred in a temperate or tropical region.

Our hypothesis is that all cold archipelago adaptations should appear similar in the subsistence sphere as a result of climatic variables being expressed most directly in man's life through control of flora and fauna upon which man depends, given a hunting/gathering level of technologic development. As hunters and gatherers living in restrictive cold archipelagoes, islanders will tend to utilize similar animals and plants and develop similar procurement systems related to the behavior of the animals pursued or the occurrence of plants collected.

We shall now review the Fuegian area as a similar cold archipelago environment and see if subsistence spheres there parallel those found in the Aleutians. If the Stewardian model holds, we should observe subsistence convergence from very different cultural origins rather than subsistence distinctions.


## THE CHILEAN ARCHIPELAGO: A COMPARATIVE REGION

The Aleutian archipelago and the Chilean archipelago are each unique to their respective continental masses yet in them we find strikingly similar cultural adaptations. Whereas these opposite ends of the New World were inhabited by natives of very different cultural, physical, and linguistic stocks, their technological correspondence reflects their similarity of topography, climate, marine adaptation, and isolation.

Lothrop (1928: 209–212) offers a short ethnographic comparison between Fuegians and middle- and high-arctic Eskimos. He concludes that although cultural similarities exist between these food gatherers, the Eskimo "in almost every aspect of life ... are better off then were the natives of Tierra del Fuego." Arctic conditions of snow and ice led Lothrop to see the polar "climate and environment" as limiting factors compounding the Eskimo cultural potential. Conversely, he does "not regard the climate of Tierra del Fuego as a necessarily stunting factor" in cultural development.

Steager (1965: 70) more recently alludes to the ecological similarity between the archipelagoes of Chile and the Aleutians but does not develop the comparison. In fact, the Aleutians, in contrast to mainland Alaska, Canada, and Greenland, do show many environmental correspondences. Thus, subarctic Eskimoids such as Aleuts, Koniags, and Chugach are more comparable to natives of southern South America in adjusting to cold Pacific environmental and climatic influences than Lothrop chose to emphasize. The following discussion explores the maritime responses of Fuegians in their cold archipelago habitats.

I note that many geographic and cultural correspondences may well be found between the Fuegian region and the Northwest coast but such comparisons are not included here.


*Comparative Maritime Adaptations*

The groups occupying the region most comparable to the Aleutians are the Yahgan and Alacaluf, the "Canoe Indians." Because of their similarity, they are treated here as one cultural entity. Excluded are the terrestrially adapted "Foot Indians," as the Ona and Haush (Lothrop 1928).

Before detailing their subsistence technology, we should acknowledge other similarities with the Aleuts. Poor climatic conditions and isolation mitigate against extensive archaeological reconnaissance in this southern archipelago. Early population devastation due to European disease and genocide leave almost no survivors from whom to collect ethnographic data. J. Bird (1938) is thus our counterpart to Jochelson and pioneered systematic archaeological investigations some decades ago. Gusinde (Oswalt 1973) parallels Veniaminof as missionary/ethnographer of the region during the historic period. The net result is that archeological and ethnographic data are as limited as they are for the Aleuts, and a combination of historic and prehistoric details produces only a general view of Fuegian maritime subsistence. Hopefully, this composite is no more distorted than for the Aleutian area.

The southern part of the Chilean archipelago (48°–56° South) is especially similar to the Aleutians. This area is vegetatively called the Magellanic Moorlands and includes almost all of the offshore islands and much of the mainland coast (Godley 1960: 466–473; Kuschel 1960: 544–545). Beech forests *(Nothofagus betuloides)* are restricted to sheltered spots with the dominant landscape being that of bogs, cushion plant and tussock associations, and bare rock. These moorlands are floristically very uniform throughout. Soils are permanently saturated and support very few soil organisms. In general appearance, these moorlands with their low vegetation are reminiscent of the steep, windswept Aleutians.

The depauperate land fauna is also reminiscent of the Aleutians in presenting few species. Known in the Fuegian region are only several frogs, lizards, a few land birds, foxes, two land otters, guanacoes, bats, and several rodents (Darlington 1960: 660–661). The marine life is clearly more important from man's viewpoint. Several sea lions and fur seals, sea otters, penguins, and other marine birds plus fish, marine invertebrates, and algae are available for exploitation (Mackintosh 1960: 628–629).

Table 2 briefly lists some of the similar attributes of these two archipelagoes. As with the Aleuts above, only subsistence and technologic complexes are treated. There are other similarities of religion, social organization, warfare, etc. but these aspects mirror to a lesser degree the maritime adjustment. Obviously there are differences between the groups, but what is important are the convergent characteristics which make them similar. Aleuts did not hunt penguins, use shell knives, or use open bark canoes; Fuegians did not use oil for lamp fuel, use throwing boards, or wear tailored clothing. But what we DO find are two very different groups

Table 2.   Similarities between Aleutian and Fuegian culture

| Shared traits/complexes (A=Aleutian; F=Fuegian) | Aleutian references* | Fuegian references* (Yahgan and Alacaluf) |
|---|---|---|
| **I.   ENVIRONMENT** | | |
| **A.   Area** | | |
| 1.   Linear archipelago configuration (A-51-55° N, F-43-56° S,67-76° W) | — | — |
| 2.   Long island span (A-approx. 1,050 miles from Unimak-Attu; F-approx. 970 miles from Chiloé-Navarino) | — | — |
| 3.   Many islands in archipelago (A-approx. 108 greater than ½ mile long; F-approx. 170 of same dimension) | McCartney 1972 | Bird 1938 |
| 4.   Extensive coastline (A-est. 2,990 miles; F-est. 10–12,000 miles, including islands and mainland) | McCartney 1972 | Bird 1938 |
| 5.   Many islands with fjorded, indented coasts (F-including mainland coast) | — | — |
| 6.   Geographically isolated *cul de sacs* | — | — |
| | | |
| **B.   Topography** | | |
| 1.   Islands comprise extension of mainland mountains (A-Aleutian Range; F-Southern Andes) | — | Steager 1965 |
| 2.   High, volcanic and other mountains (A-elevations to 9,370′, 48 major volcanic cones; F-elevations to 13,000′, volcanoes extend south to 47–50° S) | — | Bird 1938 |
| 3.   Sea erosion and mountains form jagged, indented coastline, often steep | — | Bird 1938 |
| 4.   Few beaches or coastal terraces (A-est. 95 percent of total coast too steep or high for settlement occupation) | McCartney 1972 | Bird 1938 |
| 5.   Overland travel difficult (A-wet meadows, heath, mountain slopes; F-thick, wet meadows, tussocks, local thick forest undergrowth, mountain slopes) | McCartney personal | Oswalt 1973 |
| | | |
| **C.   Climate** | | |
| 1.   Subarctic and subantarctic, cold, wet, foggy, sunshine rare, light-moderate snowfall | — | Lothrop 1928; Cooper 194 Kuschel 1960; Steager 1965 |
| 2.   Rapid weather changes, strong winds | — | Lothrop 1928; Cooper 194 Kuschel 1960; Steager 1965 |
| 3.   Weather affected by mixing warmer and arctic/antarctic waters (A-Bering Sea-Pacific; F-Antarctic convergence) | — | Lothrop 1928; Cooper 194 Kuschel 1960; Steager 1965 |
| 4.   Annual mean temperature: 32°–48° F; annual mean temperature range: 10°–20° F | — | Lothrop 1928; Cooper 194 Kuschel 1960; Steager 1965 |

*Sample references are listed as sources of information; environmental observations are not referenced, being of general knowledge; personal observations of Aleutian phenomena are cited such.

| Shared traits/complexes (A=Aleutian; F=Fuegian) | Aleutian references* | Fuegian references* (Yahgan and Alacaluf) |
|---|---|---|
| **D. Flora** | | |
| . Treeless coastal vegetation of meadow/moorland (A-all west of Unimak; F-south of Taitao Peninsula) | Walker 1945; Murie 1959 | Godley 1960; Steager 1965 |
| . Limited amount of vegetable materials provide supplement to diet seasonally; berries, roots, stalks, fungi, etc. | (see this paper) | Lothrop 1928; Bird 1938, 1946b; Steager 1965 |
| . Poor climate and/or isolation precludes aboriginal cultivation | (see this paper) | Bird 1946b |
| **E. Fauna** | | |
| . Minor terrestrial mammal fauna (A-foxes, lemmings, some shrews and weasels west of Unimak; F-sparse small deer, guanaco, fox, land-otter populations in southern part) | Clark 1945; Murie 1959 | Bird 1938; Darlington 1960; Steager 1965 |
| . Rich sea mammal fauna — seals, sea lions, sea otters, porpoises, whales, etc. | Murie 1959 | Lothrop 1928; Cooper 1946; Mackintosh 1960 |
| . Rich fish fauna | Scheffer 1959 | Cooper 1946 |
| . Rich marine invertebrate fauna — limpets, mussels, chitons, sea urchins, barnacles | Clark 1945; Scheffer 1959 | Lothrop 1928; Cooper 1946; Steager 1965 |
| . Rich marine avifauna — cormorants, petrels, gulls, geese, ducks, albatross | Murie 1959 | Lothrop 1928; Bird 1946b; Cooper 1946 |
| **F. Marine Environment** | | |
| . Cold seas (A-mean annual surface sea temp. 38°–42° F; F-mean winter surface sea temp. 41°–50° F; mean summer surface sea temp. 44°–57° F) | — | — |
| . Upwelling of seas; deep water around islands (A-Aleutian trench 7000+ meters; F-offshore trench 3–4000 meters) | — | — |
| . Strong shore currents by archipelagoes (A-westward on south, eastward on north; F-eastward along southern coast, northward along northern coast) | — | — |
| . Onshore kelp rich in shoal waters | McCartney personal | Steager 1965; Lothrop 1928 |
| **II. ADAPTIVE TECHNOLOGY** | | |
| **A. Hunting** | | |
| . Terrestrial mammal hunting rare to nonexistent | (see this paper) | Lothrop 1928; Steager 1965 |
| . Avifauna captured on nests at night and necks twisted, or snared at nests, or struck with bird spear; lowered on ropes down bird cliffs | Jochelson 1933 | Lothrop 1928; Bird 1946b; Oswalt 1973 |
| . Sea mammal hunting from small watercraft; seals, sea lions, whales harpooned or speared from boats (A-skin boats; F-bark canoes) | Veniaminof 1840 | Cooper 1946; Oswalt 1973 |

Table 2. (Continued)

| Shared traits/complexes (A=Aleutian; F=Fuegian) | Aleutian references* | Fuegian references* (Yahgan and Alacaluf) |
|---|---|---|
| 4. Cooperative sea mammal hunting at beach hauling grounds, with harpoons and clubs | Veniaminof 1840 | Bird 1946b; Oswalt 1973 |
| B.  Fishing | | |
| 1. Fishing by seaweed line from boats (A-bone hooks; F-quills for hooks) | Jochelson 1933 | Oswalt 1973 |
| 2. Fishing at weirs with fish spears, nets, hands | Jochelson 1933; Hrdlička 1945 | Bird 1946b; Oswalt 1973 |
| C.  Collecting | | |
| 1. Shore-edge collecting of seaweed, invertebrates, stranded whales | (see this paper) | Oswalt 1973 |
| D.  Food Resources | | |
| 1. Largely meat and fish diet; secondary birds, eggs, seaweed, invertebrates (varies in time and space); some animal forms stable throughout the year | Jochelson 1933 | Bird 1938, 1946b; Oswalt 197. |
| 2. Sea mammal oil stored, from seal, porpoise, and whale (F-Yahgan) | Veniaminof 1840 | Lothrop 1928; Cooper 1946 |
| 3. Food storage rare or precarious due to humid climate | Veniaminof 1840 | Lothrop 1928; Bird 1946b; Oswalt 1973 |
| E.  Transportation | | |
| 1. Boats make existence possible; interior largely uninhabitable | Veniaminof 1840 | Bird 1938 |
| 2. Boats used most of the year for moving, hunting, fishing, exploiting coastal zone | Veniaminof 1840 | Oswalt 1973 |
| F.  Domesticated Animals | | |
| 1. Only dogs kept; perhaps important in shore hunting | Hrdlička 1945 | Bird 1946b; Cooper 1946 |
| G.  Clothing/Decoration | | |
| 1. Made of sea mammal skins (sea otter, seals) and bird skins (A-tailored; F-capes) | Veniaminof 1840 | Lothrop 1928; Cooper 1946 |
| 2. No footwear and headwear common | Jochelson 1933 | Lothrop 1928 |
| 3. Paints of red, black, and white | Veniaminof 1840 | Lothrop 1928; Cooper 1946 |
| H.  Implements | | |
| 1. Predominance of nontoggling over toggling harpoon heads; unilaterally or bilaterally barbed | McCartney 1971 | Lothrop 1928; Bird 1938, 1946b; Oswalt 1973 |
| 2. Sea mammal hunting spear | McCartney 1971 | Bird 1946b |
| 3. Bird hunting spear with multiple points | Veniaminof 1840 | Lothrop 1928 |
| 4. Fish spear with multiple points | Veniaminof 1840 | Lothrop 1928; Bird 1946b |
| 5. Bone bird gorge | McCartney 1967 | Oswalt 1973 |
| 6. Mammal bone awls (A-fox; F-?); bird | McCartney 1967 | Bird 1938 |

| Shared traits/complexes (A=Aleutian; F=Fuegian) | Aleutian references* | Fuegian references* (Yahgan and Alaculuf) |
|---|---|---|
| bone awls (small to large with proximal end attached) | | |
| 7. Whale and other bone wedges | McCartney 1967 | Oswalt 1973 |
| 8. Bone combs with short teeth on lateral edge | McCartney 1967 | Bird 1938 |
| 9. Bone flaking tools | McCartney 1967 | Bird 1938 |
| 10. Bows and arrows | Veniaminof 1840 | Bird 1946b; Cooper 1946; Oswalt 1973 |
| 11. Chipped, ground slate and bone projectile points | McCartney 1971 | Lothrop 1928; Bird 1946b |
| 12. Chipped stone knife blades and scrapers | Denniston 1966; McCartney 1971 | Lothrop 1928 |
| 13. Polished stone ax/adze blades | McCartney 1971 | Bird 1938 |
| 14. Long, fine-textured whetstones | McCartney n.d. | Lothrop 1928; Bird 1938 |
| 15. Pumice abraders | Jochelson 1925 | Lothrop 1928; Cooper 1946 |
| 16. Rounded hammerstones | Jochelson 1925 | Lothrop 1928 |
| 17. Scraper blades of chipped stone | McCartney 1971 | Bird 1938 |
| 18. Stone sinkers | Jochelson 1925 | Lothrop 1928; Bird 1938; Oswalt 1973 |
| 19. Bolas (?) rare | Collins 1945 | Bird 1938 (?), 1946b |
| 20. Clubs for killing sea mammals | Veniaminof 1840; McCartney 1967 | Bird 1946b; Oswalt 1973 |
| 21. Marine invertebrate digging/collecting stick | McCartney 1967 | Bird 1946b; Oswalt 1973 |
| 22. Braided seaweed fishing lines | Jochelson 1933 | Oswalt 1973 |
| 23. Baleen bird snare | Jochelson 1933 | Oswalt 1973 |
| 24. Seal bladders and stomachs for storage of oil and other commodities | Veniaminof 1840 | Lothrop 1928; Cooper 1946; Steager 1965 |
| 25. Split sea mammal skin thong for harpoon, mooring, and other lines | Jochelson 1933 | Lothrop 1928; Bird 1946b; Cooper 1946 |
| 26. Skin containers | Veniaminof 1840 | Oswalt 1973 |
| 27. Nets (fish and other) | Hrdlička 1945; McCartney 1967 | Bird 1946b |
| 28. Basket containers | Veniaminof 1840; Hrdlička 1945 | Bird 1946b; Cooper 1946; Oswalt 1973 |
| 29. No pottery | McCartney 1970 | Cooper 1946; Oswalt 1973 |

II. SETTLEMENT PATTERNS

A. Population

| 1. Estimated archipelago population (prehistoric) between 6–12,000 | Lantis 1970 | Lothrop 1928; Steward 1949a (1875–1900 population) |
| 2. Estimated density of 1–4 persons per coastline mile | Lantis 1970; McCartney n.d. | Steward 1949a |

B. Habitation Sites

| 1. Large middens occupied, comprised of shell, bone, stone, artifacts and features; large ones between 10–20′ deep | McCartney personal | Lothrop 1928; Bird 1938 |
| 2. Middens covered with distinctively colored vegetation of indicator species; | McCartney and Turner 1966 | Lothrop 1928; Bird 1938, 1946a |

Table 2. (Continued)

| Shared traits/complexes (A=Aleutian; F=Fuegian) | Aleutian references* | Fuegian references* (Yahgan and Alacaluf) |
|---|---|---|
| neutral-basic pH in middens due to shell debris (F-more midden concentration in the southern part of the archipelago) | | |
| 3.  Middens show long occupation of a seasonal nature (A-up to 4,000 years; F-2–5,000 years) | Denniston 1966 | Lothrop 1928; Bird 1938, 1946a; Willey 1971 |
| 4.  Middens often pockmarked with pit house depressions 10–15′ diameter | McCartney personal | Lothrop 1928 |
| 5.  Midden sites often in sheltered spots with landing beach and access to water, wood, and kelp beds (A-driftwood; F-standing or driftwood) | McCartney 1972 | Lothrop 1928 |
| C.  House Types | | |
| 1.  Semisubterranean houses at more "permanent" middens | Denniston 1966 | Bird 1938 |
| 2.  Small temporary shelters for transient occupation, frame covered with sea lion skins | McCartney n.d. | Bird 1946b; Cooper 1946 |

converging toward one another in food habits, manufacturing technology, settlement patterns, and other areas as a result of similar environmental adjustments.

A recent article by Steager (1965) deserves attention at this point because it treats a number of important considerations dealing with Fuegian adaptation. Steager argues that (1) the Alacaluf and Yahgan have been misinterpreted as being primitives in "a harsh marginal environment from which they were never able to escape" (69); (2) that we should rather see them as well-adapted groups to an area where "there was a superabundance of easily available food for those who could cope with the unpleasant climate" (70); (3) that the sea provided abundance whereas the land was comparatively sterile of food resources (71); (4) that the Fuegians developed a kind of "throw-away" culture involving few permanent implements to be transported in their wanderings (73); (5) that a measure of success of the specialized maritime adjustment is the long prehistoric record showing only minor cultural change over time (74–75); and (6) that one reason for the homogeneity and stability of their culture over time was geographic, and hence cultural, isolation (75). While I concur on many of these points and find them analagous to the Aleutian case, I take exception to several important interpretations.

In portraying the relative ease with which Fuegians survived in their harsh environment, I feel Steager has overstated his argument. Mussels as a food source are emphasized in contrast to other animals:

Occasionally they would hunt birds, seals, or sea lions but these were not routine events. Now and then a whale was washed ashore and this, too, was duly consumed. But looming above everything else was the ubiquitous mussel, the staple food *par excellence* (72).

Others writing on food staples for the area confirm the dominance of shellfish but give more importance than does Steager to sea lions, seals, birds, and fish (Lothrop 1928: 32; Bird 1946b: 58). But I see Steager confusing a specialized food collecting organization with abundance of food resources and ease of gathering this maritime harvest. The following quotation demonstrates this point.

The littoral zone was a superb source of food for the Indians. A few hours of collecting would supply most of the day's needs and if anyone became really hungry, he had only to walk to the beach, gather some mussels or whatever else he could find, and return to the hut to cook his meal. The only pressing necessity was to keep an abundant source of food within easy reach and this was insured by never remaining in one place for very long and by collecting in shallow water as well as in the intertidal. ABORIGINAL POPULATIONS WERE PROBABLY EXCEEDINGLY SMALL, FOR REASONS WHICH WE DO NOT UNDERSTAND, and there was little danger of exhausting the food supply. An extremely nourishing high protein diet was, for all practical purposes, available in limitless quantities (72; emphasis added).

On the one hand we find an abundance of food easily collectable, but on the other we see only small groups constantly moving to keep from running out of food. I therefore doubt the statement that:

This was a highly specialized, not a primitive, economy and the Indian's relationship to this narrow zone was immensely productive. They seem to have RARELY, IF EVER, SUFFERED FROM HUNGER and this alone sets them apart from most primitive cultures (74; emphasis added).

The notion of Fuegian abundance and ease of subsistence can be traced back to the prime ethnographic source of Gusinde (in Sahlins 1972: 31):

... because THROUGHOUT THE ENTIRE YEAR AND WITH ALMOST LIMITLESS GENERO-SITY THE SEA PUTS ALL KINDS OF ANIMALS AT THE DISPOSAL OF THE MAN WHO HUNTS AND THE WOMAN WHO GATHERS. Storm or accident will deprive a family of these things for no more than a few days. Generally NO ONE NEED RECKON WITH THE DANGER OF HUNGER, and everyone almost anywhere finds an abundance of what he needs. Why then should anyone worry about food for the future! Basically our Fuegians know that they need not fear for the future, hence they do not pile up supplies. Year in and year out they can look forward to the next day, free of care ... (emphasis added).

To cite long, stable occupation in this region as a measure of their adaptive success (Steager 1965: 70) is legitimate but the measures of abundance are population size and how often the group must shift for food (Steward 1949b: 674). If we assume that small, wandering groups reflect accurately the past settlement patterns, then several observations come to mind. I suspect that given the lack of terrestrial faunal and floral food alternatives and the apparent limit to local littoral zones, Fuegians as other hunters and gatherers did indeed become hungry.

Minor and periodic shifts in weather and animal distributions could cause a drop in food, bringing on hunger and even starvation. Secondly, if Eskimo and arctic Indian physiological and ethnographic studies are applicable to similar cold-stressed natives, then a large quantity of fat or oil must be consumed for survival. Hammel (1964: 421–422, 430–431), for instance, points out the metabolic acclimatization of cold-stressed Alacaluf who wear few clothes and sleep with little protection. Their raised metabolic rate could be supported by greater than average fat intake. Because mussels contain little fat and sea mammals are in more limited supply, I suspect that oil from the latter is a real limiting factor. Whereas Steager acknowledges the use of oil for smearing over the body for protection (74), Lothrop (1928: 32, 133) more appropriately notes the storage of oil in seal bladders for food use. If we apply Liebig's law of the minimum here, it may be the oil commodity and not mussels and other invertebrates which is in shortest supply and therefore has the greatest limiting value. Finally, in terms of developing and evolving subsistence technologies, it is more important to see SOME evidence of other hunting, fishing, and collecting systems as alternative systems than to attempt to evaluate their importance. In other words, to have developed alternative systems to littoral collecting at all casts doubt on the notions that shellfish were overwhelmingly satisfying and abundant and Fuegians were so specialized at collecting them. Steager refers to the existence of tools of diversified collecting, hunting, and fishing (73), but also states that:

Fish were seldom eaten and the Indians showed little interest in them. This has bothered people a great deal although it should not for fishing is a complex activity and there was a superabundance of food available for gathering in the intertidal. Fish were an extremely inaccessible source of food considering the Indian's simple technology and were totally unnecessary in a simple hunting and gathering economy (74).

Why, then, if fish were "unnecessary" did the Fuegians pursue them with nets, weirs, baited lines, and fish spears (Table 2)? It is one thing to stress the commonness of mussel eating but it is quite another to decide, *a priori*, that fish and other marine animals were "inaccessible" due to the low technologic capabilities.

Bird (1946b: 58) points out that sea mammal, land mammal, fish, and avifaunal debris is found throughout the prehistoric midden deposits, but it is impossible to discern the relative importance of each.

I suspect Fuegians risked their collective necks in frail crafts in some of the worst seas only because the sea mammal meat and oil and fish obtained as a result of such strenuous effort was required as well as desired. Climbing down ropes into bird rookeries and attacking enraged sea lions on the beach were probably not just attempted for sport. In sum, due to the limited ethnographic information, I believe we are seeing only a pale shadow of the required hunting and collecting patterns practiced in the past. Further, the Fuegian reliance on marine mammals, fish, inverte-brates, kelp, and birds appears to be similar to the Aleut pattern outlined above.

Steager closes with a deterministic argument for adaptation:

It is highly probable that the ancestors of the Yahgan and Alacaluf were themselves very primitive people. If this is true then we can say that the environ-ment influenced this cultural pattern in that it placed only certain resources at the Indian's disposal. A settled, fishing society might have evolved but it did not. Instead, the people took to shellfish gathering because this was within their capabilities while fishing was not. IT MAY HAVE BEEN THE LEVEL OF TECHNOLOGY OF THESE EARLY PEOPLE, as much as anything else, THAT DETERMINED WHAT RESOURCES WOULD BE UTILIZED. If this is so, then the simplicity and stability of Yahgan and Alacaluf culture is as much an historical as an ecological problem (75; emphasis added).

Only after a fashion do levels of technology determine resource utilization and at the hunting and gathering level considered here, the development of hunting, fishing, or gathering systems was not only possible but, in fact, came about. I see little explanatory value in substituting some mystical cultural determinism for environmental determinism. Thus, this "ecologi-cal description" in my estimation misses the mark completely.

I believe a more accurate ecological statement would be that the "Canoe Indians" have, over a long adaptive period, adjusted their subsistence technology to maximizing the marine resources from their cold archipelago. Because land mammals and plants in large numbers of species or populations are lacking, the only viable food alternatives are marine mammals, fish, invertebrates, birds, and kelp. Watercraft were a prerequisite to exploiting the coastal zones and open water where these organisms were usually found.

ALL of these food resources have been seasonally or annually exploited because none are alone found in sufficient quantity to sustain a hunting/ gathering population. The evidence for such diversified exploitation may be seen in fragmentary forms of archaeological debris and ethnographic sketches. A relatively low population density involving small social groups and constant but ordered wandering attests to the limited food supply and danger of over-exploitation.

Change in major food proportions could likely have occurred over time but would be very difficult to evaluate from confused midden sites. Mussels, at least recently, have been important in the diet because of the low risk involved in collecting them by almost all members of the aboriginal group and because of their great quantity. But a 100 percent mussel diet, besides being dull, could not sustain a human population; oil from sea mammals was required for survival. And other marine foods such as fish and birds were collectable because of access on shore or by watercraft. Catching fish with lines or in weirs was no more difficult than diving for mussels. That sea mammals were harpooned as well as collected dead on shore is evidenced; that birds and eggs were collected in great numbers by hand or with different types of snares or spears is also evidenced. The total combination of food resources made survival possible but precarious. Until we learn of good evidence that middens were occupied for long periods during the year and that settlement size was fairly large, we may only presume that the human carrying capacity of this cold archipelago was comparatively low for hunters and gatherers.

Fuegian artifacts for the most part strongly resemble Aleutian artifacts (see Table 2; Lothrop 1928; Bird 1938; Oswalt 1973). The basic forms, indicative of function, are most similar whereas the Fuegian implements differ in having practically no decorative bone carving analogous to that embellishing many Aleutian counterparts. This artistic stylization is a step removed from function and reflects the Eskimoid carved-art tradition which was not matched in the Chilean archipelago.

Oswalt's (1973: 96–106) recent and innovative analysis of Yahgan technology sets forth what I consider to be confirmation of my cold archipelago hypothesis. After examining the nature of Yahgan artifacts and the complexes they form in use, he establishes a total of fifteen "associations" expressing animals pursued, implicitly their habitats and behavior and the implements used to retrieve them.

Although not intended as systemic summaries of Yahgan subsistence, these associations include all of the major Fuegian procurement systems. When grouped together by classes of animals, these associations match rather well the first seven Aleutian procurement systems described above.

By adding land fauna hunting and land plant collecting, which are well documented, plant gathering becomes a counterpart to the eighth Aleutian system whereas terrestrial hunting has no parallel in the Aleutians. Such hunting was of minor significance when compared to the remaining procurement systems. Land mammals were primarily used as sources of skins and furs rather than food.

Table 3 lists Oswalt's associations, including minor additions, and corresponding numbers of Aleutian systems for comparison.

Table 3. Comparative procurement systems

| Fuegian* | Aleutian |
|---|---|
| 1. Sealing:  canoe/harpoon dart/whistling (singing, striking water with paddle)/spear (club, paddle) | 1 |
| 2. Whaling:  canoe/harpoon dart/spear (sea lions and sea otter also) | 1 |
| 3. Otter hunting:  canoe/harpoon dart | 1 |
| 4. Beached sea lions:  harpoon dart/club (seals also) | 2 |
| 5. Steamer duck hunting:  canoe/sling (bird snare)/club | 3 |
| 6. Penguin (sea bird) hunting:  canoe/bird (fish) spear/sling | 3 |
| 7. Bird hunting (fishing):  canoe/bird (fish) spear | 3 |
| 8. Bird snare pole no. 1:  blind/live decoy/snare pole | 4 |
| 9. Bird snare pole no. 2:  duck bill call/snare pole | 4 |
| 10. Goose snare line:  snare set/club | 4 |
| 11. Birds sleeping on land:  torch/club | 4 |
| 12. Line fishing: canoe/baited line | 5 |
| 13. Herring fishing:  canoe/basketry trap | 5 |
| 14. Weir fishing:  weir/stick (hand retrieval) | 6 |
| 15. Mussel (crab) collecting:  canoe/mussel (crab) tongs | 7 |
| 16. Land mammal hunting (land otter, foxes, guanacoes):  bow and arrows/harpoon dart | – |
| 17. Land plant collecting:  container and ? | 8 |

*   Oswalt (1973: 105–106).

There is no direct Aleut correspondence to steamer duck hunting or herring fishing from boats. These are alternative systems depending upon a particular animal or a different way of catching the same animal. We would not expect to find a complete correspondence between the two systems groups. But whether we compare individual artifacts or the systems into which they are integrated during use, we see similarity between the Aleuts and Fuegians which attests to their parallel cultural response to like environments.

As a final word about subantarctic adaptation, we see that seasonal chances in weather do occur, corresponding to the subarctic (Lothrop 1928). We may assume that animal cycles therefore occur throughout the year and that the food resources discussed above are not constantly available. I have no detailed information about animal migrations but whales, some seals, geese, ducks, and probably many other species are present for only part of the year. The edible but insignificant terrestrial flora is available primarily during the summer growing season. Bird (1938: 260) mentions sites associated with a full range of seasonal activities, suggesting wandering in the past. This seasonal variation is comparable to the Aleutian area and is a major factor responsible for the broad-based hunting, fishing, and gathering that is evidenced in the Fuegian pattern. To better understand this subsistence adaptation, detailed zoological information would be required to assess availability and abundance of various food resources from one season to the next.

## Time Depth

Our knowledge of Fuegian prehistory is sketchy at best. Very little archaeological testing and excavating has occurred and only a few sites have been sampled by Bird (1938) or more recent workers. Willey (1971: 474–478) summarizes the Fuegian sequence as follows. The earliest archaeological material known in the region is that from Englefield Island, dating to 6500–7200 B.C. but considered by Willey to begin around 4000 B.C. The Englefield people were primarily sea mammal hunters, fishers and collectors whom Willey considers as a link with Pampean-Patagonian land-oriented hunters. This follows Barth's suggestion (1948: 197) that:

As an alternative to the generally held view, we might thus suggest that the Yahgan and Alakaluf cultures developed in Southern Tierra del Fuego, from inland cultures being transformed and adapted to marine subsistence under periods of severe pressure.

Englefield artifacts include various single-barbed bone harpoon heads, spear heads, wedges, bird-bone awls, whetstones, sinkers, and many chipped stone knives, scrapers and projectile points (Emperaire and Laming 1961). Most of these could be lost in Aleutian assemblages and represent a similar technological level specifically compatible with maritime existence.

By about 2000 B.C., the "Shell-Knife Culture" originally set forth by Bird (1938) begins, followed by the "Pit House Culture" around A.D. 500. These two cultures are poorly known in both time and space but are the immediate predecessors to the modern Alacaluf and Yahgan.

The overriding conclusion is that the original inhabitants of the Fuegian region — poorly understood as they are — are not significantly different from the ethnographically known peoples remaining there during the early twentieth century (Lothrop 1928; Bird 1938, 1946a; Barth 1948). This suggests that maritime adaptation was a prerequisite to full occupation of the southern Chilean archipelago. Further, once adapted to various marine animal systems, the more or less constant post-Pleistocene environment over the past several millennia restricted food alternatives to those extant at the beginning of known human occupation (see Auer 1960). Marginal location and narrowly defined subsistence systems reduced cultural flow into the region and thus we find a strong thread of continuity and stability running throughout the roughly 6,000-year archipelago occupation.

## THE KURILEAN ARCHIPELAGO

Another major cold archipelago is that formed by the Kuril Islands between Kamchatka peninsula and Hokkaido. References to environmental factors and cultural development are more restricted for this chain and we will not consider it here in detail. As indicated in the introduction, the Kurils are interesting to us not only because of the subarctic, marine location but also because of the closeness to the Aleutians.

At a glance, the Kurils appear very similar to the Aleutians in having no significant terrestrial fauna and in being occupied by coastal dwellers living in pit houses and utilizing bone harpoon heads, arrow points, fish-hooks, wedges, needle cases, stone adze blades, oil lamps, and other artifacts (Chard 1956, 1960). Food resources were primarily sea mammals, fish, birds, and invertebrates. Speculation has been made about direct genetic contact between the Aleutians and Kurils (Befu and Chard 1964), but further examination of this contact hypothesis is beyond our scope at present.

Suffice it to say that the general impression is that the Kuril Islands are also similar to the Aleutian and Fuegian archipelagoes in being a group of cold Pacific islands with maritime occupants. If the consensus is that Aleut-Kuril contacts did not take place, then cultural convergence is again demonstrated for cold archipelago cultures.

## CONCLUDING DISCUSSION

### *Aleutian-Fuegian Comparison*

This discussion has described the nature of the Aleut adaptation to maritime existence. It has illustrated the limitations and required specialization of cold archipelago living. A comparison of Aleutian and Fuegian procurement systems shows the adaptive similarity of those cultures to their respective environments. Procurement system comparisons avoid problems inherent in comparing only isolated, single artifacts from cultures unrelated in time and space.

Oswalt's cross-cultural comparison of technologic complexity (1973) is instructive here. He compares subsistence "components" (parts of weapons/instruments; e.g. harpoon end blade) and associations of the Yahgan, Caribou Eskimo, and Angmagsalik Eskimo. As no direct comparison is included between Fuegian and Aleutian materials, we take these other Eskimo groups to approximate Aleut technological complexity. The Yahgan are shown to use 69 different components as compared with 108 and 164 for the Caribou and Angmagsalik Eskimos respectively. An Eskimo sealing harpoon and float, for example, has 32 different components compared with three in a Yahgan sealing spear. But the apparent technologic gap is closed when we consider procurement or subsistence systems. The Yahgan have a simpler material culture than do the Aleuts and Eskimos but their similar procurement systems indicate that animal behavior guides the means of utilizing marine related species.

I have regrouped Oswalt's association totals to make them comparable to the Aleutian systems presented above. The Aleuts have eight systems, the Yahgan nine when we add land mammal hunting and plant collecting to Oswalt's original list of fifteen, the Caribou Eskimo have five (reduced from nine), and the Angmagsalik have eleven (reduced from sixteen). The greater Angmagsalik total results from land mammals such as bear being pursued as well as sea mammals, fish, and birds. But the closeness in both kind and number of systems between the Aleuts and Yahgan demonstrates their convergent adaptation to a more or less common environment. This close correspondence between groups is consistent with the cold archipelago hypothesis outlined above. It does not suggest that all cultural aspects are similar or that there are close genetic ties between the two groups.

Another needed demonstration to further substantiate the notion of similar maritime cultures arising in cold archipelagoes would entail a Kurilean-Aleutian-Fuegian comparison.

*Environmental-Cultural Interaction*

Few today subscribe to the old environmental deterministic position stating that specific cultural attributes are categorically caused by environments in which they occur. Nor is the environmental possibilistic position any more than an anthropological truism. But contemporary interest in environmental-cultural interaction (e.g. Meggers 1957) raises many questions about both cultural origin and function within particular habitats. The unclear level of abstraction used to describe causal relationships between environment and culture generates much of the problem surrounding "determinism."

Vayda and Rappaport (1968) criticize Steward's ecological approach which expresses the interrelatedness of environment and culture. They doubt that "significant correlations between..... cultural traits and ecological adaptation" exist, they contend that cause and effect are not clear even if significant correlations are demonstrated, and they question Steward's contention that "a degree of inevitability" exists for certain traits being found in certain ecological adaptations.

Depending upon the level of cultural unit compared, significant correlations or associations can indeed be shown as we have done in this paper.

If we substitute "predictability" for "inevitability," determinism and its concomitant onus is supplanted with variable degrees of probability. As Steward suggests, if we replace a negative possibilism with a positive probabilism, then we may predict within variable latitudes what subsistence adaptations are most likely to develop. A generalization like "the more marginal (restricted) the resources in an area, the more predictable the influences of environment on adapting culture" can be demonstrated in the cold archipelagoes described here. And that same generalization would apply to other areas considered marginal from man's survival viewpoint.

A full discussion of causality is beyond us here but several points are applicable. Even assuming high predictive value for certain cultures developing in certain environments, some other resource than association must be found to explain the effect of one variable on another. Subsistence is based on a human group sampling the known food universe in a particular area. As Lee (1968) and Sahlins (1972) have forcefully stressed, some hunting and gathering groups live in an affluent manner even though they may be considered from afar as barely surviving in a harsh environment. But harshness is defined in reference to possible alternative resources available through a particular technological level. Harshness may, however, be objectified and even quantified by noting how many food alternatives exist for man.

Forgetting for the moment cultural proscriptions against certain food utilization, a cross-cultural comparison of subsistence adaptation shows that efficiency usually operates to select for large or numerous food animals and plants. Efficiency is defined as food return per time and effort utilized in its acquisition. Demonstrations of efficiency can include what people actually do because their survival is based on successful exploitation which is adaptive. Presumably any hunting and gathering culture closely approximates maximum efficiency in animal or plant choices. But to go beyond circular reasoning, independent simulation studies might well rank the alternative efficiencies of food selection and techniques of exploitation.

In sum, given the behavior of an animal at a particular point in time and space, there is always a most efficient way, and less efficient ways, to collect birds, kill sea lions, or gather urchins. The ultimate causative statements for subsistence data will thus describe the predictability of food choice and, at the same time, the predictability of food acquisition techniques.

*Cultural Stability*

The stability and duration of Aleutian and Fuegian adaptation prove their success. Thousands of years of consistent culture history suggest little alteration of the basic subsistence systems developed to make these archipelago occupations possible. Climatic change is presumed to have been below a threshold sufficient to cause an alteration in spread of marine food resources. As a result of a consistently narrow latitude for resource exploitation, especially expressed in marine fauna, adaptive culture has likewise remained consistent over time.

Geographic isolation tended to restrict change at any particular time, but over a long period, both internal and external influences were capable of modifying or completely altering procurement systems. If significant change cannot be demonstrated, the existing cultural adaptations may be assumed to be operating efficiently.

ADDENDUM

Only after my paper had been typeset did I become aware — through Dr. Henry Collins — that Jenness (1953) had earlier raised the question of Fuegian-Eskimo diffusion. Jenness was struck by many "parallels" between Yahgan and Eskimo grammar and vocabulary and suggested they were genetically related. I am not familiar with any other proposals of more or less direct genetic ties between Eskimoids and Fuegians.

Lest somehow my Fuegian-Aleut comparisons be construed as supporting such a genetic tie theory, notwithstanding my brief disclaimer of such a position, let me more emphatically reject this conclusion. Spatial and temporal separation precludes any serious thesis that these maritime peoples have a common cultural base in the not too distant past.

Rather Jenness' point of linguistic parallels is another instance of convergence between Fuegian and arctic and subarctic peoples. A counterpart convergence in human biology is the raised metabolic adjustment in response to cold exposure found at both ends of the Americas (Hammel, et al. 1960; Milan 1962). The cultural/adaptive convergence has been described above. Just as these kinds of convergence may be explained without relying on diffusion, I suspect the linguistic similarities may rest on an alternative explanation.

## REFERENCES

AUER, B.
  1960   The Quaternary history of Fuego-Patagonia. *Proceedings of the Royal Society of London*, series B 152:507–516.
BALIKCI, A.
  1968   "The Netsilik Eskimos: adaptive processes," in *Man the hunter*. Edited by R. B. Lee and I. DeVore. Chicago: Aldine.
BARTH, F.
  1948   Cultural development in southern South America: Yahgan and Alakaluf vs. Ona and Tehuelche. *Acta Americana* 6:192–199.
BARTHOLEMEW, G. A., J. B. BIRDSELL
  1953   Ecology and the protohominids. *American Anthropologist* 55:481–498.
BEFU, H., C. S. CHARD
  1964   A prehistoric maritime culture of the Okhotsk Sea. *American Antiquity* 30:1–18.
BERREMAN, G. D.
  1953   "A contemporary study of Nikolski: an Aleutian village." Unpublished M.A. thesis, University of Oregon.
BIRD, J.
  1938   Antiquity and migrations of the early inhabitants of Patagonia. *The Geographical Review* 28:250–275.
  1946a  "The archeology of Patagonia," in *Handbook of South American Indians*. Edited by J. H. Steward. Washington, D.C.: Bureau of American Ethnology.
  1946b  "The Alacaluf," in *Handbook of South American Indians*. Edited by J. H. Steward. Washington, D.C.: Bureau of American Ethnology.
BIRKET-SMITH, J.
  1929   The Caribou Eskimos: material and social life and their cultural position. *Report on the Fifth Thule Expedition 1921–1924*. Copenhagen: Gyldendalske Boghandel, Nordisk Forlag.

CHARD, C. S.
1956   Chronology and culture succession in the northern Kuriles. *American Antiquity* 21:287–292.
1960   *Japanese source materials on the archaeology of the Kurile Islands.* Archives of Archaeology 7. Madison: University of Wisconsin Press.

CLARK, A. H.
1945   "Animal life of the Aleutian Islands," in *The Aleutian Islands: their people and natural history.* Smithsonian Institution War Background Studies Publication 3775. Washington, D.C.: Smithsonian Institution.

CLARKE, D. L.
1968   *Analytical Archaeology.* London: Methuen.

COLLINS, H. B., JR.
1945   "The Islands and their people," in *The Aleutian Islands: their people and natural history.* Smithsonian Institution War Background Studies Publication 3775. Washington, D.C.: Smithsonian Institution.

COOK, J. P., E. J. DIXON, C. E. HOLMES
1972   *Archaeological report, Site 49 RAT 32, Amchitka Island, Alaska.* Las Vegas: U.S. Atomic Energy Commission.

COOPER, J. M.
1946   "The Yahgan," in *Handbook of South American Indians.* Edited by J. H. Steward. Washington, D.C.: Bureau of American Ethnology.

COXE, W.
1787   *Account of the Russian discoveries between Asia and America.* London: T. Cadell. (Reprinted 1970. New York: Gustus M. Kelley).

DAMAS, D.
1968   "The diversity of Eskimo societies," in *Man the hunter.* Edited by R. B. Lee and I. DeVore. Chicago: Aldine.

DARLINGTON, P. J., JR.
1960   The zoogeography of the southern cold temperate zone. *Proceedings of the Royal Society of London*, series B 152:659–668.

DENNISTON, G.
1966   Cultural change at Chaluka, Umnak Island: stone artifacts and features. *Arctic Anthropology* 3:84–124.

DESAUTELS, R. J., A. J. MC CURDY, J. D. FLYNN, R. R. ELLIS
1971   *Archaeological report, Amchitka Island, Alaska, 1969–1970.* Las Vegas: U.S. Atomic Energy Commission.

EMPERAIRE, J., A. LAMING
1961   Les gisements des Iles Englefield et Vivian dans la Mer d'Otway. *Journal de la Société des Américanistes* 50:7–75.

EYERDAM, W. J.
1936   Mammal remains from an Aleut Stone Age village. *Journal of Mammalogy* 17:61.

FORDE, C. D.
1963   *Habitat, economy and society.* New York: E. P. Dutton (first edition 1934).

GEIST, O. W., F. G. RAINEY, *editors*
1936   *Archaeological excavations at Kukulik, St. Lawrence Island, Alaska.* Fairbanks: University of Alaska Press.

GODLEY, E. J.
1960  The botany of southern Chile in relation to New Zealand and the Subantarctic. *Proceedings of the Royal Society of London*, series B 152:457–475.

HAMMEL, H. T.
1964  Terrestrial animals in cold: recent studies of primitive man. *Handbook of Physiology* Section 4:413–435.

HAMMEL, H. T., R. W. ELSNER, K. L. ANDERSEN, P. F. SCHOLANDER, C. S. COON, A. MEDINA, L. STROZZI, F. A. MILAN, R. J. HOCK
1960  Thermal and metabolic responses of the Alacaluf Indians to moderate cold exposure. *Wright Air Development Division Technical Report* 60–633.

HARPER, F.
1955  *The Barren Ground caribou of Keewatin.* Lawrence: University of Kansas Press.

HART, C. W. M., A. R. PILLING
1960  *The Tiwi of North Australia.* New York: Holt, Rinehart and Winston.

HEIDER, K.
1972  Environment, subsistence and society. *Annual Review of Anthropology* 1:207–226.

HEIZER, R. F.
1956  Archaeology of the Uyak Site, Kodiak Island, Alaska. *Anthropological Records* 17. Berkeley: University of California Press.

HRDLIČKA, A.
1945  *The Aleut and Commander Islands and their inhabitants.* Philadelphia: Wistar Institute of Anatomy and Biology.

HULTEN, E.
1968  *Flora of Alaska and neighboring territories.* Stanford: Stanford University Press.

JENNESS, D.
1953  Did the Yahgan Indians of Tierra del Fuego speak an Eskimo tongue? *International Journal of American Linguistics* 19:128–131.

JOCHELSON, W.
1925  *Archaeological investigations in the Aleutian Islands.* Publication 367. Washington, D.C.: Carnegie Institution.
1933  *History, ethnology and anthropology of the Aleut.* Publication 432. Washington, D.C.: Carnegie Institution.

JONES, R. D., JR.
1966  Raising caribou for an Aleutian introduction. *The Journal of Wildlife Management* 30:453–460.

KROEBER, A. L.
1939  *Cultural and natural areas of native North America.* Publications in American Archaeology and Ethnology 38. Los Angeles: University of California Press.

KUSCHEL, G.
1960  Terrestrial zoology in southern Chile. *Proceedings of the Royal Society of London*, series B 152:540–550.

LANTIS, M.
1970  "The Aleut social system, 1750–1810, from early historic sources," in

*Ethnohistory in southwestern Alaska and the southern Yukon.* Edited by M. Lantis. Lexington: University of Kentucky Press.

LAUGHLIN, W. S.
1967   "Human migration and permanent occupation in the Bering Sea area," in *The Bering Land Bridge.* Edited by D. M. Hopkins. Stanford: Stanford University Press.

LEE, R. B.
1968   "What hunters do for a living, or, how to make out on scarce resources," in *Man the hunter.* Edited by R. B. Lee and I. DeVore. Chicago: Aldine.

LIPPOLD, L. K.
1966   Chaluka: The economic base. *Arctic Anthropology* 3:125–131.
1972   Mammalian remains from Aleutian archaeological sites: a preliminary report. *Arctic Anthropology* 9:113–114.

LOTHROP, S. K.
1928   *The Indians of Tierra del Fuego.* Contributions from the Museum of the American Indian 10. New York: Heye Foundation.

MAC ARTHUR, R. H., E. O. WILSON
1967   *The theory of island biogeography.* Princeton: Princeton University Press.

MACKINTOSH, N. A.
1960   The pattern of distribution of the Antarctic fauna. *Proceedings of the Royal Society of London,* series B 152:624–633.

MASON, L.
1968   "The technology of Micronesia," in *Peoples and cultures of the Pacific.* Edited by A. P. Vayda. New York: Natural History Press.

MC CARTNEY, A. P.
1967   "An analysis of the bone industry from Amaknak Island, Alaska." Unpublished M.A. thesis, University of Wisconsin, Madison.
1970   "Pottery" in the Aleutian Islands. *American Antiquity* 35:105–108.
1971   A proposed western Aleutian phase in the Near Islands, Alaska. *Arctic Anthropology* 8:92–142.
1972   "An archaeological site survey and inventory for the Aleutian Islands National Wildlife Refuge, Alaska, 1972." Unpublished report to the Wilderness Studies Branch, U.S. Fish and Wildlife Service, Anchorage.
n.d.   "Prehistoric cultural integration along the Alaska Peninsula." Unpublished manuscript.

MC CARTNEY, A. P., C. G. TURNER II
1966   Stratigraphy of the Anangula unifacial core and blade site. *Arctic Anthropology* 3:28–40.

MEGGERS, B. J.
1957   "Environment and culture in the Amazon Basin: an appraisal of the theory of environmental determinism," in *Studies in human ecology.* Washington: The Anthropological Society of Washington and the General Secretariat of the Organization of American States.

MILAN, F. A.
1962   "Racial variations in human response to low temperature," in *Comparative physiology of temperature regulation,* part three. Edited by J. P. Hannon and E. Viereck. Fort Wainwright: Arctic Aero-

medical Laboratory.

MÜLLER-BECK, H.
1967    "On migrations of hunters across the Bering Land Bridge in the Upper
        Pleistocene," in *The Bering Land Bridge.* Edited by D. M. Hopkins.
        Stanford: Stanford University Press.

MURIE, O. J.
1936    "Notes on the mammals of St. Lawrence Island, Alaska," in *Archaeolo-
        gical excavations at Kukulik, St. Lawrence Island, Alaska.* Edited by
        O. W. Geist and F. G. Rainey. College: University of Alaska Press.
1959    *Fauna of the Aleutian Islands and Alaska Peninsula.* North American
        Fauna 61. Washington, D.C.: Department of the Interior.

NEWMAN, M. T.
1962    Ecology and nutritional stress in man. *American Anthropologist* 64:
        22–34.

NISHIWAKI, M.
1966    "Distribution and migration of the larger cetaceans in the North
        Pacific as shown by Japanese whaling results," in *Whales, dolphins and
        porpoises.* Edited by K. S. Norris. Berkeley: University of California
        Press.

ODUM, E.
1963    *Ecology.* New York: Holt, Rinehart and Winston.

OLIVER, D. L.
1961    *The Pacific Islands.* Garden City: Doubleday (first edition 1951).

OSWALT, W. H.
1967    *Alaskan Eskimos.* San Francisco: Chandler.
1973    *Habitat and technology: the evolution of hunting.* New York: Holt,
        Rinehart and Winston.

PETROFF, I.
1884    *Report on the population, industries and resources of Alaska.* Tenth
        Census (1880). Washington, D.C.: Department of the Interior.

PIKE, G. C.
1956    *Guide to the whales, porpoises and dolphins of the north-east Pacific and
        arctic waters of Canada and Alaska.* Circular 32. Nanaimo, B.C.:
        Fisheries Research Board of Canada.

RANSOM, J. E.
1946    Aleut natural-food economy. *American Anthropologist* 48:607–623.

SAHLINS, M.
1972    "The original affluent society," in *Stone Age economics.* Edited by
        M. Sahlins. New York: Aldine-Altherton.

SAUER, C.
1950    "Geography of plant and animal resources," in *Handbook of South
        American Indians.* Edited by J. H. Steward. Washington, D.C.: Bureau
        of American Ethnology.

SCHEFFER, V. B.
1959    *Invertebrates and fishes collected in the Aleutians, 1936–1938.* North
        American Fauna 61. Washington, D.C.: Department of the Interior.

SINCLAIR, H. M.
1953    The diet of Canadian Indians and Eskimos. *Nutrition Society Proceed-
        ings* 12:69–82.

STEAGER, P. W.
1965 The Yahgan and Alacaluf: an ecological description. *The Kroeber Anthropological Society Papers* 32:69–76.

STEFANSSON, V.
1962 *My life with the Eskimo* (first edition 1913). New York: Crowell-Collier.

STEWARD, J. H.
1949a "The native population of South America," in *Handbook of South American Indians*. Edited by J. H. Steward. Washington, D.C.: Bureau of American Ethnology.
1949b "South American cultures: an interpretive summary," in *Handbook of South American Indians*. Edited by J. H. Steward. Washington, D.C.: Bureau of American Ethnology.
1955 *Theory of culture change*. Urbana: University of Illinois Press.

TAYLOR, W. E., JR.
1968 "An archaeological overview of Eskimo economy," in *Eskimo of the Canadian Arctic*. Edited by V. F. Valentine and F. G. Vallee. Princeton: D. Van Nostrand.

TRIGGER, B.
1971 Archaeology and ecology. *World Archaeology* 2:321–336.

TURNER, C. G. II, J. A. TURNER
1972 "Akun." Mimeographed report.

TURNER, L. M.
1886 *Contributions to the natural history of Alaska*. The Miscellaneous Documents, Forty-Ninth Congress, First Session 8. Washington, D.C.: U.S. Government Printing Office.

VAYDA, A. P., R. A. RAPPAPORT
1968 "Ecology: cultural and non-cultural," in *Introduction to cultural anthropology*. Edited by J. A. Clifton. Boston: Houghton Mifflin.

VENIAMINOF, I.
1840 *Notes on the islands of the Unalaska District*. Human Relations Area File translation of volume two and part of volume three. St. Petersburg: Russian American Company.

WALKER, E. H.
1945 "Plants of the Aleutian Islands," in *The Aleutian Islands: their people and natural history*. Smithsonian Institution War Background Studies Publication 3775. Washington, D.C.: Smithsonian Institution.

WEYER, E. M.
1930 *Archaeological material from the village site at Hot Springs, Port Moller, Alaska*. Anthropological Papers of the American Museum of Natural History 31.

WILLEY, G. R.
1971 *An introduction to American archaeology*, volume two. Englewood Cliffs: Prentice-Hall.

WORKMAN, W. B.
1966 Prehistory at Port Moller, Alaska Peninsula, in light of fieldwork in 1960. *Arctic Anthropology* 3:132–153.

# A Comparative Approach to Northern Maritime Adaptations

WILLIAM FITZHUGH

Archaeological research has reached a level at which it is increasingly possible to investigate general problems of cultural processes and development beyond the limits of a particular historical tradition. Previously, attempts to generalize from different cultural and historic contexts have been speculative due to the lack of adequate information concerning regional developments, environmental conditions, and chronology. As regional sequences become defined and external relationships are clarified the role of comparative archaeology should become a more prominent archaeological objective. Utilizing information from the natural and social sciences, it should be possible to identify and test propositions concerning regularities in cultural developments from historically distinct regions. Such a study, proposed by Steward (1955) within the context of his theory of cultural ecology, has never been systematically applied to archaeological data despite the belief held by many archaeologists that this type of generalization is the "new frontier" beyond particularistic and historically-oriented research.

I intend here to demonstrate the use of comparative archaeological studies by investigating the more salient aspects of cultural development in a relatively unified environmental zone — the circumpolar maritime regions — to test expectations of similarity between cultures which are not historically related but which share common features due to convergent evolution in similar habitats. The study reviews the data from each geographic zone and identifies common features in the light of historical and ecological conditions. Attention will be directed largely to the "core elements" (Steward 1955) of each regional expression and to its basic economic adaptation. There are, of course, many unique aspects of each cultural tradition which will not be noted and are not considered central to the basic problem of cross-cultural research in archaeology which is the focus of this article.

## COMPARATIVE ARCHAEOLOGY

Archaeologists have been reluctant to take up Steward's challenge that cultural variation within ethnographic and archaeological fields contains a series of culture-ecological types which can be arranged in terms of levels of sociocultural integration. Although there has been discussion among social anthropologists about the reality of these levels and the accuracy of their sociological descriptions (e.g. "patrilineal bands"), archaeologists, while paying lip service to the general developmental stages embodied in Steward's cultural ecology, have never set forth in any systematic way a means of determining the accuracy of the specific or even general propositions contained in the theory. More particularly, archaeologists have not attempted, except in a limited way in the case of formative and complex society developments, to test the theory cross-culturally from the world's archaeological record. Steward, for example, suggests that, given similar technological levels in similar environments, certain levels of social interaction, political structure, and religion should be expected. Likewise, the theory places general limits on the types of technological developments which should be expected in a given environment. Although ethnographic tests of these propositions have been made, with very mixed results, archaeologists have not attempted to apply their data to the problem.

There are numerous reasons why a comparative school has not emerged in archaeology. Most archaeologists work within geographically bounded zones, and the discipline does not have the history of peripatetic research that is common in many other scientific fields, including, frequently, ethnography. Regional archaeological research tends to continue to generate its own culture historical problems, and until recently few archaeologists worked in more than one area. A strong historical orientation has also dominated archaeological thought, which intensified with the use of radiocarbon dating, and undoubtedly has obscured the impact of Steward's thesis in archaeological circles. Finally, there is the severe lack of archaeological data from most parts of the world in which comparable archaeological cultures exist. Even to the present, use of comparative data is almost wholly restricted to the possible diffusion of elements or complexes, or, more recently, to ethnographic analogy. Rarely have

archaeologists adduced comparative data from other regions to the interpretations of their own data.

In addition, other more subliminal phenomena have restricted the use
of comparative archaeological information. Cultural relativism has been
a deeply ingrained tenet of modern anthropology. The uniqueness of a
culture, a historical tradition, and the peculiar idiosyncratic events which
always provide the distinctive shape of time have produced a rigorous
method of particularistic research during the past few decades which has
not been conducive to a search for parallel cultural events and processes.
Where this HAS been done, as in formative and complex society developments in Mesopotamia and Central America (e.g. Willey 1962; Adams
1966), there have been promising results.

There are other problems in the study of comparative archaeology,
such as the comparability of data units, the lack of rigorous definitions
for the limits of technological or socioeconomic complexes, and the
extent to which slight differences can be acceptable under a given comparative situation. Finally, since no two environments are virtually identical, is comparison of their cultural schemata theoretically admissible?
And, if so, do pronouncements of "similarity" merely carry qualitative
or absolute validity? In short, what are the boundary conditions and
conceptual forms for cross-cultural research in archaeology? None of
these critical questions has been considered by archaeologists, and
the result has been a lack of systematization and standardization, the
traditional Achilles heel of cross-cultural research in anthropology (cf.
Naroll 1970).

In order to provide a framework for comparative research in archaeology the concept of ADAPTATION TYPE is suggested as a useful addition to
archaeological systematics. Present theory includes the basic space and
time concepts needed for historical integration, but these do not provide
for cross-cultural comparison beyond the level of "stage" units, such as
"formative," "classic," and "developmental," which are too general in
scope and are linked closely with the American academic and native
historical traditions. Likewise, Steward's culture-ecological types are
really sociocultural descriptions and do not describe adaptation and
economic configurations. Struever's (1968) subsistence settlement system
is a useful concept when applied to a particular archaeological complex or
historical unit, but to compare culture units and traditions from different
historical and geographic areas, a new concept which links environmental
potential and technological capabilities is required.

ADAPTATION TYPE performs this function suitably since it describes a
nonspecific cultural or chronological unit which may be archaeological

or ethnological, and its particular usage may depend on the definition ascribed to it in the context of the discussion. As such its use is similar to that of the term "complex" in archaeological systematics. Further, an adaptation type may include a series of sub-type variants which may be defined to correspond with demographic and economic realities. Thus, for example, within a Northern Maritime Adaptation type one might specify Ipiutak, Rattlers Bight, Ainu, or Coast Saamish variants. The system is simple and flexible for comparative as well as functional studies and is used in the following discussion.

## NORTHERN MARITIME ADAPTATION TYPE

Cultural adaptations to marine resources have provided subsistence for hominids for at least the past 200,000 years with the most dramatic increase during the past 10,000 years. It can be assumed that adaption to these resources has influenced the structure of these societies, their settlement pattern, population density, religious expression, artistic representations, as well as their technology and transportation. Many of these societies share common elements which would appear to result from their similar economic adaptations. Remarkably, anthropologists have not investigated maritime adaptations for comparative information although they have made such studies of agricultural societies on a global scale presumably because of their position in the development of more complex social and cultural forms. In concentrating on village formative agricultural studies we overlook the fact that in some areas, such as Peru, certain areas of the Mediterranean, and northern Europe, and perhaps Japan, maritime adaptations formed the basis to which agricultural subsistence was added (cf. Binford 1968: 332). In these cases at least settled village life evolved under a maritime or seasonally maritime economy which was pre-adapted to sociocultural forms required in an agricultural economy. Thus, we may find that maritime adaptations have played a more important role in the development of complex societies than has been appreciated. Also, of course, we should expect to learn more about the organization of societies in which seasonality led to economic specialization and diversification and to the role of maritime adaptations in the development of mixed economies, trade, regional intercommunication, the development of market economies, and other topics (see Moberg, this volume).

   In short, the ramification of cross-cultural studies of maritime adaptations by both ethnological and archaeological methods has a potentially important, and heretofore unrecognized, role to play in anthropological research.

This paper is specifically concerned with comparative investigation of a widespread maritime adaptation found in most areas of the circumpolar zone, including, prominently, Scandinavia, northeastern North America, the American and Canadian Arctic and Greenland, the Northwest Coast, Bering Sea, and northeast Asian coasts and archipelagoes. Similar expressions occur in the southern hemisphere (see McCartney, this volume) but are not considered here. Besides the intrinsic value of such a query for historical and functional studies one must also ask about the role of northern maritime adaptations in wider economic relationships with adjacent areas to the interior and the south.

The Northern Maritime Adaptation type is a concept which includes a variety of cultural expressions and is not limited to a particular historical tradition or geographic zone. In northern Europe it developed as early as 8,000 years ago; in the Jamal region of the Soviet Arctic it did not begin until about 2,000 years ago; in northeastern North America it originated 6,000 years ago and lasted for 2,000 years before being replaced by a more inland economic orientation. The date of its appearance, subsequent developments, and environmental relationships in these areas is a Pandorean chest of questions.

The Northern Maritime Adaptation type may be defined as a general culture-ecological pattern in which the economic base and general cultural orientation is partially or wholly dependent on coastal and maritime resources of the northern littoral. As such it includes cultural adaptations to both arctic and subarctic waters and their cold water sea mammals, fishes, birds, and ducks. The combination of fishing and sea hunting (or "catching") is central to this adaptation type. Shellfish collecting is usually limited in its importance, becoming a strong component in more temperate maritime adaptations. In limiting the ecological zone to the arctic and subarctic seas and their adjacent rivers, we are consciously emphasizing areas of high marine productivity and relatively great ecological predictability, both of which concepts are central to the development of stable maritime adaptations in these areas (Fitzhugh 1972a).

It is suggested as a hypothesis here that northern maritime adaptations result in similar functionally-related cultural forms (primarily Steward's "core elements") due to similar requirements of northern exploitation patterns which arise independently in different parts of the circumpolar zone. Included within the northern maritime adaptation type are a number of general descriptive subtypes of the main concept. These include Modified Interior, Interior-Maritime, Modified Maritime, and Maritime adaptation types. Riverine adaptations also occur on the Northwestern Coast, in Alaska, and northeastern Asia. While not strictly or even in some cases seasonally maritime, they provide a stable economic base which is similar to that provided by maritime adaptations (Fitzhugh 1972b: 157–167).

Table 1.  General Northern Maritime and Riverine Adaptation Types

| | |
|---|---|
| 1. Modified Interior (Montagnais type) | Dual economy with seasonal subsistence on both coast and interior. Generalized interior-type technology without specialization for intensive maritime hunting and fishing. |
| 2. Interior-Maritime (Okhotsk type) | Dual economy with seasonal subsistence on interior and coast, but with more intensive maritime economy including technological specializations such as toggling harpoons. Generalized interior economy. Often lacks oil lamps, thus bound to the forest. |
| 3. Modified Marine (Central Eskimo type) | Subsistence restricted largely to the coast with specialized technology for marine hunting and fishing. Some use of coastal land resources. Oil heating. |
| 4. Maritime (Aleut type) | Total dependence on marine resources including birds and invertebrates. Oil heating. |
| 5. Riverine (Amur or Tlingit type) | Primary adaptation to riverine fishing. Additional subsistence provided by interior and coastal resources. This type integrates with all of the other types. |

In the past the study of northern maritime cultures has been cast in overly specific terms, with prime interest given to a few elements thought to be central to the problem of historical diffusion which was presumed to have linked the polar and boreal "corridors" of the Old and New Worlds. Today this concern seems to be a mere accident of history resulting from the available data from the west and north Norwegian "slate complex," the Laurentian of the Northeast, and the geographically central position of the Eskimos whose harpoons, ground slate, skin boats, and oil lamps seemed to preserve the core elements of a presumably older and widespread maritime hunting and fishing complex (Fitzhugh 1975; Simonsen 1972). Thus there had been great attention to the FACT of ground slate and bone technology in circumpolar regions and not enough research into WHY ground slate and bone provide a suitable technology for these regions. There is also a great need for functional studies, even in the case of the toggling harpoon which is not well understood, of the varieties of forms and functionally significant attributes which yield cultural rather than simple typological information. Here one might also note the sterilizing preoccupation with historical diffusionist explanations for the distribution of the key northern complexes which until recently existed in circumpolar studies. While the papers by Gjessing (1944), Spaulding (1946), and Møllenhus (1958; translated in this volume) were benchmarks in the birth, modification, and demise of a historically-related circumpolar stone age, it becomes far more significant anthropologically that most of these regions developed their maritime adaptations independently, thus affording one the opportunity for comparative study of cultural developments. It is at this level that the functional basis of Gjessing's circumpolar stone age becomes important and should not be disregarded today with the denial of circumpolar diffusion.

The final caveats to be made concern problems with the study of northern maritime adaptations. While I have emphasized the northern maritime element of those areas adjacent to the arctic and subarctic seas, six of the societies concerned utilized terrestrial resources and, with the possible exception of the inhabitants of the Kuril and Aleutian Islands and their ancestors, were not totally dependent on marine resources. Thus seasonality and population segmentation such that certain groups would concentrate to varying degrees on coastal or inland resources are important in any understanding of these societies. Finally, of course, one cannot study any society without consideration of its communication and external contacts with nonmaritime, Neolithic, or other societies. However, I believe that within the circumpolar zone taiga adaptations are sufficiently different in technological and economic requirements from partial or full maritime adaptations to constitute a quite distinct anthropological problem, despite the overlap that may occur between such groups. Likewise, I shall not be concerned here with the whole gamut of legitimate but, from present perspective, peripheral questions surrounding the definition of "maritime" and the quantification of marine and terrestrial resources utilized by different groups.

## CULTURAL ADAPTATIONS OF THE CENTRAL LABRADOR COAST: A TEST CASE

Archaeological investigation over the past five years in Labrador has resulted in a fairly detailed outline of the prehistory of this region. While specific sites and complexes are quite well known from both the island of Newfoundland and from the northern coast of Labrador, at present the most complete cultural sequence available comes from the Hamilton Inlet region of the central Labrador coast where a 5,500 year record of Indian and Eskimo cultures has been documented (Fitzhugh 1972b). It is therefore possible to discuss chronology and distribution of maritime adaptations in some detail.

The Labrador-Newfoundland area is a transitional geographic zone between the Arctic and the temperate Gulf of St. Lawrence where tundra, taiga, and boreal forest ecozones are closely juxtaposed. Maritime conditions vary from arctic in northern Labrador to subarctic in central Labrador and Newfoundland. The interior and coastal habitat is dominated by woodland or barren ground caribou, while the marine ecosystem includes all of the important northern sea mammals such as walrus, seal, whale, and polar bear, and subarctic fishes like cod, halibut, sea trout, and salmon. The coast of Labrador is ice-bound six to eight months a year, while most of Newfoundland is surrounded by pack ice from January to March, and its waters remain chilled by the Labrador current throughout the year. Marine and terrestrial resources have always been vital in the seasonal economies of these regions.

Paleoenvironmental history of this region is not well known because of lack of fossil evidence and difficulties in palynological interpretation due to the mixing of continental and maritime climatic conditions. Forest fingers extend down the northern river valleys far north of the plateau tree limit, while on the Labrador coast large variations in precipitation, soil availability, and the chilling effect of the Labrador Current produce marked vegetation changes from one region to the next.

Despite these difficulties a preliminary view of early vegetation patterns is emerging for the central Labrador coast (Wenner 1947; Grayson 1956; Morrison 1970; Fitzhugh 1973a). Briefly, it appears that glacial ice began to retreat from the coast as early as 10,000 B.P. Although ice remnants may have remained longer in pockets along the coast insulated from hypsithermal influence by the Labrador Current, a coastal strip was probably available for occupation as early as 6000–8000 B.P. To date, however, the first evidence of man does not occur until 6000 B.P. in south coastal Labrador (Harp and Hughes 1968: 44), while in outer Hamilton Inlet occupation began by 5500 B.P. (Fitzhugh 1972b), at which time mixed forest and tundra conditions prevailed. Pollen diagrams show that spruce was present on the outer coast by 6000–7000 B.P. Diagrams from the interior show a considerably later disappearance of ice, with initial tundra vegetation appearing by 6000 B.P. in western Hamilton Inlet and 5500 B.P. on the interior plateau. Here, there is a rapid transition to a forest-tundra vegetation, and later the full boreal forest at 4500 B.P.

Following development of the forest, the interior cores do not show climatic fluctuation; however, coastal cores show forest-tundra boundary shifts which may result from climatic deterioration. In addition, both

interior and coastal cores document extensive forest fire activity throughout the entire postglacial period, suggesting that fires have always been a
part of tundra and boreal ecosystems and, further, must have influenced
caribou ecology. In sum, the pollen data indicate that the only feasible
corridor for early human movement into northern Labrador was along a
coastal rather than an interior route. They also suggest that caribou may
have been concentrated within a fairly narrow band of tundra and forest-
tundra between the ice and the sea during the period 7000–5000 B.P.
Given these conditions, it is likely that the earliest human occupants in this
region would have employed modified maritime adaptations.

The cultural sequence in Hamilton Inlet may be broken into three
distinct chronological units. An EARLY PERIOD between 5500–3800 B.P.
was dominated by the slowly elaborating Labrador Maritime Archaic

Table 2.  Hamilton Inlet subsistence-settlement system types

| Type and system | Description |
| --- | --- |
| 1. Interior (Sesacit Phase, Road component) | Interior-restricted sss[1]: caribou winter economy in interior, lake and river fishing during summer. Generalized interior adaptation. |
| 2. Modified-Interior | Interior-coastal sss: Generalized interior adaptation; limited to generalized coastal adaptation. Winter caribou hunting in interior; summer lake and coastal hunting and fishing. |
| 2a.  Brinex, Charles complexes | Limited coastal apdatation in summer. Generalized winter caribou economy in interior. |
| 2b.  North West River Phase, David Michelin complex | Generalized coastal adaptation including semi-permanent camps for small game, fish, birds, seal. |
| 2c.  Point Revenge complex | Generalized coastal adaptation with more intensive use of marine environment. Larger social groups; use of Ramah chert. |
| 3. Interior-Maritime | Interior-coastal sss: Generalized winter adaptation, specialized coastal adaptation during summer. |
| 3a.  Sandy Cove complex | Seasonally specialized coastal adaptation, but with small coastal settlements. Limited trade and use of Ramah chert. |
| 3b.  Rattlers Bight Phase | Specialized seasonal adaptation to coast with semi-permanent summer occupation of large base camp. Trade in Ramah chert. |
| 4. Modified-Maritime | Coastal-restricted sss: Specialized coastal adaptation to marine resources. Some use of coastal land resources. |
| 4a.  Groswater Dorset Phase | Specialized technology for seal and walrus. Small population. Semi-sedentary. |
| 4b.  Ivuktoke Phase | Specialized technology for seal, walrus, and whale. Large winter communities. Dog sled and umiak transport. |

[1]  sss — subsistence-settlement system

tradition, a long-lived Indian tradition with a strong seasonally maritime orientation. The INTERMEDIATE PERIOD, 3800–1400 B.P., contains a rapid succession of short-lived but culturally distinct groups which are clearly interior or Shield-related, and on the coast a Paleo-Eskimo penetration from the north. The LATE PERIOD, from 1400 B.P. to the present, is again a stable period of continuous Indian occupation in which a strong seasonal maritime adaptation develops. Toward the end of this period a second Eskimo penetration, this time by historic Labrador Eskimo, occurs. The discussion below is concerned largely with the Early and Late Period cultures in which maritime adaptations were most fully developed. These adaptations are described in terms of a series of types and subtypes as shown in Table 2.

*The Early Period* (5500–3500 B.P.)

The cultural sequence in Hamilton Inlet, as presently known, begins with the Sandy Cove complex, an early component of the Labrador Maritime Archaic tradition dating about 5500–4600 B.P. Sites of this complex are common in the maritime sector of Groswater Bay in outer Hamilton Inlet and are summer stations situated in ideal sea mammal, bird hunting, and fishing locales. Winter sites of the complex have not been found but presumably exist in the caribou hunting areas adjacent to the coast. The tool inventory includes a bone industry, rarely preserved and about which little is known; the stone technology includes a combination of chipped and ground stone industries in which stemmed end blades, leaf-shaped, single-shouldered and asymmetric single-sided knives, wedges, and ground slate celts are most common. The predominant raw materials — quartz and red quartzite — are of local origin, while more limited use is made of exotic materials of which Ramah chert, originating from geological beds in northern Labrador, is significant in indicating sporadic northern communication and travel. Red ocher, limonite, quartz debris, and large pit hearths are often encountered in the excavations, but there is no evidence for dwelling structures or burials. Pollen evidence from lake sediments adjacent to the Sandy Cove sites indicates that the occupations occurred in a mixed forest-tundra environment north of the main boreal forest. The Sandy Cove adaptation is classified as INTERIOR-MARITIME (3a) on the basis of its strong summer maritime orientation and the presumed existence of winter caribou hunting in the interior.

The second unit in the Early Period is the Black Island complex, known only from one large site dating between 4500–4100 B.P. and also located in the Sandy Cove region. Preserved faunal remains indicate that seals and sea birds provided the economic basis of the site, but the tool inventory departs from that of the preceding period and contains notched and expanded base points, scrapers, and a distinct scarcity of ground slate tools. Pit hearths filled with charred and ochered blubber abound, and as with Sandy Cove sites there was no indication of dwellings or burials.

While not evident from its adaptation type, which remains presumably INTERIOR-MARITIME (3a), differences in tool typology, technology, and raw materials use strongly suggest that the Black Island complex is an intrusion from southern Labrador or Newfoundland which, following 4200 B.P., withdraws or is superseded without acculturation by a second-generation descendant of the Sandy Cove complex, known as the Rattlers Bight phase. Further, the Black Island complex arrives in the Hamilton Inlet region at the same time as the maximum northern forest expansion. Culturally, one would place the complex with a southern group of Moorehead or Laurentian-related complexes and with more distant affinity to the stemmed point tradition of the Labrador Maritime Archaic.

The final cultural unit in the Early Period is the Rattlers Bight phase of 4000–3700 B.P., known from one large and a series of small stations in the northeastern extremity of Hamilton Inlet in a more isolated marine setting than the preceding two complexes. The Rattlers Bight phase maintains and intensifies the strong seasonal INTERIOR-MARITIME (3b) type of adaptations with seals, sea birds, and fish as the dominant summer food sources. The period represents a classic type of dual coastal-interior economy which characterized the Labrador Maritime Archaic tradition. It is at this period that trade contacts and typological continuities extend from northern Labrador to southern Maine together with the appearance of an elaborate cemetery cult most notable from the bone-rich Port-au-Choix cemetery of Newfoundland and the great boneless cemeteries of Maine and New Brunswick. Indication of contact throughout this coastal zone is seen in the trade of Labrador Maritime Archaic points manufactured from Ramah chert, which in the northern regions becomes the only acceptable material for chipped stone tools. Other cross-ties include similar forms of bone or swordfish daggers, engraved slate bayonets, and animal effigies. From the superior condition of the bone artifacts from Port-au-Choix-2 (Tuck 1971) we may infer that a full complement of maritime technology, including barbed and toggling harpoons, was present at least by 3800 B.P. and that extensive ceremonialism, particularly including sea mammals and birds, was practiced (see Tuck, this volume). The expansion of cultural contacts and ceremonialism during the Rattlers Bight period coincides with the maximum northern extension of the boreal forest in northern Labrador, Quebec, Keewatin and other areas. During the latter part of this period Maritime Archaic people came into contact with early pre-Dorset Eskimos in northern Labrador. A combination of climatic deterioration and Eskimo contact may have contributed to the collapse of Maritime Archaic culture in Labrador after 3800 B.P.

In summary, the Early Period is dominated for 2,000 years by the Labrador Maritime Archaic tradition, a stable cultural continuum with a seasonal INTERIOR-MARITIME (3a, b) adaptation type characterized by a stemmed point tradition, a well-developed chipped and ground slate industry including large woodworking tools, and a bone and antler industry which included fixed, detachable, and toggling harpoons well adapted to open-water and perhaps ice-edge marine hunting. The central and northern Labrador facies of this tradition are not yet known to include extensive cemeteries. In central Labrador the earlier Sandy Cove complex of this tradition appears to evolve into a transitional complex seen in sites in Nain and northern Labrador in which ground slate and Ramah chert use elaborates at a time when there is a brief intrusion of southern notched point carrying peoples in the Hamilton Inlet region. By about 4000 B.P. the northern Maritime Archaic peoples reappear in central and southern Labrador and Newfoundland contemporaneously with the development of extensive trade contacts and ceremonialism between these regions and areas to the south. This evidence suggests that the Sandy Cove-Rattlers Bight continuum represents evolutionary stages in the Labrador Maritime Archaic tradition, which itself is a co-tradition of a larger series of regional groups of which the Black Island complex is a representative of the southern, Laurentian-related group. All of these groups were seasonally adapted to marine resources in the greater north-eastern littoral zone from northern Labrador to southern Maine from 6000–3600 B.P. In the southern regions increasing contacts are noted between these cultures and others with predominantly interior economies, while in the northern range the late persistence of glacial ice on the interior confines this tradition largely to coastal resources.

*The Intermediate Period* (3600–1400 B.P.)

During the subsequent Intermediate Period the central Labrador region was occupied by a series of discontinuous complexes with different technologies, tool types, and patterns of raw material use, whose similar-ities were confined largely to sharing a common pattern of MODIFIED-INTERIOR or INTERIOR adaptation types in which limited use and knowledge of marine resources and maritime technology is exhibited. These cultural units are not described here in detail. They include the ephemeral Little Lake complex (around 3600 B.P.), the Brinex complex (3500–3300 B.P.), the Charles complex (3300–3000 B.P.), the Road component (around 2800 B.P.), the David Michelin complex (around 2300 B.P.), and the North West River phase (2000–1700 B.P.). Sites of these complexes are rarely found on the coast. During this period pre-Dorset Eskimo culture is found on the northern coast of Labrador, and following 2800 B.P. Dorset culture expands into central and southern Labrador and eventually by 2000 B.P., into Newfoundland. This expansion appears related to cooling climatic conditions beginning around 3000 B.P. and to the lack of extensive Indian occupation on the Labrador coast.

One of the most intriguing problems of the Intermediate Period is explanation of the rapid succession of Indian cultures, which rarely persist more than 200–400 years before being replaced by different peoples and traditions. It seems likely that these groups were victims of their MODIFIED-INTERIOR and INTERIOR adaptation types which did not prove viable under what may have been unfavorable environmental conditions for caribou hunting (Fitzhugh 1972b: 167–194). It is a period in which forest fires, winter icing of feeding grounds, and, perhaps, disease are believed to have taken a heavy toll on the caribou herds. Without sufficient reliance on maritime resources these cultures appear to have had limited longevity.

*The Late Period* (1400 B.P. to Present)

The final period spans the prehistoric and historic periods of Labrador's past and, as with the Early Period, it is one which is dominated by a stable Indian tradition whose adaptation included extensive seasonal exploitation of marine resources. Presently, the tradition is seen most clearly in the Point Revenge complex of Hamilton Inlet from sites dating between 1000 and 300 B.P., with related sites extending from 1200 B.P. to the historic period known from southern Labrador and Quebec, north to Nain. These sites are commonly found at low elevations on the coast and contain chipped stone end scrapers, side scrapers and flake knives, and a wide variety of convex and flat-based corner-notched end blades. Boulder tent rings with circular and oval shapes are common, and hearth types include small circular cobble cooking fires and larger slab hearths. Continuity within this tradition is evidenced by a gradual evolution of tool styles and continuing high density of coastal sites. Faunal remains indicate a mixed summer economy of seals, sea birds, and land game, including black bear, beaver, otter, rabbit, and fox. Based on ethnographic analogy with the historic successors of the Point Revenge peoples, the Montagnais and Nenenot (Naskapi) Indians, these people were Algonkian-speakers whose winter adaptation was based on interior caribou hunting in small extended family units. Their adaptation type is transitional between MODIFIED-INTERIOR (2c) and INTERIOR-MARITIME (3a). They appear to have been as completely adapted to seasonal marine resources as the Labrador Maritime Archaic tradition, differing only in the size and intensity of their summer coastal settlement but capable of similar long-distance movements and contacts as far as northern Labrador.

As in the Early Period, this adaptation developed during a peak warm climatic period in which the forest edge moved north of its present position, facilitating Indian expansion. By 1450–1500 A.D., this culture area was restricted by the southern movement of Thule-derived Labrador Eskimos from Hudson Strait, who by 1600 A.D. had control of the Labrador coast as far south as the Strait of Belle Isle. Their expansion eventually included much of the northeastern shore of the Gulf of St. Lawrence to the limit of the harp seal and walrus distribution. This expansion deprived the Montagnais and Nenenot Indians of their traditional summer hunting grounds and precipitated a series of conflicts along the entire length of the coast now evinced by legend and macabre toponymy. With European assistance the Indians had managed by 1770 to regain control of the southern coast and the inner portions of the central coast, while the southernmost Eskimo occupation remained in the eastern end of Hamilton Inlet. However, the loss of the coast subsistence to the Indians of central and northern Labrador-Quebec imposed hardships and economic instability due partially to caribou fluctuation, which provide some analogy to the unstable Intermediate Period cultures with their Modified Interior and Interior adaptation types.

The culture history and adaptations of the central Labrador coast demonstrate several principles that are useful in interpreting cultural developments in this area and may have potential value for similar studies in other regions. These observations may be summarized as follows:

CULTURAL AND ENVIRONMENTAL VARIABILITY    Ten different Indian and four different Eskimo complexes are noted in the 5500-year sequence for central Labrador, with other recognizable units in southern and northern Labrador. This cultural diversity undoubtedly reflects the geographic and environmental complexity of this transitional subarctic region in contrast to, for example, more homogeneous culture history known from the boreal forest of interior Quebec.

RESOURCE STABILITY AND INSTABILITY    Ecological structures in the North demonstrate many similarities in terms of food web simplicity and stability when compared to temperate and tropical ecosystems. Nevertheless, significant differences exist between northern boreal and marine ecosystems which are vital in understanding human adaptations in these environments. Specifically, boreal and tundra zones are relatively unproductive and unstable and are subject to periodic population crashes due to limited food web diversity and a low number of trophic levels in the food chain. All species, from mice to caribou, undergo drastic population fluctuation resulting from forest and tundra fires, winter icing, predation cycles, and disease. In contrast, the marine ecosystem is relatively more stable and predictable with greater food web diversity and many more trophic levels than found in northern terrestrial systems. Marine food resources are more variable and are available in greater numbers throughout the year, providing that man's technological capacity for harvesting them is adequate. Hence, human adaptations to the arctic and subarctic littoral, including most terrestrial resources which are also available seasonally along the coast, have a potentially more predictable ecological base than do those of the more unstable northern interior, where population crashes or migration shifts occur periodically.

CULTURAL ADAPTATIONS    Cultural adaptations in the North have only slightly mitigated the impact of ecological instability and unpredictability Given the relatively low environmental potential of the interior, and especially for man the lack of carbohydrates needed for winter survival, cultural adaptations have had a minimal effect on softening the periodic subsistence crashes. For this reason interior peoples, both ethnographically and archaeologically, appear to have made virtually the same choices, and have made use of similar exploitative strategies. On the other hand, coastal and maritime adaptations have considerably more variability and require more elaborate extractive technologies if maximal utilization is to be made. In turn, they provide increased insurance against starvation. It is evident from the archaeological record in central Labrador, even disregarding climatic shifts, that there is a cline of cultural stability which increases as adaptation types progress from Interior to Modified-Interior, and Interior-Maritime. In subarctic Labrador those cultures with seasonal adaptations to the sea persist longer than those without strong seasonal patterns.

SEASONALITY, ADAPTATION TYPE, AND MOBILITY    Seasonal variation in food resources is the primary determinant of northern subsistence strategies and adaptation types. During the summer months when caribou are unavailable, the interior is impoverished, while seals, birds, and summer fish runs provide a concentrated source of food in coastal regions. It is therefore not surprising that this strong seasonal subsistence gradient induced the development of summer coastal adaptations since these could be pursued initially and quite productively with the unspecialized types of hunting and fishing technologies commonly found among interior peoples. However, in Labrador, the prevalence of firewood adjacent to the coast made it possible for Indian winter adaptations to exist without necessitating ice hunting and oil heating technology. The environment therefore supported two basic types of adaptations in this area: (1) a highly seasonal mixed economy of INTERIOR-MARITIME type which required flexible social groupings with capabilities for nomadic travel during the winter caribou hunting months, and with more concentrated settlement patterns during the summer months by the sea; and (2) a MODIFIED MARITIME (Eskimo) type economy in which winter ice hunting was supplemented by fishing and caribou hunting in the coastal regions. Within these two basic variants numerous modifications were possible, and in fact, are documented in the archaeological record. The lack of persistent interior adaptation types and privations encountered by Indian peoples with interior adaptation during the historic periods suggests that this was not a stable adaptation type for the eastern portion of Labrador-Quebec, and one which existed only when coastal resources were depleted by Eskimos.

## CIRCUMPOLAR MARITIME ADAPTATIONS: A SURVEY

The foregoing observations demonstrate the utility of adaptation type studies in the subarctic coastal region of Labrador. It is obvious that questions of cultural continuity and change, of regional diversity and technological adaptations, reflect a number of cultural and environmental variables which may have influenced cultural developments in other parts of the circumpolar zone. In the following discussion we will consider those areas in which northern maritime adaptations have developed, with special attention to technology, subsistence, and cultural continuity. This survey is unfortunately general because of a lack of well-controlled regional sequences in most of the subarctic maritime regions.

### Scandinavia

Maritime adaptations have been important in Scandinavia since the earliest known occupations of the Older Stone Age, dating roughly

8000–6000 B.P. These early occupations, known as Fosna culture in southern Scandinavia, Komsa in the arctic regions, and Askola in Finland, overlapped at least partly with the retreat of glacial ice on the interior. Each of these groups was based on a Mesolithic cultural tradition including a microlithic industry, which, in the absence of cherts or flints, utilized local quartz. The subsistence base varied in different regions, but moose and reindeer were undoubtedly utilized in both coastal and interior regions. However, the situation of many of these sites along raised strandlines on the Arctic coast, and in other coastal locations further south, indicates that marine foods and materials were also important, and scattered finds in the northern Baltic indicate that adequate extractive technologies, including harpoons, leisters, and nets, had been developed for harvesting fish, seals, and sea birds.

Unfortunately, poor conditions of preservation in most of these early sites preclude direct evidence or further refinement or quantification of the diet. Likewise, the internal chronology of the Early Stone Age and their regional subdivisions is not well controlled. Typological dating of the industries is difficult and few discrete complexes have been defined. Further, the lack of datable materials has required relative dating of these sites by correlation with the pollen sequence and beach level chronology.

Given the lack of information for cultures of this period, and their wide distribution through greatly varying environments, it is hazardous to make specific statements regarding Older Stone Age subsistence and adaptation patterns. Nevertheless, it appears reasonable to suggest that the general economic focus of these cultures was toward reindeer and elk hunting with more limited, and quite likely seasonal, exploitation of coastal and marine resources. From the increasing abundance of coastal sites as one proceeds toward the arctic regions one might surmise that marine economies begin to increase in importance in the northern regions. This view suggests a MODIFIED-INTERIOR adaptation for the Fosna and Askola cultures, while Komsa adaptations in coastal regions may have approached INTERIOR-MARITIME. One factor which may have influenced the development of seasonal maritime adaptations in the north is the migration of reindeer into the coastal regions at certain seasons. Such movements, if they occurred in the past, would have brought interior hunters into contact with the abundant coastal resources during part of their yearly cycle. However, the earliest occupants of northern Scandinavia may well have moved into this area with seasonal maritime adaptations which had been developed further south. The timing of deglaciation and the extent of ice-free coastal corridors between the mountains and the sea may prove important considerations in this problem.

Following the beginning of the Younger Stone Age about 5500 B.P., extensive cultural changes occur throughout the Scandinavian region. Cultural contact with northern Europe results in importation of flint artifacts and the acceptance of ceramics and domestic animals, while in the north comb ceramics and Karelian flints are introduced. Internal trade within the region is evidenced also by trade in amber and a distinctive banded purple slate, often in the form of finished cloven-hoof or moose head effigy daggers, perhaps northern counterparts of the Neolithic flint daggers traded widely in the south. Elaboration of religious ideas includes a moose cult, and pictographic, engraved and sculptured art begins to be practiced, providing glimpses of growing cultural complexity. Despite these contacts cultural diversity continues to increase to a point where, by 4000 B.P., regional culture groups can be recognized in south Norway and Sweden, west Norway, Finnmark, north Sweden, and Finland. Each has its own particular configuration including differences in adaptation and technology. Within the larger context of a hunting and gathering economy, each, however, shares elements of the greater Scandinavian slate complex and a growing importance of seasonal maritime adaptation. It is this combination which has attracted archaeological attention and has been the subject of comparisons with other circumpolar and circumboreal regions.

Recent research on the Scandinavian Younger Stone Age collections (Fitzhugh 1975; Bakka, personal communication) suggests that the core area for the slate complex stretches across northern Scandinavia from west Norway through Finnmark and the north Baltic region. In this area is found the greatest diversity of slate forms which only during the peak period of their diffusion about 2500–1500 B.C. are found in peripheral regions. The greatest number of Younger Stone Age sites have been found along the west Norwegian coast north to arctic Finnmark. Here they are found both in the fiords and among the islands in settings which indicate intensive maritime fishing and hunting activity. In sites where bone has been preserved, such as Traena (Gjessing 1943), in dry caves in the Lofoten Islands (Utne, personal communication), and the Varanger area of north Norway (Simonsen 1961), large numbers of harpoons, leisters, and fishhooks are found associated with a ground slate technology of stemmed and barbed projectiles, celts, and asymmetric one-edged knives. Food bone, at least in the Varanger sites (Olsen 1967), indicates occupations in the late winter and early spring by peoples who concentrated on cod, salmon, and halibut fishing and the hunting of various seals, porpoises, small whales, walrus, and polar bear. Many of these sites, such as Gropbakkeengen and Gressbakken, are large villages which appear relatively stable during their season of occupancy with possibilities of economic as well as religious specialization (Simonsen, this volume). Even if the actual size of these sites is reduced to account for the long periods the settlements may have been used, they still remain anomalous compared to other Scandinavian sites of this or earlier periods. It is apparent that intensive seasonal maritime adaptation provided a secure economic base for large groups of people at least along the arctic coasts. Although less intense, and occasionally directed at different marine species, this type of subsistence was important for Younger Stone Age peoples throughout the Atlantic and Baltic coasts of Scandinavia and Finland. Sites of this culture group do not extend east of the Kola Peninsula into the area of closed winter pack ice.

Although the most fascinating problems in Younger Stone Age archaeology remain to be studied (e.g. whether coastal occupation was seasonal or year-round; correlation of trade materials and routes with regional subcultures and economic specialization; influence of Neolithic cultures, etc.), enough data are available to suggest that there is a strong cultural continuum throughout this period, with few distinct chronological breaks suggesting extinction or movement of peoples. It seems likely that the Younger Stone Age cultures developed locally from the earlier cultures and that much of the regionalization and development of ceramics and materials trade results from increasing economic specialization stimulated by, if not a direct result of increasing use of maritime resources. Thus we may classify the coastal YSA cultures as having variants of an INTERIOR-MARITIME or MODIFIED MARITIME adaptation type, with a possibility that certain groups maintained totally Interior economies of fish, reindeer, and moose by means of economic cooperation with coastal peoples. This distinction persisted until historic times in the north in the form of Coast and Interior Lapp societies, which are quite likely direct descendants of the earlier cultures.

Finally, we might note that the origins of the YSA ground slate and Maritime adaptations need not be far removed from nor incompatible with the rather technologically different complexes of the Older Stone Age. Although evidence for a transition is not available from most regions, Simonsen (1961) has noted a developmental sequence from the Mesolithic Komsa culture to the Younger Stone Age complexes in the Varanger Sequence and a similar transition is noted for northern Sweden (Christiansson and Broadbent, this volume).

Because maritime adaptations had evidently begun quite early one need explain only the origins of the ground slate complex. Here our best evidence is that it results from an earlier and simpler slate complex in the

Suomusjärvi culture (Luho 1967) of western Finland around 8000–6000 B.P. Early sites in Ångermanland, northern Sweden, dating to around 5500 B.P., contain ground slate implements which may be transitional between Suomusjärvi and later Scandinavian slate complexes. Present distributional and typological evidence suggests the hypothesis that the development and spread of the slate complex occurs when this early slate technology becomes meshed with the requisites of a maritime economy with its time-consuming fish and sea mammal processing activities, tasks to which ground slate tools, with their large size and smooth, easily re-sharpened edges, are eminently suited. This hypothesis is favored by the coincidence in distribution of both the slate complex and intensifying maritime adaptation in Scandinavia around 5000–4000 B.P.

## Northwest Coast

The Northwest Coast offers a good comparative case in the study of northern maritime adaptations. Its long and exceedingly diverse subarctic coastline has a rich marine and terrestrial fauna and has been available for habitation by man for at least 10,000 years. The great productivity and diversity of this region, especially in its coastal resources, has undoubtedly been a factor in producing one of the most complex culture areas in North America, linguistically, culturally, and archaeologically. Further-more, it is an area which, due to geography, has been repeatedly influenced by developments in areas as diverse as the Aleutians, Bering Sea, the Canadian Rockies, the Columbia Plateau, and the Pacific Northwest. Finally, in terms of our present study, it is an area which by virtue of its environment has required maritime familiarity throughout its period of occupation.

Unfortunately, the area is still poorly known archaeologically with the most complete information available from the southern and northern extremes of the coast. Reports of the earliest sites known on the North-west Coast are not yet published with the exception of those in the lower Fraser Valley, belonging to the Pasika, Milliken, and Mazama phases between 12,000–6,500 B.C. (Borden 1968). Excepting the problematic and un-dated pebble tool Pasika complex, these sites exhibit strong seasonal river-ine adaptations, but there is no evidence to suggest that they are interior extensions of peoples who lived during part of the year on the coast. Comparably early sites have not yet been reported in the Gulf of Georgia section of the coast. Further north, however, coastal occupations occur at Namu, in the Queen Charlotte Islands, and Gulf of Alaska which date to this early period and contain blade and microblade industries, occasional ground shell celts, and bifacial and unifacial tools (Fladmark 1970; Hester, personal communication; Ackerman, personal communication). Ground slate implements are notably absent from these early sites, which suggest, however, from their locations that seafaring and marine resources were known. When these collections are compared with those from later coastal sites it is evident that they share more common features with early sites of the interior where microblade traditions continue throughout most of the sequence.

Documentation of the shift toward increasing use of sawn and ground slate industries occurs more or less simultaneously in the northern Northwest Coast region between 5000 and 6000 B.P. as evidenced in the Ocean Bay I collections of the Kodiak Island area (Clark 1972, and this volume), and the Takli Alder phase on the Alaska Peninsula (Dumond 1971). These assemblages commonly include a predominance of chipped stone tools, including stemmed and lanceolate bifaces and points, "wedges," rough microcores, stone lamps, and boulder flake tools. At least on Kodiak Island a maritime economy is a prerequisite for occupation, and site location and faunal information suggest that, here too, salmon, seals, whales, porpoises, and sea otters were hunted.

The following Ocean Bay II period on Kodiak Island and adjacent Alaska Peninsula is characterized by a rapid development of sawn and polished slate implements, including stemmed and leaf-shaped points and knives, single-edged knives, fishing weights, and lamps. The lack of microblades and gradual development of slate technology suggests a gradual transition between Ocean Bay I and II rather than a direct replacement of population. Furthermore, it appears that the Ocean Bay I complex is itself a transitional phase between the earlier coastal blade-using cultures noted above and the succeeding evolutionary line through Kachemak and Koniag periods with only minor variations until historic times. If so, the distinct break between the early coastal cultures and the introduction of the slate complex at southern sites such as Namu (Hester, personal communication) may indicate either rapid diffusion or population movement following 5500 B.P. At present, however, it is impossible to determine the exact nature of the movement, inception, and growth of the slate technology, although a northern origin is suspected. In short, the evidence points strongly toward a continuous sequence of cultural developments along the northern coast for at least the past 6,000 years.

On the southern Northwest Coast there is no information to document the early development of the slate complex or of initial maritime adaptations. The first appearance of slate implements in this area is in the Eayem phase (5500–3500 B.P.) in the lower Fraser Valley, in the form of both chipped and ground contracting stem points and knives. During the subsequent Baldwin phase slate is utilized only for large single-edged fish cutting knives of the ulu type. In general these tools appear to be selective additions to an interior tool complex, occasionally including microblades and burinated bifaces. However, coastal influence may be evident in the development of zoomorphic stone carving and stone beads.

The earliest data for the Fraser Delta region are from the Locarno Beach phase (3000–2100 B.P.). This complex has no clear antecedents in the Fraser Delta or Valley area and may be the result of northern influence (Borden 1970: 99). Locarno Beach is a fully maritime occupation with a highly developed ground slate industry including large single- and double-edged knives, points, and a variety of ground bone tools of similar function. Toggling harpoons, leisters, small adzes of ground shell, bone, and nephrite; combs, and zoomorphic and anthropomorphic artwork are also present. Exploitation included elk, deer, seal, whale, porpoise, salmon, and shellfish. Many of these elements continue into the Marpole phase (2500–1500 B.P.) with only minor additions such as the antler wedge-stone maul and heavy-duty adze complex for large-scale woodworking, and ascendency of the barbed over the toggling harpoon in sea mammal hunting. With the Marpole phase there seems to be a reaffirmation of the local sequence, extending back into the Baldwin phase, during which the basic configuration of Northwest Coast culture is completed. Later phases did not substantially alter this pattern, although the use of ground slate gradually declined until it was restricted largely to small endblades and rectangular, single-edged fish knives.

Cultural development on the Northwest Coast suggests several interesting observations in this review of subarctic maritime adaptations which might be summarized before turning to the slightly different requirements of arctic regions: (1) It is apparent that maritime and riverine adaptations have been important during the entire period of occupation and that seasonal use of land resources provided both meat and a source of material for the extensive antler industry. (2) Erratic sea level and isostatic fluctuations have caused the submergence of many early sites. (3) Microblade and ground shell or slate industries are not found in association in the Northwest Coast or interior cultures, suggesting that the two may be functional equivalents in certain respects. Microblades disappear from coastal complexes following the spread of the slate industry after 6000 B.P. In areas where coast and interior influences mingle, such as in the Fraser Valley, one finds sequential rather than contemporaneous appearance of the two technologies. The distribution of slate technology does not appear to be a result of raw material availability since slate is equally present in the interior. (4) Boulder chip tools are found in large numbers at interior salmon fishing sites in the Fraser Valley, and they occur occasionally on coastal sites here and in southeastern Alaska. Their function, presumably for processing fish, appears to be similar to that of the larger slate knives of the coast, while in the Kodiak Island area boulder chips may also have been used in the sawn slate industry (Clark, this volume). (5) There is no clear evidence of extensive cultural influence or population movements from the interior to the coast giving rise to the maritime cultures following 6000 B.P.; nor does coastal influence appear to provide formative elements for interior cultures. Current hypotheses suggest that early movements into the central Northwest Coast are from southeast Alaska by peoples bearing core and blade industries. Present data suggest that a ground slate complex, perhaps preceded by ground bone or shell prototype technologies, originates later in the Gulf of Alaska region and moves south after 6000 B.P. at which time it is already wedded to an intensive maritime adaptation. (6) Overall, culture change on the coast is gradual and without evidence of significant cultural extinction. The lack of significant intrusions from either the coast or the interior might be taken as indicative of mutually stable population and cultural systems in these areas, suggesting that maritime adaptations have been stable and that resources of the region have not been subject to serious natural fluctuation.

*Aleutians*

A fourth area for the comparative study of maritime adaptations is found in the Aleutian Island chain, a cold water archipelago with rich marine resources. Like the Northwest Coast and much of the Scandinavian region its waters are ice free throughout the year, thus enabling a maritime subsistence pattern without the use of ice-hunting technology. In contrast to the other regions noted above, however, the Aleutian ecozone is totally maritime and estuarine in its potential for human exploitation. McCartney and Laughlin and Aigner (this volume) note that the lack of fur- and antler-bearing land mammals requires intensive adaptation to marine resources, sea birds, and invertebrates. While these resources are largely stable in terms of availability from year to year, they undergo marked seasonality, causing human subsistence strategies to vary accordingly, and occasionally resulting in periods of scarcity. Despite such periodic events, often resulting from bad weather, the Aleutian system can be described as stable and productive. In particular, the lack of seasonal ice cover reduces the major environmental hurdle causing faunal shifts, population fluctuations, or periods when game are rendered unavailable to the hunter in more northern arctic regions.

The prehistory of the Aleutian chain is almost unknown throughout its 1,200 mile span, and especially in its western end. Only a few collections are available from several of the more important island groups, and the conditions of recovery do not permit adequate chronological or cultural analyses. Only the eastern Aleutians are better studied with Laughlin's and Aigner's excavations at a succession of large village sites, including Anangula (around 8500–7800 B.P.). Sandy Beach Bay (4300–5000 B.P.), and Chaluka (3500–4000 B.P.). Based on the evidence from these and related burial sites they hypothesize an 8,000 year continuum for Aleut culture and maritime adaptation which Laughlin (1967) believes began several thousand years earlier following the submergence of the Bering Land Bridge. As seen by these authors (this volume) the core features of Aleut material and social culture, subsistence system, and population evolved gradually without major external influence from either Asia or the Alaskan mainland. As such, it is described as a steady-state system evolving in response to internal and environmental factors in isolation from other cultural and demographic systems.

At present, however, the lack of archaeological data from most regions and periods of the vast Aleutian chain makes this claim difficult to assess in terms of Aleutian prehistory in general. It is evident, for instance, at least during its later prehistory, that the eastern Aleutian participated in the westward expansion of the ground slate industry of the Alaska Peninsula which reached Akun Island sometime between 3000–1000 B.P. (Turner and Turner n.d.: 24).

Archaeologically, there is some supporting evidence for Aleut evolution during the past 8,000 years. As noted by Laughlin and Aigner the most persistent traits include the use of stone lamps, bowls, images of the deity, and red ocher grinders and pallets, harpoons, leisters, ulus, core and blade industries (absent from Chaluka), and a variety of chipped stone projectiles, knives, and scrapers (see Laughlin and Aigner, this volume, Figure 4 for complete listing). While there is definite attribute clustering and evidence of stylistic change through this period, Laughlin and Aigner feel these changes do not reflect structural changes in the Aleut system; rather, they are a result of nonfunctional style shift. This core pattern persists through the archaeological record into historic Aleut culture.

Although the tremendous extent of unknown territory makes generalization based on archaeological research in one region rather speculative, the main points of the Aleutian case may be summarized as follows: (1) In terms of human subsistence the Aleutian chain represents an exclusively maritime region devoid of significant land resources. (2) Present archaeological evidence suggests a long and stable cultural continuum with little change in material culture, religious, social, or population systems. The adaptation type would be classified as MARITIME in our typology. (3) Cultural continuity indicates that an efficient adaptation was mirrored by a relatively stable, productive ecosystem. Environmental changes have been slight and have had minimal effect on human and natural systems. (4) Blade industries persist through much of the early period of Aleut prehistory and are replaced by bifacial chipped industries by 4000 B.P. Sea hunting equipment remains relatively stable throughout the entire period with nontoggling harpoons being the dominant form. Slate industries never become important in the eastern Aleutian sequence until after 2000 B.P., perhaps because of the lack of raw material. (5) To date there is no clear archaeological evidence of Aleut influence on Northwest Coast cultures with the possible exception of blade industries of the early, pre-slate periods. Demonstrable relationships are equally lacking between the Aleut and Bering Sea regions to the north.

### The Arctic

Archaeological research in the Arctic has a long history of publication, and the interpretation of its prehistory has recently become a very complex matter, including not only the developments of Eskimo culture over the past 5,000 years, but also questions of Pleistocene and Early Man research and the increasing complication of cultural contacts, population shifts, and environmental change. Even limiting the present discussion strictly to maritime regions of the Bering Sea, the north slope of Alaska, and the central Arctic including Greenland would entail too vast a task for this occasion. Thus only the pertinent points will be discussed, while the reader is referred to the available summations (Collins 1964; Giddings 1967; Bandi 1969). The comments here are largely reserved for those groups known as having an "Eskimo" culture, including the core features of a Maritime or Modified Maritime adaptation type with an arctic ice and open water hunting technology including predominantly toggling harpoons, oil heating lamps and cooking vessels, skin boats, semi-subterranean houses, and an ability to survive continuously beyond the northern edge of the forest.

The economy of most Eskimo groups (Taylor 1966) included the hunting of seals, walrus, polar bear, occasionally whales, fish, birds, and, among land animals, primarily caribou and musk ox. Subsistence emphasis varied both seasonally and regionally with the greatest complexity occurring in northwestern Alaska where major riverine, marine, and interior Eskimo adaptations are found. In addition, environmental potential varies across the Arctic, with the greatest diversity and productivity of marine species in the Bering Strait region. Viewed both ethnographically and archaeologically, cultural complexity and stability and population density fall off as one proceeds outward from this focal point. In the eastern Arctic, which has a far reduced human carrying capacity compared to Bering Strait, a minor nuclear area occurs in the Igloolik region. These and other minor core areas were important in preserving the continuity of Eskimo traditions in the face of environmental changes which have resulted in periodic local extinction in many peripheral arctic regions (Fitzhugh 1973b).

Three Eskimo traditions are generally recognized. The older Paleo-Eskimo or Arctic Small Tool tradition, characterized by a microlithic technology with microblades and burins and beginning by 4500 B.P., includes the Denbigh Flint complex and its local derivatives, Choris and Norton cultures, as well as its eastern Arctic Paleo-Eskimo affiliates, Pre-Dorset and Dorset. In the western Arctic the Paleo-Eskimo tradition gradually evolves into the Neo-Eskimo or Northern Maritime tradition by 2500 B.P., while it persists in the form of Dorset culture in the eastern Arctic until 1000 B.P. or later. Briefly, the origins of the Northern Maritime tradition appear linked to an increasing specialized adaptation to marine fishing and hunting, finally including whales, in the Bering Sea region. Archaeologically this change is documented by a rapid growth of population in coastal settlements comparable in size to the arctic coast sites of Norway, and the introduction in Norton culture of fishing line or net sinkers and perhaps the bladder float. Concurrent developments of Okvik and Old Bering Sea cultures in Bering Strait indicate that these changes were widespread, culminating in the establishment of Eskimo culture as known historically, including all of the major artifact types and subsistence systems, such as whaling and dog-sled transportation. Not least important in establishing the new emphasis on maritime hunting were the social and ideological changes which made increased economic cooperation possible.

A third Eskimo tradition, known as the Pacific Eskimo-Aleut tradition (de Laguna 1934; Collins 1964: 91), has been cited as a separate cultural province with a unique history. The status of relationships at an early period between the Aleutians and southwest Alaska is unclear, with some specialists insisting the two provinces have distinctly separate prehistories (Laughlin and Aigner, this volume) while others believe that they were originally unified (Dumond 1968). Present research on early sites in the Gulf of Alaska begins to show more resemblance to Anangula. However, by 5000 B.P. the Alaskan sites diverge from the Aleutian material seen at Chaluka with the development of ground slate industries. Further data will be needed to resolve these relationships.

More specifically addressing the problems of this article, the following observations could be made:

1. Eskimo cultural evolution can be traced back for 6,000 years during which a number of discrete complexes have formed and changed due to environmental shift, internal and, especially in the western Arctic, external stimuli. Despite the evidence of a number of important population movements and periodic localized extinction, especially in the eastern Arctic, the continuity and stability of Eskimo adaptations can be seen both in terms of technological complexes such as microblades and burin traditions and in adaptation complexes.

2. Arctic marine resources, especially seals, seem to have relatively stable populations, and resource fluctuation in general would appear to result largely from stochastic or directional climatic and environmental change. In this regard, ice distribution and the frequency of severe storms are the most serious factors affecting human survival in the north. While the core areas of the Arctic cannot be described as "marginal" for man, certain peripheral areas have never been able to support human life, and others appear to have sustained it only periodically. For this reason, mobility and technological ingenuity must have been early requirements of Eskimo culture.

3. The increased complexity of Eskimo cultural developments in the western Arctic and North Pacific as compared with the more isolated and slowly evolving traditions of the east reflect increased environmental potential and human population density, cultural stability, as well as increased cultural contacts.

4. No general statement can be made about Eskimo seasonal adaptations because they are extremely variable from region to region. However, overall, the relative lack of large sites and substantial winter houses in the eastern Arctic during the Paleo-Eskimo period suggests that groups here were smaller and more mobile than those in the west. While seasonal resource fluctuation occurs as well in the Bering Sea, the increased concentration of species allows exploitation within smaller areas.

5. Pertinent technological changes include the shift, in the western Arctic, from microblades and burin industries in the Arctic Small Tool

tradition about 3000–5000 B.P. to the Choris and Norton industries which retained the earlier bifacial tool and flaking styles while replacing the microblade industry with ground slate tools generally in the form of asymmetric knives and ulus. Ground slate technology, however, did not spread north of Norton Sound into the Ipiutak and Okvik/Old Bering Sea culture areas until the beginning of Punuk times, around 1000 B.P. Following this there is a rapid expansion of slate use which replaces most chipped stone tools and becomes the foundation of the lithic industry of the Eastern and Western Thule cultures, where the major tool types are ground slate ulus, asymmetric knives, harpoon endblades, and gravers. Most cutting functions, including those on bone, antler, ivory, and soap-stone, were accomplished with slate or, when available, by iron traded from Asia or Greenland, or from meteoric sources. The spread of the slate technology in Thule culture into an area in the eastern Arctic where Arctic Small Tool chipped stone microblade and biface industries had existed for over 3,000 years must be related to conscious choice and probably to increased efficiency of tool production, conservation, and utility. Distribution of raw materials cannot be a factor in its selection. Since it appears in association with the inception of large-scale whaling it is possible that it is related to the greater requirements of blubber cutting, massive butchering, and perhaps skin cleaning required for umiak and thong production.

Two other occurrences of slate grinding occur among Arctic cultures. Slate appears in most periods of Dorset culture in the form of knives and specialized scrapers. Most prominent in early Dorset, it never usurps the major role taken by the microblade and chipped stone industry. Its use appears as an experiment in a specialized class of tools and declines after several centuries. The second occurrence is a major expansion of slate grinding in the Northeast Greenland "Mixed Culture" of the sixteenth to seventeenth centuries A.D. in the Clavering Island area (Larsen 1934). Known primarily from sites on Dodemansbugten, the Clavering sites appear to be a local development, based on the simpler slate industry of the Greenland Thule and Inugsuk cultures. They exhibit a great array of polished and drilled slate forms, including ulus, single- and double-edged knives (some tanged and seemingly with finger gaps, copied from Euro-pean knives from ship wrecks or Norse contact), triangular and stemmed end blades, drills, gravers, rods, and adzes. Shortly after their discovery in the nineteenth century, the Clavering people vanished, perhaps the victims of the contemporary extinction of the northeast Greenland caribou.

*Northeastern Asia*

A sixth northern maritime region to be considered is the region extending from the Chukchi Peninsula south to Kamchatka, the Kuril Islands, Hokkaido, Sakhalin, and the Okhotsk Sea. With a few spotty exceptions it is an area whose early prehistory is almost completely unknown, where speculation, black light, and negative evidence are freely employed tools of archaeological interpretation. Nevertheless, it is in this area that some of the most pressing problems of North Pacific research remain to be solved. Primary among them is the question of the independent or common origin of Eskimo, Aleut, and Okhotsk maritime adaptations.

Within this zone three areas are known to have developed maritime adaptations. In the Chukchi Peninsula there is a full range of the later Eskimo cultures including Okvik, Old Bering Sea, Punuk, Thule, and historic Eskimo. Earlier sites of the Arctic Small Tool Tradition are not well known; neither have transitional sites relating to many of the intermediate coastal cultures of Alaska been found. Eskimo sites are confined to the areas immediately adjacent to Bering Strait and are not known beyond the north shore of Anadyr Gulf (Chard 1962: 213). To the south there is a very long stretch of coast, including most of Kamchatka, about which nothing is known. However, in the Magadan district along the northern shore of the Okhotsk Sea, sites of the Ancient Koryak culture, dating to the first millennium A.D., have produced evidence of an important maritime adaptation similar to that of Eskimo and Aleut culture, including the diagnostic elements of toggling and barbed harpoons, blubber lamps, needle cases, fishhooks, sinkers, armor plates, shovels, subterranean houses, stable villages, and suggestions of a sea mammal religious cult. An important pottery tradition is also found, and there is evidence of wooden boats and occasional iron tools introduced from the south or west. The marine resources available on this coast are extremely plentiful and include several species of seal, sea lion, sea otter, beluga, whales, and fish, while the nearby interior mountains contain reindeer, sheep, and deer. Large reindeer migrations to the coast occur annually in the spring. The culture of the Ancient Koryak is related to a third contemporaneous maritime group, known as the Okhotsk culture (Befu and Chard 1964; Ohyi, this volume), which dates between 500 and 1200 A.D., perhaps lasting until the seventeenth century in the Kuril Islands and Sakhalin. Both the Ancient Koryak and Okhotsk cultures are primarily sea hunting and fishing groups, although land game was seasonally important with domesticated pig becoming increasingly important with time. In Sakhalin, Hokkaido, and the Kurils, the Okhotsk culture was replaced by a southern intrusion of Satsumon culture, probably the prehistoric Ainu, displaced from locations in southern Hokkaido by the Japanese cultural expansions. This abrupt termination is not seen in the Ancient Koryak culture, which continues into protohistoric Koryak with substantial new introductions resulting from contacts with Bronze and Iron Age cultures. Place names suggest that a very large area is included in the ethnographic Koryak culture distribution stretching north throughout much of the archaeologically unknown regions. It should not be assumed that these areas were uninhabited prehistorically or that they may not have served as areas of important maritime developments linking the Okhotsk and Chukchi regions, just because they are unknown archaeologically.

The rapidity with which the Ancient Koryak and Okhotsk sea hunting cultures developed and spread throughout the Okhotsk Sea region and their strong similarities with Eskimo and Aleutian cultures, including such elements as harpoon types and traits, needlecases, shovels, and engraved art styles, has created considerable interest in their origins. Befu and Chard (1964; Chard 1960) have argued for a northern origin from the Bering Sea Eskimo (and possibly Aleut) cultures on the grounds that Okhotsk culture, their principal concern, is not typologically or geographically related to preceding maritime hunting developments of southern Hokkaido and Japan in the post-Jomon and Jomon cultures of the last millennium B.C., nor does it stem from earlier traditions in northern Hokkaido. Rather, they argue for its initial development in Sakhalin as a crystallization of disparate local and continental elements, such as a mainland (Amur region) ceramic tradition, and important new ideas introduced by diffusion or intrusion from the north — primarily the sea mammal hunting complex — producing an economic base for its rapid expansion. Physical anthropological evidence provides equivocal evidence for an actual intrusion of Eskimo people into this area (Befu and Chard 1964: 13). However, students of the Okhotsk and Ancient Koryak cultures such as Ohyi and Vasilievsky maintain that the Eskimo parallels, extensive as they are, do not relate to a specific Bering Sea or Aleutian complex but are found in traits scattered in different groups and periods. Further, they believe that though Eskimo influence may occur, there are significant differences in harpoon styles, pottery, and other elements which point to local, though diverse, origins. These authors have proposed the alternate hypothesis that the origins may be found in either the Amur-Maritime Territories region (Ohyi, this volume) or from an earlier period of Ancient Koryak culture known from the Magadan region, where sites with a more balanced interior and maritime economy are known (Vasilievsky 1969: 152). According to the *in situ* theories emphasis is placed on the gradual development of a maritime adaptation from either a seasonal riverine focus, such as persisted for over 5,000 years in the Amur region, or from a mixed interior hunting economy such as is found around Magadan. Recently Vasilievsky (1968) has emphasized Okhotsk-Koryak similarities with the Aleutian-Southwest Alaskan cultures, ideas which have also been expressed by Collins (1968) and which point to influence through a closer relationship at an earlier time.

In the absence of sufficient archaeological information, particularly about the western Aleutians, no resolution of this problem is available; yet it remains a crucial question, for if recent Eskimo or Aleut influence were found to have been the stimulus, one must explain why a maritime adaptation did not develop in this region of plentiful marine resources until the last 2,000 years. This would be a significant lacuna in the circumpolar maritime zone. With Jomon and post-Jomon cultures flourishing to the south, including sea hunting capabilities, and with stable riverine adapted peoples for several thousand years in the Amur River area, it seems unlikely that the potential of the Okhotsk Sea region would have remained untapped.

Secondly, within the Koryak-Okhotsk cultures several distinctions stand out when compared to other circumpolar maritime traditions. In contrast to most of these, the Okhotsk culture and its supposed ancestral cultures in Sakhalin and on the mainland were relatively sedentary in their settlement pattern, with well-constructed houses, a developed ceramic tradition, and a nearly exclusive use of marine, riverine, and estuarine fauna. Sites were usually constructed near river mouths or on spits where fishing and sea mammal hunting was good. A few summer camps are known, but in general groups tended to live in reasonably large sites which were occupied most, if not all, of the year. In most cases, only nearby land resources — generally small game — were utilized to supplement marine resources. Large land mammals were economically important only in the northern Koryak groups. In many of the island regions, such as the Kurils, large land mammals did not exist, as in the Aleutian Islands. Thus, in general, subsistence was totally maritime in nature. Undoubtedly, seasonal factors affected the economic cycle, but they seem not to have required settlement displacement or extensive land mobility as occurred in Scandinavia or Labrador. Increased population stability is one of the major results of this adaptation, as noted in the evolution of regional and chronologically distinct pottery styles and a great, bewildering proliferation of harpoon types despite the short duration period of the culture. Increased sedentarism, similar to that of Aleut and some Bering Sea groups, may have originated from possible ancestral stable riverine adaptations such as are seen in the Amur region, and also in the large mainland shell mound sites, which may be transitional between full riverine and maritime adaptations. Excepting the sea hunting complex, about which little is known on the mainland, this appears to be the route by which ceramic developments reached the Hokkaido and Okhotsk Sea regions.

In other areas, it is evident that the Okhotsk and Ancient Koryak cultures include a strong chipped stone industry largely dominated by bifacial contracting stemmed projectiles. Ground stone celts are also common. Polished slate implements are not found in Okhotsk collections except for a few points from sites on Sakhalin, the presumed hearth area for the culture; neither are blade or microblade industries found. This combined absence is reminiscent of the past 5,000 years of Aleutian prehistory.

Another important factor is the diversity of economic and technological factors in the development of the Okhotsk-Koryak complexes. Ceramics were introduced from the mainland Maritime Territories; iron was used occasionally for harpoon blades, and tenth-century Japanese swords were included in a lavish Mororo burial; the domesticated dog is found, while domesticated pigs, ultimately of mainland origin in the first millennium B.C., are found in early Okhotsk sites in Sakhalin. It is evident that there were important developments occurring in regions surrounding the Okhotsk Sea, and that economic relationships between inland, coastal, and maritime cultures must have been complex. Study of the maritime cultures, whose developments may be a partial response to pressures of these external economic changes, cannot be undertaken without reference to these events.

Finally, it is instructive to note that Japanese expansion into Hokkaido may have terminated the Okhotsk culture by forcing the Satsumon culture north into the Okhotsk region, where they are later recognized as maritime adapted Ainu, whereas their ancestors in southern Hokkaido were largely interior dwellers. Further, the Ainu utilized a limited maritime adaptation in this new environment without the specialized sea hunting complex of the Okhotsk culture, demonstrating the flexibility of economic requirements and adaptation types in the face of historical events.

*Yamal*

The final comparative zone, the Yamal region including the lower Ob River and its Arctic Sea environs, is one in which a maritime adaptation known as the Ust'-Poluj complex is reported to have existed as early as the Iron Age (around 2500 B.P.). Despite publications by Cernetsov (1935, 1953), Okladnikov (1960), and Moshinskaia (1970) remarkably little is known of this geographically important culture. Ust'-Poluj is reported to be a hunting and fishing culture with a mixed economy including, especially in its northern areas, adaptation to sea mammals, reindeer, and roe deer. Dog traction and possibly reindeer breeding are suggested. Other cultural traits include semisubterranean houses, ditch and bank earthwork "fortification," snow shovels, ice creepers, barbed harpoons, and pottery. Indications of contact with more advanced societies to the south are seen in the sporadic finds of iron and bronze tools. In the northern regions the Ust'-Poluj complex may have persisted without much change until the sixteenth to seventeenth centuries A.D. as suggested by folklore and documentary evidence of a maritime-adapted people in this area who ceased to exist shortly thereafter.

Moberg (this volume) raises a number of questions regarding the Ust'-Poluj complex which require clarification from Soviet archaeologists. In particular, its external relationships and origins are in doubt since Okladnikov originally suggested that the complex was "autochthonous" but with contacts ranging from the Kola burial sites to the Urals and China; while, most recently, Moshinskaia (1970) sees direct Bering Strait Eskimo influence in the dog traction and sea mammal hunting elements. Further, the possible existence of other hitherto unsuspected maritime adaptations along the arctic coast of the Soviet Union may eventually require reconsideration of the Eurasian diffusion hypothesis.

## DISCUSSION

*Chronology and Historical Relationships*

Figure 1 illustrates the data presently available for the origin and distribution of circumpolar maritime adaptations. Several points might be made concerning the earliest evidence for this adaptation type. First, it is evident that maritime adaptations are not recent phenomena for they appear in the North Pacific and in northern Europe and Scandinavia as early as 10,000 years ago. Second, although the nature of these early adaptations cannot be characterized in detail, they are evidently based on seasonal (MODIFIED INTERIOR) rather than specialized or intensive (MARITIME) adaptations, with land game being seasonally important. The earliest evidence of a specialized MARITIME type adaptation occurs at the

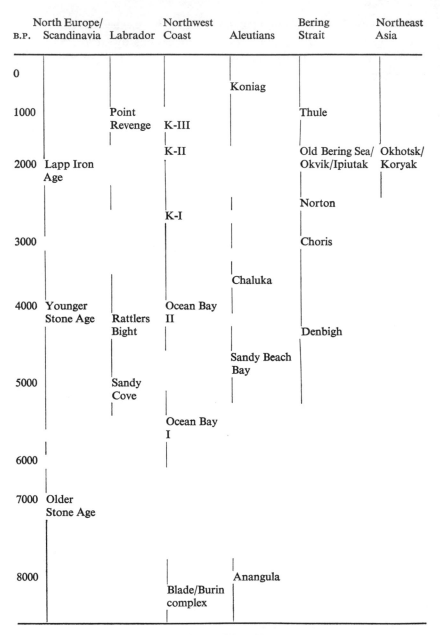

| B.P. | North Europe/ Scandinavia | Labrador | Northwest Coast | Aleutians | Bering Strait | Northeast Asia |
|---|---|---|---|---|---|---|
| 0 | | | | Koniag | | |
| 1000 | | Point Revenge | K-III | | Thule | |
| 2000 | Lapp Iron Age | | K-II | | Old Bering Sea/ Okvik/Ipiutak | Okhotsk/ Koryak |
| | | | | | Norton | |
| | | | K-I | | | |
| 3000 | | | | | Choris | |
| | | | | Chaluka | | |
| 4000 | Younger Stone Age | Rattlers Bight | Ocean Bay II | | | |
| | | | | | Denbigh | |
| | | | | Sandy Beach Bay | | |
| 5000 | | Sandy Cove | | | | |
| | | | Ocean Bay I | | | |
| 6000 | | | | | | |
| 7000 | Older Stone Age | | | | | |
| 8000 | | | Blade/Burin complex | Anangula | | |

Figure 1.   Chronology of circumpolar maritime adaptations

site of Anangula 8,000 years ago. Third, all of the early maritime adaptations appear to have developed from interior cultures in which burin and
blade industries were the dominant elements of the lithic technology. In

the Aleutian Islands, Northwest Coast, and Scandinavia this burin and blade complex persists in a seasonal maritime economy until approximately 6000 B.P.

A second stage in the development of maritime adaptations occurs about 6000 B.P. At this time there is a definite intensification of marine hunting, including an elaboration of a sea mammal hunting technology, increased coastal sedentarism (sometimes in large stable villages), economic and religious specialization, and long distance contact and trade. One of the particular features of this transition is the replacement of the burin and blade complex by bifacial chipped stone and ground slate industries.

The fullest expression of this trend is found in the Northwest Coast and Scandinavia ground slate complexes of 5000–3500 B.P. where these developments seem to result from gradual intensification of seasonal maritime adaptations established during earlier periods. However, other maritime adaptations arise in areas where there are no known antecedents, such as in northeastern North America and, slightly later, Bering Strait. While the Bering Strait developments may relate to an earlier zone of maritime interactions along the North Pacific rim, there can be little doubt that at least in the northeastern Maritimes, the North Pacific, and northern Europe and Scandinavia, maritime adaptations began as independent phenomena. Historical contacts and diffusion through the circumpolar zone cannot account for observed similarities of these three major northern maritime regions. On the present evidence contacts between these areas cannot be supported on the basis of either diffusion of specific attributes, artifacts, or industries; nor can they be explained by movements of people. Any historically derived similarities in these regions must be so general in nature that, like ground stone woodworking tools and bone and antler industries, they must pertain to man's first adaptation to the northern lake and forest zone at an earlier time than that considered here. As a result, we must consider the evolution of specific sea mammal hunting complexes including their associated harpoon and ground slate industries in at least these three regions as independent developments whose similarities result largely from functional considerations. In fact, a close inspection of ground slates (see Leroi-Gourhan 1946; Ritchie 1968; Fitzhugh 1975) and harpoon types from these regions indicates a lack of genetic similarity except in basic, functional features.

However, one cannot help remarking on the peculiarities in this second stage intensification of maritime adaptations in which slate industries become dominant. According to a widely-held belief (Shetelig 1922; Gjessing 1944; Ritchie 1968) slate grinding originated when techniques of grooving, grinding, and honing developed for bone-working in the Paleolithic were transferred to a new and more durable medium. Another theory oft touted is the "substitution theory" (Bakka n.d.) which claims that slate grinding began in areas where sources of quality flint or metal were unavailable to local inhabitants. Whatever the merits of these beliefs, and at present the derivation theory appears a sounder one, they are more concerned with the mechanics of slate grinding than with the causes for its appearance. The question to be asked is not how this occurred, but what the conditions were under which it was selected. Put in this context we are confronted with a series of coincidences in the evolution of slate complexes in the circumpolar regions. First, there is the remarkable synchroneity in the time of their appearance, around 5000–6000 B.P., in independent historical contexts in Scandinavia, northeastern North America, and the North Pacific. Secondly, in each instance the major development occurs in a northern maritime adaptation in subarctic waters, although inland expressions of a restricted nature are often found in the adjacent interior areas. Finally, with the exception of the Denbigh complex, each of the expansions of ground slate industries involved the replacement of a burin and blade complex. The coincidence of these circumstances and their surrounding context calls for more than explanation as isolated historical events. Rather a more analytical approach including adaptive and functional investigations may provide a fuller explanation of these similar developments. While the following discussion does not purport to provide answers to the problem in cross-cultural evolutionary terms certain fruitful approaches are suggested.

*Climatic Factors*

One obvious route of inquiry lies in the area of environmental factors. In particular, the sudden appearance of MODIFIED INTERIOR and MARITIME adaptations throughout most circumpolar regions raises the possibility of a unified cause, related to the onset of Atlantic (hypsithermal) climatic conditions which may have resulted in some basic shift in the relationships between land and marine ecosystems. Such an explanation might be supported if a decline in the abundance of the major land fauna of the circumpolar region, primarily reindeer and caribou, could be documented. As has been suggested for the Middle Period of Labrador's prehistory, there appear to have been times when Interior or Modified Interior adaptations were unstable due to increased incidence of forest fires, excessive winter snows or icing, or disease. That such a factor could be expressed synchronously in global terms remains to be proven, and in fact, seems unlikely; however, there is evidence of coincident growth and decline of widely separate North American caribou and moose populations over the past century which raises the possibility of similar population changes occurring throughout the northern hemisphere. Such an event might cause intensification of the maritime aspect of the earlier seasonal economies, such as that suggested for the origins of Dorset culture in the eastern Arctic (Fitzhugh 1973b). An alternate explanation for maritime intensification in Scandinavia and the American Northeast may lie in the northward movement of the boreal forest at this time, allowing peoples with less intensive maritime adaptations access to the rich unexploited subarctic seas. Quite likely, unique factors and a combination of circumstances, including climatic factors, will provide the answer to this strange synchronous development. This problem deserves extensive research as does the equally synchronous decline of the major ground slate maritime complexes in Scandinavia, Labrador, and on the Northwest Coast.

## Functional and Technological Aspects

In addition to the historical implications of this comparative study there is a series of functional and technological questions regarding the harpoon, ground slate, and projectile complexes which are the center-fold of the northern maritime adaptation type.

HARPOON COMPLEX    The detachable harpoon appears to have developed relatively early in the Upper Paleolithic as a device to hold game fast while dispatching it with a lance or other weapon. In the Mesolithic cultures of northern Europe its primary function was for harpooning fish and seals. We may expect that its distribution was widespread throughout the circumpolar zone of Eurasia, and it seems likely that man on the Bering Land Bridge possessed this implement, which, together with fishhooks and leisters, provides a core complex for northern maritime adaptations in subarctic waters.

The distribution of various types of harpoons (see Leroi-Gourhan 1946) in these northern maritime cultures suggests that environmental factors may play a role in the functional attributes of this sea hunting complex. Primarily, one finds that detachable harpoons are the basic type found in subarctic regions and that with a few exceptions (possibly early pre-Dorset) arctic hunting complexes employ the toggling harpoon and foreshaft. Nearly identical forms of toggling harpoons and occasionally fore-shafts are found in low frequency in all the maritime zones, giving further evidence of the strength of maritime technological convergence. This distinction between toggling and nontoggling types suggests a greater efficiency for the toggling harpoon and foreshaft combination in ice hunting situations where the presence of obstructions would tend to dislodge a harpoon that only penetrated part way through the skin of an animal. Arutiunov and Sergeev (in this volume) have noted a similar distinction between toggling and nontoggling forms which correspond to icebound and open water hunting locations of Eskimo sites on the Chukchi Peninsula. The invention of the toggling harpoon and foreshaft therefore may have been instrumental in the formation of Paleo-Eskimo culture and man's extension into the Arctic.

GROUND SLATE COMPLEX   A second conclusion of the study concerns the mutual exclusion noted between burin industries and ground slate tool complexes. Early maritime developments in Scandinavia, the Aleutians, and the Northwest coast include important burin and blade tools which can be assumed to have been used to work antler, bone, hide, skins, wood, and other materials. In both Scandinavia and the Northwest Coast, how-ever, this industry was replaced by one in which ground slate knives and projectiles became dominant, while in many of the adjacent interior areas the older tradition still persisted for many thousands of years. This occurrence leads to conclusions which remain to be fully tested but which appear to have general validity in functional and environmental terms.

Specifically, it appears that northern maritime cultures tend to develop ground slate tool complexes while interior adaptations do not. Cause for such an evolutionary tendency may be seen in the types of activities and functions which distinguish the two types of adaptations. Interior cultures of the boreal regions tend to be mobile groups in which large land animals such as caribou, reindeer, and moose provide most of the food and tech-nologic materials for the economy; bark rather than skin boats are com-monly used; and in general water travel is less extensive than for maritime dwellers. Consequently, skin and hide preparation is generally limited to the preparation of clothing, sleeping blankets, and occasionally tents. Cutting functions, including meat butchering, do not constitute major time investments for interior peoples. Bifacial chipped tools, flakes, and blades are sufficient instruments for these tasks.

Among maritime adapted peoples however, these cutting and processing functions are augmented by far more time consuming activities of hide preparation for boat covers, tents, and thongs, most of which are made from sea mammal hides which are extremely difficult to clean due to the thick adhering blubber layer. Finally, the gutting and splitting of fish is a task which requires long hours and sharp knives. In this type of technology some selective advantage may be gained by the use of ground slate tools to which metal tools are a close equivalent. Unlike chipped tools which require frequent reflaking and are consumed relatively rapidly, ground slate tools may be resharpened quickly during use and are not subject to rapid attrition. Furthermore, their edge is straight, without sharp serrations, and is suited for cutting soft flesh, and scraping and flensing hides where maximum pressure must be applied across a large surface and where nicks and perforations would be damaging, as for boat covers or gut clothing.

On the interior, where microblades are used predominantly for inset knives or side-armed lances there is little advantage in the use of ground slate tools. Correspondingly, they are rarely found here, even in areas contiguous to regions occupied by slate-using peoples. In some cases, as in north Norway, the use of slate may have been seasonal with another complex being used during the interior portion of the cycle. Generally, when slate diffused to interior groups it appears in the form of projectile points, while in other cases, as in the Fraser Valley, fishing sites contain slate knives only.

Many of the typological similarities noted between circumpolar slate complexes which have been attributed to historical contact are actually the result of convergence due to functional criteria such as these. Carved single-edged knives with handles, such as the banana-form type, are found in Scandinavia, east Greenland, Labrador, and southwest Alaska; stemmed and barbed projectiles have evolved in Scandinavia, the Northeast, and Alaska; ulu-type tools occur in every zone. Nevertheless unexplainable and striking similarities occur which are difficult to explain in functional terms, such as the horizontal grooves found on the blades of barbed projectiles of Alaska and Scandinavia.

PROJECTILE TYPOLOGY A review of projectile types in northern maritime complexes reveals that stemmed forms are more often associated with technologies that include toggling harpoon and lance procurement systems, as in the Arctic, where penetrations and stabbing functions are more important than laceration and holding power. Larger projectiles, often including broad-bladed and barbed forms, are more commonly found in open water areas where nontoggling harpoons and dart killing techniques are used, as in Norway and the Northwest Coast. In such cases, slender lance tips are usually found as well. These patterns suggest that greater attention should be paid to functional criteria and "invisible" technology.

## Northern Maritime Technological Complex

In cross-cultural terms there is great significance in the independent origins of these northern ground slate complexes for they indicate common developmental patterns which are potentially more important for understanding cultural processes than is the sterilizing pronouncement of common ancestry. Of particular significance is the fact that these northern cultures developed ground slate industries approximately contemporaneously within the context of a northern maritime adaptation. Although each complex varies in the typological forms employed, all share certain functional equivalents of a maritime adaptation requiring large convex edge cutting and scraping knives of the ulu type, and a variety of other stabbing, piercing, and cutting forms. So consistently are these functions translated into ground slate tool complexes in northern sea hunting and fishing cultures that it is suggested that they be considered examples of a broadly defined NORTHERN MARITIME TECHNOLOGICAL COMPLEX. Generally accompanying this complex is a woodworking industry of pecked or ground celts or adzes. The northern maritime technological complex is a cross-cultural construction predicated on the functional and adaptive requirements of a maritime hunting and fishing subsistence, which, I submit is substantially different from the technological requirements of northern boreal or tundra adaptations in the increased importance of sea mammal and fish procurement and processing. Specifically, northern maritime adaptations generally require the use of large skin or wooden boats, tailored waterproof garments, thong, and often of oil heating. Butchering and processing of marine resources toward these ends entails greater attention than needed for interior adaptations. It is suggested as a hypothesis that under these circumstances cultural selection gravitated toward the development of the northern maritime technological complex which provided a superior technology for cultures adapted to life to the arctic and subarctic seas.

This complex does not imply historical or diffusional concepts. It is a functionally adaptive complex of nonspecific cultural identification which is of use in cross-cultural developmental and evolutionary studies. Its value as a functional defined complex keyed to the subarctic and arctic littoral is that it can be analyzed with input from archaeology, ethnology, history, and functional and environmental studies.

## Social and Economic Aspects

SEASONALITY    As noted in Labrador, seasonality has an important role in maintaining MODIFIED INTERIOR and INTERIOR adaptation types such as those found in Scandinavia, the Northeast, and the Northwest Coast which could not have existed on the coast due to the absence of resources during part of the year. Only in the richest marine ecosystems, such as the Aleutians, certain areas of the Bering Strait, and perhaps the Okhotsk Sea region are there sufficient resources for a full MARITIME adaptation.

The historical importance of seasonality and settlement shifts in the evolution of maritime adaptations cannot be undervalued. It is largely through such shifts that maritime adaptations were originated by interior hunting peoples beginning to utilize coastal resources or through the increasingly coastal orientation of a riverine adaptation. Without such alternate strategies maritime adaptations would not have developed the stability to maintain themselves as they did in the North Pacific and Bering Sea. In addition, these enforced movements have resulted in fertilizing different cultural traditions across coastal and interior boundaries, eventually resulting in economic and social changes which have transformed many of these societies.

STABILITY    Conversely, maritime adaptations have provided the potential for cultural developments not found elsewhere in the taiga or forest regions of the circumpolar interior. These include:
1.   Increased absolute population density
2.   Concentration of population within seasonal or permanent settlements
3.   Intensification of religious expression through external contact (Ipiutak) and expansion of cultural sphere (Moorehead Cult)
4.   A trend towards specialization of labor and religion
5.   Expansion of culture area and intensification of external contacts
6.   Growth of trade and economic relationships beyond the subsistence area of the society
7.   Persistence of industrial traditions and artifact styles
8.   Elaboration of social structure (bilateral to clan types)
9.   Tendency toward establishment of property rights

## Propositions

The foregoing survey has resulted in a number of hypotheses which require further testing with archaeological data from the circumpolar region. As the study of cross-cultural processes and comparative archaeology in this area is only beginning, they are set forth here as tentative statements as determined from currently available information.

1. Cultural traditions of the northern maritime zone appear to have relatively great time depth and are generally free of evidence of major population replacement and cultural change. Where extensive changes occur, as in Scandinavia and Asia, they are often the result of external cultural influence from higher technological centers. In other areas culture change in maritime adaptations is slow and cumulative, and deeply-rooted cultural traditions are evident.

2. Where a variety of interior and maritime adaptations are present in the north it appears that cultural longevity is correlated with intensity of maritime adaptation. This is especially true in the Labrador area. In most other areas the state of interior and coastal archaeology does not permit positive statements to be made. Further research is needed into the relative stability and longevity of cultural traditions based on interior, modified-interior, and maritime adaptations in circumpolar regions.

3. In all of the areas considered seasonality has been extremely important in the development of maritime adaptations. In particular, seasonal adaptations requiring movements from coast to interior are characteristic of all of the northern areas surveyed except the Aleutians. Most maritime adaptations appear to have developed initially as seasonal coastal or riverine extensions of interior adaptations; while, further, seasonality and population movements have been conduits by which external cultural impulses were received and integrated. In areas where maritime adaptations did not require such movements, as in the Aleutians, population and cultural systems have been relatively stable.

4. Geographic isolation has been important in maintaining persistent cultural systems in the Aleutians. However, self-dependency has led to cultural isolation and continuity in less geographically isolated regions such as the Northwest Coast and north Norway.

5. There is a tendency in maritime adaptations toward the development of a northern maritime technological complex including the use of bone and antler harpoons, ground slate cutting and piercing tools, and often heavy wood or bone/antler working tools. The northern maritime technological complex is suggested as a cross-cultural adaptive complex geared to the requirements of a northern cold water fishing and sea mammal hunting subsistence which is distinct from technological complexes required by northern interior adaptations.

6. In most areas of the north the intensification of maritime adaptations,

increase in the size of settlement sites and regional populations, and increased sedentarism appear to be related phenomena. It is suggested that the predictability and productivity of northern maritime ecosystems provides the basis for these developments.

7.   The data reviewed here are not sufficient to assess Chard's caveat:

(1) that many people will live on the sea without making much use of it until they are initiated by outside influences; and (2) [with the situation on the Amur River in mind] that riverine peoples do not inevitably evolve into maritime ones through the operation of some inexorable cultural law ... (1962: 216).

These points deserve further consideration when more specific comparative data are available.


## Beyond Maritime Adaptations

As a final comment in this study of circumpolar maritime adaptations it is useful to consider the causes which seem to have brought these traditions to an end and the directions in which they led their respective histories and prehistories. As we have seen, the only adaptations to remain relatively unchanged — those that might be called "homeostatic" cultural systems — were those of the Aleutian Islands and the Arctic. Here the biological and cultural adaptation was stable and there was a lack of external stimuli, particularly in the form of economic factors, so that the cultural systems remained essentially the same until extensive contact with Western culture forced their transformation. Isolation has been the preservative of these traditions.

A second group of maritime adaptations might be included in the category of "intensifying" cultural systems, exemplified by the Northwest Coast cultures in which a stable adaptation permitted the elaboration and intensification of all forms of social, religious, and economic interactions, but which were sufficiently isolated from unsettling economic events so that, like the Eskimo and Aleut, they were able to preserve their cultural identity and traditions until very recently. In fact, in this case the maritime adaptation and geographic isolation served as focalizing elements in the internalization of Western influence.

A third group of cultures may be included in the framework of "evolving" cultural systems. These include the Scandinavian and Okhotsk maritime adaptations which were substantially transformed by the introduction of domesticated animals and grains together with economic intercourse with metal-using societies.

These changes suggest that there are limits to the level of cultural complexity which can be achieved by northern maritime adaptations without participation in "the civilizational process." The Eskimo, Aleut, and to some extent the Northwest Coast peoples approached these limits at their own cultural capacity. Most of these limitations were environmental, relating to the potential to stabilize the food base further and the inability to increase social and economic developments. However, in some of these regions, such as Scandinavia, new economic systems including domestic animals and grains were readily and smoothly incorporated into the previous hunting and fishing pattern because their previous maritime adaptation and settlement system was, in effect, preadapted for further intensification of the economic base. Such a development in Scandinavia felt little impact from the overall growth of the European economic and cultural scene, but other more historic cases could be cited, such as the adoption of agriculture by coastal fishing villages in Peru in the third millennium B.C. In short, the economic and cultural stability of maritime adaptations has frequently provided a basis for further complex cultural developments similar to those seen in agricultural societies. Thus we may see that maritime adaptations have served as the economic base for some of the most elaborate prehistoric cultural developments in the circumpolar zone, in addition to contributing to the cultural diversity of today's world. Investigation of the cultural potential and of the historical and evolutionary consequences of this type of adaptation should result in significant advances in our limited understanding of general anthropological processes.

## REFERENCES

ADAMS, ROBERT MC.
  1966   *The evolution of urban society: early Mesopotamia and prehispanic Mexico.* Chicago: Aldine.
BAKKA, EGIL
  n.d.   "Functional and typological aspects of Scandinavian slate points." Unpublished manuscript.
BANDI, HANS-GEORG
  1969   *Eskimo prehistory.* Translated by A. E. Keep. University of Alaska Press. Distributed by University of Washington Press, Seattle.
BEFU, HARUMI, CHESTER CHARD
  1964   A prehistoric maritime culture of the Okhotsk Sea. *American Antiquity* 30(1):1–18.
BINFORD, L. R.
  1968   "Past Pleistocene adaptations," in *New perspectives in archeology.*

Edited by L. R. Binford and S. R. Binford, 313–361. Chicago: Aldine.

BORDEN, CHARLES
1968 "Prehistory of the lower mainland," in *Lower Fraser Valley: evolution of a cultural landscape.* Edited by A. H. Siemens, 9–26. B. C. Geographical Series 9. Department of Geography, University of British Columbia.
1970 Culture history of the Fraser Delta region: an outline. *BC Studies* 6–7:95–112. Vancouver.

BRYAN, ALAN
1957 Results and interpretations of recent archeological research in western Washington with circum-boreal implications. *Davidson Journal of Anthropology* 3(1):1–16.

CERNETSOV, N. V.
1935 Drevnjaja primorskaja kul'tura na poluostrove Ja-mal. *Sovetskaja etnografija*, pages 109–133.
1953 "Ust'-Polyeskoe Vremya v Priob'e," *Materialy i Issledovaniya po Arkheologiyi SSR*, No. 35.

CHARD, CHESTER
1960 "Northwest Coast – Northeast Asiatic similarities: a new hypothesis," in *Selected Papers of the Fifth International Congress of Anthropological and Ethnological Sciences.* Edited by A. F. C. Wallace, 235–240. Philadelphia: University of Pennsylvania Press.
1962 Time depth and culture process in maritime Northeast Asia. *Asian Perspectives* 5(2):213–216.

CLARK, DONALD
1972 "The earliest prehistoric cultures of Kodiak Island, Alaska." Paper presented to the Thirty-seventh Annual Meeting of the Society for American Archaeology, Miami, Florida, May 4–6, 1972.

CLARK, J. G. D.
1946 Seal-hunting in the Stone Age of northern Europe. *Proceedings of the Prehistoric Society* 11:12–48.

COLLINS, HENRY B.
1964 "The Arctic and Subarctic," in *Prehistoric man in the New World.* Edited by J. D. Jennings and E. Norbeck, 85–114. Chicago: University of Chicago Press.
1968 Prehistoric cultural relations between Japan and the American Arctic: Eskimo and pre-Eskimo. *Proceedings of the Eighth International Congress of Anthropological and Ethnological Sciences* 3:358–359. Tokyo and Kyoto.

DE LAGUNA, FREDERICA
1934 *The archeology of Cook Inlet, Alaska.* Philadelphia: The University Museum.
1956 *Chugach prehistory: the archaeology of Prince William Sound.* Seattle: University of Washington Press.

DUMOND, DON E.
1968 On the presumed spread of slate grinding in Alaska. *Arctic Anthropology* 5(1):82–91.
1971 *A summary of archeology in the Katmai region, southwestern Alaska.* University of Oregon Anthropological Papers 2. Eugene, Oregon.

FITZHUGH, WILLIAM W.

1972a "Environmental and cultural variation in the eastern Subarctic." Paper presented to a symposium entitled "Climatic and Cultural change in the North American Arctic and adjacent regions" at the Third Annual Meeting of the Canadian Archeological Association, St. John's, Newfoundland. Edited by A. Dekin.

1972b *Environmental archeology and cultural systems in Hamilton Inlet, Labrador.* Smithsonian Contributions to Anthropology 16.

1973a Environmental approaches to the prehistory of the North. *Journal of the Washington Academy of Sciences* 63(2):39–53.

1973b Environmental factors in the evolution of Dorset culture: a marginal proposal for Hudson Bay." Paper presented to a School of American Research seminar on Dorset culture in the eastern Arctic, February, 1973, Santa Fe.

1975 "Ground slates in the Scandinavian Younger Stone Age with reference to circumpolar maritime adaptations." *Proceedings of the Prehistoric Society.*

FLADMARK, KNUT

1970 Preliminary report on the archeology of the Queen Charlotte Islands. *BC Studies* 6–7:18–45. Vancouver.

GEPHARD, PAUL H.

1946 "Stone objects from prehistoric North America with respect to distribution, type, and significance." Unpublished doctoral dissertation, Harvard University, Cambridge.

GIDDINGS, LOUIS

1967 *Ancient men of the Arctic.* New York: Knopf.

GJESSING, GUTORM

1943 *Traenfunnene.* Instituttet for Sammenlignende Kulturforskning. Oslo

1944 The Circumpolar Stone Age. *Acta Arctica* 2. Copenhagen.

1953 The Circumpolar Stone Age. *Antiquity* 27.

GRAYSON, J. F.

1956 "The post-glacial history of vegetation and climate in the Labrador-Quebec region as determined by palynology." Unpublished doctoral dissertation, University of Michigan, Ann Arbor.

HARP, ELMER, DAVID HUGHES

1968 Five prehistoric burials from Port Au Choix, Newfoundland. Occasional Publication of the Stefansson Collections, *Polar Notes* 8: 1–47. Hanover, N.H.

LARSEN, H.

1934 *Dodemansbugten: an Eskimo settlement on Clavering Island.* Meddelelser om Grønland 102(1).

LAUGHLIN, WILLIAM S.

1967 "Human migration and permanent occupation in the Bering Sea area," in *The Bering Land Bridge.* Edited by D. Hopkins, 409–450. Stanford: Stanford University Press.

LEROI-GOURHAN, ANDRÉ

1946 *Archéologie du Pacifique Nord: matériaux pour l'étude des relations entre les peuples riverains d'Asie et d'Amérique.* Paris: Institut d'ethnologie.

LUHO, VILLE
1967    Die Suomusjärvi-Kultur. *SMYA-FFT*. Helsinki.

MC CARTNEY, ALLEN P.
1972    "Prehistoric cultural integration along the Alaskan Peninsula." Paper presented at the Thirty-seventh Annual Meeting of the Society for American Archeology, Miami, Florida, May 4-6, 1972.

MOBERG, CARL-AXEL
1960    On some circumpolar and arctic problems in north European archeology. *Acta Arctica* 12:67–74. Copenhagen.

MØLLENHUS, KRISTEN
1958    Steinalderen i Helgeland. *Det Konlige Norsk Videnskabers selskabs skrifter* 1. Trondheim.

MORRISON, ALLISTAIR
1970    Pollen diagrams from interior Labrador. *Canadian Journal of Botany* 48:1957–1975.

MOSHINSKAIA, V. I.
1970    The Iron Age in the north of western Siberia and its relation to the development of the circumpolar region cultures. *Proceedings of the Seventh International Congress of Anthropological and Ethnological Sciences* 10:411–413. Moscow.

NAROLL, RAOUL
1970    What have we learned from cross-cultural studies? *American Anthropologist* 72:1227–1288.

OKLADNIKOV, A. P.
1960    Archeology of the Soviet Arctic. *Acta Arctica* 12:35–45.

OLSEN, HAAKON
1967    *Varanger-funnene IV: osteologisk materiale. Innledning – Fisk – Fugl.* Tromsø Museum Skrifter 7 (4). Tromsø, Oslo: Universitetsforlaget.

RITCHIE, WILLIAM A.
1968    Ground slates: east and west. *American Antiquity* 34(4): 385–391.

SHETELIG, HAAKON
1922    *Primitive Tider i Norge*. Bergen.

SIMONSEN, POVL
1961    *Varanger-funnene II: fund og udgravninger på fjordens sydkyst*. Tromsø Museums Skrifter 7(2). Tromsø, Oslo: Universitetsforlaget.
1972    "The cultural concept in the Arctic Stone Age," in *Circumpolar problems*. Edited by G. Berg, 163–169. New York: Pergamon Press.

SPAULDING, ALBERT
1946    "Northeastern archaeology and general trends in the northern forest zone," in *Man in northeastern North America*. Edited by F. Johnson, 143–167. Papers of the Robert S. Peabody Foundation 3.

STEWARD, JULIAN H.
1955    *Theory of culture change*. Urbana: University of Illinois Press.

STRUEVER, STUART
1968    "Problems, methods and organization: a disparity in the growth of archeology," in *Anthropological archeology in the Americas*. Edited by B. J. Meggers, 131–151. Washington, D.C.: Anthropological Society of Washington.

TAYLOR, W. E.
   1966   An archeological perspective on Eskimo economy. *Antiquity* 40:114–120.
TUCK, JAMES A.
   1971   An Archaic cemetery at Port au Choix, Newfoundland. *American Antiquity* 36(3):343–358.
TURNER, C. G., J. A. TURNER
   n.d.   "Akun." Unpublished report to the Department of the Interior.
VASILIEVSKY R. S.
   1968   The problems of the North Pacific sea hunter's culture. *Proceedings of the Eighth International Congress of Anthropological and Ethnological Sciences*, Tokyo and Kyoto 3:359–361.
   1969   The origin of the Ancient Koryak culture on the northern Okhotsk coast. *Arctic Anthropology* 6(1):150–164.
WENNER, C. G.
   1947   Pollen diagrams from Labrador. *Geografiska Annaler* 29(3–4):137–373. Stockholm.
WILLEY, GORDON, R.
   1962   "Mesoamerica," in *Courses toward urban life: archeological considerations of some cultural alternates*. Edited by R. J. Braidwood and G. R. Willey, 84–105. Viking Fund Publications in Anthropology 32. New York.

# Biographical Notes

JEAN S. AIGNER (1943–   ) is Associate Professor and Acting Head of the Department of Biocultural Anthropology at the University of Connecticut. At the University of California at Los Angeles and the University of Wisconsin (Ph.D. 1969), she studied archaeology, environmental sciences, and Chinese. Major research interests and active publication in the areas of Pleistocene Chinese hominid adaptations and subarctic human maritime adaptations, particularly in the Aleutian Islands, emphasize the theoretical paradigm of the Asiatic-New World Continuum. Since 1970 Aigner has been co-principal investigator for the research program, "Aleut Adaptation to the Bering Land Bridge Coastal Configuration."

SERGHEI A. ARUTIUNOV (1932–   ) did his postgraduate work in the Institute of Ethnography, Moscow. He has worked in the same institution since 1954. He received his Candidat of history (equivalent to a Ph.D.) in 1962 and a doctor of history (equivalent to full professor) in 1970. He did fieldwork in Japan (Ainu and Japanese) in 1960 and 1963, in Vietnam (hill tribes of Haut-Tonkin) in 1958, and in the USSR among Eskimos of the Bering Strait (1959, 1962, 1963, 1965, 1970), the latter combined with archaeological excavations. His areas of emphasis include ethnic anthropology, traditional culture of the Far East, and Eskimology.

NOEL BROADBENT (1946–   ) received his B.A. in Anthropology from San Diego State University with honors and distinction in 1968. He received his M.A. in Nordic and Comparative Archaeology at Uppsala

University in 1971 and is presently a doctoral candidate at the same institution. He has specialized in the archaeology of Upper Norrland, the subject of his dissertation, and has directed a research project since 1972.

HANS CHRISTIANSSON (1916– ) is a lecturer at Stockholm University in the Department of North European Archaeology. He received his Ph.D. in Nordic and Comparative Archaeology in 1959 at Uppsala University and was appointed Docent in 1960, a post he held until 1968. He has written extensively on northern Swedish archaeology as well as art history, a field in which he holds an M.A. He is director of the research project Nordarkeologi.

DONALD W. CLARK (1932– ) was educated at the Universities of Alaska and Wisconsin, Madison. He is now Mackenzie Basin Archaeologist at the National Museum of Man (Archaeological Survey of Canada). He is the author of several articles — for the Kodiak Island area, see articles in *Arctic Anthropology* — and of *Koniag prehistory* (Tübinger Monographien zur Urgeschichte, 1974).

DON E. DUMOND (1929– ) was educated at the University of New Mexico (B.A. 1949), Mexico City College (M.A. 1957) and the University of Oregon (Ph.D. 1962). He is now Professor of Anthropology and Head of the Department of Anthropology at the University of Oregon. His archaeological field research has been largely concentrated in southwestern Alaska; his publications have displayed an interest not only in Arctic prehistory, but in the prehistory and ethnohistory of Mesoamerica, in social organization, and in paleodemography.

WILLIAM FITZHUGH (1943– ) received his B.A. from Dartmouth College in 1964, and his M.A. (1968) and Ph.D. from Harvard in 1970. Presently he is a curator of North American Archaeology at the Smithsonian Institution. His research interests have been in arctic anthropology and ecology with specialization and field experience in the Eastern Arctic and Subarctic, especially Labrador. Major research interests center around the relationships between environments and culture change.

GUTORM GJESSING. No biographical data available.

GARLAND F. GRABERT (1923– ) was born in Indiana. He received his

M.A. from the University of Washington in 1965, and his Ph.D. in 1970. Field research in archaeology has involved salvage and historic archaeology on the Columbia Plateau 1963–1967, and in interior British Columbia, 1967. Subsequent work has been done in the San Juan and Strait of Georgia regions of the coastal area. He has been at Western Washington State College since 1967, where he is Associate Professor.

CURTIS E. LARSEN (1939– ) is Instructor of Anthropology at the University of North Carolina, Wilmington. He received his B.S. from the University of Illinois in 1964, an M.A. from Western Washington State College in 1971, and is presently a Ph.D. candidate at the University of Chicago. His research involves the interaction of human populations with natural and cultural environments. More specifically, he has conducted studies involving coastal archaeological excavations and post-glacial sea-level changes in the Puget Sound region of the northwestern United States. At the present time he is actively engaged in similar work in the Persian Gulf region. His special interests are environmental archaeology, Near Eastern archaeology, and coastal geology.

WILLIAM S. LAUGHLIN (1919– ) was born in Canton, Missouri. He received his B.A. from Willamette University in 1941, an M.A. from Haverford College in 1942, and a Ph.D. in Anthropology (Physical) from Harvard University in 1949. He is presently Professor of Biobehavioral Sciences and Chairman of the Laboratory of Biological Anthropology at the University of Connecticut. He is a member of numerous professional societies in physical anthropology, genetics, and prehistory. His major interests include the origins, affinities, and evolution of New World peoples, Aleuts, Eskimos, and Indians. He organized the first joint U.S.A.-U.S.S.R. archaeological team to do research in the United States.

MATS P. MALMER (1921– ) is Professor of European Prehistory at the University of Stockholm, Sweden. He received his Ph.D. in Prehistory from Lund University in 1962. He was Keeper of the Stone and Bronze Age department of the Museum of National Antiquities, Stockholm, 1959–1970, and Professor of European Prehistory at Lund University 1970–1973. Main publications: *Jungneolithische Studien* (1962), *Methodological problems in the history of art during the Scandinavian Iron Age (Metodproblem inom järnålderns konsthistoria*, 1963).

ALLEN P. MCCARTNEY (1949– ) is Associate Professor of Anthropology at the University of Arkansas. He received a B.A. from the University of Arkansas (1962) and an M.A. (1967) and Ph.D. (1971) from the University of Wisconsin where he specialized in arctic archaeology. He has spent seven field seasons in arctic Canada and in the Aleutian Islands of Alaska, including archaeological consulting for the U.S. Fish and Wildlife Service. He has also studied Aleut and Eskimo collections in major U.S. museums. His publications and research interests include culture history, ecological adaptations, and technology of arctic peoples.

CARL-AXEL MOBERG (1915–   ) was born in Lund, Sweden. He received his Ph.D. degree from the University of Lund in 1941. He has been Director of the Gothenburg Archaeological Museum (1957–1968) and Professor of Archaeology, especially in northern Europe, at the University of Göteborg since 1960. His publications include works on the Mesolithic and later periods in northern Europe; socioeconomic factors in prehistory (co-author, *Ekonomisk historisk början*, 1973); principles of archaeological research (*Introduktion till arkeologi*, 1969); mathematical methods in archaeology. His present research interest is the social basis in Europe during the La Tène Period.

KRISTEN R. MØLLENHUS (1922–   ) studied archaeology and Russian language at the University of Oslo, where he took his complete degree in 1953 with a dissertation on Stone Age material from northern Norway. Since 1953 he has been at the Museum of The Royal Norwegian Society of Science and Letters in Trondheim, since 1969 head of the archaeological section.

HARUO OHYI (1934–   ) was born in Tokyo. He studied at the University of Tokyo, and received his M.A. there in 1960. He taught at the University of Tokyo, Faculty of Letters (Lecturer in Archaeology, 1965–1966) and since 1966 has been Associate Professor of the Research Institute for Northern Cultures (Section of Archaeology), Faculty of Literature, Hokkaido University. His special interests include growth and succession of the cultures in northern parts of the Asiatic continent and northern North America, from Palaeolithic time to recent ages.

DORIAN A. SERGEEV (1928–   ) was born in Poltava, Ukraine. Most of his childhood was spent living with an Eskimo tribe where his mother worked as a teacher. From 1948–1953 he was a student at the University of Leningrad. After graduation he went to an Eskimo village in

Chukotka as a schoolteacher, and at the same time started ethnographic and archaeological field studies. In 1957 he became a fellow research worker at the Institute of Ethnography in Leningrad, but every year during the spring and summer he goes to Chukotka for fieldwork. In 1966 he received his Ph.D. from the University of Leningrad. Since 1968 he has been the Director of the State Museum of Ethnography in Leningrad. His main book, written in collaboration with S. Arutiunov, is *Drevnie Kul'tury Aziatskikh Eskimosov* (Ancient cultures of the Asian Eskimos), 1969.

POVL SIMONSEN (1922–  ) is Danish by birth and has received his M.A. from the University of Copenhagen. Since 1951 he has worked in Norway as leader of the Department of Archaeology at Tromsø Museum and since 1971 as professor at the University of Tromsø. His recent work has concentrated on north Scandinavian and circumpolar problems, especially within the Late Stone Age and concerning the Rock Art. His main publications are "Varanger-Funnene" I–III and VI (1959–1968) and "Arktiske Helleristninger i Nord-Norge" II (1958). His latest publication in English is "The rock art of northern Norway," Bulletin from the Vall'Camonica Center, 1947.

J. GARTH TAYLOR (1941–  ) was born in Coburg, Ontario. He received his Ph.D. in Anthropology at the University of Toronto in 1968. He has taught at the Memorial University of Newfoundland and was formerly an Associate Curator at the Royal Ontario Museum. At present he is Head of the Urgent Ethnology Section at the National Museum of Man, National Museums of Canada. He has done extensive archival, museum, and field research and has published two monographs and several articles on Canadian Eskimo and Ojibwa cultures.

JAMES A. TUCK (1940–  ) was born in Tonawanda, New York, and received his Ph.D. in Anthropology from Syracuse University in 1968. He is an Associate Professor of Anthropology at Memorial University of Newfoundland where he has been employed since 1967. His research interest is the prehistory of eastern and northern North America and he has been conducting field research in Newfoundland and Labrador for the past seven years.

RUSLAN VASILIEVSKY (1934–  ) was born in the village of Koshki, Kuibyshev oblast, USSR. He graduated in 1956 with a B.A. from Leningrad University, Historical Faculty. He received his Ph.D. in

1962 from the Institute of Archaeology in Leningrad. His main topics of study are ancient cultures of the northern Pacific; genesis and adaptation and evolution of maritime hunting cultures; genesis of Mesolithic cultures of the Angara basin. His main books are *Proiskhozhdenie i drevnyaya kultura koriakov* (1970) and *Drevnie kultury Tikhookeanskogo severa* (1973). At present he is the Head of the Field Works Department, Institute of History in Novosibirsk.

STIG WELINDER (1945–   ) was an assistant at the Department of Quaternary Geology (1966–1971) and has been, since 1972, Assistant Professor at the Historical Museum of the University of Lund, Sweden.

# Index of Names

Ackerman, Robert E., 168, 216, 223, 359
Adams, Robert Mc., 341
Adelaer, Henrich, 94, 97
Ahlén, I., 24
Ahlonen, P., 25
Aigner, Jean S., 13, 176, 181-201, 216, 361, 362, 365
Ailio, J., 33, 66
Aksënov, M. P., 115-116, 119
Almgren, O., 31
Althin, C. A., 27
Ambrosiani, Björn, 52
Andreeva, Zh. V., 104
Arbman, Holger, 52
Arne, Ture J., 87
Arutiunov, S., 159-165, 376
Åse, L. E., 22
Auer, B., 329

Baba, Osamu, 129, 140, 141, 144, 150, 153
Bader, O. N., 64
Bagge, Alex, 30, 48
Bakka, Egil, 356, 374
Balikci, A., 311
Bandi, Hans-Georg, 363
Barth, F., 328-329
Bartholomew, G. A., 302
Baudou, Evert, 45, 50, 101
Becker, C. J., 25, 26, 52, 53
Befu, H., 116, 123, 124, 329, 367, 368
Beregovaya, N. A., 67-68
Berglund, B., 22, 23, 25

Bergsland, Knut, 182
Berreman, G. D., 303
Binford, L. R., 194, 342
Björnstad, Margareta, 101
Bird, J., 317, 318, 319, 320, 321, 322, 325, 326, 328-329
Birdsell, J. B., 302
Birket-Smith, Kaj, 2, 3, 167, 222, 312
Boas, F., 273
Bockstoce, John R., 168
Borden, Charles E., 232, 233, 235, 241, 243, 245, 246, 248, 264, 358, 360
Boserup, Esther, 173
Bourque, Bruce J., 256, 258, 259, 262
Brinch Petersen, E., 26, 30
Broadbent, Noel D., 7, 47-54, 357
Broeker, W. S., 234
Brusov, A. J., 60, 62, 65
Byan, Alan L., 10, 15
Byers, Douglas S., 255, 256, 259, 261

Calvert, Gay, 232, 236
Campbell, J. M., 9
Capps, Stephen R., 206
Carlson, Roy L., 232, 243-244
Carneiro, R. L., 231-232
Cernetsov, V. N. (Černetzov, V. N.), 7, 87, 104, 105, 371
Chard, C. S., 116, 123, 124, 154, 292, 329, 367, 368, 381
Chernecov, V. N. See Cernetsov, V. N.
Childe, Gordon, 87, 104
Christiansson, Hans, 7, 47-54, 101, 357
Chubarova, R. V., 144

Clark, A. H., 304, 305, 306, 307, 308, 319
Clark, D. L., 296-297
Clark, Donald W., 170, 175, 176, 203-225, 359
Clark, Gerald H., 170, 176, 208, 210, 212, 213, 221
Clark, J. G. D., 6, 10, 12, 35, 95
Clark, Webster K., 204
Collins, H. B., Jr., 2, 3, 162, 304, 305, 306, 307, 308, 309, 321, 332, 363, 364, 369
Cook, J. P., 282
Cooper, J. M., 3, 97, 318, 319, 320, 321, 322
Cowan, I., Mc T., 230
Coxe, W., 293-294, 295, 299, 302, 304, 305, 308, 309, 310
Cressman, L. S., 235
Curtis, Roger, 269

Damas, D., 311
Darlington, P. J., Jr., 285, 317, 319
Davies, K. G., 276
Dawkins, W. Boyd, 2, 6, 15
Degerbohl, M., 24
Dekin, Albert A., Jr., 89
De Laguna, Frederica, 3, 213, 218, 220, 222, 223, 264, 364
Denniston, Glenda D., 176, 301, 321, 322
Derevjanko, A. P., 117, 201
Desautals, R. J., 304, 305, 306, 307, 308
Digerfeldt, G., 23
Dikov, N. N., 114, 170
Dixon, E. J., 282
Dmitriev, P. A., 64, 65
Drucker, Philip, 232
Duff, Wilson, 234, 235, 241
Dumond, Don E., 167-178, 208, 212, 216, 219, 221, 222, 223, 359, 365

Easterbrook, Don J., 229, 234, 242, 244
Edgren, T., 26
Eggan, Fred, 96
Ekholm, G., 31
Ekman, S., 24
Ellis, R. R., 304, 305, 306, 307, 308
Elton, Charles, 276
Emperaire, J., 328
Eyerdam, W. J., 304, 305

Fajnberg, L. A., 114
Filip, Jan, 102

Finlayson, Nicol, 276
Fitzhugh, William, 1-16, 87, 103, 255, 256, 257, 258, 261, 262, 264, 265, 339-382
Fladmark, Knut R., 216, 359
Florin, S., 25
Flynn, J. D., 304, 305, 306, 307, 308
Forde, C. D., 286
Forde, Daryll, 96
Foss, M. J., 59, 60, 61, 63
Fredén, C., 22
Fredskild, B., 24
Freed, J. A., 223
Fries, M., 23
Fujimoto, Tsuyoshi, 124-126, 128, 143, 144
Fyles, J. G., 234, 236

Gebhard, Paul H., 3
Geist, O. W., 290
Giddings, James L., Jr., 168, 169, 171-172, 211, 234, 363
Gimbutas, Marija, 103, 104
Gjessing, Gutorm, 3, 5, 6, 8, 9, 10, 12, 13, 15, 57, 58, 65, 66, 67, 69-70, 78-79, 87-98, 102, 264, 345, 356, 373-374
Godley, E. J., 317, 319
Grabert, G. F., 15, 229-249
Gracheva, G. N., 105
Grayson, J. F., 346
Griffin, James B., 170
Grjaznov, M. P., 104, 106
Gurina, N. N., 57-58, 59, 60
Gusinde, 317, 323

Hallowell, A. I., 96
Hallström, G., 42, 43
Hammel, H. T., 324, 333
Hansen, Henry P., 233, 234
Harp, Elmer, Jr., 257, 346
Harper, F., 300
Hart, C. W. M., 286-287
Haven, Jens, 269-270, 272, 275, 276
Heider, K., 282
Heizer, Robert F., 205-206, 213, 215, 219-220, 301
Hett, Joan, 183
Heusser, Calvin J., 207-208, 233, 234
Hewes, Gordon, 205
Hirakō, Goichi, 144
Holland, Stuart S., 229, 235
Holmes, C. E., 282
Honda, Katsuyo, 128
Hrdlička, Ales, 3, 197, 213, 215, 221,

223, 291, 294, 295, 299, 300, 301, 304, 305, 306, 307, 308, 309, 320, 321
Hughes, David, 257, 346
Hulten, E., 308, 309, 310
Hvarfner, H., 42, 48

Inaba, Katsuo, 142
Ingstad, Anne Stine, 103
Irving, W. N., 2, 167
Itō, Nobuo, 124, 133, 136
Itō, Shōichi, 150, 151
Ivanev, L. N., 68
Iversen, J., 23
Izumi, Seiichi, 129, 137

Jacobi, A., 215
Janson, Sverker, 42, 48
Jenness, D., 332, 333
Jochelson, Waldemar, 150, 292, 298, 299, 301, 302, 303, 304, 305, 306, 307, 308, 309, 310, 319, 320, 321
Jones, R. D., Jr., 291
Jørgensen, S., 27

Kaneko, Hiromasa, 132, 138, 141
Kapel, H., 27
Kehoe, A. B., 11
Kenyon, Karl W., 183
Khlobystin, L. P., 105, 106
Kikuchi, Toshihiko, 145
Kitakamae, Yasuo, 128, 141
Kjellmark, K., 30
Kleivan, Inge, 4
Knuth, Eigil, 175
Kodama, George, 150
Kodama, Sakuzaemon, 150, 151
Komai, Kazuchika, 129, 130, 131, 132, 144, 145
Komarova, M. N., 66
Königsson, E. S., 26, 33
Königsson, Lars-König, 22, 25, 26, 33, 53, 101
Kōno, Hiromichi, 150
Konopatskij, S., 201
Koyanagi, Masao, 142
Kozyreva, R. V., 136, 137
Krajina, V. J., 231
Kroeber, A. L., 231, 232-233, 272, 290, 311
Krog, H., 24
Kuschel, G., 317, 318

Laming, A., 328
Lane, D. S., 223

Langsdorf, 294, 295
Lantis, Margaret, 173, 175, 290, 321
Larichev, V. E., 116, 201
Larsen, C. E., 15, 229-249
Larsen, Helge, 168, 170, 366
Laughlin, William S., 2, 113, 114, 115, 119, 181-201, 216, 291, 361, 362, 365
LeBlanc, Raymond, 263
Lee, R. B., 284, 298, 331
Lepiksaar, J., 26, 33, 53
Leppäaho, J., 33
Leroi-Gourhan, A., 3, 373, 375
Liljegren, R., 22, 24
Lippold, Lois K., 176, 293
Lisianski, Yuri, 215, 220
Lönnberg, E., 31
Lothrop, S. K., 316, 317, 318, 319, 320, 321, 322, 323, 324, 326, 327, 328-329
Low, A. P., 276
Luho, V., 28, 33, 358
Lutz, Bruce J., 168

MacArthur, R. H., 285
McCartney, A. P., 11, 175, 223, 281-333, 343, 361
McCurdy, A. J., 304, 305, 306, 307, 308
MacDonald, G., 9
Mace, Robert L., 222
McGeein, D. F., 223
McGhee, R. J., 175, 259
Mackintosh, N. A., 317, 319
MacNeish, Richard S., 168
Makiuk, Joshua, 270
Malmer, Mats P., 7, 26, 41-45, 53, 101
Manville, R. H., 204
Martynov, A. I., 45
Marx, Karl, 87-88
Mary-Rousselière, Guy, 259
Mason, L., 286
Mathiassen, Therkel, 3, 102
Matthews, W. H., 234, 236
Maxwell, Moreau S., 259
Medvedeff, Dennis, 198
Meggers, B. J., 331
Meinander, C. F., 7, 26, 45, 102, 106
Meldgaard, Jørgen, 102
Merck, Carl Heinrich, 215
Milan, F. A., 333
Mitchell, Donald H., 232, 234, 235, 248
Mitsuhashi, Kōhei, 150
Moberg, Carl-Axel, 3, 5, 7, 12, 15, 41, 101-107, 342, 371
Mochanov, Ju. A., 119
Møhl, U., 24, 30

Møllenhus, Kirsten R., 3, 12, 15, 57-71, 345
Molodin, V. I., 105
Moorehead, Warren K., 255
Mörner, N.-A., 22, 234
Morrison, Allistair, 346
Moshinskaya, V. I., 7, 104, 105, 106, 371
Müller-Beck, H., 292
Munch, Jens Storm, 102, 106
Munro, J. A., 230
Murie, O. J., 290, 291, 292, 304, 305, 306, 307, 319

Naora, Nobuo, 132, 138, 148
Naroll, Raoul, 341
Nasmith, H. W., 234, 236
Natori, Takemitsu, 141
Nelson, R. K., 9
Newman, M. T., 287
Nihlén, J., 33
Nilsson, E., 22
Nishiwaki, M., 304
Nordland, O., 4
Nørdlund, P., 102
Nordmann, C. A., 92
Nowak, Michael, 168
Nummedal, Anders, 90-91, 92

Oba, Toshio, 126, 132, 141, 147, 151
Odner, Knut, 88, 92
Odum, E., 302
Ohyi, Haruo, 8, 12, 123-154, 368
Okada, Hiroaki, 137, 150
Okladnikov, A. P., 45, 66, 67, 68, 104, 115, 117-118, 137, 139, 201, 371
Okuda, Hiroshi, 147
Oliver, D. L., 286
Olsen, Haakon, 105, 356
Olsson, Ulf, 101
Onuma, Tadaharu, 128
Orlova, J. P., 68
Osborne, C., 223
Osgood, Cornelius, 222
Oswalt, W. H., 173, 287, 290, 297, 317, 318, 319, 320, 321, 326, 327, 330

Persson, Ib., 102
Petroff, I., 303
Pike, G. C., 304
Pilling, A. R., 286-287
Pronina, G. I., 104

Radcliffe-Brown, A. R., 96

Rainey, Froelich, 168, 290
Ransom, J. E., 294, 299, 301, 304, 305, 306, 307, 308
Rappaport, R. A., 331
Rasmussen, Knud, 94
Ravdonikas, W. J., 45
Riddell, F. A., 223
Ridley, F., 11
Rieger, S., 207
Ritchie, William A., 3, 373
Ross, Richard E., 168
Roussell, Aage, 102
Rudenko, S. I., 3, 67, 68, 70, 71
Rychkov, Y. G., 188
Rygdylon, E. R., 66

Sahlin, Marshall, 87, 284, 323, 331
Saitō, Tadashi, 144
Sakurai, Kiyohiko, 150
Saladin d'Anglure, B., 270
Salnikov, K. V., 66
Salomonsson, B., 25, 26
Sanger, David, 256
Satō, Tadao, 126, 129
Satō, Tatsuo, 131, 145, 150
Sauer, C., 286
Sawa, Shirō, 128, 147
Scheffer, V. B., 305, 306, 307, 308, 319
Schmidt, A. V., 3, 57, 59
Schwartz, Maurice L., 240
Sergeev, D., 159-165, 376
Sheremetyeva, V. A., 188
Shetelig, Haakon, 373-374
Shimkin, Demitri B., 104
Siiriäinen, A., 25
Simonsen, Povl, 4-5, 7, 11, 15, 75-85, 91, 92, 95, 97, 106, 344, 356-357
Sinclair, H. M., 300
Sjövold, Thorlief, 101
Smith, P. Lorentz, 93
Snow, Dean R., 255-256, 258
Solberg, O., 97, 98, 102
Sollas, W. J., 2
Sono, Toshihiko, 129, 137
Spaulding, A. C., 3, 6, 10, 15, 264, 345
Spencer, Robert F., 173
Sprague, Robert, 247
Stanford, Dennis J., 168
Steager, P. W., 316, 318, 319, 321, 322, 323, 324, 325
Stefansson, V., 300
Stenberger, M., 33, 102
Steward, Julian, 95, 96, 282, 283, 321, 324, 331, 339, 340, 341, 343

Struever, Stuart, 341
Stupart, R. F., 270
Sulimirski, Tadeusz, 104
Sumi, Hiroshi, 128, 141

Tallgren, A. M., 92, 103
Tanner, V., 97
Tauber, H., 25
Tax, Sol, 1
Taylor, J. Garth, 12, 269-277
Taylor, W. E., 289, 290, 363-364
Ten Hove, H., 23
Trigger, B., 282, 283-284
Troel-Smith, J., 25, 27
Troickaja, T. N., 105
Tuck, James A., 11, 255-265, 349
Turner, Christy G. II, 197, 291, 293, 321, 362
Turner, J. A., 197, 291, 293, 362
Turner, Lucien, 270, 305, 306, 307, 308, 309

Vajda, László, 104, 105, 106
Vasilievsky, R. S., 113-120, 138, 152, 153, 154, 201, 368-369
Vayda, A. P., 331

Veniaminof, I., 188, 196, 298, 299, 300, 301, 302, 303, 304, 305, 306, 307, 308, 314, 317, 319, 320, 321
Vuorela, L., 25

Walker, E. H., 308, 309, 310, 319
Waterbolk, H. T., 101, 103
Watson, William, 103, 104
Weiz, Samuel, 270
Welinder, Stig, 12, 21-35
Wenner, C. G., 346
Weyer, E. M., 301
Wheeler, E. P., 270
White, Leslie, 88
Willey, G. R., 322, 328, 341
Willoughby, Charles C., 255
Wilson, E. O., 285
Workman, William B., 213, 214, 218, 223, 301
Wunderlich, R., 207

Yamaguchi, Bin, 150, 151
Yonemura, Kioe, 132, 143
Yoshizaki, Masakazu, 124
Young, S. P., 204

# Index of Subjects

Activity units, 297
Adaptation type, 341–342
Adzes, 52–53; hollow-headed, 60
Afognak River, 209–210, 214
Ainu, 126, 149–150, 368
Åland Island, 27
Alaska, 9, 167–178
Alaska Peninsula, 182, 291
Alaskan adaptations, 176, 188–192, 203–225
Alaskan archaeology, 223
Alaskan cultures, 171
Alby site, 32
Aleut, 191–192, 197, 199; adaptation of, 181–200, 288, 315; archaeology of, 190, 191, 199–200; blood type of, 200; diet of, 186, 293–294, 300, 303–310; evolution of, 181–200, 362; food cycles of, 301–303; food procurement systems of, 295–298; habitats of, 182–296; hunting by, 298–299; infant mortality among, 195–196; morphology of, 192–195, 200; society of, 185, 288–292; subsistence of, 292–316; year of, 303
Aleut-Eskimo, 223, 288–290, 311–312, 364–368
Aleutian: ecosystem, 181–183; technology, 319–320
Aleutian culture, 120, 199–200, 290–292, 362; continuity of, 283, 363
Aleutians, 12, 113–120, 182, 192, 281–333, 361–363; climate of, 183–184; fauna of, 182–183, 286, 289, 290–292, 295; flora of, 183, 308–310; house types of, 322;

population density of, 311; sea level in, 184
Algonkian, 264
Åloppe, Sweden, 30
Alternate food systems, 324
Amber, 62
Amphibolite. See Schist
Amur-Maritime Territory region, 68, 153
Anangula Blade site, 188, 193–194, 201
Anangula complex, 113–120
Anangula Island, 113–120, 201, 291, 372
Ancient Koryak culture, 138, 145, 153, 367–369
Andamanese, 286
Andreanof Island, 182
Andreyev, USSR, 64, 65
Andronovo, USSR, 65–66
Angara River, 66
Ångermanälven River, 42
Angmagsalik, 330
Archaeology: comparative, 11, 339–342; direct historic approach of, 223–224, 283; ecological approach of, 212–213; of ethnohistoric resources, 283; form and function in, 192; functional studies in, 344–345; holistic approach to, 282–283; Norse, 102; systematics in, 341
Archipelagoes, 281–333; artifacts in, 320–321; cultural stability in, 329; fauna of, 284–288; settlement patterns in, 321–322
Arctic: archaeology, 103, 363–366; ecology, 3, 363–366; flora, 287; resources, 365; Small Tool tradition, 167–168,

363, 364
Arkaeologisk ABC, Denmark, 102
Arrowheads. *See* Projectile points
Art, 78–80
Artifacts: form and function of, 191–192, 326; mythology of, 159–160; polymorphism of, 165; and ritual, 159–160; shell associations of, 241, 245
Asia, 10, 367–370
Askola-Suomusjärvi, Finland, 50, 51, 355
Atka, 182
Atlantic climax forest, 24, 25
Aurora borealis, 4
Axes, 50, 51, 61, 66

Baidarka. *See* Kayak
Baikal, Lake, 66
Baltic, 21–22, 31–33
Barents Sea, 57–68
Barley, 53
Battle Axe culture, Scandinavia, 26, 31, 35, 53
Beaver, 50
Belief systems, 262–263
Bellingham Bay, 243–244
Beluga whale, 164
Beothuk Indians, 263
Beringia, 119, 184
Bering Land Bridge, 182
Bering Sea, 10, 181
Birch Bay site, 236–240, 246–247
Birnirk culture, USSR, 67
Bjurselet, Sweden, 47, 53, 54
Black Island complex, Labrador, 348–349
Blade and burin industries, 14, 372
Blade culture, 117–120
Boat Axe culture, Scandinavia, 52–54
Boats, 44, 261–262, 296. *See also* Kayak
Bohuslän, Scandinavia, 45
Bolas, 186–187
Bor II, USSR, 64
Boreal Forest thesis, 9–10
Borers, 51
Bothnia, Gulf of, 53
Boulder chip tools, 361
Bow, 65
Bronze Age, 41, 59, 106
Budun Site, USSR, 115–116

Cacheing, 53
Cairns, 45
Canoe Indians, 325
Caribou ecology, 276, 346–347
Carrying capacity, 312, 326

Cattle. *See* Domesticated animals
Central Office of National Antiquities, Sweden, 50
Ceremonialism, 349–350
Chaluka site, 188, 189, 193–194
Chekalinas. *See* Storage pits
Chilean Archipelago, 315–329
Chisels, 115–116
Choris, Alaska, 171–172
Chukotsky Peninsula, 67–68
Circumpolar Stone Age, 3, 10, 345
Circumpolar studies, 2; of adaptation, 9, 371–373; of diffusion, 4–7, 13
Climate, 164, 207, 208, 374–375
Climax areas, 231–232
Coastal adaptation, 167–178, 184–187
Coastal Archaic, 255, 257
Coastal cultures, Scandinavia, 27–28
Coastal food collecting, 186–187
Coastal Salish, 232
Coastal stabilization, 236. *See also* Sea-level variation
Cobble and flake tools, 246
Cold stress, 313, 324. *See also* Diet
Comb-ornamented pottery, 27, 33, 34, 35, 356
Convergent adaptation, 330–332
Cook Inlet, 222
Core implements, 51
Cores, 48, 115–116, 118
Cross-cultural studies, 10–11, 330–332
Cross-economy studies, 7–8, 101–107
Cultural: barriers, 182; complexity, limits of, 382; conservatism, 87, 89, 191; continuity, 216–221 (*see also* Technological evolution); convergence, 14, 265, 281–282, 317–322, 329, 373; ecology, 9, 283, 315, 331, 339–341; longevity, 380; processes, 378; relativism, 341; stability, 15, 332, 353, 364, 379; stratigraphy, 51–52 (*see also* Shoreline displacement); variation, 289–290
Culture, 203, 216–221, 224–225, 290, 342, 352–354; and environment, 281–333; environmental limits of, 283–284; material, 165, 172–173; North Atlantic, 263–265; regional differences in, 141
Culture core, 282, 283, 339–340, 343

Daggers, 68–69
Deities, 190
Demography, 273–276
Denmark, 54
De Vries effect, 25

Diet, 300, 324; in cold, 287
Diffusion, 3, 222, 344–345
Diversity, 285
Dog traction, 289
Domesticated animals, 9, 25, 53, 138–139, 148, 152, 207, 382
Dorset. *See* Eskimo
Dwellings, 62, 94. *See also* Houses

Early Norrland NTB, Sweden, 50
Ecological: continuum, 5; equilibrium, 314
Ecosystem, marine, 205–206, 224, 353
Ecotones, 9
Elk, 42, 50, 53. *See also* Moose
Englefield artifacts, 328
Enoura, Japan, 142
Environmental: determinism, 283, 325; model, 229–249; predictability, 331
Ertebølle, Scandinavia, 26, 27, 29, 34
Esan, Japan, 138
Eskimo, 67, 154, 159–165, 175, 269–177, 290, 363–366; in Alaska, 167–178; archaeology of, 102; art of, 159–160; of Bering Sea, 177, 368; Caribou, 330; Dorset, 175, 177–178, 263, 366; economy of, 164, 363–364; historical records of, 269–272; house types of, 271; linguistics of, 219; mythology of, 159; origins of, 70–71; population density among, 272–273; technology of, 70, 365–366; traditions of, 364–368
Eustasy, 234, 236, 242, 246

Fahlmark, Sweden, 47
Farming, 25–27, 28, 34, 35
Fast ice, 273, 277
Finland, 33
Fishing, 33, 50, 185, 205, 221, 261, 298–299, 320, 324; bait technology in, 66; with hook and line, 261; reef net in, 247; specialization of, 85
Flaked artifacts, 210–211
Flint, 48, 52, 53, 61, 82
Food: collecting, 26–27, 84, 101, 248; cycles, 327–328; predicting lists of, 313–314; selection, 294–295, 314; storage, 300–301; web, 296, 353
Fosna, Norway, 48, 355
Fossil beaches, 246
Fox, 292
Fox Islands, 182
Fraser Delta sequence, 241–242, 360
Fraser Lowlands, Washington, 229, 246

Fuegian, 319–320, 322, 324; archaeology, 328–329; Eskimo diffusion, 332–333; houses, 322; hunting, 325
Funnel Beaker, Scandinavia, 25, 26, 30–31, 34

Gathering, 298–299. *See also* Food, collecting
Geochronology, 247
Goats, 26, 53
Gotland Island, 31, 34
Gravers, 51
Graves, 59, 257
Greenland, 177, 285–286
Gressbakken, Scandinavia, 75–77
Gropbakkeengen, Scandinavia, 75–77, 92
Ground slate, 3, 14, 169, 217, 220–221, 244, 255, 265, 350, 362, 366, 373–374, 378; origins of, 357–358
Ground Slate complex, 376–378
Group size, 90, 95
Gulf Islands complex, 235, 246

Habitats, 183, 186–187, 197, 206
Hamilton Inlet, 345–352
Hammerstones, 58
*Handbuch*, Greenland, 102
Harpoon complex, 159, 375–376
Harpoons, 61, 160–162, 330; barbed, 141, 152, 61, 259, 328; bone and horn, 67, 68, 259, 328; toggling, 3, 152, 161, 173, 217, 259, 376
Hearths, 143, 144
Heden, Sweden, 47, 49, 50, 51
Hedningahällen, Sweden, 52
Hemmor, Baltic, 33
Higashi-taraika pottery, 142
Hokkaido, Japan, 116, 119, 123, 126, 128, 129, 142
Hokkaido University, 138
Houses, 90–91; workshop, 76–77
Hunters, 96–97, 185
Hunting, 10, 35, 248, 298, 313, 325; by boat, 184–185; cooperative, 298; evolution of, 159–165; male partners in, 185; of sea mammals, 12, 24, 28, 35, 53, 169, 184–186, 206, 219–220; of waterfowl, 204, 298–299; of whale, 274–276, 277
Hunting-collecting, 87, 89, 235, 236, 284, 286–287
Hypsithermal Interval. *See* Sea-level variation

Implements. *See* Artifacts
Indian-Eskimo relationships, 259, 270
Indians. *See* Individual tribe and culture names
Ingura, 286
Inland cultures, 27–28, 61
Ipiutak culture, 169
Isolate integrity, and dialect, 196–197
Isostasy, 234, 236, 242, 246

Japan Association of Quarternary Research, 151
Japan Blade technique, 116–117
Jettbøle, Scandinavia, 61

Kaadaraadar, 190
Kabukai site, 128–129
Kachemak tradition, 213–214, 218
Kamchatka, 68, 114, 116
Kamkeramik, 52
Kandalak Bay, 58, 63
Karalian culture, 42, 60
Kargopol culture, 61–63
Katarina Island, 59
Kawajiri-Kita-chashi site, 126–128, 132–133
Kayak, 169, 185, 296, 298
Kirkhellaren (Cathedral Cave), 92–93
Kjelmøy, 59, 63
Kodiak Island, 176, 203–225, 359; culture sequence on, 208–213; economy of, 206; ecosystem of, 204–208; fauna of, 204–206; settlement patterns on, 214
Knives, 50, 51, 58, 60, 67
Koetoi shell mound, 140
Kola Peninsula, 5, 57, 58–59
Kolyma, 67
Komsa culture, Finland, 48, 88, 89, 90–91, 355
Koniag culture, 214–215, 219–220
Koryak. *See* Ancient Koryak
Krelia, 45
Kungsladugurd, 32
Kuril Islands, 12, 126, 144–145, 216, 329
Kuvika, 83–84

Labrador, 269–277, 345–354; fauna of, 346, 351–352; flora of, 346; paleo-environment of, 346
Labrador Maritime Archaic tradition, 348–350
L'Anse aux Meadows, 103
Lapps. *See* Saames
Law of the minimum. *See* Liebig's Law

Leister points, 261
Liebig's Law, 302–303, 324
Lithic technology, 9, 50, 58, 71
Littoral exploitation. *See* Strandflats
Littorina Sea, 24
Lundfors, 47, 49, 50, 51

Magellanic Moorlands, 317
Mälar provinces, 45
Mälaren Lake, 25, 27
Man: and environment, 232–233, 249; exploitational pattern of, 183; as index animal, 181
Marine: islands, 281, 285, 291–292; subsistence and economy, 288, 361; transgression, 242–243
Marine adaptations, 14, 33, 35, 216, 224, 339–382; area of, 343; beginnings of, 235; comparative studies of, 316–320; consequences of, 200; definition of, 11–12, 343; evolution of, 192–199, 343, 369; stability of, 87, 89; subtypes of, 343–344
Maritime Archaic tradition, 257, 261, 262–263
Marpole Phase, 242–243, 246
Medelpad, 53
Microblade industry, 360
Migashi-tanaika pottery, 131
Migration, 48, 54, 130; and climate change, 177; and subsistence, 177; of women, 196
Migratory cycle, 90, 94
Minami-kaizuka pottery, 131, 142
Modlona River, 62
Mongoloid Dental complex, 192
Moose, 50
Morphology, geographic variation of, 192–195, 196
Motochi site, 146
Motomachite, 147
Moyoro shell mound, 132
Mussels, 248, 323, 326

Naiji pottery, 149
Nain Diary, 272, 276
Nämforsen, 41–42, 44
Närpes, 33
Nephrite, 58, 66
Nevin site, 255
Noodle Appliqué pottery, 124, 129
Nooksack River, 229
Nordarkeologi project, 47, 49
Norrbus, 32

Norrland, 48, 52, 54
North Atlantic: radiocarbon dates, 256–257; subsistence, 257–258; technology, 259–262
North Atlantic Archaic, 255, 262
North Bothnian implements, 51
Northern maritime technological complex, 378–380
Northern maritime tradition, 364
North Pacific cultures, 117–118
Northwest Coast, 10, 358–361; adaptation on, 229–249; chronology of, 243; cultural development of, 360–361; cultural trajectory of, 248; environments of, 229–231; projectile points of, 247; site elevation on, 239–240; site types, 246; subsistence of, 231
Norton culture, 170–174
Norton tradition, 168–169
Norway, 52, 87–98

Ob Basin, 66, 104, 105–106, 370
Obsidian, 68, 117
Occupational specialization, 75–85
Ocean Bay I culture, 208–210
Ocean Bay II culture, 210–213, 359
Okhotsk culture, 123–154, 367–369; adaptation of, 123–154; chronology of, 124–131; decline of, 145–150; distribution of, 125, 140–141; ethnic makeup of, 150; faunal remains of, 132; materials of, 132–133; origin of, 132–139, 151; settlement pattern of, 140; skeletal remains of, 150–151; stages of, 141–142
Ølby Lyng, 29
Old Bering Sea culture, 170
Omkoromanai shell mound, 151
Omnivorous flexibility, 289, 293
Onega River, 59
Östergötland, 45
Østfold, 45
Oulujoki, 33
Överåda, 30

Pebble tools, 238–239
Pechore culture, 62–63
Petroglyphs, 41–45, 96
Picks, 60, 61
Pig, 31, 33, 138–139
Pike (fish), 50
Pit-house culture, 328
Pit houses, 132, 134, 143–144, 146, 147
Pitted Ware culture, 26, 31, 34, 35, 52, 53,

54; fauna of, 30, 32–33; pottery of, 54
Point Revenge complex, 351
Population: estimates of, 271–272; geographic variation in, 198–199; increase of, 139, 174, 232; movements of, 3, 174, 218, 323; pressure, 248
Population density, 196, 269–272, 275; calculation of, 272–273; limiting factors on, 274
Port au Choix site, 255–256, 259, 349
Post-Jōmon culture, 137
Pottery, 83, 137, 140; combed pattern, 62, 63; ertebølle, 26; masatsu-shiki fumon, 129; Okhotsk, 124–131, 146; pitted, 63; Scandinavian, 58–59; Towada, 126
Pribilof Islands, 182
Prince William Sound, 264
Procurement systems, 297, 327
Projectile points, 50, 58; bone, 58, 61, 64; Nyelv (pyheensilta) type, 60; Pechora type, 63; typology of, 377–378
Puget Sound, 230
Punuk culture, 67

Quartz, 50, 51, 53–54, 57

Rat Islands, 182
Rebun Island, 142, 146
Red ochre, 51, 190, 348
Red Paint people, 255
Reindeer, 23, 89. *See also* Domesticated animals
Reindeer Island, 59
Research Institute for Northern Cultures, 126, 128
Resource: procurement systems, 295–298, 361; restrictions, 313–314; stability, 353
Risvåg, 83
Riverine adaptations, 14, 344, 358

Saames, 89, 93
Sakhalin, 68, 124, 139, 142
Sakkotsu complex, 117
Salmon, 205, 209–210, 299
Samalga Pass, 182, 184
Sanda Island, 92–93
Sandy Beach Bay site, 186, 188–189, 193–194
Sandy Cove complex, 348
Satsumon culture, 130, 131, 146, 368
Scandinavia, 23, 26, 264, 354–358; economic focus of, 355; geology of, 27; pottery of, 26; radiocarbon scale in,

25
Scrapers, 51, 57; blade, 52–53; end-, 51; keeled, 48, 51; -planes, 51;
Sea Hunting culture, 113–120
Sea-land adaptations, 289–290
Sea-level variation, 233–236, 245–246, 374; and community stability, 248–249; and site location, 234, 247
Seal hunting, 23–24, 31, 32, 33, 34, 49, 53
Sea lions, 185
Sea mammal hunting, 176–177, 206, 298, 373; netting in, 49–50; technological uses of, 14
Sea otter, 185–186, 220
Seasonality, 50, 90, 94, 232, 236, 328, 345, 355, 379; in Alaska, 168, 169, 210; Aleut, 293–295, 303, 312, 328; and community cooperation, 236; Eskimo, 273; and food shifts, 296, 312; as marine adaptation, 14, 29, 32, 34; North Atlantic, 262, 263, 273, 350, 351–352, 353–354; and petroglyphs, 96
Seasonal round. *See* Seasonality
Sedentarism, origins of, 369–370
Semiahmoo Spit site, 236–240, 247–248
Seri, 286
Settlement pattern, 7, 47–54, 91–92, 190, 380–381; in Alaska, 168, 169, 190; and economy, 143, 221; in Hokkaido, 140; in Norway, 75–76; and shore displacement, 47, 49, 51–52; stability of, 173, 177; in Stone Age, 75–76
Shamanism, 4, 78–80
Sheep, 26, 53
Shellfish, 258, 299, 343
Shell-Knife culture, 328
Shell middens, 237–243, 370
Shigir culture, 64
Ship Rock Cave, 199
Shiretoko Peninsula, 131
Shoreline displacement, 51–52
Shumagin Islands, 182
Siretorp site, 29–30
Skåe, 54
Skellefteå kommun, 47, 53
Skellefteå River, 49, 51
Skolte-Saames, 97
Slate, 48–49, 50–52, 59, 62, 65, 67, 69, 209, 212, 217; area limits of, 60, 68; associations of, 356; sawing of, 211; use of, 57–71
Slate Culture theory, 69–70
Slate-quartz technology, 48–49
Slate technology, 50, 211, 216, 359–361

Slate weapons, 212–213
Social and Ecological Gradient, 96–97
Social systems, 96; development of, 342; and ecological conditions, 94–95
Society, 76–85; "original affluent," 87, 331
Sørøy, 75
Sotmyra site, 30
Spearheads. *See* Projectile points
Specialization, 84–85; 95–96, 357; as arrowsmith, 83–84; in fishing, 85; in pottery, 83; as tradesmen, 80–82
Starodupskoe (Sakaehama) site, 136
Steppe. *See* Taiga
Stockholm University, 50
Stone: drilling, 217–218; sinkers, 49–50
Strandflats, 187–188
Subsistence, 232–233, 244, 331, 352; in Alaska, 177; alternatives, 282, 311; components, 330; crashes, 353; as diagnostic trait, 172; efficiency, 332; and population levels, 311; rubrics, 297–298; settlement system, 341; utilization spheres, 297
Sumar site, 244–245
Sunderøy points, 65
Sundsvall, 53
Suomusjärvi, Finland, 33, 49, 60, 358
Susuya pottery, 133–136
Svalings, 31

Tadushi site, 118
Taiga, 9–10, 345
Tanaina culture, 222
Tasmanians, 287
Technology, 203–225, 259–261, 377; and climate, 163; and resource use, 325; and social reorganization, 173; and subsistence, 264
Thule: migration in, 175, 177–178; tradition, 169–170, 366
Tierra del Fuego, 315–329
Time-slope hypothesis, 5–6
Tiwi, 287
Tobinitai site, 131
Tokoro-chashi site, 144
Tomarinai site, 126
Tomsk, 45
Tool styles, 351–352
Tōsamuporo site, 128
Trade, 35, 53, 80–82, 85, 203, 356
Tradesmen, 80–82
Traena, 92–93
Transhumanism, 173

Tundra, 67

Uelen site, 161, 162, 163
Ulu, 67, 218
Umiam, 169, 185, 272, 276, 278
Umqan burials, 195–196
Unimak Island, 291
Ural Region, 64
Ushkovo site, 116–117, 118
Ust' Poluj, 7, 104–107, 371
Utoro site, 143–144

Varangerfjord, 75, 92
Västerbjers, 32–33

Västerbotten, 47, 48, 49, 50, 51, 52, 54
Vegetation, 22–24
Visby, 32–33
Vladivostok, 68
Volga-Oka Region, 60

Walrus, 164
Whetstones, 50, 51, 53
White Sea culture, 59–60

Yahgan culture, 328–329, 330
Yamal region, 370–371
Yukaghir, 9